10,000 NOT OUT

THE HISTORY OF THE SPECTATOR 1828–2020

DAVID BUTTERFIELD

UNICORN

TO D.S.M.
ARCHETYPE
OF INTEGRITY

Published in 2020 by
Unicorn, an imprint of Unicorn Publishing Group LLP
5 Newburgh Street
London
W1F 7RG

www.unicornpublishing.org

ISBN 978-1-912690-81-7

10 9 8 7 6 5 4 3 2 1

Printed by Fine Tone Ltd

Contents

Foreword

BY MATT RIDLEY

When Dominic Lawson became editor of *The Spectator* in 1990, he asked me if I would like to be his deputy. Of all the roads not taken in my life, this one has intrigued me the most. I would probably have made a hash of it, I had a great time doing other things instead, and Dominic's biggest scoop involved the downfall of my own uncle. Yet the frisson of excitement that the prospect of working at *The Spectator* sent down my spine was unmistakeable.

The combination of eloquence and irreverence, of influence and independence, of not taking itself seriously, of wearing its learning lightly, that *The Spectator* represented then and now was like nothing else in public life, let alone journalism. As Charles Moore once said: 'When I first read Alexander Chancellor's *Spectator* when I was at university, it was a bit like *On First Looking into Chapman's Homer*: I recognised at once an exhilarating air of freedom.'

David Butterfield's absorbing history of *The Spectator*, to celebrate its 10,000th edition as the oldest magazine in the English language, reveals that this theme of freedom has always been there. *The Spectator*, from its very first issues, stood for freedom and has done ever since. As Butterfield recounts of Robert Rintoul, the paper's founder, 'his paper supported, in a word, freedom – not just freedom of choice for working men and freedom of conduct for all British subjects, but also freedom for the colonies, freedom for West Indian slaves, freedom for those trapped in serfdom on the Continent and in Russia, freedom of the press, and freedom of religion.'

In the Corn Laws debates, the young *Spectator* stood resolutely for free trade. 'Long have I seen that few men, few Liberals, believe in liberty: but you I think are one,' wrote W.E. Gladstone to Richard Hutton, *The Spectator*'s long-standing co-editor alongside Meredith Townsend. The paper's object was to protect 'the right of free thought, free speech, and free action, within the limits of law, under every form of Government', wrote the two editors in the 1860s.

Even when liberty fell out of fashion at the end of the nineteenth century and radicals became instead enamoured of the power of the state to represent and protect the people, *The Spectator* stood unfashionably apart. The protectionist, wrote St Loe Strachey, editor in 1905,

'finds it easy to forget that trade is a[n] exchange, that foreign trade is a for[m] of mutual co-operation by which eac[h] side may profit, that the sale of impor[ts] in our free markets is conditioned b[y] the purchase of our exports, and, abov[e] all, that market—'the place or system [of] exchange'—is best when it is allowed t[o] grow and develop according to its ow[n] free laws of individual demand an[d] supply.'

A century later it was Fraser Nelso[n] who stood up most strongly for freedo[m] of the press when the Leveson inqui[ry] almost led to state censorship. 'N[O]' shrieked his cover on 23 March 201[?]. This book shows that *The Spectator* h[as] stood throughout its history for the liber[ty] of the individual against the power of t[he] state. In the 1820s that placed it on the le[ft] of the political spectrum; in the 2020[s] places it on the right. *The Spectator* w[as] quick to spot, and champion, all sorts [of] causes: gay rights in the 1950s under I[an] Gilmour; Margaret Thatcher in the 197[0s] under Patrick Cosgrave; a referend[um] on Europe in 2003 under Boris Johns[on]. There were mistakes of course. T[he] *Spectator* went gaga over Mussolini a[nd] even showed some warmth for Sta[lin] during its least impressive period.

Its editors were nearly always men (no women yet) of eccentricity, courage and eloquence who make great copy in themselves. Two Johnsons, two Lawsons, a Chancellor and two future Chancellors, some industrial drinkers and romanisers, some churchy monks. Its prize columnists included two who went to prison, Edward Gibbon Wakefield and the incomparable Taki. Geoffrey Wheatcroft told a story of how at one of The Spectator's notoriously bibulous Thursday lunches Spiro Agnew was confused when Barry Humphries left the room and returned as Dame Edna. Kingsley Amis said 'the chief problem with the Spec side is not getting arseholed whenever I go there.' Said one early commentator: 'There is a personal flavour about this newspaper which differentiates it from its contemporaries — a strong individuality, in singular contrast with the somewhat colourless method of other newspapers', a remark that is just as true today.

For a naïve undergraduate in the 1970s, the contrarianism of many columns was a revelation. No conventional wisdom escaped rethink. My first memory of The Spectator was getting absolutely furious with a (genuinely) terrible article about Darwin by Christopher Booker, who later became a friend. Soon after, I recall my bafflement at articles by Auberon Waugh. They were so vicious and over the top that they were surely not meant to be taken seriously. Or were they?

This particular form of journalism, in which exaggeration allows you to get away with making a point while not being held accountable for it, because you are being both funny and absurd, has since been perfected by Rod Liddle and James Delingpole among others, though it was also part of the secret of both Jeffrey Bernard and Taki.

Leave the last words to the person who will almost certainly be The Spectator's most famous editor, even if the magazine runs another 10,000 issues, Boris Johnson: 'In the glutinous consensus of New Britain, The Spectator is a refuge for logic, fun and good writing. It challenges the orthodoxy, whatever that happens to be. It will continue to set the political agenda, and to debunk it.'

Preface

It is an unbroken rule of publishing that a magazine does not last for 10,000 issues. If it is founded to fight a cause, that battle is typically won or lost after 100 issues, and often little more than a footnote of history after 1,000. If it is founded to fill a gap in the market, within a generation that gap will have been filled to satiety, or the notoriously fickle market will have moved on to other things. If it is founded to be the public clarion of one or more individuals, it is rarely destined to live beyond their own mortal lifespan. Even if a magazine skilfully and successfully evolves in tandem with an ever-changing world, it is most improbable that it will survive many thousands of issues: the dangers of financial ruin, proprietorial reinvention, governmental suppression and public indifference are likely to rear their heads soon enough. Never should it be forgotten that, in any given week, the game could be up for good, if the readership decide that they would, on reflection, rather be reading something else.

Check the small print of *The Spectator*'s contents page, however, and you will see the casual remark that you are holding an issue numbered 10,000 – or thereabouts. The unbroken rule of the press is now proved, as all laws should be, by an outstanding exception. Founded in 1828, *The Spectator* is now the oldest weekly magazine in the world. For 192 years it has somehow managed to turn out a number every single week, however improbable or impracticable that task.[1] Its first number was on sale before the electric motor was invented, before Morse code was codified, before Darwin had boarded the Beagle, before the Metropolitan Police was established, before the first Boat Race was held, before the Palace of Westminster burned to the ground, and before the future Queen Victoria had even turned ten. *The Spectator* was thus at hand to mourn the deaths of Lord Liverpool (1770–1828), George IV (1762–1830), Hazlitt (1778–1830), Goethe (1749–1832) and Talleyrand (1754–1838). Even the Duke of Wellington, though pilloried as the nation's bumbling Prime Minister when the virulently anti-Tory *Spectator* first appeared, continued to be a regular reader until his death, in 1852. The paper in turn gave its old adversary the unprecedented honour, as a non-Royal, of marking his death with a black-bordered front page.

The Spectator, then, has been spectating for some time. It has witnessed the reign of eight British monarchs and the rise and fall of fifty-five prime ministers. Twenty-four of these thirty-five men and women (some holding the office more than once) have contributed to its pages, whether Liberal, Labour or Tory: twelve (Asquith, Lloyd George, Macdonald, Attlee, Macmillan, Douglas-Home, Heath, Major, Blair, Cameron, May, Johnson) have offered articles, while the other dozen as far back as Gladstone have written lectures or letters. Chancellors of the Exchequer have always found the need to read *The Spectator* – and all but one of the last twenty-one holders of that office, Labour and Conservative, have written in the magazine; the current prime minister – lest we forget – edited for half a decade. Politics has, by contrast, been an incidental feature to good, readable writing. It is not a mere statistic that sixteen Nobel Laureates for Literature have written in its pages, including George Bernard Shaw, Thomas Mann, T.S. Eliot, Bertrand Russell, Jean-Paul Sartre, Gabriel García Márquez and Harold Pinter.

When *The Spectator* reached its first century, in 1928, the Prime Minister Stanley Baldwin's after-dinner speech was broadcast live to the nation. Even the paper's main weekly rival was compelled to confess that *The Spectator* had always seemed to have been part of the fabric of Britain:

We have been brought up to regard it as a timeless institution, like the City

Corporation, the Bank of England, and the House of Lords. It is strange to realise that, until a hundred years ago, Britain had to muddle along somehow without the weekly discipline of *The Spectator*.[3]

Well, Britain has since muddled along with *The Spectator* for another ninety years and now faces a world far more different from 1928 than that year was from 1828. There is no easy explanation for how the magazine has achieved its astonishingly irrepressible survival. Doubtless a mixture of good writing, bloody-minded grit and genuine luck have been major factors; but there has also been, from its very first year of appearance, a public acceptance that *The Spectator* is here with a job to do.

What is that job? Some would glibly answer, 'To keep the Tories in power'. Indeed, the modern *Spectator* is sometimes dismissed as the in-house journal of the Conservative party, or an anachronistic medley of right-wing, navel-gazing Little Englanders. But a read through any issue of *The Spectator* will soon put paid to that wilful oversimplification and cynical guesswork. Not only has the magazine always been without a formal link to any political party, but its political affiliations have ranged in response to the state of the nation: it has been Radical, Liberal, Liberal-Unionist, Conservative, and on occasion even Labour. More tellingly, for most of the last hundred years, its duty has been to defend a conservative, liberal and avowedly independent outlook. It has always been worldly, but always British; it has at every turn been a stout defender of the Union, but able both to look within for insight and to look without for inspiration.

Yet, despite its long and distinguished past, *The Spectator* lacks a general account of its history. Two books, it is true, have tackled particular periods in its career: in 1928, a lavish centenary volume appeared under the name of Sir William Beach Thomas, although it was mostly written by Katharine Leaf (later West);[4] in 1998, Simon Courtauld published a history of the subsequent seventy years.[5] The first work gives a colourful account of *The Spectator*'s first fifty years, but drops off markedly in focus and interest after 1880. The second volume is a work of exemplary detail and clarity for the period 1953 until the mid-1990s: Courtauld's account of *The Spectator* in the Sixties, Seventies and Eighties is unsurpassable as a chronicle of the magazine's complex inner workings. The two books between them thus give only a sketch for the period from 1880 to 1950, though these decades saw the establishment of *The Spectator* as an institution of British life, its alignment with Conservative (and, in part, Liberal) politics, and its gradual transformation from a newspaper to a magazine.

This book therefore aims to give a more balanced history of *The Spectator* from its foundation through to the present day. Since what was thought and said in the heat of the moment often transcends in value and interest the cold analysis of the historian, I have given copious citations throughout from the paper/magazine, from advertisements, from rival titles in the press, and from correspondence (public and private). Although there are periods when the journal was of especial influence in society, or on the point of collapsing under financial pressure, I have attempted to pace the account as evenly as possible over the decades, and indeed over its twenty-five editors. In periods of particular upheaval – wartime austerity, economic depression, political unrest – I have done no more than outline the important public role that *The Spectator* played, aware that in each case it would require a book-length treatment to do justice to so rich a subject. This, then, is simply a digest, written in the hope that it both answers some questions and raises others that we have forgotten to ask.

I

RINTOUL AND THE RADICALS
1828–1858

No Scottish printing apprentice has the time or the temerity to daydream that he will, in later life, see a mountain named in his honour on the other side of the planet. And yet, for one lad toiling with the finicky business of setting, inking and pressing type up a backstreet in Edinburgh, such a feat was destined to be a mere footnote to his future achievements. By the time of his death, this jobbing printer had transformed the newspaper scene in Scotland, created the most influential weekly in Victorian England, and played an undeniable role in reforming the British nation, the British Empire, and the world that was to come. To understand how *The Spectator* first emerged into that world, it is necessary to unearth the man who moved behind it.

ROBERT STEPHEN RINTOUL (1787–1858) came from nowhere: his family was unknown to wider society,[6] and his birthplace, the village of Tibbermore near Perth, is known only to proud locals and Civil War historians.[7] After basic schooling in nearby Aberdalgie, the young Rintoul threw himself straight into the world of work. For several years he was apprenticed to James Ballantyne in Edinburgh, the publisher and friend of Sir Walter Scott. But in 1809, an opportunity opened up on the Tay, at the snappily named *Dundee, Perth, and Cupar Advertiser; or, Perth, Fife, and Angus Shires Intelligencer.*[8] The issue of 17 March 1809 closes with his first mention in print: 'RINTOUL, Printer'. Although founded only eight years earlier, this weekly newspaper had fast won for itself the reputation of being a journal sympathetic to the burgeoning movement of reform politics. The proprietors, James and Paterson Saunders, evidently had confidence in young Rintoul's talents, for within two years he was promoted to the role of editor, aged twenty-four.

As Rintoul gained in confidence and freedom, he sedulously reworked the *Dundee Advertiser* into a streamlined and pointed tool of commentary. To the first column of the four-pager he introduced a 'Summary of Politics'; this move, and its subsequent finessing, made Rintoul the 'pioneer' in British journalism of a new, comment-driven style of article – what was to become the 'leader'.[9] He scrupulously reworked the paper's contents, character and appearance; as colleagues recalled, 'he attempted to elevate the compilation of a newspaper into an art.'[10] Before long, he had doubled the *Advertiser's* readership from the mere 600 he inherited; what is more, his political aspirations had attracted the notice of an increasingly influential set of Scottish intellectuals. Under Rintoul's editorship the *Advertiser* became a Radical organ whose voice travelled far beyond its geographical remit – and weighed heavy wherever it landed.

The task was not slight. Scotland at the time stood as an almighty bulwark against reform, shackled by an anachronistic system of societal control. Self-electing councils in the burghs ensured that vested financial interests were fiercely protected; citizens were subject to an aggressive system of penal law, steered by tyrannical judges and waved through by timid jurors; the Kirk saw little interest or incentive in shaking up age-old practices, however harsh and intellectually indefensible. In the Dundee of the early nineteenth century, when its population hovered between two and three thousand, the governing 'popular' party was congenitally averse to change. Aware of this, the reformers saw that the route to progress lay in freeing up the educational system; they fought to improve the provision of elementary and burgh schools, but progress was grindingly slow. Meanwhile, a more strident political movement to promote the true cause of the people was emerging from the Whig elites of earlier generations, a force that could at last challenge the long-standing Tory governance of the Perth burghs. Its leading figures were William Ramsay Maule (1st Baron Panmure), MP for Angus, Charles Lord Kinnaird and his brother Douglas, George Kinloch of Kinloch, Francis Jeffrey and Henry Cockburn – all men of broadly Whiggish outlook. Not only was Rintoul adopted into their social milieu but he secured several of them as contributors

The Dundee Advertiser at the start and end of Rintoul's editorship (1809, 1825)

to the *Advertiser*: besides Kinloch and his unfailingly aggressive articles, regular contributors included the author Robert Mudie, the poet Thomas Hood, and 'Scotland's greatest nineteenth-century Churchman',[11] Thomas Chalmers, the celebrated champion of the urban poor.

The *Advertiser* – now closing with the all-encompassing 'Edited, printed, and published, by R.S. Rintoul' – was perfectly placed to be the primary conduit for this new reforming force of liberalism. In tandem with it, Rintoul willingly published several other works in vigorous support of reform, including the sermons and parliamentary speeches of the evangelical abolitionist Samuel Horsley.[12] From 1814, Rintoul and Kinloch led the campaign for the management of Dundee's all-important harbour to be wrested from the incompetent grip of the Dundee corporation: Rintoul not only published the architectural proposals of Thomas Telford, but used the *Advertiser* to press the case hard and with success. Somewhat unsurprisingly, local Tories felt the need to found a rival newspaper in 1816, the *Dundee Courier and Argus*. In the meanwhile, Kinloch campaigned more widely across the Scottish political scene, all the while keeping his friend 'Radical Rinty' – a.k.a. 'The Incendiary' – in sync with the latest developments.[13]

In 1818, Rintoul met another Scottish radical, Joseph Hume, newly elected as MP for the Aberdeen burghs; this was destined to be a transformative moment, for Hume would become Rintoul's primary ally and patron over the next four decades. In 1819, a warrant for arrest came his way, for publicising the rabble-rousing speeches of Kinloch so readily. He narrowly escaped prosecution, which did no harm to his reputation: such was the local confidence in Rintoul's ability and integrity that in that same year he was sent to London to represent the cause of the Guildry and Trades Incorporations of Dundee before the Select Committee on the Royal Scottish Burghs (1818–20). For his 'zealous discharge of the duties entrusted to him' he was rewarded with a gold snuff box and the freedom of the town.[14] However, Rintoul's outspoken journalism was not without

A portrait reproduced from a contemporary watercolour miniature (artist and location unknown); Rintoul's signature from 1828

controversy. He had to face down several lawsuits, th[e] most notable coming in 1824 from Patrick Anderso[n], the Provost of Dundee, rankled by the allegation that h[e] had mismanaged a substantial educational bequest. Th[e] editor told the facts as they were – and won the case.[15]

Perhaps it was this high-profile court-case, perhap[s] it was Rintoul's increasing political frustration, that le[d] in early 1825 to his falling out with the newspaper's chie[f] proprietor, the solicitor James Saunders. Rintoul, as [it] happened, had been headhunted by the team settin[g] up *The Westminster Review* in London – led by Jerem[y] Bentham. He did not accept the offer, but his mark o[n] London society had evidently been made.[16] In search [of] a new opportunity closer to home, he headed once mor[e] to Edinburgh and became involved with a new week[ly] venture. The *Edinburgh Times* first appeared on 2[?] January 1825, a paper 'conducted on liberal principle[s] and printed (by a local firm) on 'the largest size permitte[d] by Act of Parliament'. Whether Rintoul founded th[e] paper, or joined it after he left the *Dundee Advertis[er]* in mid-February 1825, is unclear; likewise uncertai[n] is when Rintoul left, probably several months befo[re] the paper merged in May 1826.[17] The *Edinburgh Tim[es]* gained a good reputation for its economic outlook, an[d] even secured an article on wages and profits from Joh[n] Stuart Mill.[18] But, despite the high hopes, the ventur[e] was not a success: many of its reports were reprinte[d] in other papers, north and south of the border, but i[ts] circulation could not push beyond a mere 400. For th[e] failure the British public should be infinitely thankful: Rintoul came to see that prospects were unhappy in Scotland, and took the advice of his friend Douglas Kinnaird to head to London. This brave move – at the age of thirty-nine, with a wife and two young children in tow – proved to be permanent.

In the 1820s, the capital was a magnet to those clamouring for change. The crucible of Reform was heating up: Robert Peel was reshaping the penal system, William Huskisson was clearing away trade protectionism, and Parliament was in genuine turmoil. As the fifteen-year Tory premiership of Lord Liverpool came to its end, the Canningite-Whig Ministry of 1827– stood ready in the wings, ready to challenge long-held tribal devotions, to repeal the Test and Corporation Acts, and to deliver Catholic Emancipation. Kinnaird and Hume airlifted Rintoul into the editorship of a new weekly, *The Atlas*, a 'general newspaper and journal of literature', which first appeared on Sunday 21 May 1826. There seems to have been genuine excitement in the editorial claim that this new periodical would be 'the largest newspaper ever printed' on a sheet 'nearly double the size of *The Times*',[19] using bespoke 'printing-machines ... worked only by the power of steam'.[20] The paper was a lively sixteen-pager that sought 'to concentrate in one sheet the various matters of fact and speculation which are at present scattered through many, and which no newspaper of the common size can contain.' Nevertheless, it was observed ruefully in the first issue that 'Even the ATLAS will not hold every thing'.[21] It avowed 'no politics of its own', instead creating under the heading of 'The Politician' its own so-called 'newspaper parliament', by reproducing and rephrasing the opposing arguments of the ablest political writers of all parties'. Perhaps more remarkably for the time, it proudly declared that its literary pages would be 'wholly independent of interested influence', written to please readers not booksellers.[22] *The Atlas*, with Rintoul at its helm, duly emerged to be one of the very first Sunday papers to combine news and politics with reviews of literature, art and science. Although the great majority of its contents was reproduced from the dailies of the

The Atlas masthead (1826)

preceding week, it included occasional 'essays and jeux d'esprit', the first of which was 'Of dogs in general, and Sir Walter Scott's dogs in particular'.

Rintoul used his opening editorial article of 1827 (buried in the middle of the paper) to announce the value of such a large-scale format: 'we may consider ourselves indebted to the amplitude of this Journal, that it is as well a *record* of all passing events, as an active *commentator* and *observer* on every thing which may interest or instruct.' As to politics, 'we hope also to have a party, but the members of it are the mere lovers of truth, who prefer a view of things as they are, to any flattering or any distorted representation of them.' In practice, the paper's Whig politics – and Benthamite sympathies on social issues – were thinly disguised. Kinnaird, one of the original sponsors,[23] knew that Rintoul would serve as an energetic and accomplished editor. And so it proved: *The Atlas* allowed him how to secure and manage a large and diverse team of original and outspoken writers, including considerable arts coverage. The paper enjoyed an impressive circulation of 5,000, but it certainly did not pull its punches in criticism.

The very first issue called the Royal Academy's exhibition 'the severest trial of the eyes and the patience known to this nation', containing 'a thousand abortive attempts at pictures'.[24] Its freedom from publishers' influence also attracted rapid notice: a contemporary said that 'in point of fairness and apparent independence of Booksellers, the reviews of *The Atlas* are ... valuable, and are written with great talent and acuteness.'[25] And its blows did land. When William Hazlitt, for instance, read that he had 'the ingenious art of selling his literary production four or five times over',[26] he devoted one of his trademark essays to lashing back at the ignorant criticism of 'The editor of *The Atlas*'.[27] Nor was it long before formal lawsuits emerged from wounded authors.[28] It may be, however, that such legal wrangling in public was not to the taste of James Whiting, the lead proprietor; it is probable that external pressure was mounting to afford certain works or publishers a rather easier ride.

What is clear is that Rintoul felt he was no longer able to act as the editor he intended to be. On 8 June 1828, he resigned from *The Atlas*, privately confiding that his resignation was 'in consequence of attempts to vulgarise and betwaddle the "Atlas" – contrary to our compact, and to the line of conduct which gave that paper its literary character.'[29] As a sign of the remarkable sway he held over his writers, '*all* the literary contributors' – those charged with original writing – left *The Atlas* with him.[30] Without missing a beat, he set about creating a new weekly – and on terms that would not stay his hand. First he found suitable premises to rent west of Fleet Street at 159 Strand, looking directly on to St Mary le Strand; this was the base of his new publisher, the bookseller Frederick Westley. Then, to allow himself an exclusively editorial role, he employed the newsagent Joseph Clayton to act as printer, producing the paper at the press of William Clowes, on Stamford Street across Waterloo Bridge.

After four weeks' hard graft he was ready to launch the first sixteen-page number of his fourth – and indeed final – weekly journal. On 1 July, an announcement spread across the London press:[31]

TO be published on Sunday next, price 9d., the First Number of THE SPECTATOR, a Weekly Journal of News, Politics, Literary, Dramatic, and Musical Criticism, &c., by the late Editor and principal Contributor of the "Atlas" newspaper.—Printed by Mr. Clowes. Published by Mr. Westley, 159, Strand.

A couple of days later there followed a much fuller advertisement, adding that the paper would also have 'the aid of other Literary Associates'. Rintoul, its evident author, declared that readers would find in this venture the best elements of *The Atlas*:

> in general conduct, the same undeviating impartiality; in Politics, the same temperance, and determination fairly to appreciate and faithfully to exhibit the conflicting opinions of the day; in Literary, Dramatic, and Musical Criticism, the same spirit and honesty; in the Essays on general subjects, and the lighter commentaries on men and manners, the same endeavour to blend amusement and instruction; in a word, the same pens guided by the same principles – the same mind in a renovated body.

But it also made clear the substantial differences and advantages afforded by the paper's fresh start:

> In form and arrangement indeed, the new paper will be very unlike the old one: for the Editor recommences after an experience of two years, and

The location of *The Spectator*'s first premises (1820s; 2020): 159 Strand

after the consideration of many suggestions which have occurred in the course of it... [*The Spectator*] proposes to keep his eye on every event or question which can affect the interests or sympathies of any class whatever... The variety of its contents will eminently adapt it for circulation in the country, and in families; for while it is hoped in each branch to satisfy the wants of those who only look to one branch – as the politician to politics, the lover of literature to books, the playgoer to the drama – it is the design of the editor to combine them into a proportionate whole, to gratify the taste of the general reader. And that this Paper may be submitted to the most indiscriminate perusal, without distinction of sex or age, the scrupulous may rely on the preservation of a moral tone, which will always render *The Spectator*, at least, a harmless intruder into the domestic circle.[32]

To advertise the event more broadly, Rintoul wrote to his long-standing acquaintance in Scotland, William Blackwood, the eminent publisher of *Blackwood's Magazine*. After announcing that he had 'begun *The Spectator*, also on the neutral ground in politics, but decided in its criticisms', he made clear his ambitions beyond London: 'I have ordered you ten copies of the first number. Help me to some publicity in the North.'[33]

However, for all Rintoul's evident enthusiasm, this was a difficult period to start so ambitious a venture. First, newspapers had to struggle under an oppressive burden of tax: there was a 4d stamp duty on every issue printed, alongside the charge to the publishers of 3s 6d for every advertisement taken on, and 3d for every pound of paper used. Secondly, the London market was already overcrowded with established titles; beyond the problem of finding a niche, it required considerable capital to publicise a new title and win it a sufficient readership to keep it afloat. Thirdly, the task of distributing a paper beyond the metropolis was slow, expensive and uncertain, and challenging the dominant provincial titles on their own terms was an uphill struggle. Fourthly and finally, given the relatively high cost of newspapers

as a commodity, enterprising middlemen had emerged to offer the popular service of reading rooms, where, for a small sum, a wide array of newspapers and periodicals could be perused over coffee and crumpets; for others, the library, the common room, or the club provided a similar reason not to take out anything so expensive as a subscription, decreasing yet further the scope for profit.

It was thus no simple matter to get people to purchase a new paper – especially when it was the second priciest weekly in town: because of its considerable range and scope, *The Spectator* appeared at the challenging price of 9d (now some £2.50), just undercutting its inevitable rival *The Atlas* at 10d. In fact, Rintoul privately confessed that this price was still too low: only the full shilling (12d) would have covered his costs. As with his two previous titles, the paper was printed on one large sheet, but the paper tax put space at a premium. From the start, *The Spectator* thus faced an awkward balance: on the one hand, to cram in as much text as possible on to every page, with no space conceded to headlines or images; on the other, to provide a more elegant and easy reading experience than the chaotic and crabbed columns of contemporary papers. Rintoul's hope was that *The Spectator* would offer such breadth and depth of news and comment as to make an admittedly costly purchase on Sunday a more satisfying prospect than the more expensive acquisition of a daily paper through the week.

The name of *The Spectator* was Rintoul's own choice. It was, of course, not an idle one, but a bold appropriation of the celebrated predecessor founded by Joseph Addison and Richard Steele (1711–12). That original series, issued six times weekly, launched into the realm of journalism the short essay form, both prompted by contemporary events and informed by history and literature alike. The 555 issues of its first series covered all and sundry topics, real and fictitious: society, morals, culture, fashion, philosophy and politics. Protected by a beguilingly playful and chatty style, each puckish salvo deflated the puritanical pretensions of the age. A given week could laud heroic humility (no. 340), reprove women taking snuff (no. 344), and outline the transmigrations of Pugg the monkey (no. 343). The self-assured ease of each foolscap theme captivated and curated polite society under Queen Anne.

The series vividly embodied a fully-formed literary character – Mr Spectator, a dispassionate observer on the world, shaped by years of travel, study and reflection. Crucially, his freedom from political partisanship allowed open and unfettered comment, both in his own voice and refracted through his fellow clubmen – the hapless country squire Sir Roger de Coverley, the affable man-about-town Will Honeycomb, and the industrious merchant Sir Andrew Freeport.

Within two years *The Spectator* had folded, stymied by stamp tax and flagging inspiration. Several hands attempted successors, most notably Addison himself, who (with the aid of Pope and others) published eighty more essays in 1714.[34] But the original was established as a quintessential classic, passing through over a hundred editions in its first century;[35] Macaulay equated its popularity with that later enjoyed by Scott and Dickens.

There had, in the intervening years, been plenty of other *Spectator* imitations in Britain and beyond, but no such title had endured.[36] Rintoul's plan was different: unlike his predecessors, he resurrected the title of *The Spectator* without qualification. It is possible that Kinnaird supported the choice by recalling the wish of his late friend Byron to start 'a periodical paper, something in the *Spectator* or *Observer* way'.[37]

Although not so presumptuous as to declare itself a continuation, the paper from the outset made plentiful reference to Addison and Steele.[38] Despite manifest differences in form, there is no doubt that the new *Spectator* sought to revive their spirit. Under Rintoul and his nineteenth-century successors the paper and its correspondents talk of 'Mr Spectator' and 'Dear Spec' in the unmistakable idiom of the original. The initial 'Mr Spectator' is cited as 'our esteemed namesake' and 'grave prototype'. The autonomous swagger of the first *Spectator* is reflected from the very beginning: it is presumably deliberate that the first issue of Rintoul's paper not only mentions Addison and his 'precepts' but reappropriates the heading 'Works of the Learned', which Addison had pointedly mocked (Spec. no. 457).

Even the paper's striking gothic masthead closely reflects that in Bisset's popular 1793 edition of the Addison-Steele *Spectator*:

As one who was certain that he would not embark upon a political career himself, but would perch as a Scotsman amid and above the hubbub of London life, the role of wry spectator was destined to suit Rintoul and his paper well.

The first issue of the new *Spectator* appeared on Sunday 6 July 1828, covering in rich detail the events of the preceding week. The very first paragraph set out its objectives with clarity and confidence:

> The principal object of a Newspaper is to convey intelligence. It is proposed in the SPECTATOR to give this, the first and most prominent place, to a report of all the leading occurrences of the week. In this department, the reader may always expect a summary account of every public proceeding, or transaction of interest, whether the scene might lie at home or abroad, that has taken place within the seven days preceding the termination of our labours; which, we wish it to be remarked, close on *Saturday* at midnight.

Everything that happened worth reading, Rintoul was keen to stress, would be reported. Contemporary advertisements for the new title were keen to stress the novelty of this reboot of the newspaper model:

> Its Plan is entirely new, comprising – 1. The whole News of the Week, so selected, sifted, condensed, and arranged, as to be readable throughout. 2. A full and impartial exhibition of all the leading Politics of the Day. 3. A separate Discussion of Interesting Topics of a general nature, with a

view to instruction and entertainment at the same time. 4. A Department devoted to Literature, consisting of independent Criticisms on New Books, with Specimens of the best Passages. 5. Dramatic and Musical Criticism. 6. Scientific and Miscellaneous Information.

This formula, the very DNA of *The Spectator*, still lives on without significant mutation.

A closer look at the first issue gives a clear sense of this cocksure newcomer. Each of its sixteen pages carries two columns chock-full of text. The first five pages cover news, moving from general topics to parliamentary business, followed by interesting extracts from the press. These opening accounts were certainly thorough: news from the court informs readers that 'the King's giraffe is given over by the physicians. The complaint seems to be general debility, with an especial weakness in the knee-joints.'[39] There follow seven 'Topics of the Day', each the equivalent of a leading article. These, like the rest of the contents, are unsigned, and would remain so for the next hundred years of the paper: reflections from *The Spectator*'s collective perspective are couched in the editorial 'We'. The topics first broached are 'Parliamentary Representation in Ireland', 'The Theatre – War in Turkey', 'The Last Fashion of Morality', and 'The Ungentility of Suicide'; the last three are instead reviews of artistic news: 'Play-Wrights and Managers', 'Comédie Française – Mademoiselle Mars', and 'The Music of the Season'.

Next come four pages under the heading of 'The Literary Spectator'; two pages concern Robert Walsh's *Narrative of a Journey from Constantinople to England*, most of which is given over to long extracts in small print. A good taste of the paper's critical canons is given by the programmatic article opening this literary section, 'Works of the Learned for 1827–8':

> Since the direct influence of literature upon the wellbeing of society has been discovered, the practical utility of books is the standard by which they are tried. Before this power was perceived, learning in itself, and for itself, was a fine thing: a book *per se* was a monument, sacred to the memory of its author, if to nothing else. To walk along the aisles of a college library, and to deviate into its stalls, is to visit a churchyard...

Rintoul, a man who had little time for the lofty posturing of ivory-towered grandees, was decidedly a man of action. Accordingly, his *Spectator* would judge literature on a utilitarian basis: it needed somehow to change the world – or at least shape the mind for the better. Throughout his career, Rintoul was fond of quoting a remark he heard at Panmure House in Edinburgh from his friend Joseph Hume about the 'reformist' politician Sir Francis Burdett: 'He talks well, but what has he *done*?' As an editor, he resolutely dismissed maudlin navel-gazing, seeking instead to report concrete change. The literary broadside continues:

> Much has been printed – more reprinted; but what has been added to the existing stock of ideas? What will live? What deserves to live? How much is already dead?... In running over the publications in literature during the season, we shall estimate them according to the knowledge they have contributed, the pleasure they produced in the perusal, or the ability they display. *What has been DONE?*

This initial prospectus of Spectatorial principles makes clear that they apply not only to non-fiction – works of history, travel, science – but even to novels and poetry. Yet, despite his avowedly haranguing tone, Rintoul acknowledges that 'we presume no ignorance in the reader; doubtless he knew something before the First Number of the *Spectator* fell into his hands.' But, when it comes to poetry, he is markedly more stringent:

> We have no poetry; and in criticism, much so called, but nothing that deserves the title... Poetry is as rife as criticism, and equally worthless.

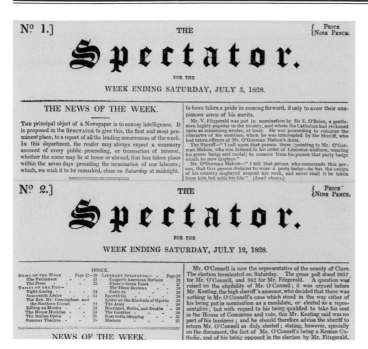

The first paragraphs of the first two numbers of *The Spectator*

The Spectator would give no place to false puffery, cynical log-rolling and execrable 'paid paragraphs' penned by wily publishers. Still, the reader is given a small concession; overleaf, on page 12, is printed the first piece of verse in *The Spectator*. It is a 'song' from *The Bride*, a tragedy by the Scottish poetess Joanna Baillie: fittingly, it is an exhortation to practical optimism over rational pessimism.[40]

The closing pages move back into chronicling facts of the week: one carries news of the military, commerce, and births and deaths; the next reproduces information from the 'London gazettes'. Neither of these features, already replicated in so many other titles, was to last long. News from the markets and the financial world, by contrast, has retained a continual presence. The last two pages carry advertisements – the lifeblood of any paper's success, which in this early phase are limited entirely to recent literature. Perhaps to ensure that every carefully constructed page won equally careful an inspection, the first issue is unique in the paper's history for carrying no list of contents.

Such a miscellany, then, was *Spectator* no. 1. It would be untrue, however, to say that its appearance brought London society to a standstill. Its initial circulation was in the hundreds, not thousands; although many of its reports and leaders were quick to find syndication the paper was limited to a three-figure circulation for its first two years.[41] Rintoul himself knew full well that a serious and expensive paper would take some time to build up steam. Nor should we overestimate what stood as a good sales figure: in 1828, *The Times*, much the biggest-selling daily, managed only 8,000 nationwide the biggest-selling weekly, the virulently Tory *John Bull* dominated that field with a sale of some 6,000 copies and the readers of *The Atlas*, now edited by the spirited Irishman Robert Bell, would need some encouragement to change their Sunday paper.

Nevertheless, the young *Spectator* began with some swagger. Astounded at the morbid fascination of the press with the murder of Maria Marten – shot dead by her lover in 1828 – Rintoul published a satirical account under the shrill header 'Points of horror!!!!':

> The taste for murder in the enlightened public of Great Britain ... is so extravagantly eager, that murderers will come to be held in the light of public benefactors... We should never get through the cares of existence without a good supply of crime; our cases of police prevent us from being nationally that dullest of things and greatest of monsters, a perfect character. If the public will have Sunday papers adorned with pictures, let them aim at gratifying something better than a morbid curiosity ... shall we not enlist the Hogarth of our day, the inimitable Cruikshank, to illustrate our notions of the picturesque?[42]

The following page published four engravings by Cruikshank, commissioned at the princely sum of twenty guineas, which depicted increasingly lurid reimaginings of the murder, the trial and the auction of grim mementoes from the crime scene.

After his first few months of hard toil, Rintoul wrote again to Blackwood with greater confidence. Having set out *The Spectator*'s 'straightforwardness and the preference of plain strong sense to affect

10,000 NOT OUT

elic-hunting after Maria Marten's murder (G. Cruikshank)

nery or to Cockney simplicity', he proceeds to set out
ae paper's prospectus:

we do not profess to discuss politics, though we record them historically – and, I think, with unwonted impartiality, our motto in every thing being 'fair play'; secondly, when we do happen to deal with an abstract principle, which is commonly classified as belonging to the department of political science, we take it up rather as a branch of Ethics, and follow it out regardless whether the results may seem more to favour one set of political opinions, or the opposite. In short, we have nothing to do with Party. Is it not right that there should be *one* paper in England to maintain this position? I do it honestly, and from temperament: I mean my *aim* is honest, however imperfect the attainment.

There is no cant in *The Spectator*. No indecency. No impiety. May I add, *no trash*, and *not much dullness?* We have already obtained, even from fastidious critics in high station, the soubriquet of 'The *Gentleman's* Paper'; no bad distinction in these times.

You will observe it would be a mistake to consider the *Spectator only* as a literary periodical: it is a <u>newspaper</u>, and miscellany of general entertainment; and its criticisms on *Literature, Music, The Drama*, together with the essays and off-hand remarks on morals, manners, and points of humour, may be regarded as an addition to as perfect a compilation of *newspaper information* of every kind that respectable and cultivated families would desire, as ever has [been] contained in one sheet of paper. Not a subject or event of importance is omitted; not a paragraph is taken from other papers without a useful inspection and purification – indeed, most are rewritten.[43]

Rintoul closes with a pious flourish: 'there is not one of us – myself, contributors, or supporters as capitalists – who is not even more anxious that our success should tend to elevate and improve the tone of the newspaper press.'

The mention of financial supporters raises the question of how *The Spectator* funded its foundation. While Rintoul did provide some money himself, a far greater sum came from his wealthy backers, keen to promote a sophisticated weekly with an enlightened attitude to reform. The primary support came from William Dixon (1788–1859), the coal magnate from Govan, but considerable sums were stumped up by his old friends Douglas Kinnaird (1788–1830) and Joseph Hume (1777–1855). Dr Thomas Southwood Smith (1788–1861), the sanitary reformer, and Charles Day (1782–1836), the shoe-blacking tycoon, also gave appreciable backing in the early years. This may seem an excessive deployment of financial firepower, but the accounts made for grim reading. In the first two years, *The Spectator* lost some £7,500 (c. £500,000) per annum – to say nothing of the costs of finding and appointing premises. A sense of Rintoul's real panic about the paper's prospects can be gleaned from another letter to Blackwood, this time from September 1829:

The circulation is very considerably higher than when you were in town, and it keeps up – with a tendency to increase – which no other paper in London does at this time of the year. Still it is *far from paying*; and I suspect, in confidence, what I foresaw and told you nearly a year ago, that its success would be a question of *resources*. The undertaking, planned on a great scale and for long endurance, must be of slow growth. It must succeed, and greatly too, if I can provide the funds, say for a couple of years longer; but mere ordinary success will not support *The Spectator*.[44]

A price-rise was soon deemed unavoidable. To mitigate the bad news, readers were informed on 15 May 1830 that the newspaper would expand by 50 per cent in size, from sixteen to twenty-four pages, allowing it 'to devote a larger space to topics of general interest'. Lest the reader be in doubt, *The Spectator* asserted that

> it is universally received as THE BEST FAMILY JOURNAL in the empire.[45] We may add, that the cost at which it has attained its present character, is unequalled by any journal of the same description. The changes which we have announced will add very materially to the expense. To afford the proprietors an adequate remuneration, the price will be raised to a Shilling.

It was no embarrassment for *The Spectator* to seek to pay its way – but the price of that was a paper costing double most of its weekly rivals. Rintoul's proposed solution was to enclose the paper inside a striking cover of lucrative advertisements, but the fear that sensible readers would simply discard this pointless wraparound discouraged prospective advertisers. The actual change in form was minor: once the dust had settled, from 5 June 1830, the paper continued to run three full pages of advertisements, now arranged and indexed by topic. The contents proper covered the same range as before, but took advantage of the new space to expand in scope.

The Spectator's first offices on the Strand did not survive long. In 1829, the newly founded King's College London forcibly purchased several buildings along the south of the street, including that occupied by *The Spectator*. The following year it was demolished to make way for an archway into the campus, itself destroyed in 1972 by the unfortunate arrival of the Strand Building. Rintoul rapidly found premises nearby, by moving on to Wellington Street, which ran from the Strand to Waterloo Bridge, along the course of present-day Lancaster Place. The range of buildings on the west side of the road, owned by the property tycoon Thomas Goodall of Brighton, was not much to look at, but already had a good pedigree in journalism. On its arrival at 4 Wellington Street, *The Spectator* found itself in the fine company of *The Examiner* and *Westminster Review* next door. A year later, Joseph Clayton took over from Westley the role of publisher, and by 1832 had established his own printing press at 7 Windsor Court, across the Strand opposite Somerset House.[46] As for the paper proper, in December 1831, presumably as a cost-cutting measure, it moved into Rintoul's family home at the south end of the block (no. 9).[47] Here, with views of Somerset House to the east, the Savoy Chapel to the west, and Waterloo Bridge to the south, *The Spectator* would spend its next ninety years.

Not many families of four have had to accommodate the working offices of a national weekly, along with its chief staff, in their humble abode. This tall townhouse was, unsurprisingly, designed for residential purposes: even its staff would later describe it as 'huggermugger', 'dingy' and 'like something in a novel of Dumas'.[48] Its five floors each contained one room, and were accessed by a steep turret staircase. Rintoul and his family lived on the top two floors; the two below were given over to the newspaper and its publisher, and the ground floor to servants' quarters. That original building, famously shining white on Wellington Street,[49] is now demolished, its foundations long lost beneath the sprawling hulk of Brettenham House (erected in 1932).

Perhaps Kinnaird had always entertained a longer-term plan in luring Rintoul from Edinburgh to *The Atlas* – namely, to use that title merely as a training ground for his protégé to learn the arcane but high-octane business of Fleet Street journalism. For London did indeed have

Wellington Street, *The Spectator* office (1830–1920; pic. 1907)

revolutionary, a proto-socialist or an anti-establishment demagogue. Instead, he was a staunch individualist, committed to the belief that, once the people have been suitably educated, they have the right to live and do as they desire – and as their education advises.

A small uplift in circulation came in May 1829, when *The Spectator* swallowed up *The Sphynx*, a weekly founded in 1827 by James Silk Buckingham. Having also established the literary weekly *The Athenaeum* in January 1828, Buckingham soon realised that he could not maintain both titles. In the public announcement of the incorporation, he wrote that '*The Spectator* presents, perhaps, the most perfect analysis and epitome of news that have ever been attempted in a weekly paper ... of its literary talent it may truly be asserted, that no periodical of the present day surpasses it in the acuteness, soundness and fairness of its criticisms, or in the infinite variety with which its pages constantly abound.'[50] So spake the salesman, but other contemporaries were also quick to acknowledge *The Spectator*'s success. One doyen of the newspaper scene recalled that 'so early as the first year of its publication, [it] acquired a high reputation, both for the independent course it pursued on political and indeed on all other questions, and the intellectual character of its articles.'[51] Blackwood's *Maga* at last responded to Rintoul's requests for support and acknowledged that *The Spectator* 'is impartial. It is a fair, open, honest, and manly periodical.'[52] *The Globe*, then a radical evening paper, saw other features worthy of commendation, describing the title as 'distinguished among its weekly contemporaries for its perception of the ludicrous in manners, and its piquant, yet not malignant, satire upon the foibles of society.'[53] Addison and Steele, it seems, had found a worthy successor. In August 1829, *The Spectator* used its own advertisement to record that it had 'completed its year of probation, and acquired a distinguished rank among the Journals of the Metropolis.' It proudly reminded readers of its aim to be 'the most *informing*, the most *amusing*, and the *fairest* of all Newspapers.'

Yet Rintoul was well aware that he needed *The Spectator* to circulate in a broader ambit than the talking

ace for an avowedly radical periodical. *Blackwood's Magazine* ('Maga', 1817–1980) was the venerable vehicle educated Tories, *John Bull* (1820–92) of their ultra-nservative, nationalist brethren; *The Examiner* (1808–), after its high-minded early years, had come to align elf with the establishment, supporting many aspects Liberal Party politics. *Tait's Edinburgh Magazine* was on to be founded (1832–61) as the organ of educated higs, but it would have little spirit for popular reform. he *Spectator*, by contrast, keenly clamouring for reform all kinds, found that no specific political faction s appropriate: the Tories were too conservative, the higs outmoded, and the Utilitarians out of step. ntoul's politics were led by concrete issues of the day, t dogmatic party politics: he was not a Republican shops of London. An advertisement of the following year cast an ambitiously broad net:

> There is food for every palate. There is News for the Old Lady, Literature and Fine Arts for the Young One; the Father of the Family is presented with every subject that relates to his interests, national or individual, discussed or reported; while the pursuits, tastes, and pleasures of his Sons (if they be rational), are as sedulously catered for... There is no class to which the SPECTATOR can come wrong; it is as well adapted for the Farmer as the Fine Gentleman, for the Mechanic as the Publicist, the Tradesman as the Magistrate or Clergyman.

Fine talk. But evidently not quite every Tom, Dick or Sally wanted to spend their precious 9d on 'a weekly journal of news, politics, literature, and science'.

Although *The Spectator*'s sales figures were slow to improve, its influence was rife. Articles from *The Spectator* were widely read – and widely reprinted by press and journals throughout the country. In particular, Rintoul was both amused and frustrated that politicians evidently read *The Spectator* (among other titles) while disdaining its importance. Privately, he noted that the start of the Parliamentary session was 'when our *proper* public comes to town'[54]; publicly, he railed in *The Spectator* that

> The tone in which newspapers are usually mentioned in the House of Commons is absurd. Men who cannot breakfast without one, in the evenings pretend to be hardly cognisant of the existence of such things. Men who in private life look to them for their sole stock of opinions, are found in public sneering at their contents.[55]

Such spikiness did not go unnoticed. As early as 1830, *The Spectator* was being personified in political cartoons. In Henry Heath's skit we find Rintoul, amid a bevy of newspaper editors, acting as a spokesman for

press freedom. 'No tyranny', he declares, 'can arres the march of intellect – knowledge is strength – th French have set us a good example.' To the left stand James Scarlett, the Attorney General, who had unjustl gagged and shut down dissident elements of the Londo press. He provocatively lights a cannon with 'a powe unknown to Magna Charta'. Stuffed under his arm i a bundle of further charges: 'Censorship of the press 'Licence to print acts', 'Gag<g>ing Act', 'Repeal habea corpus' and 'Warrants to search'. The Prime Ministe the Duke of Wellington (far left), stands by in voca support. Rintoul's *Spectator* (right), not yet two years ol is thus depicted as a chief bulwark against such attack on the free press as were already under way in Franc from the Count of Polignac (here standing in the rear)

A core principle of *The Spectator*'s foundation w that it be non-political. However, the growing agitatio for parliamentary reform, and the chaos following th resignation of Wellington in November 1830, we drawing the paper ever deeper into political activism The make-or-break moment for *The Spectator* – wheth it would ride the crest of the wave or be submerge for good – was provided by the advent of the Gre Reform Act, that fundamental overhaul of Britain electoral system. The Bill's troubled progress throug the Commons in the summer of 1831, and its repeate rebuffing by the Lords later in the year, had stirred the nation to fever pitch. But *The Spectator* tried to tack the matter with level-headed pragmatism: 'the Natio wants good laws and the instruments wherewith to obta good laws are good members of Parliament.'[56] After t new Parliament passed the bill in July 1831, the pape focus turned squarely upon the Lords, who sensed th this could be the end of an all-too-comfortable era.

The Spectator realised at an early stage that it cou best aid the cause of reform not by lecturing its reade but by educating them. It allowed itself, in effect, to ser as the publisher of political fact-files that piggy-back on the paper itself. These supplements, always suppli gratis, were guaranteed an interested – and often invest – readership. An 'Anatomy of the House of Commo first appeared as four pages of tables on 23 October 18

AN_ENGLISH_ESSAY._on the_ POLIGNAC _SYSTEM!!_

Henry Heath on the suppression of the free press (1830)

before re-emerging in a corrected twelve-page form in the first fortnight of 1831. These tables cut through the smoke and mirrors of Parliament, painstakingly analysing each of its members by his constituency's size and method of suffrage, however dysfunctional; what is more, it revealed who had relationships with members of the peerage, and who held vested interests in the military, the law and commerce. Never had so much targeted political information been set before a public that had never been so engaged.

With the political temperature rising, the first column of the opening issue of 1831 spelt out Rintoul's problem: 'It is difficult to be a SPECTATOR in these times.' It continued,

The history of 1830 is the history of the progress of national liberty and public opinion. *We* are of

the people, feel with them, and hope for them... For our parts (and it is with no idle vanity) we maintain that the duties of a public instructor, for such is a newspaper, are high, and that his responsibility is painfully great – his power at the present day is universally admitted to be immense ... varied talents, and the devotion of much skill, unassailable integrity, and high and generous views, are absolutely essential to the formation of a true public advocate and teacher in a journal... We do not hesitate to point out, that the *Spectator* is no ordinary compilation, thrown together without taste, order, and almost without effort... In our capacity as Spectator, we see every thing; in that of Reporters, we communicate all we can learn, in the way best fitted to the ears that hear; as Critics, we discern and decide in all cases where doubt may occur; as Teachers, we offer the tribute of our study, our education, and our knowledge; and it would be difficult to find the question which, in the course of the year, we do not at least aim at throwing light upon.[57]

Thus fired up for action, *The Spectator* imagined itself as 'a bundle of intelligence germinating hands and eyes in all directions – the hands springing out like the sons of earth, each armed with a pen.'[58] By March, Rintoul had felicitously coined perhaps the most famous slogan in *The Spectator*'s history: 'The Bill, the whole Bill and nothing but the Bill.' After its first appearance, on 12 March 1831, this call-to-reform would reappear countless times in the press, in popular prints and in the parley of frustrated citizens across the country.

Rintoul had attended the founding meeting of the Parliamentary Candidate Society that same month, sitting alongside J.S. Mill, Francis Place, John Arthur Roebuck and Major Aubrey Beauclerk. To encourage the nation to think critically, *The Spectator* introduced a series of eighty-eight biographical sketches of MPs deserving support ('Trustees of the Nation').[59] But although it was fully in the fray, the paper was fully aware of the dangers of preaching:

a newspaper that should attempt to dictate must soon perish ... if it dictates, it dies... Newspapers

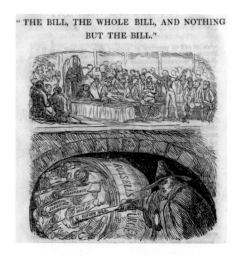

"THE BILL, THE WHOLE BILL, AND NOTHING BUT THE BILL."

A contemporary Anti-Reform pamphlet (anon., London, 1831)

are but an instrument to express the opinion of their readers on either side of whatever may be in question; and, taken all together, where the Press is free, they constitute the public voice.[60]

It nevertheless celebrated the increased influence of the press – 'free, enlightened, active and powerful beyond all comparison with former time.'[61] By this point *The Spectator* felt the need to make explicit its manifestly political position. On 21 May, an article entitled 'To our Non-Political Readers' confessed plainly that

it is difficult to be a *mere* spectator in times like these. It is all very well, in the piping times of domestic content, to sit still and report progress; but when, as in the great business of Reform, every thing is at stake it is the duty of even neutrals to arm... It is sometimes *criminal* not to take a side – there are cases in which he that is not with us must be against us. Such is the grand struggle that is now agitating the country from its centre to its remotest corners... No, no. In ordinary times, we consider ourselves of the Commissariat department, and confine our cares to supplying provisions for the camp; but who, when all is at issue, can stand upon a hill and gaze upon the varying fortunes of the battle?... Those times of

The Spectator, 12 Mar. 1831

pleasant companionship with our public will soon return, and we shall hail them with delight, – none will hang up all the signs of hostility with more genuine satisfaction than ourselves. But let us earn our repose.

When the Bill was voted down by the Lords in October, riots broke out across the land. As *The Spectator* grimly observed, 'The House of Lords is hastening to euthanasia because of its want of correspondence and sympathy with public opinion.'[62] The paper's reporting of weekly news became increasingly sardonic: 'The writers of the Opposition press talk of constraining the people by an Anti-Reform Ministry. Constrain the whirlwind with my lady's fan!'[63] Having succeeded in the past, *The Spectator* tried its favoured tactic of education. To expose the vested interests of the Lords, and their clandestine control over the Commons, the paper worked up – in eye-watering detail – its 'Anatomy of the Peerage'. This arrived in two instalments in November 1831, before crystallising, in updated form, as a twenty-four-page 'Christmas supplement' for the issue of 31 December. Edward Bulwer-Lytton, the novelist and incipient politician, gushed with approval:

What admirable documents they are!... It is by efforts like these, made at great risk – at enormous expense – with a noble direction of judgment that consults what may instruct the People, and disdains to pander for lucre to their prejudice and their passions – it is also by philosophical and practical principles, applied to the matter of such facts, and calling the chaos into harmony, that we are made deservedly proud of the better portion of the English Press... [They have] called Wisdom to the breakfast-table, and brought home the best part of ethics (political knowledge) from the closet to men's daily understanding and ordinary business.[64]

More succinctly, for the *Northern Whig*, it was 'one of the most valuable manuals of political knowledge

that has yet been submitted to the public, in a cheap form.'[65] Yet, despite the avowedly political nature of its end-of-year 'Anatomy', Rintoul wished to make clear the restricted scope of his paper's aims:

But let it be remembered, that while we are anxious to better what we have, it is no part of our plan to lose what we have got. The *Spectator* is of the Conservative order: and so is our Constant Reader. In all our advocacy of new measures, and our explosion of old Tory doctrine, one leading feature will be found to mark our proceedings – respect for the sanctity of Property, the most holy and venerable of civil institutions. If our Constant Reader will rely upon guidance, he need not fear that a single iota of his possessions, be they small or large, will ever be shaken out of his hands. Let not good-natured people run away with the idea that there is any connexion between amelioration and a war upon wealth. This is a base insinuation of the enemy.

Full of festive play, *The Spectator* gave itself a hearty back-pat:

We have not only been wise among the sapient, but we have been, and continue to be, courteous and gentle. Though we have thrown ourselves into the foremost of the fight, our warfare has been chivalrous – we have taken no mean advantage: our object has been general good, and our arguments as general: we have combated with principles, not persons: we have attacked the reason, not the feelings of individuals... We have shivered not a few lances, and unhorsed many a foe; but after the fiercest contest, we could have shaken hands with our antagonist, and boldly asked him if all had not been fair. Is it not true, most Constant Reader; and can many journalists make the same appeal?[66]

In the early months of 1832, *The Spectator* fought as hard as the medium allowed to get the Bill at last over the line, openly backing the proposal for William IV (celebrated as 'a second Alfred' and the 'most popular king in the world')[67] to create pro-Reform peers who could sway the Lords. That drastic measure proved to be unnecessary, once the Bill finally limped through the Lords, and gained royal assent that June. Rintoul – and others – celebrated in the belief that without *The Spectator*, the Bill would never have become law. That is clearly fanciful; but it is hard to deny that the fight would not have been so effective, so well-focused and so swift in coming without the strenuous activities of Rintoul and his team.

The paper did not rest up. Instead, with parliamentary reform achieved, it pressed on with its mission to teach Britons to petition for a better system. It issued a trio of 'Keys to Political Knowledge': I: The Working of the House of Commons (29 Sep. 1832), II: Public Expenditure (3 Nov. 1832), III: Taxation (2, 9 and 23 Feb. 1833). The progress of all these efforts was tangible: not only were the surveys widely shared and discussed, but the years 1830–2 saw a tripling of the paper's circulation, from some 600 to 1,800. And, as a most satisfying mark of their shared success, Rintoul's long-standing friend and ally, George Kinloch, entered Parliament as the first MP for the new constituency of Dundee in January 1833.

However, this stark transformation of *The Spectator* into an avowedly political organ forced it to forgo its neutral persona. Although it was in no sense the voice of any given party, its commitment to social and civil reform could hardly be disguised. Advertisements dropped the claim that it was 'the best journal for respectable families', and some founding proprietors felt compelled to sell up their shares. But, far from shrinking back in this Age of Improvement, Rintoul simply bought up their stakes and pushed on with his cause. By the close of 1833, in fact, he had become the paper's sole proprietor, allowing him a free hand hitherto unknown in his career.

The Spectator and its burgeoning readership were soon to feel considerable disappointment at the stalling pace of reform. The Whig ministries of Grey and Melbourne in the 1830s achieved far less than was hoped. Rintoul soon apprehended that, to achieve real change,

it would be necessary to usher along the populace beyond Westminster Palace. Despite his impatience about Britain's slow progress, it would not take long for other major causes to fall into *The Spectator*'s lap.

Aside from its political agitations, the paper had successfully established itself as a journal of polished writing on all manner of topics in life, literature and the arts. Rintoul was acutely aware that such writing – often timeless in nature – was of equal, if not greater, potency in retaining readers than the fervid dissection of transient political disputes. In order to secure the best writing of this kind, he would often pay some £40 (c. £3,000) for copy for each issue. On occasion, he would offer £10 for a single contribution – an almost unparalleled sum for the period. The results were worth the expense. A judgment for 1837 is typical for its approval:

> *The Spectator*'s style is clear, easy, and close; and its articles are usually remarkable for their acuteness, their good sense, and for the important information embodied in them. They display an entire mastery of the subject discussed, and often excite our surprise and admiration because of the new light in which the writer puts it, when we had thought that everything had been advanced which human ingenuity could bring to bear on it... 'The Spectator' is, perhaps, the most striking exemplification afforded by the weekly newspaper press, of what political economists call the division of labour. There are several gentlemen distinguished as writers on political and literary subjects, regularly engaged for it; and each has his own department. Mr. Rintoul is what is called the conducting editor; that is, he has the option of accepting or rejecting what articles he pleases.[68]

On the one hand, Rintoul never forgot the lesson of Addison and Steele that news could and should be disseminated and discussed without forgoing literary taste, elegant style and gentle humour. On the other, he was not prepared to let good writing obstruct *The Spectator*'s ideological goals. For Rintoul and his paper, supported, in a word, freedom – not just freedom of choice for working men and freedom of conduct for all British subjects, but also freedom for the colonies, freedom for West Indian slaves, freedom for those trapped in serfdom on the Continent and in Russia, freedom of the press, and freedom of religion. In fact, on this last count, Rintoul's religion, however tightly held, was lightly worn: the paper at once supported the Established Church and encouraged Catholic emancipation – one contemporary even described Rintoul himself as 'Pro-Catholic'.[69] It did not push a specific denomination to the irrational exclusion of others.

The all-important goal of *The Spectator* was to create an efficient and transparent system of government, so that the people could vote and live as they chose. To secure that, it passionately supported not just the Reform Bill but the extension of the franchise, the shortening of Parliamentary terms, the secret ballot, the reworking of the postal system, and the implementation of self-determined systematic colonisation to improve the lot of British subjects at home and abroad. No reader of *The Spectator*, familiar with this consistent outlook, could be surprised that it gave its backing to the Abolition of Slavery Act (1833) and the Municipal Corporations Act (1835), defended the Tolpuddle Martyrs in 1834, and expressed some middle-class sympathy with the cause of the Chartists in their first thrill of 1838, even publishing the 7,000-word text of the People's Charter *verbatim*.[70] Its role in the successful campaign against the 'taxes on knowledge' secured the lowering of stamp duty from 4d to 1d in September 1836; as was only proper, *The Spectator* instantly returned to its original 9d – a price it would not rise above for the next 125 years.

In 1835, when the political success of Rintoul's *Spectator* had become widely acknowledged, he was invited back to his foster city of Dundee. The city hosted an extravagant dinner to thank him for his services towards securing liberal reform. *The Scotsman* records that Rintoul was 'presented with an elegant silver tea service, as a mark of the high estimation in which his political principles and powerful advocacy of the liberal cause are held by the people of Dundee.'[71]

The Spectator's ballot box proposal, 25 Feb. 1837

Despite these public successes, however, the private finances of *The Spectator* were causing worry. The paper was feeling the pinch, presumably under the pressure of lost subscribers and disenchanted advertisers. Debts increased as its circulation stalled, floating precariously between two and three thousand copies per week. Ironically, however, the large debts that Rintoul had built up saved the paper from a buy-out. First, in 1836, the 'Metropolitan Company', a committee of radical politicians and journalists looking to set up a new daily newspaper, considered buying *The Spectator* and transforming it into a daily. When they determined on the course of starting a fresh title, *The Constitutional*, and Rintoul's name was considered as an editor, his poor management of finances was one of the chief objections raised.[72] Later, in 1837, he found himself reaching out to Whig friends, including another radical politician, George Grote.[73] As the Tory press smelt blood, Rintoul feared he would be bought out by them if he failed to find radical support. Harriet Grote records that the purchase was ruled out because of the debts: they were not prepared to 'feed the cow for others to milk'.[74] Although the negotiations came to nothing, they seem to have hardened Rintoul's stance against the sham reformers who supported the Whigs. In turn, the paper's own strategy for reform moved away from parliamentary and political procedure to trade and the economy.

These proprietorial problems aside, Rintoul's reporters continued to keep their ear close to the ground, ready to pounce on political malpractice. For instance, a leader of December 1836 begins wryly: 'Somehow or other, cabinet secrets will ooze out.'[75] What follows reads like a modern *Spectator* political column, reconstructing the allegiances and rankling dissatisfaction among Melbourne's back-bitingly dysfunctional cabinet. An editorial in the *Manchester Guardian* was quick to attack the paper for its improper conduct in reporting such private matters: it was 'not patriotic' – and, besides, 'we do not think it very likely that "cabinet secrets" should "ooze out" in the way the *Spectator* would have the public believe.'[76]

But *The Spectator*'s sense of propriety was more geared towards its lofty goals than any political cabal. To the consternation of many, the paper railed increasingly against Melbourne's toothless Whig ministry – and had no time for 'his lucky Lordship' constantly cosying up with 'his beloved Mistress' Queen Victoria.[77] Instead it favoured the cause of the Philosophical Radicals, supporting the breakaway of Sir William Molesworth and John Arthur Roebuck. Such a move soon brought about some striking overlap with the Tory opposition in its criticisms of the government. In 1837, it shocked readers by reflecting that 'a Conservative Government, however composed, will be found very much preferable to a "Reform" Government, merely so called, existing upon many pretences... Practical improvements, we are satisfied, will be more attainable under a Government ostensibly opposed to "Reform," than under a "Reform Government" *merely so called*.'[78] Not for the first or last time, the paper confused its readers by its failure to support a consistent party line.

Reacting to Tory gains in the Whig election victory of August 1837, *The Spectator* had to be frank with its readers. A long leader headed 'The Spectator's Policy and Position' began:

A journal, published but once a week – debarred by its price and the nature of its contents from circulation amongst the millions – never under the obligation of patronage from any Government, nor at any time the organ of a party or sect, but always representing the individual opinions of its editor and sole proprietor, – a paper thus inherently destitute of the means by which influential journals commonly acquire their power, is just now the observed of all observers. We venture to say that there is no previous example in the history of periodical literature, of such a journal as the *Spectator* obtaining so much notice from its contemporaries, as has been bestowed upon us during the last three or four weeks... Why is so much importance attached to the sayings and doings of a humble weekly paper?

Having set out the nature of his paper's opposition to Melbourne's tactics, Rintoul continued:

The mere partisans and parasites of the Government, therefore, have had a strong motive, and have now a stronger one, for seeking to intimidate the *Spectator*, to run it down by abuse, to deprive it of weight and authority with the public, and above all, to disparage it with those sincere Reformers, who, being very much disappointed and vexed, hardly yet know whether to wreak their wrath on those who have cheated, or on him who endeavoured to warn them.

He could not hold back from explaining how this principled stance had helped the paper's standings:

We are independent and plain-spoken – that is the foundation of our present consequence, not to say influence. If we please the Tories by exposing Whig pretences, and displease the Whigs by showing how they have played and are playing the game of the Tories, the fault is not ours in either case: nor, considering our abiding attachment to Reform, let who may desert or oppose it, will either party be much gratified to learn, that the circulation of the *Spectator* has been steadily growing during the last year and a half, and was never so large, for any corresponding period, as during the last half-year.[79]

This, Rintoul continued, was despite the '*intimidation* of a cross kind' arising from the 'threats of pecuniary damage ... privately directed against the proprietor of this journal by Whig and Whig-Radical partisans.' The triumphant statement that follows may be taken to enshrine *The Spectator*'s quintessential position:

Had the *Spectator* virtually set itself to sale – flattering the prejudices, and the unreasoning hopes of well-meaning Reformers – ... there is no question that, in trading phrase, the journal might have 'done better', and, instead of more than holding its ground, have perhaps considerably extended it. But there are such things as sincerity and self-respect; and the *Spectator* is prepared to sacrifice something for them, even if it should turn out in the long run that honesty is *not* the best policy. Our course was not chosen for profit, and we were prepared for loss; but the reverse has happened.

Still, the paper was acutely aware that its mordant lectoring would not find favour with all who took it. As an apologia of sorts, a leader of 1838 – pointedly titled 'We would be kind' – observed that

political journalists, like doctors and surgeons, live by the evils they seek to remove ... it is our vocation – though perhaps not our nature – to snarl and snap and make ourselves disagreeable. We *would* be kind, but are not suffered. Believing well of human nature, we are nevertheless compelled to be in a perpetual state of objection to it – to be its accusers and prosecutors; while others, more fortunate in their selection of objects, have the pleasing task of recording its bright redeeming points, and playing the Plato to our Diogenes. Alas! That we should be so implicated in the storm as sometimes to overlook the rainbow![80]

The article concluded, rather playfully:

Perhaps some crafty or despotic minister, whom we, in the discharge of our public duty, may be in the bait of denouncing in harsh and unceremonious language, may be all that is estimable in private life. No doubt. We, too, in our private capacity, may be all that is bland and mellifluous. Who knows?

Over the next few years, as the prospect of a Tory government led by Sir Robert Peel increased, *The Spectator* continued to be criticised for its increasingly hostile attitude to All Things Whig. More controversial were its positive reports of Tory policies – and indeed its growing Conservative readership. Rintoul, however, remained unapologetic in putting principle ahead of party:

Truth, and what is more, truth in its just proportions, is our aim, whether in facts, political opinions, or criticism. That we always succeed in this aim it would be presumptuous to affirm; but if there is a body of Conservatives who will bear with the blows we frequently deal at the politics of their party, in consideration of their general belief in our integrity, so much the better for society. A class of readers who will submit to opposition to their prejudices from respect for a spirit of free enquiry, is far more respectable, both morally and intellectually, than pretended Liberals, who require a journalist, as the price of their support, to suppress unpleasing or disadvantageous truths; to sink down into their unscrupulous advocate of their party; to go with all their gullibility, and to change his course with every change of their caprice, or every necessity of their baffled blundering or intrigue.[81]

He had reason to be confident. By 1840, the circulation of *The Spectator* had successfully climbed to its then highest figure, of 3,500, making it the second most popular weekly after the indefatigably rabble-pleasing *John Bull*. But not all of Fleet Street was happy with Rintoul's hard-won success. The *Weekly Chronicle* (1836–67), a younger rival, asked its readers that year, 'What brought this great luminary amongst us from the North? What proofs has he given of practical superiority, in the affairs of this sublunary world?'[82] It proceeded to dispute both the political and commercial integrity of *The Spectator*. Rintoul was never in a mood to let such swipes go unchallenged; in a remarkable article of March 1840, he gave his most detailed defence in print of what he was working towards:

> The *Spectator* never expected a very high numerical sale; for it never formed its plan with that object, or descended to the arts by which it is attained. The price alone must shut out our journal from the market of the populace; and the subjects treated of, the manner in which they are treated, and the absence of scandalous reports or indecent news, are equally distasteful to the rich vulgar. In addition to these drawbacks, our course has not been one to stimulate circulation. We are the organ of no party; we run counter to the prejudices of all parties; and instead of lending our columns to the propagation of delusions, it is one great cause of the *dead set* made against us by the organs of the Government, and all the journals the Government can in any way influence, that we expose *them* on fit and proper occasions.[83]

Responding to the challenge about the paper's circulation, he was open: it is 'a property of no great money value, it is true, but in the creating of which, much money as well as labour has been spent.' But he strenuously rejected the idea that sales figures were the best metric of the paper's importance:

> The influence of the *Spectator* is irrespective of the number of copies printed and purchased; it arises from the class of minds it operates upon, and from its influence more or less direct over the views of other journals. We are read, too, (unluckily for our profit!) by many who do not *buy* – in too many reading-rooms and clubs, by too many rich economists who make one paper pass through several families. And, no bad judges of the rationale of circulation, advertisers seem to understand all this.

Many *Spectator* readers, there can be no doubt, supported the government of the day; after all, it was the Whigs (they reasoned) who had passed the Bill. By contrast, on the eventual accession of Peel to his second prime-ministerial term in 1841, the paper grew steadily more enthusiastic in praising his aims, if not those of the Tory party more broadly. By 1842, 'A Puzzled Admirer' was writing to the editor demanding clarity on *The Spectator*'s political outlook. To the query 'What do you aim at in your perpetual sarcasms against the Whigs?' Rintoul (for it can hardly be anyone else) responded as follows:

> At exposing humbug; at teaching men not to lean for support on broken reeds, nor to shear swine for wool, nor to look for grapes off thorns or figs off thistles... The Reform Bill was sought and supported not as an end in itself, but as the means to another end – as an instrument whereby to obtain and keep in office wise and capable Ministers. The Whigs, who were neither wise nor capable, insisted upon being kept in office because they had given us 'the Bill'... The whole subsequent career of the Whig Ministers may be described as a series of vague Liberal speeches and no-doings.[84]

Of Peel, by contrast, 'His peculiar mission is to d[...] (Here speaks a Rintoul.) Although Peel's first ter[m] brought outrage from *The Spectator* – the opening lead[...]

of 1835 cried 'Down with the Tories!' nineteen times[85] – now that he was in the prime position to enact change for the better, it lent its tentative support. As to its broader outlook on the British people, the paper declared:

We believe that if the material condition of the people can be improved, their craving for knowledge will be rendered more sharp; and we believe that every advance they make in knowledge will enable them to improve their condition and render that improvement permanent... Perhaps we are too unimaginative to be dazzled by rank and station and their attendant shows; but we cannot sympathise with the morbid dislike which some entertain towards them; the country will have them; we are contented, and can look on sometimes admiring and sometimes laughing at them. We frankly admire great and good qualities in men, and despise the empty affectation of them. For a desirable end we will coöperate with any man, and will labour in vain with nobody.

Fired with its missionary zeal to educate, *The Spectator* continued to issue a range of supplements to inform the nation and slowly steer policy: on postage reform (9 Mar. 1839), saving the sugar trade by abolishing slavery and establishing free labour (15 Apr. 1843), repealing the Corn Laws (25 Jan. 1846), making railway gauge uniform (2 and 9 May 1846), and colonising New Zealand (4 Jan. 1845) and Ireland (3 Apr. 1847). But its keenest backing in these years was given to a supplement that emerged from the work of a long-standing friend. In 1840, the Radical MP Joseph Hume assembled and chaired a committee of the Board of Trade on import duties. Its conclusion was clear: that free trade should be implemented across the board to abolish invasive and unjust protectionist tariffs. *The Spectator* had long been convinced of the advantages brought by the international division of labour – as first set out by Adam Smith and David Ricardo – and of the need for free trade alongside 'systematic colonisation'. For Britain under the grip of the Corn Laws, the freedom to trade needed fighting

for. Since the committee's 300-page report was unlikely to find an attentive readership, a digestible thirty-two-page summary was whittled from it and served up for mass circulation. It appeared as a supplement to the first *Spectator* of 1841, which announced:

The subjects of the Supplement published with this number of the *Spectator* are not held to be so popularly attractive as personal lists or tales of scandal; but they are of far more importance. Their object is to increase the material wealth of the country – to give everybody more, and to take less from each.[86]

The supplement sold tens of thousands of copies, dwarfing its typical circulation. It was distributed to all mayors, councils and corporations throughout the country, and sent to hundreds of officials abroad, including every American senator. Its contentions went on to shape the Liberals' pro-free-trade budget of 1841, a budget that proved to be too challenging for the nation's squirearchy, still pulling rank at the ballot box. By July 1841, *The Spectator* was irritable and impatient:

Free Trade and Financial Reform are mere words in the mouths of the leaders of both parties. Any House of Commons we can have at present – with the present constituency, in the present temper of that constituency – will be found utterly worthless for great legislative purposes.[87]

The following year, the deliberate heel-dragging of Parliament was still the source of intense frustration:

The only two political parties in the country are equally what is called 'conservative' – equally bent upon keeping matters in the main as they are.[88]

Although the Tory government was staunchly against repeal, Peel was gradually becoming converted to the cause. In 1845, against the backdrop of the incipient Irish Famine, he shocked his party and the country by declaring himself against the Corn Laws. As that bill came before Parliament, *The Spectator* announced its watershed importance:

> Let the measure pass, and free trade, with only such imperfections as time will easily remove, is the law of the land; protection a tradition of the past, traced only in ruins doomed to rapid decay.[89]

The paper followed the debate in intimate detail – and fired a rocket at Benjamin Disraeli when he misrepresented John Stuart Mill (an occasional *Spectator* writer) as a supporter of protectionist tariffs.[90] When Peel at last passed the bill – a move that swiftly terminated his political career – *The Spectator* expressed genuine pity for 'the most conspicuous martyr of emancipation from party thraldom':[91]

> The Corn Bill is safe – but its author is sacrificed. The Corn Laws are abolished – but so is Peel... There must be something rotten in the thing called Party which can force from office the very man whom the country would choose, at the very height of his popularity and power.[92]

On Peel's death four years later, the paper gave a genuinely warm valediction. Having dismissed him in the heat of the 1830s as a man 'totally unfit for the task' and 'not worthy to hold the station' of prime minister, whose 'pretentions to conversion are false, hollow and insincere',[93] it now praised his admirable ability to evolve:

> Among modern statesmen his career is singular for the completeness of the political change in himself. It may teach those who desire to emulate him, that it is never too late to learn; that *courage* is *sage*, and that the candour which revises the convictions of youth and dictates an altered course will survive the hasty misconstruction of the day if it be steadfast in its purpose; that a public policy suggested by close observation, based upon fact, and supported by the sanction of the nation, is irresistible.[94]

Alongside electoral reform and free trade, the other major cause *The Spectator* promoted in its early decades was that of colonial reform. As so often with the paper, it was not doctrinaire dogma but new ideas from unexpected quarters that led it to make the case. In this instance, however, the origins of the campaign were truly bizarre. Edward Gibbon Wakefield (1796–1862) had overplayed his hand as a dandy and a cad. In 1816 he had eloped with Eliza Pattle, an orphaned heiress in Chancery. After her untimely death, he raised the stakes in 1826 by abducting and forcibly marrying the fifteen-year-old Ellen Turner, a yet wealthier heiress. After a clandestine ceremony, he was caught red-handed and ring-fingered at Calais, and was jailed for three years in Newgate prison. Once he was incarcerated, his thoughts focused on his immediate environment: he read widely on the penal system and formulated fresh ideas for its improvement. From his cell he rapidly issued a flurry of articles and pamphlets on capital punishment, emigration and the colonies.

In 1829, Rintoul was struck by an anonymous series in the *Morning Chronicle*, entitled 'A Letter from Sydney'. These epistles advanced a markedly novel plan of colonisation, designed primarily to incentivise the typical, law-abiding British citizen to start a new life abroad. *The Spectator* wasted no time in declaring this 'the best scheme of colonization that has ever been submitted to the public', and 'one of the highest triumphs of human ingenuity'.[95] On learning through private enquiry that the notorious Wakefield was the Blighty-based author, Rintoul did not baulk at starting a productive correspondence. In April 1830, *The Spectator* turned out an eight-page supplement entitled 'The cure and prevention of pauperism, by means of systematic colonization'.[96] (This, as it happens, was certainly not to be the last *Spectator* article penned by a jailbird.) Rintoul at once wrote to Blackwood in the hope that Christopher North (the Tory *nom de plume* of John Wilson) would promote the cause more widely across the nation.

In July 1831, when reviewing Wakefield's work on penal law, Rintoul was moved to write:

If ever man redeemed the wrong he had done society, by conferring upon it a vast benefit, it is Mr. WAKEFIELD. We would call upon all generous minds to forget that this enlightened and ingenious inquirer had ever been detained within the walls of a prison, except for the purpose of a philosophical investigation.[97]

From Wakefield's release in May 1830, right through his emigration to New Zealand in September 1852, Rintoul and he remained close friends and allies in the promotion of colonial reform, both being early and active members of the newly founded National Colonisation Society. In short, Wakefield argued that people from every class of society, not just convicts, should be encouraged to settle in and improve the colonies. To increase options for investment among the labouring and middle classes, the wastelands of sparsely inhabited or entirely uninhabited colonies should be made commercially profitable. Government-owned land should be sold to Britons at a fair price, and the proceeds should serve as funds for their emigration; the colonies, once established, should be self-governing. In fact, Wakefield's scheme of 'systematic colonisation' proved to be the basic template for the modern Commonwealth. It helped shape colonial practice in South Australia, gave Wakefield an active and influential role in Lord Durham's transformative Commission on Canada, and led to the successful British colonisation of New Zealand.

At first, The Spectator was the only keen supporter in the press of such substantial colonial reform. Yet, for all the ridicule it received, the paper continued pressing the cause against a wilfully obstructive Colonial Office. As it later lamented, in an early acknowledgment of the 'brain drain' phenomenon, 'it is the systematic misrule of the British colonies which sends emigrants to the United States of America.'[98] In 1839, when The Spectator issued as a special supplement Lord Durham's report on Canadian colonisation, it described the document as 'without any exception, the most interesting state paper that we ever saw.'[99] It was certainly read by the right people: one year later, Canada followed its core

recommendation in passing the Act of Union.

In December 1838, Wakefield founded The Colonial Gazette, a journal specifically dedicated to reforming the colonies. Within nine months it was being published under Rintoul's auspices from The Spectator offices on Wellington Street. Rintoul wrote to Blackwood not long after the transfer that 'it promises soon to stand to the press in the Colonies much in the same relation that the Spectator bears to the provincial press of this country – supplying much of its matter, and considerably influencing opinion.'[100] This was not an empty puff for The Spectator: as a contemporary Irish paper wrote, 'the articles of the Spectator were more generally transferred to the columns of the provincial journals than those of any of its contemporaries.'[101] Until the Colonial Gazette ceased, in January 1847, the two titles published many columns drawn – with minor tweaks – from each other. On 14 September 1839, before the boats of the New Zealand Land Company set out to found their new colony in Wellington and beyond, lively toasts were given at a grand dinner aboard ship. The toast 'The Public Press' was directed at the guest of honour, R.S. Rintoul.

Wakefield set the highest store by his friend's advice: he later asserted that Rintoul's opinions on colonial matters were 'worth mine over and over again'.[102] In a public letter to his editor, he confessed that 'I should have done nothing at all, if you had not constantly helped me during the years when the pursuit of systematic colonization was a continual struggle with difficulties.'[103] To this Rintoul appended the note, 'the kind of merit which the Spectator seeks not to disclaim, is simply that of not being frightened by the novelty of a scientific proposition; and, of having, when examination has assured us of its solidity, held by it until others had become as convinced of its reality and of its practical nature as we are.'[104] By 1852, when Wakefield at last emigrated to New Zealand himself, having failed to persuade Rintoul and his family to do so, he bade adieu for the last time to 'his truest and best friend'.[105] His family shared this adulation: when Wakefield's son, Jerningham, was touring the South Island of New Zealand in 1840–1, he encountered an imposing peak of 5,700ft overlooking what would become the port of Nelson. As he needed to christen it somehow, the name of sufficient stature that came to him was Mount Rintoul. What the humble editor made of this titanic gesture is not recorded, but the name is now destined to endure with the peak.

Yet, for all its fight for emergent causes, *The Spectator* knew when to draw the line. The paper was not swayed to support direct action amid the revolutionary troubles in 1848, and kept a level head throughout what proved to be a watershed moment for so many regions on the Continent. When that year Thomas Francis Meagher was leading the Young Rebels of Ireland, the paper warned that

A sincere and earnest respect for political freedom demands that the ignorant shall be protected against the machinations of those vanity-stricken men who emulate the lunacy of Courtenay Thom, and that the peaceable shall be secured against excesses foreknown to the guardians of the public peace.[106]

Rintoul, who often used his newspaper to declare his sincere respect for 'the sanctity of property', was never going to thrill at mob-rule. Instead, a greater focus that year was upon reform of the civil service, led by a formidable series of letters from Arthur Symonds, the Registrar of the Metropolitan Buildings Office. These five 'Letters on the Obstruction of Public Business' were transformative in reforming Whitehall administration in the hope that efficient transparency might replace stubborn opacity.[107]

It would be wrong, however, to regard *The Spectator* as a mere political lobbyist. Although its front half was filled to the gills with news and politics, perhaps the most read and most widely circulated elements were its literary and artistic reviews, which occupied the majority of the paper's rear. From the outset, *The Spectator* was a keen reviewer of contemporary books, assessing some two or three hundred each year. Its activity in this field steadily increased, and by 1851 the throughput of titles

was sufficiently large to require the launch of a monthly 'literary supplement' that expanded the issue by eight or more pages. (This appendix went on to form part of *The Spectator* until 1931, when it was reshaped into a quarterly, seasonal feature.) Rintoul, although only one of many reviewers, did not swerve from his firm conviction that the artist was 'a public servant, whose existence could only be justified if he did good to others through his art.'[108]

Despite this rather reductive attitude to artistic invention, *The Spectator* soon gained the reputation of critical independence in producing reviews that were 'often severe, but seldom unjust'.[109] In opera, Verdi and Piave saw *La Traviata* (1853) castigated for 'sensual profligacy and moral degradation'; of Lord Tennyson's *Princess*, a poem on a 'subject which narrow, uninteresting, unnatural and absurd', the critic said 'namby-pamby is the true characteristic of the execution'.[110] In fiction, Edward Bulwer-Lytton's *Pelham* (1828) was mocked as 'sheer baby-fancy'.[111] Emily Brontë's *Wuthering Heights* (1847) was dismissed as 'too coarse and disagreeable to be attractive'; Charlotte Brontë's *Jane Eyre* (1847) was reprimanded for its 'low tone of behaviour'. And when a fellow author had her (anonymous) novel *The Fair Carew* (1851) dismissed as 'mere literary smartness', Charlotte told George Smith that the review was

a much more honest notice – though infinitely stupid. The poor man used what faculties he had – but the faculty of judging a work of fiction is not among his talents. That worthy critic has no perception for originality of thought or nicety of delineation: he is blind as a bat and profoundly satisfied with his blindness. However... the 'Spectator' has treated the 'Fair Carew' with much more respect than it treated 'Jane Eyre'; of the latter – its most salient remark was that the conception and characters of the book reminded him [the critic] of nothing so much as the grotesque and hideous masks of apes – wolves and griffins to be found in the carved works of certain old Cathedrals. It was in his estimation a morbid monkish fancy – a thing with the head of an owl – the tail of a fox and the talons of an eagle.[112]

Although Rintoul advertised that in his paper all artistic works were 'criticised with freedom and spirit, but with candour and kindness',[113] he warned one of his chief literary critics that 'The Spectator is not enthusiastic, and must not be!'[114]

Inevitably, not all readers could find themselves in agreement with the stern criticism dished out by Rintoul's Spectator.[115] Owing to its frequently exacting reviews, the satirical medley Punch (founded in 1841) often published skits on how The Spectator was afflicted with 'incomparable frigidity' and should change its name to the Cold-Water Advocate;[116] any critic for the paper 'may go on with several lines of praise; then he inevitably comes to a "but", and this is sure to be a cold-water butt.'[117] Casualties, the Punch wags maintained, were frequent in The Spectator offices: the printer gets chilblains, the staff constantly slip on ice, and the editor's ink needs to be kept boiling in a saucepan.[118] In 1841, the poet Richard Horne sent his volume Chaucer Modernized to Rintoul along with 'Cockle's anti-bilious pills'. On the box was written, 'To be taken one hour before the book is reviewed'; on the book, 'This mixture to be taken one hour after the pills.'[119] Horne elsewhere depicted Rintoul being served 'a superb plate of thistles, which he munched with natural relish'.[120] A short-lived American review observed that The Spectator has the reputation of being the most cold-blooded journal in existence. It has no more geniality than Babbage's calculating machine.' That this criticism had some deeper cause is revealed by the description of the Rintoul as 'a cannie Scot of the worst description, being heartless, selfish, mean, grasping and bigoted; he is consequently a first-rate man of business, and has secured the fortunes of his paper.'[121]

Given these stiff and stuffy strictures, it is perhaps surprising that, in 1850, Rintoul accepted the suggestion of Ford Madox Brown, relayed via Lowes Cato Dickinson, to take on William Rossetti as the paper's art critic, a position he held until 1858. As a co-founder of the Pre-Raphaelite Brotherhood, Rossetti wrote for The Spectator the first declaration of that movement and its principles in the public press.[122] Its enthusiasm was predictable for the author but somewhat surprising for the paper. In architecture, too, Rintoul's Spectator was influential. Indeed, it is one of many quirks in the paper's history that Crystal Palace – the building of the Great Exhibition, and now the district and its football team – was a glib term propagated among polite society by its sceptical assessment of Joseph Paxton's architectural project.[123]

Alongside its increasingly detailed coverage of literature, theatre, opera and the visual arts, The Spectator still found space regularly to discuss the mores of society and the changing fashions of Victorian Britain. A contemporary press directory used terms that would have well described the Spectator of Addison and Steele:

Cold, shrewd, sagacious, searching are its strictures on men and manners: never characterised by warmth – yet redeemed from dullness – nay, rendered pointed and piquant, by the sharpness of their edge, the acuteness of their satire, and the bitterness of their application.[124]

Correspondence played from the earliest days of The Spectator a very lively role. One of the first readers to have their letter published in full was Charles Lamb (22 Nov. 1828, above the initials 'C.L.'), who lamented others' editorial meddling in Shakespeare's verses. Rintoul soon made clear by example that he was content to publish, often in unabridged form, even those letters that strongly disagreed with – or dismantled – the paper's previous arguments. Among the most energetic and prolix correspondents was Daniel O'Connell, 'The Liberator' of Ireland. The first of his four letters to the paper, published as a 'correspondence extraordinary' in November 1833, caused a flurry of political interest, not least for the author's humorous tone.[125] The pleasantries were not to last: as the course of Ireland and The Spectator drifted farther apart, O'Connell (and his son John) regularly slandered Rintoul and his paper in his speeches: he 'was a Liberal at one time, but now is the worst kind of Tory – one professing liberality, but practising the very worst species of despotic principles.'[126] As for 'the mongrel *Spectator*', it 'could not be said to represent any party in particular, except that of the sour black-hearted writer, a fellow with an odd name, Rintoul.'[127] Such even-handed honesty would become (and remain) a staple of *Spectator* correspondence pages, although a formal 'Letters to the editor' section was not made a regular feature until 1850.[128] But on 15 June that year, it should be said, a letter appeared from Karl Marx, Friedrich Engels and August Willich, who wrote to protest that they were not anti-Prussian dissidents plotting assassination in London. The editor's heading, 'Prussian Spies in London', did not bespeak great sympathy. In subsequent years we find Charles Kingsley promoting Christian socialism and university reform,[129] or Alexis de Tocqueville arguing (in translation) for reform of the British military, although Rintoul politely withheld the 'French gentleman's' name.[130]

Rintoul's energies were relentless on every imaginable front. However, despite evident signs of being a workaholic – after all, he literally could not quit *The Spectator* of an evening – and indeed something of a control freak, he wrote a lot less for the paper than many of his successors in the editorial chair. Instead, as a long-standing colleague recalled,

> He suggested the papers, he supplied suggestions as to the mode of treating them, he carefully and critically analysed every article, and urged its writer to revision with a view to make it as perfect as possible. In the news department there was the same labour; in the selection, condensation, and arrangement of the intelligence he took an active and unwearied part.[131]

The publisher Alexander Macmillan recalled that Rintoul

> used to dwell on the necessity of his contributors, if they would be really effective, 'writing bullets', and not beating out their shot to flat ineffective

sheets. The larger the surface in proportion to the mass the less the impression made.[132]

This is in keeping with the paper's reputation for cutting to the chase: as a Scottish newspaper later recalled, 'I was usual to hear public men say, "If you want the whole question put in a nutshell, get Rintoul to do it."'[133]

John Hunter, an Edinburgh lawyer, privately described him in 1839 as

> the very *beau idéal* of a newspaper editor, keeping all his assistants (much superior men to himself) in dire subordination and imparting a unity of tone to the whole by his knack of touching up and cutting and carving. When all is done he fancies he has done all.[134]

As others recalled, 'not a line appeared without M Rintoul's supervision',[135] and

> From its first line to its last, all its pages seemed as if written by the same hand … all that appeared bore his stamp, and breathed his ideas. He had always the happy knack not only of winning coadjutors, but of keeping them in order.[136]

His *Spectator* staff conjectured with good reason th

> No journal perhaps was ever before so thoroughly edited as the *Spectator* of Mr. Rintoul; not a line or word was passed over as a matter of course; every line and word passed through the alembic of his brain.[137]

Perhaps uniquely in *Spectator* history, Rintoul's contr was such that the staff saw little of one another: 'F so identified his paper with himself', another journal remarked, 'that his contributors only knew *him*; they we not acquainted with each other.'[138]

Leading figures on the team were John Tyls Wicksteed, who served as sub-editor, the reform author John Wade, who was the primary leader-writ and the poet and diplomat Henry Southern.[139] Thornton Hunt, son of the controversial essayist Leigh Hunt, joined the staff in 1840, and became increasingly involved in the political writing. At times he served as sub-editor, and – on the rare occasions when Rintoul did take a holiday – as acting editor; on one occasion he brought in his friend G.H. Lewes, the partner of George Eliot, to help with editing copy. William Smith Williams – the man who first recognised the merit of *Jane Eyre* – was a prominent critic of art, theatre and literature; in the 1850s, George Brimley, librarian of Trinity College, Cambridge, became the primary literary critic. Among his regular music critics were George Hogarth, Egerton Webbe, Edward Holmes and Edward Taylor, Gresham Professor of Music; the appearance of musical notation, and sometimes entire pieces, was common enough in the early *Spectator*.

Rintoul – or his paper – manifestly grew to be something of an intellectual magnet. He could persuade Thomas Carlyle to write on Ireland,[140] J.S. Mill to review George Grote's monumental *History of Greece*,[141] Grote to discuss the state of Switzerland,[142] or J.A. Roebuck the failings of Lord Durham's administration in Canada.[143] Albany Fonblanque, although primarily based at *The Examiner*, made occasional contributions. Richard Whateley, the Archbishop of Dublin, and William Maccall wrote regularly on religion and ethics. Other Scottish writers alongside Maccall included the future editor of the *Daily News* William Weir, the future editor of the *Dumfries Times* and *Birmingham Journal* Robert Douglas, and the celebrated humorist William Maginn. While rivals alleged that Rintoul gave preferential treatment to Scottish writers,[144] others recalled his one-nation remark that 'a perfect newspaper required a Scotchman as editor, Irishmen as reporters, and Englishmen to write the leaders.'[145]

There is no question that *The Spectator* was Rintoul's life – as it inevitably feels for any committed editor. He would not leave London during a parliamentary session, and did not take a holiday at all for the first thirteen years of his tenure. Only in later periods would he allow his family to escape with him to their summer house

in Lochee, suburban Dundee. Nevertheless, he could occasionally be seen about town, having descended from his chaotic Wellington Street eyrie. He crops up orating to working men in 1836; delivering part of a public lecture series on national education in 1839; at the inaugural dinner of the Scottish Society in 1849; as a delegate for Sir Arthur Helps's Health Fund to petition Palmerston in 1854; and on bibulous nights out with the theatrical crowd of the actor William Macready. Beyond his contributors, and his political allies mentioned already, his circle of friends included the radical politicians Sir William Molesworth and Charles Buller, and the literary circles of Lord Tennyson, Robert Browning, W.M. Thackeray, Laman Blanchard and Bryan Procter. There is evidence, however, that Rintoul deliberately avoided a high-profile presence in society so as to preserve his hard-won editorial impartiality. Edward Quillinan, William Wordsworth's son-in-law, remarked,

> I don't quite understand Rintoul's point. Making it a rule to avoid authors, he makes it a rule to exclude himself from the best intellectual society – that is, if he applies his rule rigorously. If he means that he avoids the small cliques of authorlings and criticlings who puff one another and abuse every one else, I quite understand him and 'small blame him,' as the Irishman says.[146]

Nothing so far has been said of Rintoul's family. This is not by chance: remarkably, although the Rintouls literally lived in the *Spectator* offices, their private life remained exceedingly private. That was not without reason. Rintoul had married his wife, Henrietta (1785–1860), while working in Dundee. Whereas Rintoul was Scottish-born and -raised, Henrietta's story was rather different: born to Henry William Atkinson, Provost of the Royal Mint, she grew up in the Tower of London. At the age of eighteen she married a well-to-do barrister, William Doidge Taunton, with whom she had three children; in 1809, however, she separated from her husband; the following year the House of Lords found her guilty of adultery with another young barrister, Bargrave Wyborn. Divorced from her husband and children, she presumably returned to live with the Atkinson family, now resident in the new Royal Mint building on Tower Hill. When and how she reached Dundee, and when she first became acquainted with Rintoul, is unknown.[147] By 1826, however, she and her husband headed south to London with their two young children, likewise called Robert (1821–91) and Henrietta (1824–1904). Since Henrietta senior grew up, and indeed was seven years married, within a mile of Fleet Street, perhaps the move seemed less daunting to her. At any rate, she was not unknown in London society; just as Charles Dickens recalled a visit of his fellow journalist Robert in 1836, Mary Hogarth, his sister-in-law, noted in the same year that 'Mrs Rintoul is quere as ever and her two sweet children as interesting.'[148] The relationship between Dickens and Rintoul subsequently soured, not least because *The Spectator* repeatedly dismissed Dickens's novels as vulgar, low-brow and humourless.[149] While it is clear that the Jarndyce v. Jarndyce case of *Bleak House* (1852–3) was inspired by the dispute over the legacy of one of *The Spectator*'s founding sponsors, Charles Day, it may only have been contemporary tittle-tattle that Dickens called Rintoul 'squint-owl'.[150] In 1846, when a newsagent accidentally sent him a copy of *The Spectator*, Dickens exclaimed to a friend: 'Of all the papers going, they couldn't have picked me out a more unlikely one.'[151]

As to the children, Robert used the connections of his mother, finding a job at the Royal Mint, now run by her brother Sir Jasper Atkinson. After the Company of Moneyers was dissolved in 1851, he joined the army, rising to the rank of major with the 4th Dragoon Guards, until he sold his commission in 1887. His sister Henrietta was a remarkable woman. Although she published nothing under her own name, she seems to deserve in her own right a place in the history of the paper. An admiring friend later recalled that

> Mr Rintoul was fortunate in being father to a
> devoted daughter who, from an early age, gave

Rintoul and his wife Henrietta (c.1855)

him valuable assistance in his editorial work. While still a young girl, and for the space of some few weeks when he was suffering from severe illness, she filled the editorial chair herself, and did so with ability.[152]

Other reports note that she regularly worked alongside her father through the night that preceded the paper going to press. It is regrettable that, since no evidence survives, we cannot know just how many paragraphs appeared from Henrietta's hand in the 1840s and 1850s. But her involvement with luminaries of the artistic scene is clear: she had an on-off relationship with William Rossetti for almost ten years (1851–60). Although they were twice affianced, their marriage was stymied by Rintoul's fatherly disapproval. On the death of both her parents, however, Henrietta left poor William baffled by terminating the relationship. As he later recalled, 'consequent upon her grief for her mother's death, she viewed with dismay the idea of forming any new ties, and she preferred that the engagement should be regarded at an end.'[153]

Rintoul's wife Henrietta died shortly after him in September 1860; after his death she had moved Darlaston Hall, Staffordshire, to stay with a long standing friend of the Rintouls (and Rossettis). Neither on nor daughter married. The younger Henrietta later spoke of her life as empty after she left the world of *The Spectator*, dying a spinster in 1904. The family now lies as one in Highgate Cemetery, buried without fanfare in a grave that is at once untended and unvisited.[154]

But Rintoul as an editor leaves behind in those who knew him a lively character sketch. To William Rossetti, he was 'a short, sturdy man, with a large head, well moulded, and full of character and resolution. He ... spoke with the rich Scottish intonation, but unmarked by provincial peculiarities.'[155] To Wakefield's niece, he was 'the large-browed, gentle-mannered editor of the *Spectator*, who must never be spoken to upon a Friday', when the paper was being put to bed.[156] Wakefield's son described him as 'one of the men of his age who, more than any other out of Parliament, imparted the earnestness of his own character, and his hatred of *shams*, to the leading men with whom he associated in literary and club life.'[157] (Rintoul's own

club was, unsurprisingly, the Reform, to which he was elected in its first few years.) To Carlyle, he was a 'rational, candid decisive man':[158] although others noted that his 'Scotch deliberateness and self-possession of manner'[159] rendered him 'constitutionally as well as editorially of a phlegmatic nature',[160] 'never was a kinder heart concealed under a somewhat brusque and peremptory exterior.'[161] Most could not get close to the man: 'Nobody, we will venture to say, ever understood Rintoul, but they said he was wonderfully clever.'[162] To those who did know him, he was 'a man of firm integrity, reliable wisdom, and cheerful habit, undemonstrative, but sincere, ready enough to do a kind thing, but utterly averse to artifice.'[163] 'Neither the frowns nor the smiles of the great had ... the least influence upon [his] mind',[164] since he 'saw that integrity and ability are the only legitimate sources of success for a journalist.'[165] As one national newspaper concluded, 'A more just and shrewd appreciator of men and things,

Rintoul in his mid-fifties (Hill and Adamson, c. 1843)

a more honest and sincere man, and a more kind and trustworthy friend, we have never known.'[166] Even the paper he founded and then abandoned, *The Atlas*, could observe after thirty years of rivalry that he left behind 'the name of a highly accomplished gentleman, an honest politician, and a good man.'[167]

The last years of his editorship were not easy. Although the paper had saved costs by dropping its later Sunday edition in 1850, the removal of the final stamp duty in 1855 had opened the door to a slew of penny papers. The appearance of the *Daily Telegraph* that year, which soon halved its price to 1d, swiftly dominated the field of the dailies. In 1856, the *Morning Star*, founded by John Bright and Richard Cobden, won a keen readership as a penny daily of radical politics. More pressingly, the entry in 1855 of the *Saturday Review* – a clever and worldly paper that treated contemporary politics with a refreshingly flippant outlook – encroached upon the established readership of *The Spectator*. External observers felt that the paper, having won most of its battles, had less to fight for.[168] Even *Spectator* writers conceded that they were losing some sparkle: a leader of 1856 complains that 'the present state of English politics must necessarily appear flat and uninteresting to men trained amid the conflicts of parties and the contrasts of principles which characterised the period from the close of the great French war in 1815 to the final settlement of the Free-trade controversy in 1852.'[169] With nothing to fight, Rintoul's edge was being blunted and circulation gradually sliding. Although precise figures are irretrievable, the high point of his paper's sales was probably reached in the mid-1840s, with a figure of around 4,000 copies. Rintoul, of course, regularly complained that five times more people read the paper than actually bought it.

By the time he had completed his seventieth year, in 1858, after almost an unbroken half-century of editing weekly papers, Rintoul was burnt out. Although he had been telling friends of an imminent retirement for some fifteen years,[170] declining health at last forced him to give up the post. Even to the last, however,

he retained his bite. There is good reason to believe that the last thing that appeared from his pen was a riposte of 6 February 1858 relating to provocative comments he had made on the sub-par professoriate of Scotland. *The Spectator* for 23 January had worked up a comparative table of the established professorships at English, Irish and Scottish universities, analysed by subject. Observing his native country to be patently behind the curve, Rintoul had lamented 'the stagnant pool of Scotch complacency and apathy as regards education... What a shame, that in a land that has given more genius and shed more lustre on English literature than perhaps one people ever did for the fame and universality of another, there should not be one special Professor of the English Language and Literature!' This attack rankled with his adversary William Fleming, the Glaswegian Professor of Moral Philosophy, who indulged in some decidedly special pleading. Rintoul was unmoved:

> The paucity and trifling nature of the corrections sent us, show, we think, that our table was surprisingly correct, considering the very scanty materials from which, so far as Scotland is concerned, it was compiled.[171]

It is fitting that Rintoul's last words in print not only defend *The Spectator* but echo his first days in Dundee when he made his name by holding to account the various Scottish institutions that fell below his exacting standards.[172]

Rintoul would have read with contentment *The Spectator*'s entry in the *Newspaper Press Directory* of 1857:

> This journal, for thirty years, has occupied a leading position amongst the weekly press of the metropolis; and in variety of matter, clever and forcible writing, and perspicuous and business-like arrangement, it is excelled by none, and approached by very few, of the London newspapers... The impartiality that gives so much force to its political views, imparts immense value

to its literary criticism, which never descends into mere eulogy on the one hand, nor abuse on the other; discerning, industrious, painstaking, it elicits every excellence, and exhibits every characteristic feature, of a work.

Aware that his race was run, and that he could not give more vim to his beloved paper, Rintoul sold it in February 1858 – after overseeing 1,546 issues. The buyer was a young and bright chap, John Charles Addyes Scott; the price paid is unknown, but the majority of the sum seems to have been given to Rintoul – the sole proprietor for quarter of a century – in the form of a healthy annuity. Scott's attraction to Rintoul was perhaps the financial stability he could bring to the title: his annual income was rumoured to be at £10,000 (now some £1,000,000). For his own part, Rintoul doubtless hoped to enjoy well-earned retirement with his family; but, the reins at last handed over, his health declined sharply in the following weeks, exacerbating a heart condition that had troubled him for a few years. On 22 April, aged seventy-one, he died.[173] Remembering the man in a long and affectionate obituary for *The Spectator*, Rintoul's erstwhile colleague William Weir wrote:

His labours in this journal are an enduring monument of his unswerving rectitude, his unflagging industry, and, a disinterestedness rare even among the class of teachers and instructors of their kind. His name will ever occupy a prominent place in the biography of those, who, in silence and obscurity, and with vizor down, have marshalled the strong forces of the now sovereign power of public opinion.[174]

John William Parker, proprietor of *Fraser's Magazine*, wrote that Rintoul

Did more than almost any other man of our time to raise the tone of journalism and journalists. Many of those who were trained in his school are now the conductors of leading papers in London and the provinces, and are carrying out the principles they learned from him.[175]

Perhaps most fittingly, Edward Owen Greening, co-founder of the *Social Economist*, recalled a decade later:

In days when weekly journals in England were newspapers, and not, as now, reviews, the *Spectator* was the most perfect newspaper that ever existed. We never had such another journal as that which Mr. Rintoul produced... If newspapers circulate in Elysium Fields, we have no doubt that Mr. Rintoul is the first 'gentleman of the Press' there, and issues a *Spectator* which every Disembodied minister in the land of shades is under the necessity of consulting.[176]

II

AN UNEASY INTERREGNUM
1858-1861

Writing in 1928, Sir William Beach Thomas was forced to record of *The Spectator*'s new owner that 'of the Mr. Scott who purchased it almost nothing is known – perhaps he deserves to be forgotten.'[177] That *The Spectator* could pass from the hands of one of the most revered journalists in Britain, if not the world, to someone whose identity could not survive even two generations is nothing short of remarkable. But this is indicative: the paper was about to enter a shadowy three-year period in which it would lose much of its lustre, forgoing its independence and, in turn, its integrity.

The Scott in question was the twenty-seven-year-old Lord of the Manor of Ratlinghope, Shropshire. For all his grand family lineage, JOHN CHARLES ADDYES SCOTT (1830–88) was an unlikely purchaser of *The Spectator*. The financial side of proceedings is simple enough: Scott's father, Robert Wellbeloved (later Scott), sometime Liberal MP for Walsall and a keen free-trader, died in 1856, leaving John to inherit his considerable estates in Staffordshire, Worcestershire and Shropshire. For a man whose twenty-first birthday party won three columns in the county paper,[178] the bank balance would scarcely have registered the acquisition (at a few thousand pounds). It is much less easy to explain the editorial side. It would be natural to assume that Scott was a keen reader of *The Spectator*, and perhaps that he was an occasional contributor to the paper during the 1850s; one may even hazard that Rintoul was on friendly terms with Scott's father, given their political sympathies. But for all these possibilities there is no evidence.

To come to the facts that are available, Scott had passed through Edgbaston Proprietary School to Manchester New College, a dissenting academy still based in Manchester before its transfer to Gordon Square, London, in 1853. He matriculated as an exhibitioner in Classics, but magnanimously requested that the money won be transferred to the other successful candidate, who was in genuine need of it. After a stellar career, winning prizes across the board, he graduated with the highest honours in Classics and Mathematics in 1851. His interests evidently ranged wider than the curriculum: in the previous year, when the college was undergoing public inspection, Scott was chosen to deliver a speech to the assembled grandees on 'The effects of the increase of manufacture on the intellectual and moral character of a people'. As a result of his undergraduate success, Scott secured a Mathematics scholarship to University College London. In 1854 he took his MA and served alongside Richard Holt Hutton as examiner for the Hibbert Trust. Two years later, he was elected a Fellow of UCL, a post – with apparently few essential duties – that he held until his death in 1888, aged fifty-seven.

Few, if any, readers would have detected that the issue of 13 February 1858 was the first produced by hands other than Rintoul's. It was issued in the same form, from the same offices, the same printer and the same publisher. Doubtless its writing staff was almost entirely unchanged, and the collective house style had more than enough momentum to endure. The only detectable change was the introduction of a sub-leader called 'Brief notes on a number of things', a rather unprepossessing title that would not have passed muster with his straight-talking predecessor. Perhaps others felt the same, for this series of miscellaneous remarks ceased in April. What did attract the attention of rival observers was the favourable notice suddenly given to new publications. Already by mid-April, the *Illustrated Times* exclaimed that the paper, owned by someone 'whose name is unknown in the press-world', was 'seeking for an increased circulation by puffing advertisements!'[179]

It is unclear what was going on behind the scenes. Evidence suggests that, for the first few months, the long-standing deputy editor Thornton Hunt served as Scott's co-editor, before deciding that his partner's staunch commitment to abolishing slavery worldwide rendered his own position untenable. Whether some none of the leading articles of this period were written by Scott himself is unknowable, but the many editorial responses to 'Letters to the editor' are certainly his own. They reveal a man fully prepared to defend himself against criticism and stand his ground in the best fashions of *The Spectator*.

After Rintoul's death, the quiet change of ownership – which had been reported only in April[180] – could hardly be hidden from the public. Accordingly, an article in the issue of 1 May asserted:

> We shall be faithful to that preference for deeds over words, which, as the readers of the memoir in this issue will see, early became the master-thought of [Rintoul's] work. We shall put forth no programme, and shall not attempt to justify that expectation of our predecessor by promises. It will be best seen in future doings rather than in present words of the *Spectator*, whether we shall be unmindful of the duties and the responsibilities, which are laid on those who succeed to the post and the labours of Robert Stephen Rintoul.[181]

Perhaps ironically, Rintoul's *Spectator* did not itself require radical reform. However, one so aware of the footsteps in which he followed was soon to conclude that his feet did not fit. By December 1858, after some ten months in the task, Scott entered private negotiations to sell up the magazine. Perhaps the task was more onerous than anticipated; perhaps his subtle changes and innovations had elicited private rebukes of unbearable vigour; perhaps the appeal of his villa in Naples, where he was to die, proved irresistible. At any rate, his last issue appeared on Christmas Day that year, whereafter he turned to other business. Fittingly for one reputed to be sharp as tacks, Scott conducted a successful business as a nail magnate. In his later years, he published *A Few Words on National Policy* (1865), which in reality contained quite a few words on what Britain's policy should be in Europe. Although this would have set him up well for the *Spectator* of the future, his only subsequent contribution seems to have

J.C.A. Scott in later life, alongside his wife Mahlah (m. 1863), whose voice transformed her from nail-maker to opera-singer

been a letter on the judgment and foresight required for first-rate chess playing.[182] His one poetic effusion – *Beehives: A Pastoral* (1877) – is not read.

Although Scott's purchase price of *The Spectator* is unknown, he obtained £4,200 (c. £500,000) for it when it left his hands in January 1859. The press were reporting by the end of that month that the new purchaser was Thornton Hunt, now prepared to return as chief to his long-standing employer. In a sense, this was true. But those who knew the man, renowned for his precarious impecuniosity, would have realised that the money was not his own. Few, however, could have predicted the astounding truth: the money was provided by foreign sources for political propaganda. The purchasers were Benjamin Moran (1820–86), then Assistant Secretary to George Dallas, the American ambassador at the American Legation (i.e. the US Embassy), and James McHenry (1817–91), an American railway financier then based in Liverpool and London.[183]

Moran was keen to get the British press on the side not just of his ambassador but of his President, the Democrat James Buchanan Jr (pres. 1857–61). In August 1858, he had lamented to his diary that Americans in Britain were 'unrepresented at the fountain head of civilization, Christianity, and commerce, while all other nations have their organs. We are abused without the means of defense, and misrepresented without the power of corrections... An organ under proper control would be invaluable to an American Minister here, and I would sooner be its editor than Envoy to the Court of St. James.' As it turned out, Moran did not have to wait long for a prize catch to come his way. The negotiations for *The Spectator* began with Scott on 17 December that year and were completed on 5 January 1859,[184] although the paper had practically changed hands by the close of 1858.

The purpose of the purchase was clear: to secure an English journal that would stealthily promote the cause of the Buchanan administration. While the British press was united in its pro-abolition stance, Buchanan had to keep the peace with his power base in the slave-owning South: he therefore acknowledged – with almost all the developed world – that slavery was morally wrong, but cited the need to preserve the Union as a good reason for doing nothing drastic to end it. Dallas represented his policy of dilly-dallying well when he said of slavery to Lord Brougham, 'you can't get rid of it without consequences more dreadful than the thing itself.'[185] But, in order to disguise American influence on a venerable organ of British independence, it was necessary to leave the business of editing to an established English journalist.

That choice did not prove difficult, for THORNTON LEIGH HUNT (1810–73) had been friends with Moran since the early 1850s. His c.v. suggested him as much the most natural fit – and Rintoul himself had brought Hunt on to the staff almost twenty years earlier. His previous work on reformist papers presumably aligned his politics well: he had served as a sub-editor of *The*

Constitutional, for which Rintoul had been mooted as a founding editor, before editing the *Cheshire Reformer* and *Glasgow Argus*. His passions – for social reform and free speech – would have chimed entirely with Rintoul's. During the next twenty years, Hunt was terrifyingly prolific in several corners of journalism; like his predecessor, he was briefly editor of *The Atlas* in the 1840s. If this move to a quondam rival tested their relationship, it must have been severely tried by his co-founding another rival weekly in 1850. *The Leader*, an outspokenly radical organ, was begun with the philosopher and critic George Henry Lewes; when the latter entered a relationship with George Eliot, Hunt promptly did the same with Lewes's wife Agnes, later fathering four children; like Lewes, too, he did this in spite of a long-suffering wife, mother to his brood of ten. Lewes laconically observed that Hunt, 'in spite of his physiognomy, had his way with women'.[186] Since *The Leader* (1850–60) was also based on Wellington Street, Hunt presumably found himself in and out of *The Spectator* office very regularly. Most importantly of all, however, from its foundation in June 1855, Hunt had been serving as acting editor of the *Daily Telegraph*, a position that he held until 1873. His days, even by Rintoul's standards, must have been quite desperately frenetic.

Still, Hunt was forged in the *Spectator* mould by Rintoul. As the journalist George Holyoake later recalled of Hunt's training:

On Friday Mr. Rintoul would give him a Parliamentary paper for which there was space for two columns. It would transpire that that space was not available, and the *précis* would have to be re-written to reduce it to a column and a half. At a late hour it would be found that there was room for only one column, when the *précis* had to be reduced again – not by el[l]ision, but by rewriting.[187]

Alongside his established track record, Hunt's appeal to Moran was doubtless enhanced by his claim, in private, that he, not Rintoul, suggested the 'Topics of the day' for *The Spectator*.[188] This may be presumed an embellishment. It probably was due to Hunt's journalistic instinct, however, that, from his first issue of 1859, he reduced *The Spectator* in price from 9d to 6d. A contemporary journal followed its praise of Rintoul's *Spectator* as 'the best compiled general newspaper in the world' with a worry that his successor's price reduction was 'in accordance with the spirit of the times in a financial sense, but we are certain in no other.'[189] An anticipatory notice in the issue of Christmas Day 1858 pressed the claim that the change in price would bring no diminution in the paper's content but rather beneficial improvements:

By a gradual, but not we trust, a slow process, the reader will find the information supplied to him in the several departments of the journal more complete than it has yet been. He will be deprived of nothing that he has been accustomed to look for in our pages, but he will from time to time find additions introduced on a plan of consecutive improvement. That plan had received the approval of the Founder and late Editor of the *Spectator* just before his own retirement; and he handed it to his successors for adoption. Circumstances have hitherto delayed its execution; but it will presently speak to the reader for itself.

We have reason to believe that the *Spectator* will possess an enlarged interest, and that it will be supported by an increasing number of readers. The present price, exceptional among political papers of the highest class, would operate restrictively in this extension of usefulness, and hence the reduction.

But the aspect of the journal will remain unaltered; and politically the *Spectator* will be what it has been from the first, – a Liberal paper, perfectly independent of every party.

It is to be gravely doubted that, after thirty years pursuing his own line, Rintoul approved any such

Thornton Hunt (Samuel Lawrence, 1849)

change, and certainly none representing foreign concerns; that he instructed Scott to enact them; and that his *Spectator* would call itself straightforwardly 'Liberal' (so capitalised). Hunt, it seems, was pulling a fast one.

Within the first month of his editorship, Hunt chose to call on his famous father as a contributor – a man held in high repute by literary London, but in low esteem by Rintoul himself.[190] *The Spectator* proudly ran Leigh Hunt's sixteen-part series 'The Occasional', exceptionally published under his own name and sometimes as part of an extended supplement, which was much read and much discussed.[191] It was to be the last work he produced before his imminent death, in August 1859. The paper, however, was not selling well, not least because of its unmissable but unexplained *volte face* with regard to America and abolitionism; as one historian has noted, its 'commentary on American affairs read like a Buchanan administration propaganda sheet'.[192]

Few *Spectator* readers could have failed to howl when they read an early article of Hunt's tenure. On 15 January 1859, *The Spectator* ventured a leader on the news that an American citizen had been caught illegally importing 400 slaves from Africa, for which he was unlikely to be punished. Rather than giving the paper's typically stark condemnation of any perpetuation of the indefensible institution of slavery, the writer strove hard to lay some blame on the North for not properly respecting the concerns of the Southern States. After one-and-a-half columns of mealy-mouthed muttering, it is – *mirabile dictu* – only Buchanan who comes out of the piece at all untrammelled.

The new American focus, and pro-American outlook, of *The Spectator* was unmistakable. In fact, such was the volume and accuracy of the material provided that Moran – a budding journalist as a younger man – was very probably the writer of much of it. His name, there is no doubt, is often shoehorned into the paper's columns without obvious cause. For instance, his contribution to a work of American history is celebrated with a full-page review as a 'remarkable essay' whose author 'adds to the force of his writing by singular modesty of statement and an unfailing taste';[193] the reviewer seems unconcerned that he names Moran throughout, whereas the contributions to the printed book were anonymous. Among other cases we find: a paragraph describing Moran's memorial to his deceased wife among the miscellaneous news;[194] a column on the Fourth of July celebrations which Moran helped organise;[195] and, amid the three stated attendees at Leigh Hunt's funeral, the name of Moran himself.[196]

President Buchanan is consistently defended as the master of balancing competing and dangerous forces. When he was openly challenged by American abolitionists, *The Spectator* sang his praises as a President

> who has alone displayed the capacity, the courage, the will, and the elevated national virtue, to administer the affairs of the Republic for the Republic, without being carried away by the extreme unworthy on either side – to govern the Union for the Union, not in the spirit of a malignant and traitorous disunion.[197]

Unsurprisingly, too, Moran and McHenry's *Spectator* was keen to highlight the virtue of those in the Anglo-American diplomatic corps:

> In these days, men who are called to the administration, of England and America alike, are gentlemen and men of the world, who know the people with whom they have to deal, the interests which are influenced by their conduct, and the responsibilities imposed upon them.[198]

The change in editorial control was noticed in man a quarter. For example, John Bright, the radical MI told a Liverpool crowd of reformers in November 185 that, on reading a recent copy of the paper, he had t exclaim, 'What a declension from the time when M Rintoul conducted the *Spectator* to the gentlema whoever he may be, who now manages its economic department!'[199] As circulation slipped and cost mounted, its losses proved to be considerable. Ove the course of the next two years, Moran had to pour further £2,000 into the project.[200] Brash advertisemen strove vainly to promote the journal's standing all th more. In 1860, it advertised, in somewhat brusqu fashion, that it

> was the FIRST OF ALL THE JOURNALS OF EUROPE to publish ACCURATE INTELLIGENCE OF POLITICAL EVENTS OF THE HIGHEST IMPORTANCE... In order to remove any self-created obstruction to the Circulation of the Paper, its original exceptionably High Price has been REDUCED TO SIXPENCE.

In March 1860, however, Hunt joined the *Morni Chronicle*.[201] This venerable daily, founded in 176 and renowned for its celebrated team of writers th included Hazlitt, Dickens and Mill, was in a yet mo parlous state. The cause of its decline was likewi foreign influence: in December 1859, Napoleon I Emperor of France, had secretly acquired the tit Over the next thirteen months he spent £23,000 the concern. Most of this astounding sum, howeve was being clandestinely pocketed by the America (but Parisian-based) Henry Delille, nominated as agent by Napoleon's private secretary Jean-Franço Mocquard.[202] It proved hard to keep a lid on t astounding prostitution of a London paper: by M 1860, the press was circulating stories of the w who tried to buy a copy of the *Chronicle* with a franc, explaining, 'I thought you took French money.' The rumours, in fact, went farther – that there was hidden French influence exerted upon *The Spectator* itself. 'In literary coteries,' a London correspondent told Scottish readers in the spring of 1860, 'the *on dit* now is that the paper mentioned is in the direct interest of the French Emperor. Certainly it has become entirely Napoleonic.'[203] The evidence for this is scanty but not negligible: it may well be that McHenry's financial support, derived from his shadowy activities in Paris, was bankrolled by Napoleon. Both McHenry and Moran were on social terms with Serjeant Glover, who first sold the *Chronicle* to Napoleon after offering up its pages to the American Legation;[204] with Delille, who carried out that purchase;[205] with the Duc de Persigny, Napoleon's Ambassador in London (1855–8, 1859–60);[206] and with George Francis Train, another bombastic railway magnate, who decades later claimed – albeit with some impossible details – to have helped engineer the Emperor's acquisition of *The Spectator*.[207] One provincial paper felt comfortable to state in June 1860 that the *Spectator* and *Chronicle*, 'both edited by Mr. Thornton Hunt, are understood to have become the property of the French Government'.[208] Whether it was part-puppet for the Americans, or for the French as well, *The Spectator* in 1859–60 was in no sense its independent self.

Given the major demands upon his time that the *Daily Telegraph* and the *Chronicle* required, it may well be that Hunt's move in March 1860 started severing his ties with *The Spectator*. At any rate, by October of that year, his health failed, and he headed to America for a two-month tour, where he was doubtless rewarded for his good service. The press then concluded (incorrectly) that Hunt had to sell up his shares in *The Spectator*. As it was, perhaps from a date in March itself, the editorship of the paper had passed into the hands of GEORGE HOOPER (1824–90).[209] Hooper had been a sub-editor under Rintoul from the early 1850s, as well as a regular writer for *The Leader*. In the wake of this transfer, the press noted a clear shift in *The Spectator*'s

George Hooper in later life

attitude towards France: 'The politics of the paper have changed; from being violently Napoleonic, it is now violently *anti*.'[210] It is true that Hunt's *Spectator* had been better disposed than most to Louis Napoleon – but Hunt was always a contrary fellow before the taking of any coin.

Despite this change in personnel and (in part) editorial stance, the paper's finances did not improve. In October 1860, Moran met George Hooper and a Mr Middlemas 'about the present condition of The Spectator. From all appearance, there is little hope of saving the property; but I am sorry that Cheltnam has not behaved well. It seems he concealed the true state of the business, which is much worse than he represented.'[211] Charles Smith Cheltnam (1823–1912), Hunt's brother-in-law, had been appointed as manager of *The Spectator* in 1859, a position presumably created by Moran to stem his alarming losses; in the wake of this evident dressing down from the boss, Cheltnam also hotfooted it to the *Chronicle*.

Meanwhile, at *The Spectator*, money-saving measures were required. From 26 October, a 'New Novels' section was introduced, evidently designed to give favourable puffs to new publications as per private bidding: in eighteen months, the famed independence of *Spectator* literary reviews had been seriously vitiated. Editorially, however, the paper was in good hands – although the pro-Buchanan railway-related blizzard of material continued unabated. Hooper could write with verve and deploy an admirably broad array of knowledge. His particular expertise was as a writer on military matters: his monographs on Waterloo (1862),

Wellington (1890) and (curiously enough) the defeat of Napoleon III at Sedan (1887) sold with considerable success. Leaders from 1860 include support for middle-class women taking up work, universal education, care for the blind, and distrust of the overbearing power of the Vice-Chancellor of the University of Cambridge.[212]

Alongside some forty years' total service on *The Spectator*, Hooper was a celebrated leader-writer for the *Daily Telegraph*, after successful spells editing *The Globe* (1861–5) and the *Bombay Gazette* (1868–71). His obituary notice in *The Spectator* was sincere in its praise:

> We never knew in the profession a more absolutely upright man, or one whose heart was more sound; while his judgment, in spite of a certain fire of temper, was completely free from the taint either of prejudice or rancour.[213]

One wonders how often the tempers flared at the editorial helm. Nevertheless, *The Athenaeum* recorded that

> Mr. Hooper's house was for years a gathering place for journalists and men of letters, and those who have spent many delightful evenings in the society he collected about him will not soon forget their genial host, whose stores of information were not more remarkable than his kindliness and his uprightness of character.[214]

By the beginning of 1861, Moran despaired of *The Spectator*, confiding to his diary on 3 January that 'it don't pay, never did since Hunt became its owner'.[215] He and McHenry at last decided to sell up: having met their shadowy associate Train (for unknown reasons) on 7 January 1861, Hunt was given his instructions two days later as the public-facing figure, and, on 19 January, the sale was completed.[216] The operation was over but the damage was done. The slide of *The Spectator*'s standing is attested by the fact that its circulation had fallen distinctly – perhaps to below 2,000 – and that its saleable value had more than halved, to a mere £2,000. Thus ended much the most curious and uncharacteristic

phase in the paper's history – an unhappy twenty-five months in which it lost its stability, its leadership and its independence. Perhaps *The Spectator* had tongue firmly lodged in cheek when it gave notice, in 1874, of Moran's transferral to Lisbon:

> No man so distinctively and essentially an American has been more influential in London... The wildest American patriot has never accused Mr. Moran of not pushing his country's claims far enough, and yet he has always been accepted here as a true and worthy friend of England.[217]

III
THE MORAL MAZE
1861–1886

The very survival of *The Spectator* depended upon the purchaser it now found: with its reputation damaged and its readership ebbing away, only the most formidable of editors could steer it back to health. Happily, the new owner was a man preternaturally well-disposed to journalism, who lived and breathed editorial verve. MEREDITH WHITE TOWNSEND (1831–1911) was undoubtedly unusual: forged in Ipswich and finessed in India, he was sparky, savvy, contrary, romantic, even mystical.

The contemporary press – to varying degrees dependent on *The Spectator* for guidance and copy – knew that the paper sorely needed salvation. Thus the incoming proprietor-cum-editor was received as a potential ray of hope. One Scottish paper noted optimistically that 'The *Spectator* has long been in a moribund state; but Mr Townsend has ability, energy, and money, and perhaps may revive it.'[218] But another periodical, extending the metaphor, later recalled that 'the best newspaper doctors would have pronounced it beyond hope of restoration to health and strength.'[219] Townsend applied all his powers, but conceded that it was a 'heartbreaking task ... to work up a newspaper that had lost so much ground.'[220]

Despite the several hands through which the paper's proprietorship had passed, its premises had remained unchanged. Yes, attentive readers of the paper will have raised eyebrows on reading, in 1860, that *The Spectator*'s address had shifted from 9 Wellington Street to 1 Wellington Street. In reality, the world had reordered itself around the paper, deciding it would be better to renumber the street's properties from *The Spectator* offices upwards. Despite the unwelcome upheaval of recent years, the continuum of Rintoul's foundation survived intact – in long-serving staff, long-standing features and long-subscribing readers. What is more, a living and breathing remnant of Rintoul was still in evidence on the premises. For Henrietta,

his daughter, had managed to retain her quarters in the attic room throughout the last three short-lived editors.[221] What Townsend's reaction was to finding this rather highly-strung thirty-something pining in the rafters is unknown, but he did initially consent for her to continue lodging at the premises. Soon enough, however, this awkward *ménage* proved unworkable and he paid her a pretty sum to head elsewhere. She never forgave the paper.

Townsend was not a man of conventional manners or habits. Born in London and schooled in Ipswich, at sixteen years of age he somehow found himself teaching Greek to Scottish teenagers. The results were disastrous – and within the year he had readily accepted the invitation of his uncle, John Clark Marshman, to take up journalistic work in India. This brave decision changed his life. He at once started writing for the *Friend of India*, founded in 1835 and based in Serampore, a little north of Calcutta. In 1852, at twenty-one, he succeeded Marshman as its editor, becoming owner the following year: over the next decade he wrote almost all of the paper, thus raising a little-known English-language journal of the Indian subcontinent to the predominant conduit for Anglo-Indian relations. In 1856, Lord Dalhousie, the retiring Governor-General of India, referred to Townsend affectionately as 'the little man at Calcutta', and in the following year thanked him as one of those 'who stand by me at a time when, literally fettered and gagged, I am deprived of all power of defending myself.'[222] At this time Townsend was appointed as the Indian correspondent for *The Times*, having never filed a sentence in Britain.[223] But, far from being a flag-waving colonial, he was throughout his tenure acutely and sensitively aware of how the native communities felt. Fluent in Bengali,[224] strong in Hindustani, and on nodding terms with several other tongues, he learned from many involved conversations with local peoples to be sceptical of the long-term prospects for British rule in India. His articles forecast better than most the Indian mutinies of 1857–8.

Townsend's health failed soon after the exacting

Townsend (L) in India with his munshi

troubles of this period, and he was forced to return to Britain in the spring of 1860. Although he would never be of robust health – life insurers at the time refused to 'accept the life' – he was energetic in casting about for new prospects in the British press. After some failed bids for minor titles, he leapt at the prospect of acquiring *The Spectator* on hearing that it was for sale. Having sold up his assets in India, he evidently had the requisite funds for the purchase: £1,000 was paid in pounds, the remaining half arriving in six-monthly instalments converted from his hard-won rupees.[225]

For the first five months after the acquisition in January 1861, Townsend operated as *The Spectator*'s sole editor; his predecessor George Hooper stayed on the staff, as presumably did several other core writers, 'almost all of whom [were] Oxford men'.[226] But this new presence at *The Spectator* was immediately apparent. From the very first issue under his control, of 26 January 1861, his Indian expertise and globalist outlook were in evidence: the lead book review concerned an Indian pamphlet entitled 'An Appeal by the Indigo Manufacturers of Bengal to the British Government'. More strikingly, there was a complete reversal in the paper's attitude to Buchanan's administration, now in its dying days: the soft, rose-tinted view of America was replaced with a palpably icy stare. The president

was categorically dismissed as a mindless and negligen[t] leader driving his country into civil war. Townsend'[s] strident leader is simply headed 'The America[n] Bourbon'. Not just the outlook but the actual look o[f] the paper soon changed. As well as an improvemen[t] in the typeface, the balance of content shifted: th[e] opening 'News of the Week', which had under Rintou[l] sometimes sprawled over a dozen pages, was shortene[d] to three focused pages. With space thus freed up[,] Townsend added more 'sub-leaders', i.e. articles afte[r] the political commentary that ranged cheerfully ove[r] all and sundry subjects.

Within a fortnight, the printers and publishers ha[d] also changed. The long-serving Joseph Clayton, wh[o] had printed *The Spectator* from its very first issue, an[d] served as publisher since its hundredth, left the trade;[ ]Townsend therefore took on Alfred Edmund Gallowa[y,] then in the early phases of his career, who could pri[nt] the paper in Beaufort Buildings, sitting off the Stran[d] where the Savoy Hotel now stands. Galloway's servic[e] allowed Townsend to expand the title from twenty-fou[r] pages, its size for the last thirty years: on 9 Februar[y] 1861, the paper grew to twenty-eight pages, the last fi[ve] of which were revenue-boosting advertisements. [A] Townsend then claimed with commendable confidenc[e:] 'The addition of four pages to our space enables us [to] improve the type, and throw the News into a connect[ed] form, which we believe our readers will find infinite[ly] more satisfactory.' The 'News of the Week' was no[w] written as a single narrative, seamlessly stitch[ed] together, rather than an apparently random amalga[m] of entirely disparate and dispassionate fragments [of] fact. *The Spectator* at once shed much of the dress o[f] mere 'newspaper'.

Despite his spirited efforts, however, Townse[nd] seemingly underestimated the work required [to] revivify *The Spectator*: soon he was eager to fi[nd] someone who could share the editorial reins. As [it] happened, an episode during his final months [in] India proved transformative for the paper's fate. F[irst,] in 1859, Townsend had chanced to meet the Libe[ral] politician James Wilson, freshly embarked at Que[e]

Victoria's bidding to reform the byzantine Indian tax system. On learning that Townsend aspired to enter the newspaper business once back in Blighty, Wilson's thoughts turned to *The Economist*, the worldly journal he had founded to support free trade in 1843. Since Walter Bagehot, his newfound son-in-law, was flying high at this paper, Wilson promoted the name of *The Economist*'s frighteningly clever but seriously spiritual editor, whose talents were not ideally suited to that paper. This man, he told Townsend, should be signed up as soon as the chance arose. And so it was, in the early months of 1861, that Townsend invited Richard Holt Hutton to the *Spectator* office. The two men, however different in outlook and experience, quickly clicked in conversation, and Hutton was offered the co-editorship before the goodbye handshake. As he worked his way down the steep spiral staircase of 1 Wellington Street, Townsend called after him, 'I say, have you got any money?' The response – 'Not much' – was good enough, and Townsend offered him a share in the proprietorship. Thus began, from June 1861, one of the greatest and happiest relationships in the history of journalism.

Richard Holt Hutton (1826–97) was a thoroughbred Yorkshireman, born in Leeds but conveyed to London aged nine so that his dissenting family could salvage a suitable education. On the advice of his father, a Unitarian minister, Hutton passed through University College School before entering University College proper: the prospect of Oxford and Cambridge was quite out of the question, given their mandatory doctrinal tests. Hutton's eyes were opened wide: he later suspected that UCL was 'a much more awakening place of education for young men than almost any Oxford College'.[228] But such was his frenzied pursuit of learning that Francis Boott worried at the time he 'would kill himself by overwork unless kept from study'.[229]

Yet Hutton could not rest up: before taking his MA in 1849 with a gold medal in philosophy (just like his younger predecessor at *The Spectator*, Scott), he visited Germany twice, in the winters of 1846–7 and 1848–9. On the latter occasion he studied under the classical scholar Theodor Mommsen, then quite possibly the most learned man in Europe. This Rhadamanthus of Berlin recalled that the young Hutton 'took away from my lectures not only all the knowledge that I could give him, but much mental nutriment for which he was indebted to his own genius.'[230] For the rest of his life, Hutton kept a curious eye on fast-developing German thought.

His ambition to follow his father in becoming a Unitarian minister seems to have been frustrated by his uncompromisingly learned sermons. Instead, perhaps more appropriately, he was appointed Vice-Principal of University Hall, a new Unitarian hall of residence for UCL students. When the Principal, Arthur Hugh Clough, resigned in 1851, Hutton was promoted to his post. But, just six months later, his health collapsed, and he travelled to Barbados to cure inflammation of the lungs. Further tragedy struck: he and his wife caught yellow fever, from which she soon died. (Townsend, too, had lost his first and second wives to ill health in the 1850s.) On his return to Britain, Hutton co-edited *The Inquirer*, a weekly Unitarian paper, from 1853 to 1855; throughout the period 1850–5 he was also the lead editor of the *Prospective Review*, a theologically focused quarterly. In 1855, when that title was relaunched – in part with the support of Lady Byron – as the *National Review*, he served as co-editor with his undergraduate friend Walter Bagehot for the next seven years. Hutton had during that time turned his focus to *The Economist*, where he acted as editor from May 1857, a post held – with some difficulty – until May 1861. Throughout that period the predominant force among the magazine's writers was Bagehot, whose position was solidified in 1858 by marriage to Eliza Wilson, daughter of the proprietor. By late 1860, Hutton – never a natural economist – was starting to wonder about returning to education. But when the call came from *The Spectator* a few doors down, the editorial freedom it afforded was evidently irresistible.[231] Thus, in 1861, 'two of the cleverest men in England, and two of the most refined gentlemen in the world'[232] were united in harness.

There is no doubt that Hutton's arrival brought to *The Spectator* a new moral gravity, tinged with a profoundly religious solemnity. It must be Hutton's doing that, by 1862, *The Spectator* had tweaked its official subtitle. Rintoul's original 'Weekly Journal of News, Politics, Literature and Science' had become a 'Weekly Review of Politics, Literature, Theology and Art'. The shift to 'Review' marked a decline in its obsession with news, the explicit advertisement of which was now comparatively otiose; politics was brought to the fore, religion given its own focus, and the cold survey of the progress of science (for Rintoul, technology) replaced with a broad-minded interest in Art. Of these fields, theology brought the major shift in gear. As one devoted reader recalled, 'religion had never been prominent in the journal, but Hutton at once began to preach, and he preached to a great and listening and picked audience until he died.'[233]

The output of the two men over the next four decades was prodigious: it would be no exaggeration to say that each wrote something in the region of 8,000–10,000 articles and reviews for *The Spectator*. In the typical week, Townsend wrote two political leaders (usually on foreign affairs), one sub-leader, and one review; Hutton normally wrote one or more leaders (usually on domestic affairs),[234] a sub-leader, and one or more book reviews. The 'News of the Week' was co-written, but so elegantly interwoven that even the keenest reader could not apportion paragraphs to their authors.

Most pressing, for wavering readers of the paper, was the need to restore a morally and intellectually defensible position on the rapidly fragmenting United States of America. By the time Abraham Lincoln was sworn in as Buchanan's successor, in March 1861, the long-building momentum towards civil war had become irreversible. Contemporary British opinion on the ensuing conflict is crude and unedifying: the cause of the North found strikingly scant support in the Victorian press. It was a brave decision, then, for *The Spectator* – along with the *Daily News*, Charles Dickens's radical creation, and the *Dundee Advertiser*, Rintoul's former paper – to declare its unwavering opposition to the South. The co-editors were unite in their aim, although their priorities differed: fo Townsend, the Union had to be preserved to kee the American project alive; for Hutton, slavery in a its forms had to be abolished. The pair thus stoo resolutely against the nation's intelligentsia, whos admiration for the Confederacy's patriotic prid was fuelled by economic pragmatism: equality an freedom are all well and good, but the textile trade Lancashire needs affordable cotton.

Townsend, for one, was having none of th scaremongering: in his very first issue, of January 186 a sub-leader on 'The supply of cotton' began: 'It is hig time that this cotton question should be thorough! discussed, if we intend to avoid a panic as dangerous a as expensive as the wildest apprehension of a maritin defeat.'[235] Drawing upon his first-hand experienc Townsend recommended the expansion of the cotto trade into India to 'emancipate England, at once, fro dependence on the South'. More importantly, his oth sub-leader on Buchanan the 'Bourbon' dismissed t dilly-dallier for his too-late-in-the-day leadershi 'The great fact in the intelligence from the Unite States is that, at last, Mr. Buchanan has a mind, or ha a mind, of his own.' After outlining his 'irresolutio and 'weakness', Townsend moved to the crux of t matter:

Apart from either the economical or the political aspect of the question, there is one which may be more formidable at the moment – the moral aspect. The party which regards slavery as sinful may be small, but it must grow. The party which regards slavery as an evil, which must be checked by limiting the area of slavery, is large and is expanding.

He then closed, damningly:

For this fearful complication [of imminent civil war] no man is more answerable than Mr. Buchanan, and he will probably fulfil Mr. Cobb's prediction, and take his place in history as the Last President of the United States.

Soon after the news of the war's onset reached Britain, Townsend declared in June 1861 that Britain was being 'taunted with servility to cotton, with false pretences of liberality, and with a wicked delight in the suffering of the States.'[236] The Spectator reasserted the fundamental principles at stake:

the quarrel, cover it with cotton as we may, is between freedom and slavery, right and wrong, the dominion of God and the dominion of the Devil, and the duty of England, we submit, is clear.[237]

The Spectator's attitude to General Robert E. Lee, eventually general-in-chief of the Confederate forces, stood out markedly. Although he was both slave-owner and slave-captor, the British press at large lauded his Christian virtue, military strategy and stout support of the 'noble cause'. Hutton and Townsend, however, condemned him for his long-standing defence of something that he privately knew – so they claimed – was ethically unjustifiable and fundamentally wrong. By contrast, although the paper was at first sceptical of Abraham Lincoln as a leader ('a rather vulgar personality'),[238] it recognised soon enough that his motivating cause was admirable.

As the conflict wore on, The Spectator looked around and lamented that 'the educated million in England have become unmistakably Southern'.[239] Even The Spectator's own readers turned their backs: subscribers fell below a thousand for the first time since the paper's very earliest years, and the title almost collapsed. Nevertheless, many were prepared to see the moral good, such as J.S. Mill, who wrote privately to the editors in 1863 that he could not 'omit the opportunity of expressing the very high estimation, both moral and intellectual, in which he holds the Spectator, under its present management.'[240]

Throughout the conflict, the paper received special correspondence from 'A Yankee': behind these satirical and jaunty letters was the American journalist and scholar Richard Grant White. With his caustic humour, White fostered transatlantic support for the Union, although his grim attitude towards race relations later caused a public falling out with the editors. A front-page paragraph told readers:

We publish, though with regret, a letter from our able 'Yankee' correspondent expressing in full measure the hatred felt by many persons in the North towards the negro. As a sketch of opinion it is valuable, but we can endorse neither his facts nor arguments. He says the 'loathing' between the two races is so deep-seated that amalgamation is impossible; we say that one-third of the slaves are, as appears from their colour, the result of that amalgamation. He says the presence of negroes in Congress is impossible; we say that it is found easy in Jamaica.[241]

Another correspondent who toured America in the crucial year of 1862 was 'An English Traveller': this was Edward Dicey, a far-roving Cambridge graduate then on the staff of the Daily Telegraph. Aware of this scoop from the front line, The Spectator advertised that his letters would be

of a somewhat novel character, containing week by week, not news, but a thoughtful account of the political situation, and the progress and effects of the war, as they present themselves to a cultivated Englishman.[242]

Bolstering such front-line commentators was the expertise of the former editor, George Hooper, a man remarkable for his prescience. The tale has long been told in The Spectator office that Hooper,

a civilian but with an extraordinary flair for strategy, divined exactly what [the Union general William Tecumseh] Sherman was doing when he started on his famous march. Many years afterwards General Sherman said that when he started with the wires cut behind him, there were only two people in the world who knew what his objective was. One was himself and the other, as he said, 'an anonymous writer in the London *Spectator*.'[243]

As contemporary rumour had it, the sole champions of the North in Britain were Queen Victoria, the Duke of Argyll, and *The Spectator*. Thus alienated from public opinion, the paper's circulation reached its deepest nadir in 1862. A contemporary journal recorded rather sharply that 'nobody took it in, and nobody read it.'[244] Charles Darwin was reduced to the lamentation that 'we have no paper like the old Spectator in Rintoul's time';[245] Thomas Hughes, author of *Tom Brown's School Days*, later wrote a reminder of this stark isolation to the *New York Tribune*:

> From the very first the United States had the staunch advocacy of the soundest portion of our press ... the *Spectator* fought for you at the risk of absolute ruin; for its circulation is chiefly among the very class which was most unfriendly, and whose prejudices were faithfully represented by the *Saturday Review* and the *Times*.[246]

Given their unstinting commitment to the cause, the editors did not mince words when the news of Lincoln's assassination came through in April 1865: thus died 'certainly the best, if not the ablest, man ruling over any country in the civilised world ... whose short but glorious career ... will place him for ever among the noblest rulers of the world.'[247]

The paper's worldly outlook, well established under Rintoul, was demonstrated by the increase of foreign correspondents and travel writers beyond theatres of war. In March 1862, a series began from 'A Frenchman', evidently a writer of political standing and – as if a riposte to the recent history of *The Spectator* – no admirer of his emperor. These innovations, described by contemporaries as 'features somewhat new in weekly journalism',[248] caused an instant sensation. Even more successful was a series penned by Hughes charting his travels in Europe and America, under the *nom de plume* of 'Vacuus Viator' ('idle wanderer', a tag from Juvenal). The feature was immensely popular, and eighty-odd pieces would appear until it came to its natural close in 1895.[249]

Amid the political crises of the early 1860s, the paper shifted its politics slightly, at least in name. The *Newspaper Press Directory*, which had faithfully recorded *The Spectator*'s outlook as 'Liberal, Independent' in previous years, changed under Townsend and Hutton to 'Whig – Philosophical'. In the following year, the editors sought to clarify their position in a widely circulated advertisement:

> The paper is the organ of no party, coterie, or individual. Its object is simply to express, in every department of life, the thoughts of educated Liberals – the only thoughts which in England are apt to find inadequate expression. Consequently in political principle the Spectator is thoughtful Whig, but with a more decided tendency towards reforms at home and the extension of orderly freedom abroad than the old Whigs were supposed to have. Since its establishment, however, it has subordinated all party interests to the general welfare of the people.

The notice proceeded to affirm the editors' intention 'to do battle against all forms of intolerance and religious repression'. More strikingly, they wanted the paper to serve as an essential intellectual tool – 'to correct that vagueness and bewilderment of thought which the constant receipt of news in little morsels had such a tendency to produce.' The 'News of the Week' was described as 'three pages composed of short pungent paragraphs, containing the entire history of the week, told not in minute detail, but in the way which a clubman of good information would relate

he news.' As an expression – perhaps embellished – of
heir financial security, the pair declared that they had
'staff large enough to ensure a reasonable certainty
hat every topic discussed shall be treated by some
ne who makes it a topic of special study.' A slightly
ater advertisement, often re-issued throughout their
enure, promoted *The Spectator* as the 'Independent
iberal Newspaper'. To validate that independence,
he editors made clear that they, and they alone, were
n charge:

> The Proprietors, who in 1861 purchased the
> *Spectator*, have since that date conducted it
> themselves. They are therefore exempted from
> many influences which press severely on the
> independence of journalism, and have from the
> first made it their chief object to say out what they
> believe to be truth in theology, politics, and social
> questions, irrespective not only of opposition
> from without, but of the opinion of their own
> supporters. Their object is to reflect the opinion
> of cultivated Liberals, but in the matter of the
> American War they fought against the mass of
> the very class they are trying to represent, and
> were finally acknowledged by them to have been
> in the right.

he paper's object, it continued, is to protect

> the right of free thought, free speech, and free
> action, within the limits of law, under every form
> of Government ... and in social questions, to urge
> the faith that God made the world for the people
> in it, and not for any race, class, colour, creed, or
> section, with all the consequences to which that
> principle leads.

People seemed to be taking notice. The well-
nnected publisher Alexander Macmillan wrote of the
aper in 1863 that 'since Hutton ... has taken it, it seems
me generally to have got back its old vigour. I think it
iite the best paper going.'[250] The great Etonian tutor
William Cory Johnson confessed at the time, 'I now
read the *Spectator* ... and I find myself once more heart
and hand with the true lovers of freedom.'[251] Spurred by
such enthusiasm, Hutton made particularly strenuous
efforts to promote *The Spectator*'s literary side, which
had lapsed under the narrow-minded proprietorship
of Moran and McHenry. The expansion of the paper's
size had allowed for a commensurate growth in reviews,
which focused primarily on English literature. For
those who moved in this world, the improvement was
palpable. In 1861, for instance, Wilkie Collins wrote to
Galloway, the paper's new publisher:

> the paper is excellently conducted – the literary
> portion of it (which I may perhaps claim to pass
> an opinion on) being written with an intelligence
> of appreciation and a fairness of judgment, which
> some of *The Spectator*'s weekly contemporaries
> would do well to emulate.[252]

This view was held more broadly: Leslie Stephen told
Thomas Hardy that 'the *Spectator* has really a good
deal of critical feeling. I always like to be praised by
it.'[253] Samuel Butler told Darwin that the 'very strong'
review of his *Erewhon* did much to shift copies.[254]
And there is an ambiguous affection in the fact that
Robert Louis Stevenson called *The Spectator* 'his
grandmother'.[255] Galloway, however, failed to achieve
the success that he sought for the paper, and jumped
ship after eighteen months. It must have taken some
persuasion to get John Campbell, in August 1862, to
board a vessel that seemed slowly but steadily to be
going under. In actuality, however, the partnership
somehow worked wonders, and Campbell – who
printed the paper on Exeter Street across the Strand –
valiantly served in this post for thirty years.

One of the most important pieces that Hutton
wrote was penned in his first month at the helm. It
was prompted by an account of newspaper abuses in
the task of criticism, penned by John Grote, brother of
George.[256] Hutton's response reads as a programmatic
manifesto of how he understood his duty as public

critic in a position of national influence. Unlike many romantic English contemporaries, he emphasised the importance of privileging the modern over the historical, the present over the past. Most importantly, he argued for the need for a public commentator or reviewer to acquaint themselves with what seems challengingly unfamiliar:

All true criticism on worthy subjects does involve effort, and considerable effort. No one can fairly judge what another has done without genuine study of something which is generally in some degree alien to one's own thought. And it is so much easier to stay at one's own centre and rail at another man for not coming to us, than to migrate to his point of view, that criticism is always tending to degenerate into a list of excellent reasons why an author should have been other than he is in order that he might have written his book from a centre of conviction similar to our own, instead of the one which he has chosen... Unless [the critic] can enter into the wants of his generation, he has no business to pretend to direct its thoughts.[257]

But Hutton's outlook as a critic was shaped fundamentally by his theology. He believed that the free, intuitive and creative spirit of the mind was an echo of God's will, and that literary imagination was the primary canon of literary excellence. This undergirded his entire perspective on the artistic world: if excellent art was the reflection of a healthy mind, works that fell foul of his criticism were diagnosed as the tell-tale symptoms of psychological disorder. The 'controlling intellect', by contrast, despite its being so fetishised in Victorian culture, was something to be tempered, not venerated. Accordingly, substance always outweighed style. An impressive leader appeared from his hand in the first *Spectator* for 1870, simply headed 'Style':

It is to the second and third-rate men that perfection of style is of first-rate importance. To

them it every day becomes of higher moment. They will not be read by the great mass unless, by potency of style, they smooth the reader's path, and lure him on... In the long run, real popularity is the test of real merit. The reputation of a clique is always treacherous and fleeting. That of the bookstall alone endures until the end.[258]

Because of – or in spite of – its lofty sentiments, Hutton's literary criticism was widely celebrated. Gladstone, for instance, called him 'the first critic of the nineteenth century'.[259] Appraising the combined effect of Hutton's theological and literary writings, Owen Chadwick rightly observed that he 'turned *The Spectator* into the most revealing guide to the progress of the human mind'.[260] Contemporaries, too, saw *The Spectator* as 'the educated Englishman's lay preacher and instructor';[261] 'it does good in discussing religious questions, in showing up the enormous and selfish influence of the aristocracy, and in fighting for the intellectual ranks rather than for the moneocracy.'[?] This higher moral authority was not, of course, the *ex nihilo* creation of the Hutton-Townsend tenure. In 1857, the last phases of Rintoul's long service, one had made the tongue-in-cheek remark:

How delightful, like the philosophic *Spectator*, to sit in one's arm-chair, looking down on all things, divine and human, and utter sentences of solemn instruction to a small knot of readers willing to pay a high price for one's weekly wisdom![263]

But Townsend and Hutton were well aware of the dangers of taking literary criticism – and themselves – too seriously. This is particularly well evidenced by a splendid parody of contemporary philological and textual scholarship, in which the true but latent meaning of 'Hey Diddle Diddle!' (as preserved in a mysterious ancient inscription) is explored with pseudo-academic ridicule:[264]

The inscription reads thus:

```
HEYDIDDLEDIDDLE
THECATANDTHEFIDDLE
THECOUIUMPEDOVERTHEMOON
THELITTLEDOGLAUGHED
TOSEESUCHFINESPORT
ANDTHEDISHRANAUAYUITHTHESPOON.
```

In old writing of this sort, where there is no distinction of words, the first point naturally is to ascertain if any particular combination of letters occurs more than once, as the chances that it is a distinct word will of course be very great. Here the letters THE occurring some seven times, gave the desired key to the whole. No one could doubt that they represented a common, and yet an important word;

The *Spectator*'s team of critics shared similar tastes: Tennyson, Eliot, Kingsley, Thackeray and Longfellow usually received positive reviews; at last, after decades of antipathy, it also came round to Dickens. George Eliot was sufficiently pleased by Hutton's review of *Romola* to write, 'you have seized with a fulness which I hardly hoped my book could suggest, what it was in my effort to express.' Less fortunate, for the most part, were the Brontës, Brownings, Arnold, Stevenson, Pater and Wilde. The debut work of the last – *Poems* (1881) – filled the reviewer 'with alarm' and led to the firm conclusion:

Mr. Oscar Wilde is no poet, but a cleverish man who has an infinite contempt for his readers, and thinks he can take them in with a little mouthing verse. Perhaps he is right for the moment; but this we can say with some confidence, that the book is the trash of a man of a certain amount of mimetic ability, and trash the trashiness of which the author is much too cultivated not to recognise quite clearly.[265]

Nevertheless, it was a significant development of the Townsend-Hutton *Spectator* to give over considerable space to poetry. Rintoul's paper had been less interested in publishing verse; when it did, it was more taken by ephemeral doggerel on political matters than the emotionally charged, and often awkwardly long, offerings from contemporary poets. But the new co-editors were keen to promote fresh poetry, successfully recruiting the likes of Robert Buchanan, A.C. Swinburne, Alfred Austin, Robert Bridges, Austin

Dobson, Aubrey de Vere, Coventry Patmore, J.A. Symonds, J.K. Stephen, Hilaire Belloc, Mary Coleridge and William Watson.[266] A particular coup came in 1878, when Matthew Arnold passed on to Hutton a copy of Samuel Butler's 'A Psalm of Montreal', a satirical swipe at the philistinism of a Canadian museum. So racy was the tone for the Victorian *Spectator* that, unusually, the poem appeared without attribution.[267] Butler had already set out his stall on satire in the paper: when he read that his satirical novel *Fair Haven* (1873) involved falsehood, he fired off a letter: 'to be accused of lying by the *Spectator* is far too serious a matter to be ignored.' Offended at his reviewer's obtuseness, he ventured that a 'writer cannot write for everybody; he must assume a certain amount of apprehensiveness on the part of his readers, and is justified in leaving children and stupid people out of his calculations.'[268]

An interesting case study of *The Spectator*'s literary criticism in the 1860s is provided by Algernon Charles Swinburne. In the last gasps of Hooper's editorship, *The Spectator* reviewed two Swinburne plays, *The Queen Mother* and *Rosamond*. It came to the conclusion that he had

some literary talent, but it is decidedly not of a poetical kind... Honey and rosewater verses are, we imagine, what Mr. Swinburne holds to be quite wrong in poetry; but he has mistaken reverse of wrong for right. In feeling and in thought, the daring, the disagreeable, and the violent, are in these dramas, substituted for boldness, beauty, and strength. We do not believe any criticism will help to improve Mr. Swinburne. He writes, as we believe, upon a strongly rooted bad principle. He will not, by such dramas, convince the world that it has always been wrong about poetical beauty, and that he has come to set us right.[269]

Happily, for Swinburne, *The Spectator* changed hands almost immediately after this rebuke, and he found Townsend and Hutton a much more accommodating pair. As a result, seven of his first eight published poems appeared in the paper over the following year.[270] Trouble was not far to seek, however. In 1862, Hutton described George Meredith, Swinburne's housemate and fellow pre-Raphaelite, as a poet 'without literary genius, taste, or judgment', and complained that his latest work, *Modern Love*, 'treats serious themes with a flippant levity that is exceedingly vulgar and unpleasant'.[271] Swinburne leapt to Meredith's defence in an alarmingly long letter, published in full on 7 June 1862. A few quotations will reveal his anger:

> Praise or blame should be thoughtful, serious, careful, when applied to a work of such subtle strength, such depth of delicate power, such passionate and various beauty, as the leading poem of Mr. Meredith's volume.

Most outrageous, he said, was the reviewer's (i.e. Hutton's) claim that Meredith was insincere on moral matters:

> The present critic falls foul of him for dealing with 'a deep and painful subject on which he has no conviction to express.' There are pulpits enough for all preachers in prose; the business of verse-writing is hardly to express convictions; and if some poetry, not without merit of its kind, has at times dealt in dogmatic morality, it is all the worse and all the weaker for that.

Hutton's editorial coda – given, of course, within anonymous parentheses – recorded his 'personal respect to our correspondent, whose opinion on any poetical question should be worth more than most men's', before underlining that his own unequivocal judgment followed from 'the most careful study of Mr. Meredith's book'.

Having already been a successful reviewer for *The Spectator* (of Victor Hugo, among others), Swinburne now tried to have his revenge by foisting on the paper a hoax review – of a fabricated and fabulously sadistic French poet, 'Félicien Cossu'. Only once the review had reached galley proofs did Hutton's monocular patrol alight on the impostor.[272] The relationship between poet and patrons thus proved short and sweet. Swinburne wrote the following year to his friend Richard Monckton Miles:

> I don't want to send any more to the *Spectator*; I don't approve of their behaviour (e.g. never sending one's own articles, and taking back books sent for review — notamment four volumes of Les Misérables) and their principles offend my moral sense.[273]

After the dust had settled from the change in ownership, some more inventive measures were adopted to grow the readership as finances required. The first *Spectator* of 1863, for instance, was a double issue, half of which was formed of a twenty-four-page supplement on 'The Royal Families of Europe'; two months later, to mark the marriage of Prince Edward to Alexandra of Denmark, another double issue appeared, this time with nineteen pages on 'The Princes of Wales in their personal and political relations to the crown and the nation'.[274] Both supplements covered their substantial production costs with ten pages of adverts, although the latter also required the one-off mark-up to a shilling (1s 2d stamped). Punters had to pay for their historical indulgence.

Buoyed by these crowd-pleasing experiments, the editors served up for the next decade weekly slices of history. This began with a no-detail-spared survey of the 'governing families' of England (thirty families), Scotland (twelve) and Ireland (fifteen).[275] In part, this was a breathless account of the great landed gentry of the United Kingdom. The emphasis, however, lay on *governing*: the series sought to show the extent to which, for better or worse, a crop of aristocratic families had been at the tiller of British government for centuries past. The series began with a territorial map of where such influential families lurked when down from London,[276] and took a full three years to have its say (June 1863–June 1866).[277] But before readers could draw breath, here followed the 'Provincial History of England', a blow-by-blow, county-by-county narrative of the nation's past. This took another four years to roll off the press: after being trailed for two months on the front page, it ran until 1870.[278] For good measure, the monarchy was then given a dusting down in the chronological series 'Estimates of the English Kings' from William the Conqueror. The editors' intention was

> that they might assist in supplying a want which has been felt by many readers of English History, of some more distinct conceptions of the English Kings as living men than are supplied by the incidental notices scattered through the record of their reigns, or by the meagre and often incongruous summaries of qualities which precede or conclude the narrative of each reign.[279]

The history lesson at last came to its close by stopping (at a respectful remove) with George III, in April 1872.[280]

This, among other novel ventures, achieved apparent success. After so hairy a start, circulation ticked up in 1864 towards 2,000, and that year *The Spectator* turned a profit for the first time since 1857. In 1865, the *Dublin University Magazine*, while granting that Rintoul's *Spectator* had been 'a marvel of sub-editing', declared Townsend-Hutton's *Spectator*

> now the most eccentric and original journal in London. There is a personal flavour about this newspaper which differentiates it from its contemporaries – a strong individuality, in singular contrast with the somewhat colourless method of other newspapers. In reading the *Saturday Review* you seem to be dealing with a committee. The *Spectator* gives you the idea of a man arguing with you, and a rather determined man too.

In part, the increased appeal of *The Spectator* came from its authoritative and cogent leaders. For Townsend and Hutton shared both genuine political verve and the canny ability to unpick the strings of those in power. Hutton had very much earned his stripes in this field. Most prominently, he produced in 1865 a series of parliamentary sketches for the *Pall Mall Gazette* – of which he was almost made the first editor.[281] Presumably it was the informal and chatty nature of these portraits that made them inappropriate for the anonymous *Spectator*.[282] Anthony Trollope observed at the time that 'nothing probably so good in their way has ever before appeared in the columns of an English newspaper... I doubt whether in them all the critic can put his finger on a single material mistake.'[283] Here was born the playful but honest art of parliamentary sketch-writing. Hutton was thus ready to bring that same analytical scalpel to his hebdomadal dissections of British politics in *The Spectator*.[284]

For some, it was sufficient to remark, 'Mr Hutton is the *Spectator*'.[285] But, although he had great influence as a political, religious and literary voice, perhaps a more closely read part of *The Spectator* was Townsend's celebrated sub-leaders. These essays – usually falling between 1,000 and 2,000 words – were sparkling pieces of writing. One long-term staffer regarded their author as 'one of the most brilliant historical and political leader-writers that ever served a weekly journal'.[286] Townsend's instincts for current affairs that mattered were indeed famous. Another called him 'a sort of Jules Verne of politics, seeing at a glance how a slight modification of actual facts might change the map of Europe or remodel the structure of society.'[287] To John Buchan, a later colleague, he was 'clearly a holy man, a *guru* of some sort, with his old-fashioned courtesy of speech, and his gift of delivering gnomic judgments which annihilated space and time.' Another even ventured to call him Hutton's 'more brilliant colleague'.[288] Townsend's successor as editor was yet stronger in his praise:

> It is my honest belief that he was, in the matter of style, the greatest leader-writer who has ever appeared in the English Press. He developed

the exact compromise between a literary dignity and a colloquial easiness of exposition which completely fills the requirements of journalism. He was never pompous, never dull or common, and never trivial... No one could excite the mind and exalt the imagination as he did. And the miracle was that he did it all the time in language which appeared to be nothing more than that of a clever, competent man talking at his club. He used no literary artifice, no rhetorical emphasis, no elaboration of language, no *finesse* of phrase. His style was easy but never elegant or precious or ornamented. It was familiar without being commonplace, free without discursiveness, and it always had in it the note of distinction... He never appeared to preach or to explain to his readers. But though he had all the air of assuming that they were perfectly well-read and highly experienced in great affairs, he yet managed to tell them very clearly what they did not and could not know. He could give instruction without the slightest assumption of the schoolmaster. In truth, his writing at its best was in form perfect journalism.[289]

This is all true. There was much, in fact, of the modern tabloid leader-writer in him. He combined sensationalist expression with colloquial language, common-sense truths with challenging ideas – all underpinned by deep learning, exotic experience and a technicolour imagination. As colleagues recalled, 'qualifying words were an abomination to his strong imagination': he 'did not deal in greys' but wrote with a 'nervous, vivid, almost violent style', which 'leaped to metaphor rather than wandered in simile'.[290] 'Dreamy' and 'screamy' – words which few would associate with Victorian journalism – were among his favourite splashes of colour.[291]

Each week, Townsend's unsigned pieces – always bashed out within two hours – were eagerly devoured and keenly debated, keeping *The Spectator* on the lips of the nation. 'I have myself known families', a veteran of journalism recalled, 'which would as soon have don[e] without dinner as have missed their weekly "portion[s]" of Hutton or Townsend.'[292] Even with 2020 vision, hi[s] style still reads as lively as ever, and his inventivenes[s] saves most pieces from anachronism. Turn to hi[s] leaders on London being imprisoned by snow, o[r] blown up by gas, or on human responses to a gale i[n] the face, and the words feel as fresh as when they firs[t] were set in type.[293] Townsend was, of course, capable o[f] deep thought in spite of his racy style: his article o[n] the purpose of pain packs plenty of punch, concludin[g] that 'a painless world would be a world of worthles[s] men and women'.[294] In the last years of his editorship[,] the complaint was made that Townsend was 'perhap[s] the ablest living writer whose name is practical[ly] unrepresented in literature'.[295] It is an embarrassmen[t] that his articles, among the most celebrated essay[s] of the High and Late Victorian periods, have n[ot] once been gathered for publication, however parti[al] or inadequate the selection.[296] He is one of the mos[t] unjustly forgotten figures in journalistic history.

Hutton's style was – and remains – more challengin[g]. His sentences – long, sprawling and qualified at eve[ry] turn – 'went tottering on, bent double under all the[] burden of thought'.[297] Although they were mercifull[y] free of jargon and high-flown abstractions, each claus[e] was weighed down with earnest meaning, so the goin[g] was slow and the chance of fallers high. *The Tim[es]* tempered its praise with unease:

It was as if within the folds of the long-drawn, sinuous, complex involutions of a style never swift, sometimes prolix and toilsome, there was a subtle aroma; something not felt by the uninitiated was there to satisfy and refresh certain minds in their troubles.[298]

Writing at a generation's remove, Virginia Woo[lf] revealed her impatience more than her taste[,] attributing to Hutton 'a voice which is as a plague [of] locusts – the voice of a man stumbling drowsily amo[ng] loose words, clutching aimlessly at vague ideas.

Hutton did indeed write as his thoughts tumbled forth, but those thoughts emanated from a plentiful sump of much-pondered, carefully weighed cogitations. One of his closest friends, if truth be told, was the parenthesis: reserve and caution always held him back from the devastatingly sweeping judgment – the thoughts with which Townsend awoke and fell asleep. At times, it seems, he was almost too clever for the syntax into which he was born. Still, the sense remains with every paragraph that, as one admirer sagely noted, 'all his articles, literary or political, are noticeable quite as much for their power suppressed as for the power put forth.'[300] This seems wholly appropriate for a man 'bearded and somewhat Socratic in countenance'.[301]

Style aside, Hutton's range was immense. He did not limit himself to parliamentary politics, literary reflection and religious meditation: under his influence *The Spectator* became an early and vocal campaigner for women's education, the reform of working standards and animal rights.[302] He was always open to blue-sky conjecture – witness his frequent reflections on extra-terrestrial life, where 'Martials' lurk on that mysterious planet[303] – and followed developments in science closely, if sceptically.

The stark difference between the two editors' approaches to leader-writing has been well expressed: 'Townsend looked upon life as a drama played in a great theatre and seen from the stalls. To Hutton, life was more like some High Conference at which he himself was one of the delegates, and not merely a spectator.'[304] But, for all their unquestionable differences, Hutton and Townsend fell out only once – the cause is unknown – and their mutual friend Bagehot was at hand to pacify them. When the two men could not reconcile their views in private, they sometimes took the fairest cause available to them in public: to write two adjacent leaders as two sides of the coin mid-toss. Turn to the issue of 15 April 1871, for instance, and the leading articles open with 'The future of France I: the dark side'; this is immediately followed by 'The future of France II: its brighter side'. The two pieces are manifestly from different hands; predictably enough,

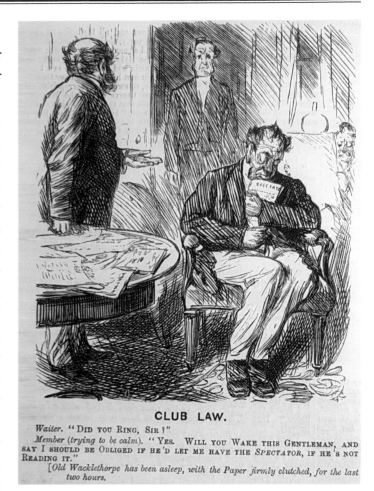

CLUB LAW.

Waiter. "DID YOU RING, SIR?"
Member (trying to be calm). "YES. WILL YOU WAKE THIS GENTLEMAN, AND SAY I SHOULD BE OBLIGED IF HE'D LET ME HAVE THE *SPECTATOR*, IF HE'S NOT READING IT."
[*Old Wacklethorpe has been asleep, with the Paper firmly clutched, for the last two hours.*

Punch cartoon, 25 Apr. 1868

Hutton took the bleaker and Townsend the rosier view of the crisis. Both men were always ready to defer to the other's talents: Hutton was often heard to say of an issue that 'the best part was t'other fellow's', whereas Townsend regarded Hutton as operating on a wholly different plane from him.

One point on which the men conspired to agree was in keeping the franchise away from women. When a petition arose to amend the Second Reform Act so as to give women with property the right to vote, which received vocal support from a *Spectator* regular, J.S. Mill, the editors opined that women were not sufficiently invested in the political sphere to have won the vote. In June 1866, Hutton's stuffy leader on 'The women's petition and congress' closed with the following Catch-22: 'Women must show a glimmer of diffused political capacity before they talk of their general political rights.' This elicited furious correspondence from the incipient women's suffrage movement, with Frances Power Cobbe haranguing the editors for their intellectual narrow-mindedness: 'I should be ready to wager that among the most constant readers of the *Spectator* ... there were to be found at least as many ladies as gentlemen.'[305] She closed with one more petition, that 'you will still treat us on some other principle than that of the traditional schoolmaster, who strictly forbade his boys to enter the water till they prove beforehand their *capacity* to swim.'

Over the next year a spirited exchange of letters touched on the issue, mostly from female correspondents.[306] Nevertheless, *The Spectator* was still of the conviction that

> even in the middle classes, the widows, wives, and daughters of very few men, not Members of Parliament, take the slightest interest in politics, or could show even that very bare and trivial amount of interest and intelligence with regard to politics which an average man, qualified in the same way, could usually show. Man for woman, living in the same class of house, and qualified by the same rental qualification, —no one, in his senses, would doubt that the average man's political interests and notions would be far in advance of the average woman's of the same level.[307]

These worries ultimately came down to the different intellectual prospects of men and women, which required separate educational streams:

> Is it not true that women's minds are proportionally finer and more quick of apprehension on the side of taste and art, and weaker on the side of mere intellectual grasp, — feats of logic, retentiveness of memory, tenacity of hold on first principles, —than men's? If so, can the best general education for the two sexes be identical? For our own parts, we believe that no general education is good which does not leave behind it the highest acme of a real gain in *power* and *resource* which it is possible to give... What we fear from too absolute an identification of the general education of young women with the present education of young men, is that it would not instil into the former the full sense of power and resource which they are capable of receiving. It would neglect the side of their minds on which they are superior to men, and hammer away at that side on which they are inferior to men, and so discourage them.

Robust, if then widely held, views. Still, it should be remembered that *The Spectator* was guaranteed n[o] receptive audience. On the contrary, competition ha[s] only increased in recent decades. Throughout th[e] Townsend-Hutton tenure, *The Spectator* jostled wi[th] three other intellectual weeklies: *Athenaeum* (founde[d] 1828), *Saturday Review* (1855) and *Academy* (186[?] appearing first monthly then fortnightly, but week[ly] from 1873). By 1870, *The Spectator* had fought its way ba[ck] to the head of the pack; the regrettable spell of 1858–[6]0 seemed to have been politely erased from journalist[ic] memory. The paper's circulation had accordingly rise[n] to match its high point in the 1840s, at somewhe[re] around 4,000. That figure grew steadily over the ne[xt] fifteen years, but would not break 10,000 until the ve[ry] end of the century. A press historian, writing in 18[?] spoke of the paper as then being at its very best:

> it never at any period stood so high as it does as the time I am writing. It has never allied itself with any party in the State, but has treated, and still treats, all the political questions of the day in accordance with its own convictions of truth and right. I have never yet met with the man who, no matter how much he might be opposed to the views of the *Spectator*, ever doubted its honesty or questioned its great ability.[308]

Readers in high places were indeed taking its words seriously. In 1872, for instance, during his first spell as prime minister, *The Spectator* had quoted with surprise a remark that its Liberal hero, William Gladstone, made at a meeting of the Society of Biblical Archaeology. He there confided to his fellow bookworms that

> every day must begin for me with my old friend Homer – the friend of my youth, the friend of my middle age, and of my old age – from whom I hope never to be parted as long as I have any faculties or any breath in my body.

Such literary fervour from the country's leader raised even contemporary eyebrows. The *Saturday Review* averred that Gladstone 'cannot eat his breakfast until he has read his lesson for the day out of it'.[309] The *Daily Telegraph* expressed its wonder 'that a statesman upon whose hands devolves the charge of this Empire should, in the midst of toils and labours under which most men would utterly break down, find time not only to continue the studies of his youth, but to prosecute them with a vigour and an energy which even the keenest Heidelberg professor might envy.' It proceeded to liken him to Alexander the Great, 'who never slept without a scroll of the "Iliad" under his pillow.'[310] *The Spectator*, for its part, gave a highbrow account of how the Homeric *Weltanschauung* infused Gladstone's politics, concluding:

> The public spirit which is so great in Homer, the gloom of that perpetual conflict which is yet so dear to Homer's heroes, and the simplicity and directness of that political power which they wield, are all characteristics which have a natural fascination for the modern statesman; and the last of them has probably that special fascination for Mr. Gladstone, which the grander and simpler primeval forms of power always have for the highly organised intelligence of a subtle and elaborate civilisation.[311]

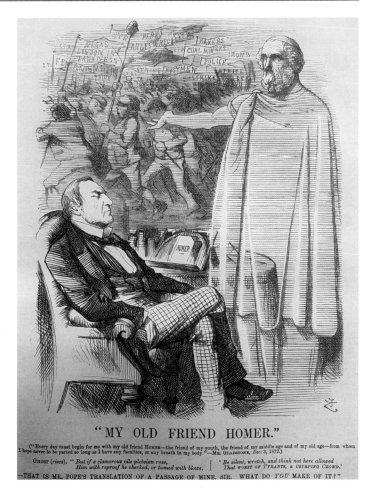

"MY OLD FRIEND HOMER."

("Every day must begin for me with my old friend HOMER—the friend of my youth, the friend of my middle age and of my old age—from whom I hope never to be parted so long as I have any faculties, or any breath in my body."—MR. GLADSTONE, *Dec. 3, 1872.*)

GHOST (*rises*). "*But if a clamorous vile plebeian rose,* | *Be silent, wretch, and think not here allowed* | *Him with reproof he checked, or tamed with blows,* | *That worst of TYRANTS, a USURPING CROWD.'*"
—THAT IS MR. POPE'S TRANSLATION OF A PASSAGE OF MINE, SIR. WHAT DO *YOU* MAKE OF IT?"

Punch cartoon, 14 Dec. 1872

The wits of *Punch*, by contrast, sketched the ghost of Homer pestering a sleeping Gladstone for his views on a crowd in civil unrest – described, after Pope's famous translation, as 'that worst of tyrants, the usurping crowd'.

Gladstone's innocuous admission of his private literary passions proved to be a PR disaster. Aware he had to act swiftly, he set *The Spectator* – and the nation – straight by firing off a letter to the paper, which duly headed the next week's correspondence columns:

> I wish to say that the reporter has been led, probably by some careless or indistinct expression of mine, into an error. What I said was that every effort to examine the question raised on that day must begin for me with Homer ... as to my beginning every day with Homer, as such a phrase

conveys to the world a very untrue impression of the demands of my present office, I think it right to mention that, so far as my memory serves me, I have not read Homer for fifty lines or for a quarter of an hour consecutively during the last four years, and any dealings of mine with Homeric subjects have been confined to a number of days which could readily be counted on the fingers.[312]

Business, then, before pleasure for the premier. Indeed, Gladstone's diary confirms that September 1872 brought him fresh Homeric draughts, his 'first course of this medicine since 1868'.[313] Still, however hard-pressed the Homer of Hawarden was by the demands of government, one notices with admiration and amusement that he nevertheless found time here and there to turn out five books on his epic hero.

Gladstone, of course, was not the only leading light of the day to address the nation via the paper's correspondence pages. Alongside the usual suspects, letters appeared from the likes of Charles Darwin (on natural selection, 18 Jan. 1873), Thomas Huxley (on the possibility of miracles, 10 Feb. 1866), John Tyndall (on scientific truth, 17 Feb. 1866), Millicent Fawcett (on preaching as unproductive labour, 24 May 1873), Cardinal Newman (on his early relationship to the Roman Church, 5 May 1883), J.S. Mill (on Thomas Hare's plans for electoral reform, 29 Apr. 1865), Jacob Bright (on the problem of Portuguese colonialism, 14 Apr. 1883), William Morris (on the lack of allegory in his work, 20 July 1895), and Samuel Clemens – or rather Mark Twain. The last wrote amusingly about the danger of plagiaristic publishers:

I only venture to intrude upon you because I come, in some sense, in the interest of public morality, and this makes my mission respectable. Mr. John Camden Hotten, of London, has, of his own individual motion, republished several of my books in England. I do not protest against this, for there is no law that could give effect

to the protest; and, besides, publishers are not accountable to the laws of heaven or earth in any country, as I understand it. But my little grievance is this: My books are bad enough just as they are written; then what must they be after Mr. John Camden Hotten has composed half-a-dozen chapters and added the same to them? I feel that all true hearts will bleed for an author whose volumes have fallen under such a dispensation as this... Sometimes when I read one of those additional chapters constructed by John Camden Hotten, I feel as if I wanted to take a broom-straw and go and knock that man's brains out. Not in anger, for I feel none. Oh! not in anger; but only to see, that is all. Mere idle curiosity.[314]

We must return to politics: the British press wa[s] exercised to differing degrees by the Eastern Crisis [of] the mid-1870s, when Ottoman Turks murdered up [to] 15,000 Balkan Christians. As an important strateg[ic] ally to the United Kingdom, however, Turkey was n[ot] challenged on the matter by the Tory governmen[t;] worse still, the Prime Minister, Benjamin Disrael[i,] flatly denied the truth of such grave allegations. Whe[n] news of the Bulgarian atrocities reached its zenith – the summer of 1876 – *The Spectator* did not temper i[ts] criticism:

We wish we could bring fully home to our readers the serious, even the disastrous consequences which will arise to the British Government from the attitude which Mr. Disraeli, and Mr. Disraeli alone, even in his own Government, has assumed about the Turkish atrocities. That attitude will affect the position of Great Britain and its influence throughout the world, and in Turkey itself may help to produce a catastrophe which we do not hesitate to say we believe to be approaching at the full pace of modern events.[315]

The Powers of Europe must not stand by and plead the malignity or the imbecility of his

Government as an excuse for letting the cruelty and rapine and lust go on... Mr. Disraeli's manner ... has been the very reverse of earnest. If he had been dealing with canards of a grossly improbable and purely indifferent character, he could hardly have demeaned himself with less sense of the gravity of the issue and of the solemnity of the tragedy on which he was questioned.[316]

The Spectator, for its part, could call upon its regular correspondent Malcolm MacColl (later Canon of Ripon), who was then on a fact-finding tour of the Balkans, from where he filed correspondence relaying to the paper's aghast readers the horrific deeds afoot.

In 1876, Hutton and Townsend acquired on their staff another writer of some future renown. In a hurry at twenty-three, H.H. Asquith found that he could enliven his lacklustre Bar career by penning spirited articles for The Spectator. He served on and off as a leader-writer on domestic politics and legal matters (especially when the editors took their holidays), and also pulled his weight in the reviewing department. His first article, 'The English Extreme Left' (12 Aug. 1876), sympathised with the desire of the Liberals' 'Radical wing' to split at last from their party. Since, however, 'no third Party has ever been able to stand its ground in England', Asquith gave the sage, if dull, advice to maintain 'the rude dichotomy of English Party politics'. Over the next eight years his lively leaders covered all manner of subjects, including 'College Heads' (1 Oct. 1881), 'Gladstone and Free Trade' (15 Oct. 1881) and 'Banks, and their Customers' (13 Oct. 1883).[317] By the end of 1884, however, after penning some sixty pieces, Ol' Squiffy was feeling the pull of politics proper, and duly left to climb the greasy pole. With typical journalistic irony, he would later lead not just the Liberals he had counselled in print but the nation whose Sundays he had complemented. In fact, his hard-won route – from Spectator page to prime-ministerial power – would be followed by many figures: the same transition was later made by MacDonald, Macmillan, Heath,

Cameron, May, Johnson and – rather more curiously – Blair and Brown.[318]

Asquith evidently enjoyed his decade in Wellington Street, forming an intimate relationship with the editors. Following Hutton's death, he called him 'my oldest and best friend amongst literary people'.[319] With a rare insight into the private practice of his two employers, he later recalled that

ostensibly, they had nothing in common; Townsend, with his courtly Anglo-Indian air, tapping his snuff-box, and walking up and down his room, emitting dogmatic paradoxes: Hutton, more than short-sighted, looking out on external things through a monocle with an extra-powerful lens, and talking with the almost languid, donnish air of one who had in old days breakfasted with Crabb Robinson and sat at the feet of Arthur Clough. I was often in and out of this curious laboratory, passing from one floor to the other, and now and again foregathering in colloquy with both of the respective occupants. There would be a free and animate clash of discussion, usually about the subjects of the forthcoming number, always ending in an *entente cordiale*; and they would return to their dens, and each set to work to hammer out in totally different styles their joint handiwork.[320]

For all their difference, though, the result in print was a genuinely unified whole. A contemporary reader said that the paper 'could hardly be more homogeneous than it is in tone, if week by week it flowed from the pen of one man from first to last.'[321] This uniformity was helped by the fact that, as Asquith himself recalled, the paper was 'written almost from cover to cover by the two proprietors'.[322]

We owe to Harry Quilter, the paper's idiosyncratic art critic (1876–87), much the most vivid sketch of the two men at the height of their influence. Hutton, he says, was by no means a milksop, and could be very angry on occasion. He kept discipline among his contributors with an iron hand; personally speaking, I never sat down on the little sofa in his office, to discuss a forthcoming article, without feeling as if I had been 'sent for' by the head master. He rarely or never altered articles, but rejected them without the slightest hesitation if he disapproved of their tone. His co-editor, on the other hand, had far less of the moral bias, and when Hutton was away on his holiday would pass any article that was good enough from a literary point of view, and of an article he was a most admirable judge. He was a quaint, excitable, and exceedingly untidy little man, with his waistcoat half-unbuttoned and covered with snuff, which he took copiously the whole time, and he had a trick of speaking as if he were furiously angry on the slightest provocation. It was, however, a mild, fretful, spluttering sort of anger, quite different from the great roar of Hutton, and to see the two men together was curious indeed. Imagine a thin, elderly lion turned into a short-sighted man, and set down at a high desk, writing busily, apparently with his nose as well as the pen, so closely was the head approached to the manuscript; imagine I say, this metamorphosed king of beasts, writing at break-neck speed, with grunts and ejaculations, and continual replacements of an eye-glass, and tossings of its grey mane, and sheets of copy flying all over the room when they are finished; and then fancy amidst it all, a little round-about brown figure, pacing incessantly up and down the little room, snuffing furiously, and talking with a brilliant exaggeration of statement that now and then provoked remonstrance, and now and then a shout of laughter from the seated figure.[323]

Another observer recalled how, despite the difficulty of the task and the notorious illegibility of his own hand, Hutton served as the most scrupulous proofreader for the paper:

having only the use of one eye, and that of defective vision, it was necessary for him to bow his head to within a few inches of his objective in order to guide his pen along the paper. The marvel to me was the immense amount of writing he got through each week besides his proof correcting, usually done at the window looking on to Somerset House, the proof being held in his left hand, on the window shutter, where he could get the light: there he would stand and work until he had finished his revision.[324]

Although in the early days Townsend and Hutton were without question the dominant writers of the paper, as their tenure progressed they could call upon an increasingly formidable host of contributors. Such was the joy they took in good writing that they would sometimes pay double on receipt of a particular pleasing contribution: since Hutton looked after the finances, he had a free hand to tweak fees as he fancied. The names of Bagehot, Hughes and Swinburne have already been mentioned. But regular writers included Daniel Lathbury, co-editor of *The Economist* (1877–8) who wrote a sub-leader each week, the jurists Frederic Pollock, A.V. Dicey, Lord Bowen and Lord Coleridge the theologians F.D. Maurice, James Martineau and Dean Stanley, the social reformers J.M. Ludlow Frances Power Cobbe and Emily Faithfull, the novelists Cashel Hoey, Margaret Oliphant, Snow Wedgwood and Emilie Barrington, the dramatist Herman Charles Merivale, the literary men James Macdonell, Edmund Gosse, H.D. Traill, J.S. Blackie, John Hutton and John Morley, the great classicists of the day Benjamin Jowett and Richard Jebb, and the incomparable oenophile George Saintsbury. Co-ordinating what books went where was the paper's first literary editor, Alfred Church, a great populariser of the classics; throughout his forty years in that post he often expressed unalloyed delight at the successes of Dean (Richard William) Church – no relation, as it happens, but this was the man whose surname landed him a job at *The Spectator* thanks to Hutton's misdirected admiration.[325]

However, most of these leading lights were forcibly hidden preserving the *Spectator* bushel: unlike many other rival weeklies, the editors remained committed to preserving contributors' anonymity. For Townsend, [it] helped diminish the influence of personality, 'by exempting the writer from certain provocations, and by subjecting him to certain moderating influences'.[326] For Hutton, 'signed journalism ... tends to foster petty [v]anities more effectually than unsigned.'[327] Only special [c]ases – like their close friends F.D. Maurice and J.M. [L]udlow – were granted the occasional indulgence of [si]gning their contributions.

The High Victorian period was an age of doubt as [w]ell as of progress, as correspondents with *The Spectator* [re]gularly attested. Science was steadily shaking faith in [C]hristianity: scrutiny of nature was undermining the [ar]guments for intelligent design; biblical criticism was [ch]allenging the truth of scripture; and astronomical [di]scoveries were making planet Earth seem increasingly [le]ss special. For the first time in its history, it seemed, [C]hristianity and its core doctrines were becoming [so]mething that could be side-lined, if not ignored. In [th]e case of Darwin, for instance, his *Origin of Species* [fir]st suffered strident criticism from Adam Sedgwick, [wh]o expressed his 'detestation of the theory' and its [w]onderful credulity ... that a lemur might easily be [tu]rned into a bat'.[328] But, as the dust slowly settled, *The [Sp]ectator* gradually moved towards accepting his core [th]eories; an important trio of long letters from Edward [Fr]y (then a QC) gave reassurance in 1872 that, if [D]arwinism be true, it can be adequately accommodated [wi]thin a theological system.[329] Still, for all the march of [sci]ence, the editors of *The Spectator* were determined [th]at faith would not lose pride of place.

Neither Townsend nor Hutton had a conventional [rel]igious upbringing. The former was born into [Sw]edenborg's Church of the New Jerusalem, the latter [in]to hard-line Unitarianism, denying the divinity of [Ch]rist. Both drifted inexorably towards Anglicanism [in] later life, but with some significant colouring. [To]wnsend was profoundly – if hazily – influenced by [In]dian spiritualism; Hutton long supported the Broad

Church movement of F.D. Maurice but, inspired by J.H. Newman's High Anglicanism, was said to be attending Roman Catholic Mass in his final years.[330] Yet this is to speak of the men; Swedenborgianism or Unitarianism or Sacerdotalism found no place in *The Spectator*'s editorial 'We'. Each writer did, nevertheless, approach religion in his characteristic fashion. A *Spectator* article – when penned by Townsend – could begin, 'God, then, governs as well as reigns';[331] or – when penned by Hutton – intone magnificently:

> Revelation is the true answer, and in a sense the only answer, to agnosticism... Of course, if we insist on knowing God as completely as God has shown us that he knows us, we shall all be agnostics. There is nothing more impossible than for man to fathom the riddles of this most unintelligible world. But the question for us is not whether we can understand it, but whether there is or is not one who understands us and has shown us, in the individual life through conscience, and in the national life through the teaching of the chosen race, that he has the key to our most secret thoughts, though we have not the key to any of his except those which he engraves upon our hearts and carves indelibly in the story of one perverse people.[332]

In such a fraught climate, *Spectator* readers were naturally anxious to join the debate over fundamental religious issues when opportunity arose. A brace of controversial articles of 1872 provided just such a chance. That year, Francis Galton published his 'Statistical inquiries into the efficacy of prayer' in the *Fortnightly Review*.[333] The debate had gained force from the widespread wonder that public prayers for the Prince of Wales's good health seemed to have won God's aid in December 1871. The ever-sceptical John Tyndall suggested in a subsequent article that a 'prayer gauge' should be set up to measure the outcome of hospital patients' health over a period of three years, some of whom were routinely prayed for, some not.

Hutton hit back at such a 'covert sneer' made up 'of thinly-veiled scoffs':

> we should be much surprised to learn that any man who had really given up his mind to thoughts of this kind at all, had ever regarded his prayer as a sort of petty dictation to God, the effect of which might be measured like a constituent's pressure on his representative in Parliament, by the influence it exerted on the issue. You pray, if you pray in the spirit of Christ at all, not for a specific external end, but because it is a deep relief to pour out your heart to God in the frankest way possible to limited human nature, and in the hope that if your *wish* is not granted, your *want* may be.[334]

Spectator readers worldwide were quick to give impassioned arguments and intimate anecdotes to support or reject the question of whether prayer did work, should work, or could never work. The discussion – firing on all cylinders from all quarters – filled dozens of columns throughout August and September 1872.

Despite *The Spectator*'s close association with *The Economist* – where Hutton was a former editor, and Townsend a regular political correspondent – it did form and project its own positions. Like Rintoul, they were staunch advocates of free trade. Over recent decades, however, the commensurate surge in British imports was immense: in the 1830s, 2 per cent of grain was imported; by the 1880s that figure was 45 per cent. Occasionally, pressed by poor harvests or dips in trade, British belief in free trade wavered; to some it looked increasingly out of step with countries such as Germany and America that were advancing rapidly behind their protectionist barriers. Sporadic calls arose for 'fair trade' – the imposition of reciprocal duties on goods from countries that levied their own tariffs. Nevertheless, in 1875, Hutton set out coolly and clearly the long-term benefits of a free trade policy, warning that 'the first and most plausible way, to the ignorant observer, of "encouraging" commerce is Protection. It requires a good deal of study and of intellectual tenacit to keep clear of the plausibilities of the Protectiv fallacies.'[335] Five years later, he repeated that warning:

> There can be no question that the great mass of the people of England do not understand Free-trade. They were induced to adopt it 'through their stomachs,' and not through any intellectual process whatever, and a very slight taste of commercial depression was quite enough to set people talking about 'one-sided Free-trade,' and the folly of allowing England to be made a receptacle for the cheap exports of foreign nations... Anyone who remembers the winter of 1869–70 will call to mind the complaints that were then made about foreign competition, and the agitation against 'Free-trade without reciprocity' which was set on foot by the carpenters, who were at that time rather closely pressed by the importation of window-frames from Sweden, ready-made.[336]

It would be another quarter-century before *T Spectator* had to flex its muscles on the principle.

Townsend was always keen to keep *The Spectator* the forefront of debate. More than one staffer recal his frequent observation that 'I've noticed that we' doing best when we're in hot water.'[337] Despite th feisty attitude towards his paper, however, he h little time for engaging with society outside his tv beloved spheres – *The Spectator* and his family (a wif son and two daughters). By contrast, Hutton (who h no children) was more widely known among figur of the day. Most importantly, he was a foundi member of the Metaphysical Society (1869–85), whe he kicked about the Big Questions in the compa of Tennyson, Gladstone, Huxley, Tyndall, Ruski Balfour, Manning and select others. He was also celebrated host of regular parties at the Devonsh Club, where his free-flowing supply of champag came second to the conversation as the most sparkli presence in the room.

Politically, *The Spectator* became increasingly open in its support of the Liberals as the Townsend-Hutton tenure advanced. Gladstone's first two prime-ministerial terms (1868–74, 1880–5) saw the paper propound its outlook with unparalleled confidence. As a contemporary newspaper jested, 'We have often thought the government of the country should be shifted from Downing Street to No. 1 Wellington Street.'[338] Certainly, the paper's admiration for Gladstone had risen almost to the point of idolatry by the mid-1880s. The man whom Rintoul's *Spectator* praised as 'an exact reasoner, an honest politician, a warm-hearted patriot' in the days of the Aberdeen Budget of 1853[339] had since grown into their near-perfect statesman over the next thirty years. His great adversary Disraeli, by contrast, had been dismissed as early as 1846 as 'that spoiled child of Parliamentary fashion'.[340] But *The Spectator*'s established ties were to be tested by another political crisis in the wings: when the Irish Question came to the fore, Gladstone strenuously advanced the case for Home Rule, much to the shock of the English establishment. While his decision split the Liberals in two, it failed to cleave apart Townsend and Hutton, who were as one in their keen support of the Union. There was no defensible course open to *The Spectator* other than to adopt its usual practice, of putting principle ahead of party. Gladstone and his wing of the Liberals could no longer be supported.

The gravity of this decision was made all the heavier by Hutton's long-standing personal friendship with the Grand Old Man. Soon after their split, Hutton confessed to him:

I can hardly tell you how difficult my work as a journalist has become to me, since I felt compelled to take a different view from yours on the Irish question. Instead of enjoying it as I used to, it has become all duty work ever since.[341]

So prolonged and impassioned was *The Spectator*'s opposition to the Home Rule Bills that more than one contemporary judge wondered whether Gladstone's motion would have passed, had the paper only fought for the other side. When the Second Bill was defeated, by a majority of thirty, on 8 June 1886, Hutton offered commiseration in that week's leading article:

His ablest colleagues alienated; his oldest friends dismayed; a Bill which was to tranquillise Ireland for ever, lost; a Parliament rendered useless before it had actively lived; the Liberal Party, 'the greatest instrument of progress ever constructed,' shattered to its foundation; the country filled with hostile passions; all enemies rejoicing and all progress suspended, —the moment that followed the division must have been a melancholy one for the proud old man, conscious of utter rectitude of purpose, and certain that his plan was only too far-sighted for the clamouring multitude around.

And yet, despite this grave and lasting separation on such an emotive issue, Gladstone's respect for Hutton and his paper was unshaken. He wrote to his friend, 'Rely upon it, I can never quarrel with you,' adding later the candid remark that 'Long have I seen that few men, few Liberals, believe in liberty: but you I think are one.'[342] Gladstone next wrote a letter to *The Spectator* to protest that his nuanced view of Home Rule was improperly understood. This he apparently did anonymously, above the initial 'Y'.[343] The closing paragraph is worthy of citation:

It is amazing to see the bitter feeling of the time against Mr. Gladstone. He may be mistaken, he may be deluded, he may be mad; but surely he is disinterested. He has faced the splitting of an enthusiastic united party, the loss of friends, the furious abuse of enemies, at an age when he might well have chosen to end his public career in peace, as full of honours as of years. Grant that there is in him a hope of completing the work of reconciliation between the sister-islands which he has so long laboured at—who can call

Townsend and Hutton in the 1890s

this an ignoble ambition?—while he can, at best, have but a faint and doubtful prospect of himself living to enter upon the Promised Land?

But, despite these irresoluble disagreements, Gladstone remained a close friend of Hutton. He confided in correspondence that his respect 'for Mr Hutton is so great that I no longer venture to read his pages'.[344] Still, he later declared in public:

Much as I deplore the policy of the *Spectator* on the Irish Question, I recognise the same sincerity which marks all its writings. It is one of the few papers which are written in the fear and love of God.[345]

IV
SPECTATORIAL CERTITUDE
1886–1920

────────

The decision to oppose Home Rule, Gladstone and his government arrested *The Spectator*'s steady rise in circulation. The many readers who instinctively put party allegiance before ideological dogma rapidly cancelled their subscriptions, as once again an editorial point of principle set sales sliding. It is probable, too, that Asquith's exit from Wellington Street the previous year was encouraged by his political differences on this critical issue. His decision, however, proved to be very significant for the paper's future. For, in 1886, JOHN ST LOE STRACHEY (1860–1927) was invited to take up Asquith's post. That role required a mixture of political leader-writing, reviewing and standing in as co-editor when Townsend and Hutton each took their consecutive six-week holidays in summer.

The son of a Somersetshire squire, St Loe (as he was universally known) was a curious mix of political agitator and polymathic Quixote, who channelled some of the vivacity of his uncle, the poet and critic John Addington Symonds. Schooled at home, he spent his formative years knee-deep in an ancestral library stuffed to the rafters with English literature. For the rest of his life he would quote poetry as naturally and instinctively as his date of birth. While reading History at Balliol he was reputed to be a rabidly left-wing oddball with a prodigious memory: the undergraduate verses of his day said of Strachey, 'There is no line of any poet That can be quoted, but I know it.' Soon, however, the introduction of new ideas and outlooks from men raised in a different world moved him towards a committed Liberal outlook. He duly took a First.

Left unstimulated by the career at the Bar that stretched ahead of him, he instead pursued his passion for journalism. His father, Sir Edward, 3rd Baronet, had been a frequent contributor to the paper earlier in the century, and had won St Loe an introduction to the journalistic Dioscuri. Strachey's political outlook helped to land him a place at the table: he was not just a Liberal, or just a Liberal Unionist; he was, in fact, co-editor of the *Liberal Unionist* (1887–92). This, 'a fortnightly journal to represent the views of the Liberal and Radical Unionists on the Irish question',[346] could scarcely have been more up *The Spectator*'s street.

Strachey was open-minded, hard-working and wide-ranging: in his early years at *The Spectator* he was also writing a weekly piece in *The Economist*, and serving as a leader-writer for the *Standard*; in the 1890s he also found time to edit three volumes of the biannual *Cornhill Magazine*.[347] His first two *Spectator* articles – one steering the Conservative Unionists towards optimism, the other on the Privy Council and the Colonies[348] – caused a remarkable stir in the office and across the country. From this point onwards he wrote for the paper, almost without a break, for the next forty years; *The Spectator* – in a phenomenon we have encountered more than once already – soon became his life.[349]

In 1888, Hutton's wife Eliza suffered a carriage accident from which she never recovered. He therefore worked regularly from home to provide care: she would play chess with him, but would utter nothing beyond 'Hello' and 'Goodbye'.[350] Although contemporary newspapers reported the rumour that he was set to retire, he fought on. But as his own health waned in the mid-1890s, Strachey's activity increased. In 1894, to reflect this rise, his salary was more than doubled to £1,200 (*c.* £100,000). After Eliza's death in March 1897, Hutton's forces rapidly ebbed away. The last article from his hand, 'The great colonial experiment', appeared on 26 June. Having outlined the challenges of peacefully maintaining the empire, he concluded that, given the inevitable differences of voices in that amalgam,

We must see how very difficult the task will be, what self-control it will require to suppress the dissonances, to avoid entering on subjects on which agreement will be impossible, and yet to secure a hearty co-operation in extinguishing slavery, in protecting freedom, and in stimulating the nobler enterprises of the human race. The full development of democracy involves, we suspect, one of the greatest difficulties of our growing Colonial Empire.

His last words in private correspondence were 'Dear Townsend, God bless you.'[351]

On 9 September 1897, Hutton died; like Rintoul, he was seventy-one. Townsend reported the event at the outset of the next *Spectator* with moving brevity:

> Our readers will be grieved to hear of the death of Mr. R.H. Hutton, so long one of the editors of this journal. After an illness of many months, marked by severe though intermittent sufferings, he passed away quietly in sleep during the afternoon of Thursday, the 9th inst. His colleagues are forbidden by pledges which they cannot break, either to write a memoir of him, or, within the range of their influence, to permit any one else to do so. They can therefore only record their grief at an event which, in the case of the writer of these lines, terminates an unbroken friendship of thirty-six years, and a literary alliance which, at once in its duration and completeness, is probably without a precedent.[352]

No more could be said. Townsend said nothing more; Strachey said nothing more. Even now, the three book-length accounts of Hutton's life and work languish unpublished in libraries of the American Midwest.[353] Although Hutton strongly forbade any written eulogy,[354] many tributes for the man nevertheless emerged from all quarters. *The Times* spoke of him as 'one of the few spiritual teachers, the group of men always small, of whom counsel is sought in the perplexities, doubts, and conflicts of life.'[355] A paper of his native county said, 'He was the "Spectator;" and the "Spectator" is the best newspaper in the world for thoughtful people.'[356] Even a rival weekly, the Conservative *Speaker*, had to confess the truth that 'if English journalism has a chief he is

to be found in Mr. Hutton'.[357] To Herman Merivale, he was 'the greatest journalist and most all-round brain' to John Morley 'the finest and bravest critic of this generation', to William Watson 'the greatest spirit I have ever known'.[358] The poem 'To Richard Holt Hutton', written by the last of these, ended:

> And not uncrowned with honours ran
> My days and not without a boast shall end!
> For I was Shakespeare's countryman;
> And wert thou not my friend?

The Spectator Hutton left behind was in an excellent state. The *Daily Chronicle* did not shrink from calling it 'perhaps the greatest power in critical journalism that England has ever known'.[359] After three decades of committed co-editorship, its circulation had climbed doggedly from below 1,000 to above 10,000. Writers of the 1890s could declare that *The Spectator* had fully re-established its place as 'the most entirely respected newspaper printed in the English language',[360] whose fairness is 'absolutely unmatched in the annals of newspaper literature'.[361] Lord Randolph Churchill approvingly dubbed it 'a modern Rhadamanthus' that 'censures in the most impartial manner politicians of different shades and parties'.[362] The novelist Margaret Oliphant – whose short-lived 'Commentary from an easy chair' (Dec. 1889–Nov. 1890) was one of the few marked failures of the Townsend-Hutton tenure – called it

> a journal which, amid all the chops and changes of modern journalism, stands with the personality of a man (or might we say two single gentlemen rolled into one?), amid the organs and mouthpieces of popular opinion … [they] have retained a character, an honesty, and a personality far above the level of the ordinary newspaper.[363]

The 1890s was a decade in which the lofty moral grandeur of nineteenth-century intellectuals clashed with the increasingly cynical and playful outlook he century that loomed. In the Age of Decadence *The Spectator* was not a natural fit.. A significant marker of one era giving way to another was the retirement, in 1894, of Gladstone, *The Spectator*'s erstwhile hero. The paper seemed genuinely stumped by a future without him, mourning

> the dimness which has come over the political vision of all the English world, while it endeavours to realise the change which the passing-away of Mr. Gladstone will produce in the scene of Parliamentary life. His has been so emphatically the leading figure, whether for good or for evil, in the politics of the last quarter of a century, that the mere notion of his departure bewilders and beclouds the vision of every one who tries to imagine the scene without him.[364]

To several observers, *The Spectator*'s readership was also starting to seem a relic of an era slowly fading from view. They were 'a public sheltered in leafy rectories and in snug villas from the headlong decisions and rowdy activity of the world';[365] 'gentle souls, fond of flowers and birds; more particular about the appointments of their dinner tables than the food the dishes contained ... middle-aged and declining gracefully to a future existence for which they were fully prepared.'[366] There was a growing sense that the paper had become too slow to apprehend and appreciate the new age dawning; increasingly late notices of published works of literature did little to counter this impression. 'It is better', Walter Besant noted in an affectionate piece, 'to review books when they come out than a twelvemonth later.'[367] Once the same work was unwittingly reviewed twice, first as a 'regrettable book', then as 'the best story' that the author 'has yet given the world'.[368] In 1895, when a translation of Mommsen's *History of Rome* was given notice as if its contents were new, thirty-three years after their first publication, widespread mockery was almost a civic duty.[369] One Oxford wag turned to verse for the task:

> Ah! Philosophic friend, for you
>   Years are not, earlier or later;
> Time stands, there is no old or new,
>   Worlds change, there is but one 'Spectator.'[370]

The occasionally backwards outlook of *The Spectator* was often compounded by some of Townsend's more outrageous articles. An 1895 sub-leader on 'The Negro Future', for instance, is almost unreadable for its imperious and unquestioning racism.[371] Not only did it argue for the inferiority of African peoples but it expressed the pessimistic belief that their future as a world race may be shorter-lived than that of others. Mary Kingsley, the young ethnographer whose travels in Africa had prompted *The Spectator*'s reflections, wrote in to oppose some of the more unhinged assertions. While the 'Correspondence' (her first publication) shared the widespread Victorian belief that Africans were culturally inferior to other races, she argued that she did 'not believe the African to be brutal, or degraded, or cruel. I know from wide experience with him that he is often grateful and faithful, and by no means the drunk idiot his so-called friends, the Protestant missionaries, are anxious, as an excuse for their failure in dealing with him, to make him out.'[372] For all Townsend's faith in Indian autonomy, his broader view of the wider world remained desperately dark.

In 1897, Townsend came under pressure from Alfred Harmsworth (later Viscount Northcliffe), flush from the stratospheric success of his halfpenny *Daily Mail* (founded in 1896), to sell Hutton's side of the proprietorship. Strachey, who had long been assured that he would inherit Hutton's editorial seat and shares, was instead offered the purchase; this he was able to secure only with substantial loans, mostly from his family. The original plan was that he and Townsend would be co-proprietors on the tried-and-tested model, but with Strachey inheriting complete editorial control. After some negotiation, the better course emerged to be for Strachey, in 1898, to buy up Townsend's shares as well, a feat that took him to the very brink of his

Synopsis of Writers for July, 1898

	LEADERS	SUB-LEADERS	CORRES.	POETRY.	BOOKS.	TOTAL.
Mr. Townsend	12	4	✓	✓	✓	16
St. Loe Strachey	8	1	✓	✓	✓	9
D. C. Lathbury	4	✓	✓	✓	✓	4
H. Clarke	5	3	✓	✓	1	9
C. J. Cornish	✓	4	✓	✓	✓	4
C. L. Graves	✓	1	✓	✓	4	5
~~J. J. Dutton~~						
B. Kidd	✓	✓	✓	✓	1	1
Sir M. E. Grant Duff	✓	✓	✓	✓	1	1
Mrs. Alicia B. Little	✓	✓	1	✓	✓	1
Rev. T. P. Powell	✓	✓	1	✓	✓	1
Mr. J. Powell	✓	1	✓	✓	✓	1
Mrs. Lathbury	✓	✓	✓	✓	1	1
Mrs. Strachey	✓	✓	✓	✓	1	1
H. Russell	✓	✓	✓	✓	1	1
Miss Townsend						
Prof. Church	✓	✓	✓	✓	2	2
C. Whibley	✓	✓	✓	✓	1	1
H. Merivale	✓	✓	✓	✓	1	1
Sir A. Lyall	✓	✓	✓	✓	1	1
B. Mallet	✓	✓	✓	✓	1	1
H. C. Beeching	✓	✓	✓	✓	1	1
S. Lane Poole	✓	✓	✓	✓	1	1
C. Adeane	✓	✓	✓	1 in.	1	1
R. J. Alexander	✓	✓	✓	3½ in.	✓	1
Miss Christie	✓	✓	✓	2 in.	✓	1
~~Stephen Phillips~~	✓	✓	✓	2 in.	✓	1
E. V. Lucas	✓	✓	✓	5 in.	✓	1
~~Sir C. Strachey~~	✓	✓	✓	7 in.	✓	1
L. J. Higgs	✓	✓	✓	3 in.	✓	1
E. Kemble	✓	✓	✓	✓	1	1
Col. Trevor	✓	✓	7	✓	✓	1
~~H. J. Palmer~~	✓	✓				
T. Raines	1	✓	✓	4 in.	✓	1
Clara Henderson	✓	✓	✓	✓	7	1
W. Ward	✓	✓	✓	✓	7	1
~~W. G.~~ Hubbard	✓	✓	✓	✓	1	1
G. Strachey	✓	✓	✓	✓	7	1
~~H. Sargent~~	✓	✓				
Miss March Phillipps	✓	✓	7	✓	✓	1

Current Literature.— July.
(other than Prof. Church)

	COLS. – IN.	
Mrs. Strachey	1 – 0	?
Mr. Patchett Martin	– 4	
~~Sir C. Strachey~~	– 3	
Mr. Wallace	– 2	5
~~Miss Strachey~~	1 – 5	4
Miss Townsend	– 7+	12
Miss Price	– 4	10
Mr. Ludlow	– 3	8
Master of Ruthven	– 8	½
~~St. Loe Strachey~~	– 5	
Miss Christie	– 10	25
Mr. Cornish	– 4	10
Mr. H. Russell	– 6	14

Magazines.— July. *Inch.*

Mr. Townsend	×
Mr. Strachey	×
Miss Townsend	– 7
Mrs. Strachey	– 6

Poems

Strachey's file of contributors, July 1898

inancial capabilities. In June 1898, *The Spectator* was launched as a limited liability company, with a capital of £84,000. Strachey, having now invested everything in the success of the paper, duly doubled his own salary o £2,400 and gave it his all. To his great credit, the amble paid off. His meticulously kept records of ontributors and payments show how carefully the roject was run: as well as revealing the names behind he veil of anonymity, they show that – most unusually or the day – Strachey paid male and female journalists qually.[373] The formula worked: astoundingly, within a here two years of his editorship, he had doubled the irculation of *The Spectator* to above 20,000.

For the next ten years, until 1908, Townsend served s a leader-writer, producing one or two general articles ach week. Although the paper had in previous decades lways kept a close eye on politics, at home and abroad, oth he and Hutton came in their later years to operate : some remove from the cut-and-thrust world of arliamentary machinations. Strachey, by contrast, was political terrier, who delighted in bringing to the fore lively, invested and refreshingly optimistic account f the week's politics. His interests were not limited to le workings of Westminster; he was also passionate out Britain's relationship with the rest of the world, pecially America and the Commonwealth.

When Strachey took up the proprietorship, the paper as still produced in much the same way as when it first ppeared. The printers – despite some changes in the 90s[374] – sent large printed sheets to the Wellington reet offices, where a team of expert ladies folded em into shape. Purchasers of *The Spectator*, therefore, d to cut several edges to unlock the issue's contents. orse still, if held improperly, the paper swiftly fell art. Only the smartest of households had a butler at nd to iron and sew it for the reader's convenience. or Strachey, this archaic inconvenience would not do. e therefore took measures to ensure that the paper is sewn before being dispatched to newsagents and bscribers. Such small changes garnered considerable d widespread gratitude.

By 1899, Strachey's increasingly prominent public role was widely acknowledged. The *Daily Mail* reported – perhaps with a tinge of envy – that

> the watchword of the *Spectator* – 'Independent Liberalism' – exactly fits its latest editor... Mr. Strachey and the *Spectator* serve a small public, whose demands it is not irksome to obey, and so they have been able to defy the shocks of chance and change... They have been able to remain themselves because they are sure of their public.[375]

A columnist in *Country Life* that year confessed:

> I am often asked why the *Spectator* flourishes so much, and whether there is room for another weekly of the same kind. Frankly, I do not think there is. It flourishes because it is consistent, and always sound; and has got its constituents well within its grip. But the demand for that kind of journal is limited, and to start another would be a long, and, probably, also a disappointing business.[376]

By 1900, the circulation of *The Spectator* was three times that of its closest rival among the 'intelligent weeklies'. It was at this time, most of all in its history, that the paper rested 'on the breakfast table of every vicarage in the country',[377] its very pages conjuring up 'the spectacle of the rectory garden with a yew tree in the middle and the girls in their pink frocks round the lawn-tennis net'.[378]

Still, despite the great and good among the paper's readership, Strachey felt no qualms about exposing corruption and sleaze among the upper echelons. An ardent believer in W.T. Stead's definition of the journalist as 'the watch-dog of society',[379] Strachey caused widespread shock by uncovering the secret payments Cecil Rhodes had made to the Liberal Party in 1888 to abet the progress of his various interests in the Empire.[380] When the future prime minister, Sir Henry Campbell-Bannerman, read of these allegations, he fired off a letter to *The Spectator* declaring 'that the story is from beginning to end a lie and that your deductions are therefore false'.[381] Accordingly, the Rhodes correspondence with the Liberals' manager Francis Schnadhorst was published in full, showing that cash had indeed been given by Rhodes in the belief that it would secure a non-evacuation policy in Egypt.[382] Many papers and politicians (H.H. Asquith included) criticised *The Spectator* for its outspoken indiscretion, but many more saw it as a fair exposé of grubby dealings. A decade later, when David Lloyd George, Rufus Isaacs and other members of the Liberal Government were implicated in the Marconi scandal, *The Spectator* was no less ruthless in revealing their unethical behaviour.[383] But this was no gutter-press mudslinging. Strachey had no interest whatsoever in pandering to the baser curiosities of the public at large. Instead, he was confident that the keen and candid discussion of the pressing issues of the day would find a commensurately committed readership. 'It is no use', he later observed, 'to set up a man of straw and call him The Public and then to fawn on the puppet of your own creation.'[384]

Describing himself as a 'strong anti-Little Englander' and a 'Democrat Imperialist', Strachey kept throughout his tenure a very close eye on global politics. In particular, he keenly watched the ominous rise of European powers. The columns of 'Vigilans sed Aequus' ('Watchful but fair'), published in 1902–3, did much to reveal how Germany was moving inexorably towards war. Their author, the classicist and *Guardian* journalist William Thomas Arnold, died soon after the columns appeared, and was thus spared the grim truth of his forecast.

Following the retirement of D.S. MacColl as the paper's art critic in 1895, Strachey placed his own brother, Henry (Harry), in the post, who at least had the credential of being a painter. Running an anonymous journal certainly helped downplay any public cries of nepotism: Strachey's wife, son, daughter, son-in-law, sister and cousin all wrote in the paper at various points. Among other active staff of the period were W.E. Garrett Fisher and Wilbraham Cooper, with the Irishman Stephen Gwynn acting as a regular leader-

writer. Strachey also profited greatly from the wit and wisdom of Charles Lancom Graves, who from 1899 played the multifarious role that both he and Asquith had under Hutton and Townsend. Graves (uncle of Robert) had started writing for the paper in 1894 but was known to Strachey through his work at both the *Liberal Unionist* and *Cornhill*; his main outlet, however, was *Punch*. Townsend, aware of such an encouraging pedigree, told him that he should help in 'lightening the incorrigible seriousness' of *The Spectator*, which he did with vim until 1917.[385] Alongside his scrupulous work as chief sub-editor, Graves reviewed literature and music, occasionally contributing verse – but was not let loose on politics. He was, however, given free rein for one of the most amusing – if admittedly niche – series in the paper's history. In 1894, he published comic rhyming translations of Horace's odes, freely reworked in the mouth of Gladstone the bard. These instalments of 'The Hawarden Horace' proved a great success, and sold well when reprinted together. Not many now, perhaps, will laugh at the opening stanza of *Odes* II.14 (*eheu fugace Postume, Postume*), addressed to the bellicose statesman Sir Ellis Ashmead-Bartlett:

> Ah, Ashmead, Ashmead! Waning fame
>   Nor art not eloquence can stay;
> A dog, though hyphenated by his name,
>   Can only have his day.

But such versatile wit is very rarely sustained so successfully. In the joint hands of C.L. Graves and T.E. Page (a celebrated sixth-form master at Charterhouse) the classics had and have never been handled better in *The Spectator*.

Other long-standing contributors included D.C. Lathbury, Harold Cox and C.J. Cornish, who frequently offered up sub-leaders. A more famous staff member of the time was John Buchan. Although long cloaked in anonymity, he was a prolific contributor in the first decades of the twentieth century, filing over 800 pieces between January 1900 and March 1934. The majority of these articles dated to before the Great War, and articular the period 1901–7 when Buchan served as the aper's first 'assistant editor', overseeing a large portion f leader-writing.

In 1902, Strachey followed Rintoul's example in cquiring a second title. His own interests led him to he *County Gentleman,* a journal of country sports based onveniently close by at 3 Wellington Street. Although e was a keen sportsman and rider himself, Strachey's im for the new acquisition was broader: it was to serve as vehicle to promote his various schemes for improving ritish life beyond the city. Over the next five years, e editor Eric Parker, already of the *Spectator* stable, hampioned many of Strachey's ambitious causes, which the latter often gave additional support in is primary paper.[386] In 1904–5, for instance, the two urnals ran a competition for the best cottage that could e built with a budget of £150 (*c.* £15,000). The contest ught to highlight Britain's dire need for improvement rural accommodation and to prove that cost-effective onstruction was not beyond the country's capabilities:

The Exhibition will show what modern ingenuity can do in the way of cheap housing. It will also show how systems of building with special materials long established in various localities can be used and adapted for a wider area.[387]

his 'Cheap Cottages Exhibition' was duly held on land Letchworth in July 1905, hosted enthusiastically by e Garden City Company. It proved to be such a success some 70,000 visitors made their way there – that plans on crystallised for establishing a new city on the inciples Strachey espoused: inexpensive, inoffensive ousing – and a community where alcohol was banned om sale. Three-quarters of the houses built for that mpetition are still standing, and Letchworth Garden ty has never looked back.

Under the editorship of Townsend and Hutton, *The ectator* had increasingly directed its interests beyond e human sphere, devoting frequent sub-leaders to e animal world. In 1890, a weekly column on country e was commissioned from C.J. Cornish, a master at

St Paul's. He was followed in this role by Eric Parker, and then Sir William Beach Thomas. Between the three of them, they wrote a weekly digest of country matters for sixty years. Throughout the 1890s, in particular, *The Spectator*'s animal-loving readers would frequently submit to the letters pages tales of interest about their pets or chance encounters with wildlife. Such was the frequency of correspondence on this front that, in 1895, Strachey published a collection of *Dog Stories from the 'Spectator'* (1895). The subheading revealed his wide-eyed wonder: *being anecdotes of the intelligence, reasoning power, affection and sympathy of dogs.* The first chapter bore the presumably unique heading in world literature of 'Syllogistic Dogs'. No one could prevent the appearance soon after of *Cat and Bird Stories from the 'Spectator'* (1896).[388] Stanley Baldwin, when Prime Minister, publicly recalled that

there has never been any cat from Caithness to Cathay or from Portobello to Pernambuco which has behaved more oddly when on its own than those cats which have written to the *Spectator.* There has been no dog which has barked in the Empire or outside it whose oddity of manner or eccentricity of deportment has not been brought into the *Spectator.*[389]

The temptation for hoaxers proved irresistible. To take one instance of many, on 14 November 1896, this curious letter appeared:

Sir, – I send you the following story of my fox-terrier dog. This little animal has formed numerous curious friendships during its lifetime, but the latest is perhaps the most curious of all. It is not permitted for dogs to remain in this College during the night, and so I keep mine at a house some distance off. Every morning the dog comes of its own accord to my rooms, and is accompanied on its morning walk by a cochin-china hen and a kitten belonging to the man with whom the dog is left during the night. The hen and kitten always leave the dog at the College gates, as they are not permitted to enter.

The letter was signed from Balliol, Oxford, by E.S.P. Haynes, then reading Law. Haynes himself was shocked to find the letter standing above his name and wrote to tell *The Spectator* that it was a slanderous forgery. It then emerged that a club had been in existence for several years among Balliol undergraduates, whose sole purpose was to invent dog stories for the pages of *The Spectator*. The most outlandish suggestion read at each meeting was duly sent off for publication, often with the name of an (unaware) undergraduate to boot. Many others were quick to mock Strachey's strange fascination in this regard. Owen Seaman wrote of 'the stolid *Spectator*, bewildered with fabulous bow-wows',[390] and *Punch* had Strachey declare:

> Unless and until an Englishman possesses a dog, or, failing that, unless and until he has contributed a dog story to the columns of the *Spectator*, he cannot be admitted to have reached the full stature of his manhood.[391]

In later life, Strachey sighed that he 'had got rather bored by the amount of jokes, diluted till they contained no more than .0001 of wit-alcohol, about the *Spectator*'s dog stories.'[392] History does not record whether he kept a straight face on receiving a submission from the parodist Stephen Leacock, in which a sighting of the 'pulex hibiscus' bird is reported by the retired major 'O.Y. Botherwithit'.[393]

Back in the real world, Britain's international trade policy was hanging in the balance. Despite their staunch opposition to the idea in previous decades, by the early twentieth century the Conservatives were promoting protectionist measures. The flashpoint came in 1903, when Strachey's long-standing friend Joseph Chamberlain, now Secretary of State for the Colonies in Arthur Balfour's administration, told a crowd in Birmingham that his proposed 'tariff reform' would abolish unemployment and improve living standards.

The Spectator was once more forced to back its principle and not its private acquaintances. But by defending both Unionism and Free Trade, Strachey was left with no political party to support. His paper, long committed to allowing the world's peoples to interact with as little restriction as possible, became the most ardent British campaigner against Chamberlain and his Tariff Reform League. Once more, the circulation inevitably fell – and it would take twenty-five years to win back so large a readership.

Yet the great advantage of Strachey's proprietorship was that it gave him the freedom to pursue an unpopular policy – even to financial ruin, if he so chose. As Alfred Harmsworth observed at the time, 'it would not matter to Strachey if Mrs. Strachey were his only reader. He would go on sticking to his Free Trade policy in the *Spectator* as strongly as ever.' Strachey expressed this steadfast commitment in a letter to Winston Churchill, stating that he was 'prepared to fight this thing out even if it ruins the *Spectator*. It won't of course do that but may cost me half my readers, and I am quite prepared to see it do so.'[394] Churchill in turn gave the reassuring response that '*The Spectator* will be on the winning side as well as on the right side.'[395] And so, setting sales figures aside, Strachey told his readers in no uncertain terms that

> It is the duty of all who care for Free trade, who believe in the principle of tariff for revenue, and who do not imagine that a tax can be converted into a money-making machine, or that a country can be rendered richer by increasing the cost of living to its inhabitants, to oppose Mr. Balfour's Administration, and to force it to resign office and appeal to the country without delay.[396]

For a man described by his own family as 'the least factual, or at any rate the least numerical thinker',[397] his dogged diligence in pursuing this fight is impossible not to admire. Along with Buchan, Strachey had become an energetic member of the Political Economy Club (founded by Mill in 1821), whose very *raison d'être* was ree trade. Among his army of private correspondents, he former prime minister Lord Rosebery conceded *The Spectator*'s 'extraordinary weight and influence on uch matters'.[398] Bertrand Russell used the letters page f *The Spectator* to argue that international trade could e compatible with an increase in wages and working onditions (30 Jan. 1904). In due course, almost every ubsequent *Spectator* issue of the 1900s contained an npassioned but well-reasoned defence of this doctrine. or instance, in 1905 Strachey challenged the thinking f 'The Protectionist' who

St Loe Strachey, 1905

finds it easy to forget that trade is an exchange, that foreign trade is a form of mutual co-operation by which each side may profit, that the sale of imports in our free markets is conditioned by the purchase of our exports, and, above all, that market—'the place or system of exchange'—is best when it is allowed to grow and develop according to its own free laws of individual demand and supply ... the true policy of international trade must be 'to fight foreign tariffs by free imports' ... no system but the free exchange system can enable every nation to produce those things which it can produce most profitably. Thus is the labourer benefited, as his labour is made more productive.[399]

When recalling this campaign in his autobiography, .rachey confessed, 'I felt as strongly about Tariff eform as I did about the dissolution of the United ingdom.[400] It is a sign of the man's commitment to the use that he stood as a Free Trade Unionist candidate r Edinburgh and St Andrews Universities, even though an outsider his failure was effectively pre-ordained. the election of January–February 1906, when *The ectator* returned to advocating tentative support for e Liberals, Chamberlain's policy not only split the iberal Unionists apart but caused Balfour's Unionist-onservative coalition to lose to a Liberal landslide. n hearing the news, Strachey's friend Theodore oosevelt, then President of the United States (1901–9), nfided his own view:

As for protection and free trade, I am confident that protection would be most damaging to Great Britain. As regards the United States, I think I once told you that I am on this point rather an economic agnostic.[401]

Roosevelt had been a frequent and willing correspondent with Strachey for several years. In one letter he noted with wide-eyed approval, 'It is curious how exactly you and I agree on most of the great questions which are fundamentally the same in both countries.'[402] In 1902, he invited Strachey and his wife Amy to the White House, where the editor was hosted and hailed as nothing short of a leading statesman. Strachey thereafter maintained impressively close ties with America, even when they became considerably challenged under the strains of World War I.

In 1906, Strachey was fired up by the suggestion of a Lieut.-Col. Alsager Pollock to show the bumbling War Office the inadequacy of their worn-out ways. The proposal was to train up a hundred teenage lads of no military experience to war-readiness within six months. If anyone of able body could be prepared for battle so swiftly, he reasoned, the whole infrastructure of the British Army could be reworked to a more efficient model. The 'Spectator Experimental Company' was funded by readers' donations: £4,500 soon flooded in – from the Duke of Bedford, Waldorf Astor and the everyman. The would-be soldiers were 'ordinary young men of the working class with a natural ambition to do well in civil life, and also with the healthy young Englishman's liking for soldiering'.[403] They were drilled 'in tactical exercises, in shooting, signalling, gymnastics, trenching, bridge-building' – and *Spectator* readers were regularly debriefed about their exploits.[404] Nevertheless, Pollock was clear that the project's 'intention is to train soldiers, not to attempt "cramming" them'.[405]

Some observers suspected that *The Spectator*'s fighting stock were not random recruits but carefully selected specimens. But Strachey was quick to make clear that the men were 'excellent examples of young Englishmen, but thousands just as good could be found in any part of the kingdom. They are not in any way picked men.'[406] The company's virtues were advertised by some public manoeuvres; in others – such as mock battles against the Coldstream and Grenadier Guards – Pollock gravely observed that most of the force would have been lost.

Nevertheless, within five months of training at their Hounslow Heath barracks, the men had undergone 'immense improvement, moral, intellectual, and physical', and were deemed 'fit to take their place with any Regular battalion at the front or elsewhere'.[407] As Pollock later claimed, the difference between an average army recruit of six months' training and an SEC initiate was that 'between a costermonger's donkey and a Derby horse'.[408] Not just the military top brass but even King Edward VII inspected the men, a curious observer of what he called 'an experiment of national importance'.[409]

The Spectator congratulated the soldiers for their 'very hearty' co-operation: 'every one acted with the sense that he was performing an important piece of public work, and gave far more than could be expressed in pounds, shillings, and pence.'[410] The experiment had real impact: not only did more than a third of the recruits go on to join the regular army, but, in 1907, Lord Haldane, after discussing the success of the SEC with Strachey, drew up the Territorial and Reserve

Douglas Cochrane, 12th Earl of Dundonald (L), inspecting the SEC with Pollock (1906)

Forces Act, which duly established the Territorial Arm[y]

There is no question that Strachey permeated a[ll] aspects of his *Spectator*, especially after the retireme[nt] of Townsend in 1908. As he confessed to a friend, h[e] had 'absolute control and responsibility' for a paper h[e] owned 'lock, stock and barrel'.[411] But not all admire[d] the results of this forthright approach. David Lloy[d] George, for instance, never saw eye to eye with *T[he] Spectator*, which he dismissed as 'the organ of th[e] anarchist party'.[412] Since the paper turned its back o[n] the Liberals, and supported the Unionists at bot[h] elections of 1910, the Chancellor of the Exchequer sa[w] his controversial plans for financial and parliamenta[ry] reform rubbished each week. The antipathy betwee[n] the two men came to a head in October 1910, when a[n] audience in Crediton was told that '*The Spectator* is edite[d] at present by an exceedingly pretentious, pompous, a[nd] futile person', who (he continued rather ironically), '[if] you do not accept as gospel the ill-informed platitud[es] which he preaches, instantly makes personal, offensiv[e] and stupid attacks upon you.'[413] The nub of the proble[m] for Lloyd George was Strachey's lecturing the workin[g] classes on the need for thriftiness without admonishi[ng] wealthier citizens in the same way. '*The Spectator*', [he] added, 'is not a sort of paper that the working ma[n] takes in as a rule. It would be rather hard, I think, o[n] a working man, after a week of arduous toil, that [he] hould afterwards have to read *The Spectator*. Flesh and lood could not stand it.'[414] Strachey was shocked but ot baited, instead calmly observing:

> We confess to finding the temptation to answer Mr. Lloyd George in detail very strong; but we have come to the conclusion that to do so would not be consistent with the traditions of the *Spectator*.[415]

In private, meanwhile, he wrote to Rudyard Kipling celebrate the publicity such an attack brought, which ould have cost him £1,000 'in the ordinary way of usiness'.[416] He continued to advise his readers to vote t the Liberals, throwing his full support behind alfour's Unionists once they at last granted what *The* ectator had long demanded: a national referendum on e contentious topic of their tariff reform programme. though the Unionists failed to win both elections of 10, Strachey continued to fight the Unionist cause ainst Home Rule in the years that followed, again ggesting a referendum on the issue and again losing e debate. His desperate hopes of a centrist third rty emerging, which could defend the Union and its stitutions, while advancing the cause of free trade, mpounded the failures – before the Great War moved e focus elsewhere.

To return to Lloyd George's Crediton speech, one her observation attracted widespread criticism. A ter received from a reader in Burnley complained that e Chancellor was

> hardly correct in referring to the *Spectator* as the organ of the wealthy. Now I am a young man working my way into the solicitors' profession, as did Mr. Lloyd George before me, and I, along with many others in this part for whom I can speak, and who are by no means wealthy, are regular readers of the *Spectator*. I get it second-hand through a local library, and I should like to wager that there are far more readers of your paper among my own class than among, say, the *nouveaux riches* cotton manufacturers here.

Without being at all snobbish, might I suggest that the line of demarcation between readers and non-readers of your paper is an intellectual rather than a monetary one?[417]

Tempers always simmer, of course – and twenty-five years later Lloyd George would come round to *The Spectator*, writing a lead cover piece on 'The case for public works'.[418]

Strachey often repeated the idea – already evidenced to some degree by Rintoul and Townsend – that a journalist should have no friends. Indeed, he was so immersed in his paper that his family generally referred to him as 'Ed. Spec.' after his ubiquitous ripostes to the correspondents who filled his copious letters pages. But, for all his immersion in the fourth estate, he was a remarkably popular figure. If everyone did not necessarily love him, everyone knew him – and many found it hard to tell him 'no'. Lytton Strachey, for instance, St Loe's cousin, wrote some eighty pieces for *The Spectator* in the years before the war (1904–13), primarily reviews of literature and theatre. He and his family were not, however, very close devotees of his paper: they came to apply the word 'spectatorial' to any 'particularly pompous and respectable pronouncement'.[419] Lytton's brother James claimed that *The Spectator* then 'represented St Loe's opinions, expressed St Loe's policies and, most striking of all, was written in St Loe's literary style, with his unmistakable editorial first person plural.'[420] As another contemporary observed, Strachey's 'spirit breathes in every line'.[421] It is indeed true that Strachey took greater control than his predecessors over the topics on which leaders should be written. Although he would usually nod through literary reviews and most sub-leaders without alteration, he was notoriously keen that leader-writers produce something that chimed with the paper's consistent line and style. Contributors would often find sentences rewritten, or curiously embellished; worst of all, some columns would appear unchanged, save for the addition of a final paragraph – a summative peroration – introduced, without consultation, by Strachey. It was later said that his control was something beyond the usual editorial sovereignty; his rule more nearly resembled a theocracy. He exercised a positive moral ascendancy over his contributors and his public. Never could an editor have said with greater justice 'Mon journal c'est moi'.[422]

His successor as editor wrote that Strachey's political ideas

were poured out with a vehement reiteration that produced a deep impression and marked the man who could not be ignored. You might agree or disagree; you might curse this unceasing dogmatist; but you had to listen ... if he had to choose between ruining his paper and abandoning a principle which he thought essential, he would choose the ruin.

Such a uniform outlook of one paper – week in, week out – was naturally ripe for parody. Even the staff had a go: in the first decade of the twentieth century, John Buchan and Raymond Asquith (son of Hubert) produced a complete mock issue, which included Spectatorial sub-leaders on 'God', 'Bridge' and 'Field-mice'. But Strachey's over-protective attitude to his paper rankled in some quarters. In 1911, for instance, the ever-incandescent novelist Frank Harris found himself utterly outraged. For Strachey had regarded his *English Review* article on 'sex morality'[423] as so shockingly obscene that *The Spectator* would refuse to acknowledge that journal in its columns thereafter. Letters of objection flew in from all quarters. But the titanic scale of Harris's rage can be gleaned from a few quotations from his vitriolic letter (printed in full):

You are the very type of a muddle-headed, half-educated, self-important, and silly creature, who probably by purchase has got hold of a weapon too sharp and too heavy for his feeble-foolish hands... You, St. Loe Strachey, take me to task and read moral lectures, with all the authority of your

Punch and Judy show... English morality indeed: Piccadilly Circus at night and the *Spectator* as censor. There is a pit fouler than any imagined by Dante, a cesspool bubbling and steaming with corruption and all shining with putrid iridescence of hypocrisy – that pool is English morality, and one of the foul bubbles on it the *Spectator*.[424]

In October 1911, three years after his retirement and fifty years after he had resurrected the paper, Meredith Townsend died. Although so influential in steering public opinion, he nevertheless perished without having cast a vote in any British election. His last years had been spent in deepening delirium and relative immobility. Strachey's obituary notice declared him 'one of the greatest of English journalists in his own or any preceding age':

He possessed in the first place – and this is perhaps the *sine qua non* of journalism – the power to interest his readers... He never ground out his articles as if they were engendered in the inside of some terrible barrel-organ or vast musical box worked by steam or electricity. No doubt we shall be told that his writing was much too oracular. So perhaps it was; and yet it was this oracular touch, conveyed without pomposity or mental swagger, which made his work so arresting.[425]

Townsend's daughter Cecilia recorded that he 'hoped his work in the next world would be to co-edit with Hutton a better *Spectator*' – but he would add sadly, 'it can't happen; Hutton will be so much above me there'.[426] Nevertheless, that same daughter later came to be recognised as Strachey's best writer of sub-leaders: whether tackling religion, society or literature she mixed irony and wit with an arrestingly unique philosophy on life – 'a saint with a spice of malice', one colleague had it.[427]

In the years 1910–12, *The Spectator* campaigned against the 'White Slave Trade' in Britain, which related primarily to women forcibly employed for sex, had bour, or both.[428] As in decades past, the paper made itself an effective campaigner to change the law, in this case helping secure the Criminal Law Amendment Act 1912. But Strachey was conscious of the real travails of the working class as much as the desperate underclass. He commissioned a series by Stephen Reynolds called 'Seems So', which sought to provide a 'working-class view of politics'. A noble idea, but rather naïvely conducted: Reynolds's field research amounted to long conversations with some Devonian fishermen; their salty assessments of current affairs were then reworked into fictionalised dialogues that purported to showcase what the everyman thinks, once the pointy-headed theorising was pared away. For his own part, Strachey filled his own correspondence pages with a seventeen-part series of 'Letters to a working man', covering topics such as 'The State and the Individual', 'The Family' and 'The Unemployed' from his essentially Whiggish outlook. The collection was expanded and published in 1908 under the title *The Perils of Socialism*, with a dedication to Roosevelt to boot. Though addressed to a real man – an ex-miner in Somerset – the conceit did not convince everyone. 'We are not sure', the *Sociological Review* commented, 'that the form of letters to a correspondent, who does not himself appear, is the best in which to present views on Sociology to the public. There is an air of unreality about it.'[429] But such was Strachey's unflagging optimism in the worldly wisdom of the individual – and his ability to improve his circumstances without state intrusion.

Regrettably, the same outlook led Strachey's paper to be one of the most staunch opponents of a universal Old Age Pension. The argument was financial, not moral: without a contributory system, the necessary rise in taxes would ruin the fight for free trade. Proposed welfare reforms, unemployment benefits and free school meals received similarly stern dismissal, although he found reasons to support a National Insurance scheme. Strachey stood in near constant opposition to the growing influence of trade unionism and the burgeoning Labour party, and rejected many projects of the Liberal government: despite Asquith's services to *The Spectator*, the paper was at times sceptical, at times appalled, at his increasingly paternalistic and protectionist approach to the British people.[430] Somewhat inconsistently, Strachey remained forthright in his attempts to restrict alcohol and gambling, proudly publishing a letter from Sir Edward Fry (28 May 1910) that bolstered his criticism of Cadbury's and Rowntree's for their indirect support of newspaper racing tips.

In August 1913, Strachey once more took it upon himself to catalyse housing reform. On this occasion, he encouraged *Spectator* readers to enter a new 'Model Wooden Cottage' competition, where contestants had to design the best house on a strict budget of £100. The contest had a curious twist:

> I am going to make a sporting offer to all devisers and inventors and patentees of cheap methods of building ... I will allow any man who gives proof of good faith and good sense to show his mettle by putting up a model £100 cottage on my land. If his cottage will satisfactorily stand the test of wind and rain for a year, and show that it can keep them out and that it is not merely a butterfly house, I will purchase it from him for the £100 expended upon it, plus £10 for a year's loss of interest on capital. But I am to be the sole judge as to whether the cottage is a satisfactory one from the point of view of weather-tightness and general stability... If I am not willing to buy the cottage because in my opinion it is not a sound and weathertight cottage, I will undertake to give the man who built it the land on which it stands for nothing, and of course a reasonable means of access to it ... I do not want on the one hand to encourage the complete building crank, while on the other I do not want to dampen the ardour of the man who really has something in his scheme, though at first sight it may look rather wild.[431]

To inspire ideas, Strachey wrote several pieces of colourful correspondence 'to the editor of *The Spectator*' (i.e. himself) in which he outlined and illustrated his own successful construction of a weatherboard cottage for £110.[432] The eventual winner, in 1914, was the young architect Clough Williams-Ellis; hundreds of copies of his plan, specifications and method of construction were subsequently put on general sale.[433] Doubtless to Strachey's delight, Williams-Ellis went on to marry Amabel, his daughter, in 1915.[434] It was a son-in-law of *The Spectator*, then, who would go on to produce the astoundingly inventive and playful Italianate architecture of Portmeirion.

Events in the wake of the assassination of Archduke Franz Ferdinand were documented carefully and warily throughout 1914. When Austria-Hungary looked as if it was bringing Europe – and the world – into ineluctable conflict, the paper made clear that its avowed reluctance to fight could swiftly give way to a tenacious commitment to end the war properly. It wrote on 1 August that

> the Government have been doing the right thing in the right way, that is to say, they have done their very best to stop the war or to minimise its effect, but, at the same time, and with a minimum of provocative action, they have clearly indicated that we do not mean to play a selfish or a narrow part. If the worst comes to the worst we shall stand loyally by our friends and our virtual engagements – a policy dictated alike by honour and by self-interest ... at least we can feel in this country that we have done nothing to provoke the strife and that we shall be fighting in self-preservation and fighting with honour and honesty.[435]

Once war had been declared later that month, the case for war with Germany was made clear:

> If the Germans win, there will be no place left in the world for the little independent nations. They know that they will always have genuine friends and protectors in Britain, not out of policy, but out of the British creed that they have a right to live. Quite apart from our own safety, we ardently desire that they shall continue to exist, because

Recurrent Advertisement, 1915

we hold that both in the matter of liberty and moral and intellectual progress they are of the greatest possible use to mankind. We have no desire to see the earth monopolised by some three or four great nations. Free competition is as good in the political as in the economic world ... we enter the battle as a nation with a perfectly clear conscience. We are not striving for dominion, nor to deprive any other Power of its just rights or of its independence. We are fighting the good fight of freedom.[436]

As the conflict spread, Strachey launched hims[elf] wholesale into activities to support the cause. He w[as] genuinely, if naïvely, convinced that this would be t[he] war to end war. As High Sheriff of Surrey (1914–15), created a list of 250,000 fit war reservists (the 'Veteran[s'?] of which the War Office had lost proper record.

much of wartime, the paper underwent a 25 per cent reduction in size because of paper restrictions, paring back what often stretched to forty-four or forty-eight pages to a mere twenty-eight. Revenue decreased as advertisements were necessarily scaled back, or replaced with straightforward injunctions in support of the war effort. In connection with this, *The Spectator* ceased allowing adverts for intoxicants, since Strachey felt that they could make no desirable contribution to the cause. By contrast, for the first time in its history, the paper allowed advertisements (for more conscripts and more efficient domestic rationing) to appear in its front half. Month by month, the paper became a louder and clearer rallying voice for a nation under arms.

Strachey's old friend Evelyn Baring, 1st Earl Cromer and former Controller-General in Egypt, had often written for the paper. But in 1915 he produced his most influential series of articles under the banner *Germania contra Mundum* ('Germany against the world'). These set out in stark rhetoric the reasoning – and also the foolhardiness – of German ambitions.[437] Yet, despite his patriotic support of the cause, Strachey was adamant about maintaining fair conduct throughout. He took pains, for instance, to defend the just treatment of German prisoners:

We shall not do any good to the people who have suffered so deeply in Belgium and France by making unfortunate and innocent Germans and Austrians suffer equal miseries. Such action would not be justice, but crime and folly.[438]

For much of the war, Strachey held a remarkable series of weekly meetings at his London house, 14 Queen Anne's Gate. Aware that Americans were struggling to obtain reliable news to relay home, he created a summit of journalists where they could meet leading figures from the government and the military. The first gathering, in the critical early days of September 1914, saw Prime Minister Asquith address an array of writers, including Edward Price Bell of the *Chicago Daily News* and Edward Marshall of the *New York Times*. Later

meetings played host to Sir Edward Grey, Lord Haldane, Lord Buckmaster, the Archbishop of Canterbury, Admiral Sir Reginald Hall (Head of Intelligence at the Admiralty), and the American Ambassador Walter Hines. One regular attendee described Strachey as 'the best friend American newspaper men had during this war'.[439] The last of the meetings occurred, in May 1917, at the *Spectator* office itself on Wellington Street.

Despite these efforts, Strachey's pro-Americanism was frustrated by the lacklustre attitude of the Americans in the earlier stages of the war. In two leaders of January 1915, he recorded the paper's 'acute anxiety and alarm at the way in which we are drifting towards the danger of a collision with the United States',[440] prophesying 'a collision of spirit between those who at their ease contemplate the legal subtleties connected with contraband and neutrality, and those who are fighting for their lives and for all that is dear to them with a powerful and remorseless enemy.'[441] More pointedly still, he compared the 'cold indifference of the United States Government on the moral issue' unfavourably with the sacrifices that Lancashire cotton workers had made during the American Civil War, when they put the cause of the North against slavery ahead of their own imminent starvation. The increasingly tense relationship between America and *The Spectator* would later improve again; in fact, Strachey would have formative discussions with President Woodrow Wilson about the prospect of forging a League of Nations, and subsequently enjoy dinner at the White House with President Calvin Coolidge (in 1925).

Nor was the editor content with doing his part in print. He took pains to visit the front three times, in Ypres twice (May and Nov. 1915) and the Somme once (Aug. 1916). His direct encounters helped secure for the paper one of the most popular and moving accounts of life on the front line: the letters of Lieutenant Donald Hankey, younger brother of Maurice, the secretary to Lloyd George's War Cabinet.[442] Written under the moniker of 'A Student in Arms', these letters ran from October 1915 to April 1916, to great effect. Through such meditations on the daily possibility of self-sacrifice,

Hankey anonymously became one of the most read and respected figures on and off the front line. His style was honest and unadorned, but infused with a calm and noble spirit:

> A captain said a few words to his men during a halt. Some trenches had been lost. It was their brigade that had lost them. For the honour of the brigade, of the New Army, they must try to retake them. The men listened in silence; but their faces were set. They were content. The honour of the brigade demanded it. The captain had said so, and they trusted him. They set off again, in single file. There was a cry. Someone had stopped a bullet. Don't look round; he will be looked after. It may be your turn next.
>
> They lay down behind a bank in a wood. Before them raged a storm. Bullets fell like hail. Branches were carried away, great tree-trunks shattered and split. Shells shrieked through the air and burst in all directions. The storm raged without any abatement. The whistle would blow. Then the first platoon would advance. Half a minute later the second would go forward, followed at the same interval by the third and fourth. A man went into hysterics, a pitiable object. His neighbour contemplated him with a sort of uncomprehending wonder. He was perfectly, fatuously cool. Something had stopped inside him.
>
> A whistle blew. The first platoon scrambled to their feet and advanced at the double. What happened no one saw. They disappeared. The second line followed, and the third and fourth. Surely no one could live in that hell. No one hesitated. They went forward mechanically, as men in a dream. It was so mad, so unreal. Soon they would awake...[++]

On 12 October 1916, Hankey fell in the Somme. His last letter, along with an editorial note by Strachey, was not only printed in *The Spectator* but issued separately

St Loe Strachey (W. Rothenstein, 1924)

in leaflet form; thousands of copies were thus put in[ ] circulation among the Allied forces.[+++]

Alongside such front-line reporting, *The Spectat[ ]* became a particularly well-known vehicle for th[ ] anguished and contemplative verse that the cris[ ] inevitably prompted. Among the contributors ea[ ] week were Thomas Hardy, Siegfried Sassoon, Aust[ ] Dobson, Émile Cammaerts, Laurence Binyon, Iv[ ] Gurney, Katharine Tynan, May Byron and Alfr[ ] Noyes.[++] One of the most popular poems of the Gre[ ] War, Lucy Whitmell's 'Christ in Flanders', appear[ ] first in *The Spectator* on 11 September 1915. It lat[ ] became so widely quoted – both in the press and t[ ] pulpit – that the printers ran off leaflets to be bought[ ] bulk (in batches of fifty or a hundred) and sent to troo[ ] in the trenches. It is estimated that some 50,000 cop[ ] were sold, in America as well as Europe.

Strachey's own powers, however, were best deploy[ ] in organising resources back in Britain, and his journ[ ] became a primary tool for that task. Among the sever[ ] appeals he ran was 'The Spectator Home Guards Fun[ ] which raised over £3,000 for the Volunteer Traini[ ] Corps. More significantly, Strachey realised that *[ ] Spectator* could also help maintain a sense of collect[ ] purpose for those on the front. A frequent advert[ ] 1916 encouraged readers to buy additional subscriptio[ ] in order to send *The Spectator* on to soldiers:

He or she who gives the 'Spectator' as a present will give a weekly pleasure to the officer or soldier in the trenches, or to the officer or soldier abroad, or to the civilian man or woman at home... When the first reader has finished with the 'Spectator' it will give equal pleasure to those to whom it is passed on. It is a special mark of the 'Spectator' that it is never thrown away, but passes from hand to hand like a book or magazine, until it is worn out.[446]

Wellington Street from the south (1896)

Although fighting only from the editor's desk, the stress and strain of the War caused Strachey's health to collapse in 1917, due primarily to pernicious anaemia. He was forced then and subsequently to retreat from his beloved paper for several months, during which periods John ('Jack') Atkins, assistant editor since 1907, operated as acting editor.

Since Strachey threw himself – and thus his paper – so enthusiastically behind the war, some contemporaries in the more moderate and pacifist press criticised him for jingoistic bellicosity. This feeling was perhaps intensified by his running a full-page illustration of Britannia Victrix – the colossal statue that John Flaxman proposed for Greenwich in 1799 – in the post-Armistice issue of 16 November 1918. Amid the guilt-pangs that followed the conflict, Strachey remained unrepentant about the role he had played:

Brettenham House, now dominating the west side of Lancaster Place (2020)

I refuse absolutely and entirely to apologise for the war, or to speak as if I were ashamed of it, or of the part which as a journalist I played in regard to it before it came or while it was in progress. The war was not only necessary to secure our safety, but it was, I am as fully convinced as ever I was, a righteous war... The war was a terrible evil, and we have suffered very greatly, but once more I refuse to be apologetic in regard to our method of carrying it through.[447]

Yet, for all the man's fighting talk, the Great War had ground Strachey down, a strain from which friends felt he never properly recovered. On returning to *Spectator* work, he seemed to have lost much of his spark and drive: his interests, too, were drifting elsewhere, and the paper was slowly coming loose from its moorings.

As Britain dusted herself down to stand in a world that was irrevocably changed, the sedate self-confidence of *The Spectator* and its timeless truths seemed somewhat out of kilter. From the end of the conflict, circulation figures started to fall swiftly, dropping by a third in three years to 13,500. While this number hid the tragedy of subscribers falling in battle, the alarming

13 York Street in 1922, by Clough Williams-Ellis

with the brave new world, he included the following tongue-in-cheek recollection of its premises:

If you turn out of the Strand into Wellington Street you can hardly fail to notice a certain house which is painted white. There are many houses which are painted white, but the white of this house is more white than the whiteness of any other house. It is like a house dressed in a surplice – a house that stands in conscious rebuke of a naughty world, wearing the white paint of a blameless life. The impression will be deepened when you read the legend inscribed in modest characters across the front, 'The Spectator', and realise that over the threshold Mr. St. Loe Strachey must pass daily to the pained contemplation of the wickedness and folly of men.[++9]

The Spectator, of course, was sure to find a way continuing some tradition, and installed itself th August in a suitably white house a hundred yards nort These premises, at 13 York Street (now 15 Tavisto Street) just south of Covent Garden, had allegedly on been the home of a quondam *Spectator* contribute Leigh Hunt, father of a former editor. Although t previous occupant (*The Insurance Record; and Actuar and Statistical Inquirer*) did little to inspire the mind, t new site soon proved to be a happy breeding ground f some genuinely innovative ideas.

decline required the dual remedy of fresh content and fresh talent. Although Strachey was wholeheartedly committed to the belief that 'the things that are new are not true and the things that are true are not new',[++8] that doctrine was proving increasingly out of fashion.

It was indicative of the fast-changing world that, in 1920, the government enacted plans to widen Wellington Street to ease traffic congestion and improve the ailing bridge infrastructure. Since this was not an age of architectural conservation and cultural blue-plaquery, the *Spectator* offices underwent compulsory purchase and, after a decade's delay, were eventually demolished in 1930. Thus, after over ninety years' peace, the paper was forced to leave Wellington Street behind. When A.G. Gardiner wrote his ill-tempered attack on Strachey's *Spectator* as an organ of 'unctuous rectitude' out of step

V
AN OLD VOICE IN A NEW ERA
1920–1953

Having toiled for the best part of forty years on the paper, Strachey was in no mind to let it slide. But, in an age of wireless radio, international press networks and increasingly ubiquitous advertisements for rival titles, *The Spectator* needed to up its game. In February 1920, it announced three major changes: a rise in cost, from d to 9d (at last reversing the desperate move made right back in 1859); the introduction of business and finance columns, previously deemed ungentlemanly; and revamped criticism of poetry, drama and the rapidly emerging arts.

The rise in cost was essential to arrest the paper's falling revenue in subscriptions and, by extension, advertising. As to broaching money matters, Strachey was characteristically unapologetic:

It is imperatively necessary that at the present moment the mind of the nation as a whole should be turned to Finance. Men and women in the pre-war days might be excused for leaving such matters to experts. Now we must all bend our minds to the nation's business and strive to control it for good in the only way that such control can be exercised – *i.e.*, through knowledge. The Poet, the Artist, the Man of Science, the Idealist must one and all stoop to conquer the foe – the universal wolf of Industrial Ruin which besets our path.

Arthur W. Kiddy, indefatigable editor of the *Banker's Magazine* from 1894 to 1944, provided the majority of financial comment. These columns appeared first in 20 under the pseudonym 'Onlooker', before Kiddy became in the following June the first signed columnist *Spectator* history.[450] Always filing his letters from 'the City', he soon won a keen following, although his romantic strictures were not necessarily to the tastes of the paper's readership. In 1931, when *The Spectator*

was running a series of competitions in which readers offered limericks about recent issues of the paper, the parodist William Hodgson-Burnett successfully turned to the man for inspiration:

I admire Arthur W. Kiddy
(Though the figures he quotes make me giddy),
    If it wasn't pure chance
    Made him take up Finance.
Why did he? Why *did* he? *Why* did he?[451]

As to the revival of its poetic criticism, Strachey's decision was doubtless influenced by his children, Amabel (1893–1984) and John (1901–63), who were both closely involved in the post-war artistic scene. The leading article declared that

we have now got an authentic poetic atmosphere both here and in America – wherever indeed the English language is spoken – and the *Spectator* means to do its best through its review columns to let its readers hear week by week of the new singers. We mean, that is, to abandon our omnibus reviews of 'Minor Verse' – forty nightingales in a nest, *horrescimus referentes!* – and give a weekly notice of such verse as must be taken seriously.

We do not suggest for a moment that all the new tendencies in verse are good, or will last, or ought to last. We do not intend to 'wonder with a foolish face of praise' merely because a man or woman writes daringly, rhymes madly, or is as free with his prosody as his oaths. A writer may defy all the rules of decency, syntax, prosody, and sense, and yet be a thoroughly bad poet.

Crucially, readers were assured after all of these announcements, 'there is to be no change in the *Spectator* but only development.'[452]

In the summer of 1921, Strachey appointed an enterprising, globally connected figure by the name of Evelyn Wrench to act as the paper's first 'business manager'. Drives to increase subscribers became frequent, new advertisers were pursued with greater zeal, and advertisements for *The Spectator* appeared more often in an increasingly broad range of newspapers and magazines. In addition, *The Spectator* chose to pay out no dividends to the proprietor for three years (1922–4). For a paper propounding financial expertise, the optics were sub-ideal when, in October 1922, it lowered the price again to 6d, after the eighteen-month experiment at 9d. The accompanying leader reported that a fall in paper costs made the reduction possible, but enjoined readers to help the journal 'very largely increase' its circulation. Readers were given step-by-step encouragement:

1. Let every existing subscriber to the SPECTATOR find us another.
2. Let every casual purchaser become a regular subscriber.
3. Let everyone who is in the habit of reading the SPECTATOR in a club, library, or reading-room determine to become a weekly buyer.

Rintoul would have been thrilled. But to arrest any fears in the long-standing reader that this suggested an undue – and unspectatorial – interest in lucrous profit, Strachey went on to reassert the paper's fundamental principles of editorial independence:

The views expressed by us, whether right or wrong in themselves, are not the resultants of external and undisclosed influences – official or financial, political or propagandist. Not only does no commercial Magnate, but also no Ministry, no Party leader, and no social 'movement' or 'organization' play the part of the predominant partner in our columns...

We believe that what readers want from us, especially in the region of politics, is not an echo of their own opinions, nor that of some Party Junta or Chief, but the opinion of an independent

Advertisement, Oct. 1922

body of men, trained in the observation, the interpretation, and the general diagnosis of public affairs – a body of men whose desire is to act as the honourable and confidential servants of their readers...

In a very real sense we consider our readers to be our masters. But these masters, though entitled to our obedient attention and to a constant and vigilant care for their entertainment and information, are not entitled to a servile attitude on our part. The service we offer and are proud to render is a free man's service. Above all, we desire to act (as, indeed, our readers expect) as the watch-dogs of the community.[453]

Noble though these sentiments were, *The Spectator* continued to press hard the cause of its finances. By the close of 1922, it was asking readers to say when purchasing goods in stores 'that they had seen the advertisement in the *Spectator*', in order to encourage the placing of adverts in the paper, and thereby raise the price that such space could command.[454] The journal's first page was now prepared to tell readers, 'There is no better New Year's present than a year's subscription to the "Spectator".' Cap was very much in hand.

These rather infra dig tactics, combined with an improvement in the typeface, worked: from 1921 to 1923, the circulation rose by 40 per cent, from 13,500 to almost 19,000. But more still needed to be done. *The Spectator* boldly launched a 'life membership' scheme, whereby readers could pay a lump sum to guarantee an issue through their letterbox every day until they died. Prices naturally had a sliding scale: 15 guineas for those under forty-five, 13 guineas under fifty-five, 11 under sixty-five, 9 under seventy-five, and a mere 5 guineas for any older reader who wanted to take their chances. For several reasons, however, the under-forty-five subscriptions proved hard to shift. Indeed, despite some of the new features, the paper's advertising campaign of 1924 – rather unhelpfully billed 'The Man in the Armchair' – echoed the nineteenth century more than it talked up the twentieth:

Picture, if you please, a somewhat heated debate; the scene – a club, a drawing-room – where you will. Opinions are declaimed; arguments are hastily advanced to be as quickly demolished.

Then the Man in the Armchair speaks. His quiet, fluent talk, his tolerant attitude towards the other side, his keen perceptive instinct that quickly probes the weak point of the opposition's case, his easy pleasant wit, his moderation and restraint – above all, his obvious sincerity – combine to make his words carry conviction and command respect.

In the world of journalism, the personality of *The Man in the Armchair* can be found in THE SPECTATOR. Plain-spoken, yet without rancour; critical, but never hyper-critical; unsensational, yet vigorous; it expresses its news and views in a manner as easy and pleasant as that of a clever man at his club…

THE SPECTATOR has a wide range of vision. It claims to be the best labour-saving device in the world of news and thought. Can the busy man afford to be without it?[455]

Despite such grandstanding, many, it seems, decided not.

For all his literary immersion, Strachey's tastes were certainly behind the curve: Rudyard Kipling, Thomas Hardy and Joseph Conrad were the just-about-contemporary writers he prized above all, and all three duly contributed to his *Spectator*, in prose and verse – with Kipling serving as an occasional 'correspondent' on 'village rifle clubs'.[456] It was telling, too, that Sir Arthur Conan Doyle was a frequent letter-writer, whether on South African cricket or trade protectionism.[457] In the first two decades of the century, as the *Times Literary Supplement* (founded 1902) increasingly gained a hold on the field, *The Spectator* cannot be described as having a keen sense of the *avant garde*. In fact, both Ezra Pound ('Salutation the second', 1913) and T.S. Eliot ('Le Directeur', 1917) wrote poems explicitly mocking the conservatism of Strachey and his paper.[458] But Strachey's children helped work up a range of new features for it, including architecture, theatre and plenty of modern verse. Their fresh-faced self-assurance was reflected in the new and confident section headings 'Music worth hearing' and 'Pictures worth seeing'. Amabel had published in 1921 an *Anatomy of Poetry*, which was in many senses a manifesto in defence of modern(ist) poetry; it found a very favourable reception in *The Spectator* from John Buchan (who, irregularly, chose to sign that review).[459] Something evidently changed for the better in the paper's literary atmosphere, as Pound and Eliot both later came round to being *Spectator* contributors – writing on poetry and the Church respectively.[460] A telling remark from a usually critical contemporary suggests a subtle change in the paper's overall character: '*The Spectator* has, I think, become much more human of late – or is it that the old controversies are dead and the new controversies seem to us who are middle-aged of so little moment?'[461]

Given the pressing need to raise its circulation, this was no time for the paper to turn down significant scoops. And in the closing days of 1923, a remarkable piece came its way. Amethe McEwen, a *Spectator* correspondent abroad, succeeded in eliciting a message from someone notoriously beyond journalistic reach: Benito Mussolini. In her introductory note to the piece, transcribed from a conversation at the Palazzo Chigi in Rome, she recalled:

> Mussolini listened to me with a look of half-humorous incredulity and rapped out, somewhat to my discomfiture, an accurate enumeration of all the opportunities of understanding Fascismo that there had been during the past years.[462]

Mussolini's speech was run as the first leading article of 1924 and was presented as his collective message for the British nation. The interview was preceded by a proud editorial note:

> This message has been sent through the SPECTATOR by His Excellency Signor Mussolini, Prime Minister of Italy. It is addressed to the people of England who desire truly to understand the meaning of Fascismo, and the new inspiration of Italy.[463]

The piece itself – only a couple of hundred words in length – appeared first in English then in the original Italian. Its most important sentences ran:

> Italian Fascismo was not merely a political revolt against those outworn and incapable governments which had become a menace to the development of Italy, and under whose rule the authority of the state had fallen into decadence and decay. It was also a spiritual revolt against old systems of ideas which were bidding fair to corrupt the sacred principles of Religion, of Patriotism, and of the Family. As a spiritual revolt, therefore, Fascismo was a direct expression of the people of Italy...
>
> Whoever has eyes keen enough to read into the heart of Italy's story will be able to understand and appreciate Fascismo. Those

Advertisement, Jan. 1924

who know neither Italy nor her history, and who remain untouched by the purity and greatness of spiritual things, will never understand.

The Spectator had been around long enough to b[e] acutely aware that such a movement could be soon vitiate[d] for worse, whether by the power-hungry autocrat or th[e] hero-hungry populace. We may be unsurprised that M[s] McEwen would, after successful service as a Germa[n] translator, later divorce her husband (an RAF captain) [to] marry Leo Graf (Count) von Zeppelin, and re-emerg[e] as a pro-Nazi broadcaster from the pathetic comfort [of] a Viennese *Schloss*. Instead, the paper chose to name i[ts] leading article, immediately after Mussolini's addre[ss] 'The spirit of Fascism'. This mixed a genuinely optimist[ic] assessment of the movement's support for working-cla[ss] living standards with open scepticism about its slidi[ng] into something to be feared:

> A Democratic Dictatorship such as Mussolini [has] has set up and desires to maintain may very likely suit the nature and instincts of the Italian people. In any case, that is their affair and not ours. We only know that Dictatorship would not suit the English people. In our opinion it is a

danger because, even when it is founded on noble things, it may rapidly degenerate into evil.

The piece closed on a more optimistic note:

Signor Mussolini will find no difficulty in working with our Government, and the British people will find none in understanding the spiritual significance of his message to them.

These words, easy to read as Old Strachey at his most naïve, have not aged well. Still, it was characteristic of the editor in his later years to embrace with enthusiasm movements that seemed to portend greater opportunities for the individual. In fact, there may be more going on in this case: although the piece was signed by Strachey, it is possible that his son John was influential in commissioning or promoting the interview. Later in the same issue, it was John who signed off a favourable review of Mussolini's political speeches. A political rift was emerging on York Street: while Strachey senior ended up describing his politics as 'left centre', Strachey junior was veering in the 1920s towards the genuinely revolutionary Left.

Two years later, Mussolini was in *The Spectator* once more, interviewed in Italy by Wrench's cousin, Francis Yeats-Brown. Again, this was a rather wide-eyed piece detailing the impressive aura of power that Il Duce emanated. Under the heading 'The New Italy Incarnate', Yeats-Brown records his impression that Mussolini 'would not willingly harm a mouse'.[464] Other than for revealing his interest in what circulation *The Spectator* had, the interview is a hollow piece of star-struck veneration. Many a reader must have wondered what on earth it was for. Needless to say, as world affairs unfurled and unravelled in the following years, *The Spectator* came to reject Mussolini and the spectre of Italian Fascismo in no uncertain terms.[465] Instead, the paper was starting to promote a new vision of politics, which tallied with the evolution of inter-war Conservatism. An influential series of four articles by Noel Skelton, the journalist and burgeoning

politician, appeared in the spring of 1923 under the name 'Constructive Conservatism'.[466] Their collective thrust was to outline and encourage a fresh political framework, in which the British were enfranchised to have a direct stake in the buildings and land they occupied. The idea caught on: the term that Skelton coined and pitched – the 'property-owning democracy' – has underpinned Conservative thought ever since.

Two further decisions of the 1920s catalysed *The Spectator*'s gradual evolution. The first was its willingness to acknowledge, even to embrace, new media. In 1924, Iris Barry (a *nom de plume* for her native Crump) began as the paper's regular film reviewer; as such, she became 'the first film critic on a serious British journal'.[467] She wryly recalled her early years in the post:

On the *Spectator* I was seeing about a dozen or more pictures a week, and actually being paid to see them. It was a bit bewildering at first and not a little frightening for at that time I was, I suppose, a horrid little egoist – as jejune as they come: I took my responsibilities as weightily as the late Mr. Gandhi and I firmly believed that my slightest qualifying adjective might raise grave doubts amongst countless thousands as to whether they should invest their shillings at the Strand Palace or forget it all with a pint of bitters at the Elephant and Crown.[468]

Her biographer, Robert Sitton, recorded how trail-blazing this work was:

Iris saw many of the seminal films of the period with fresh eyes, not knowing which, if any, eventually would take their place among the canons of a new art form. Her writing and analysis is sophisticated, substantial, and surprising for a self-taught critic who seems to have derived great benefit from her informal contacts and conversations with the important British modernists she knew.[469]

Barry soon became part of a 'power couple' in *The Spectator*'s back pages through her marriage to its literary editor, the poet Alan Porter. Her contribution to the world of film proved to be lasting: in 1925, she and Strachey were actively involved in founding the Film Society in London, the great inter-war body for connecting Brits with Continental cinema. Within a few years, the *Daily Mail* saw Barry's rising star and snapped her up; by 1930, she had emigrated permanently to America, throwing herself into Hollywood society and founding a famous film studies programme at the Museum of Modern Art. Ever since Barry's pioneering columns, film has been a core feature of the *Spectator* review pages, dissected by the likes of Graham Greene, Isabel Quigly, Peter Ackroyd, Hilary Mantel, Mark Steyn and Deborah Ross.

The second decision, much more shocking to the *Spectator* faithful, was to reveal to the world at last the identity of its writers. Since its foundation a century earlier, *The Spectator* had been fundamentally an anonymous journal: its contents were unified under the one voice of The Spectator, however split that personality could seem on any single issue. Occasional names had, it is true, appeared in earlier decades: although leaders, sub-leaders and reviews had always been unsigned, a good amount of 'special correspondence' had from the outset been filed under a pseudonym or, in exceptional circumstances, above the author's initials or full name. Letter-writers to the editor always had the choice of declaring or disguising their authorship; by the close of the nineteenth century, however, the great majority of letters were written *propria persona*. As editor, Strachey had followed Townsend-Hutton in being a passionate defender of unsigned leaders and sub-leaders, even though they had become a rarity in the weekly press of the early twentieth century. Among his various arguments was the belief that 'men who write anonymously, and in the name of their paper and not of themselves, are much less likely to yield to the foolish vanity of self-assertion.'[470] But Wrench, his business manager, along with several other staff members, felt that the British public were increasingly purchasing papers for their cast of celebrity writers, not for th[e] collective wisdom of their unknowable employee[s]. *The Spectator* gradually succumbed to the growin[g] pressure of the field, and, on 24 June 1922, the firs[t] leader ('The mother's eldest daughter', on British an[d] American law) appeared above the name 'J. St. Lo[e] Strachey'. The piece, now written for the first tim[e] with 'I' not 'we', was manifestly the voice of the ma[n] not the paper. Under assurances that this is the ne[w] journalism that would sell, Strachey persisted with th[e] practice: over the next few years, each issue carried tw[o] or three signed pieces among the 'Topics of the Day[', leaving one or two leaders as the anonymous voice [of] the paper. Strachey, once more, had helped drag th[e] journal forward into the present.

Yet the world was moving faster than he could handl[e,] and in 1924 he belatedly chose to take his retiremen[t.] Although he was publicly heralded as 'the Dean [of] Conservative journalism in England',[471] his priva[te] views had noticeably drifted towards the Left. Perha[ps] he realised that forgoing control of *The Spectator* wou[ld] be prudent for its long-term health. His son John, wh[o] had worked on the paper since 1922, could have seeme[d] a natural successor: he could write, knew how the pap[er] operated, and certainly had a keen interest in curre[nt] affairs. There was one problem, however: he had joine[d] the Labour Party in 1923, and even contested the se[at] of Aston (unsuccessfully) in 1924; a small proble[m] that he was active in politics, a large one that he w[as] beginning to publish pro-revolutionary literature wi[th] Oswald Mosley, with whom he would later found t[he] New Party, before sidling up to the Communists. N[ot] only would Strachey Jr write favourably of the Russi[an] press (7 Apr. 1928), but when Stalin's *Leninism* receiv[ed] a critical review, he wrote in to criticise the review[er] (23 June 1928); the following week he had to rebut t[he] charge that he too was a Communist.

A more Spectatorial prospect for the paper was clo[se] at hand: JOHN 'EVELYN' LESLIE WRENCH (1882–196[?]). This man, 'whose name might have come out of Wau[gh] and whose manner out of Wodehouse',[472] had long be[en] known to Strachey as an active promoter of Brita[in] he Commonwealth and the Special Relationship. Although born in Northern Ireland, he had trodden he well-worn path of English education through ummer Fields and Eton, before diving straight into usiness. After some success in postcard publishing, he oined the *Daily Mail* at the start of the century. A more ignificant career step came in 1910, when he founded he Overseas League, later followed by the English-peaking Union in 1918 – both causes close to Strachey's eart. He also shared the belief of 'Ed. *Spec.*' that, for the ood of society, Britain's alcoholic drinks trade should e regulated by a disinterested, not-for-profit body. ow Strachey must have soared on reading Wrench's ecreations' in *Who's Who*: alongside 'travelling' are e everyday hobbies of 'promoting Commonwealth nity' and 'British American cooperation'. Wrench ad been road-tested as a writer since 1922, when he arted a column ('The English-speaking World') on mperial affairs. Strachey felt he could keep the paper's olitics sound and its finances safe, and handed over e editorial reins from 1 January 1925. In addition, he ave Wrench the option of purchasing the controlling are of the paper, should he later decide to. The baton, rried by one man so carefully for nigh on thirty years, d at last been passed on.

Strachey did not cut ties with *The Spectator* entirely: well as keeping a decent portion of shares in the mily, he wrote a weekly column on all manner of ings. But, in his newfound freedom, he launched mself into novel-writing and travel. As with the sad ses of Rintoul and Townsend beforehand, however, rachey's own health declined quickly after he let the per go. In August 1927 he died, aged sixty-seven – st four months from celebrating the centenary to nich he had so long looked forward. As a remarkable ibute, the following *Spectator* redeployed the black rder of mourning, previously used only on the aths of royalty and two leading statesmen, the Duke Wellington and President McKinley.[473] A four-page emorial supplement was appended to the issue, which serted plainly that 'Strachey *was* the *Spectator*'. ach Thomas observed – with curious ambiguity –

that Strachey 'sacrificed himself, and to some extent the paper, on the altar of his own excess of energy; but he did invaluable work during the war. It may be truly said of him that he died for his country.'[474] Celebration of the man's past was combined with genuine concern for the paper's future: 'we pray that those who come after him may be worthy of him and his example.' Lord Oxford and Asquith, his predecessor as the paper's deputy leader-writer all those years ago, recorded in his memoirs his wish to pay 'humble tribute to the high purpose, the fine temper, the urbane culture, and the unfailing wealth both of literary and political resource with which during his succession to Townsend and Hutton he has maintained the best traditions of English journalism.'[475]

In 1925, then, Wrench became (as he grandly styled it) Editor-in-Chief and Managing Director of *The Spectator*. By July, he (aided by his father) paid the sum of £25,000 (c. £1.25 million) to purchase the control of ordinary shares, thus establishing him also as the company's chairman. This last position, overseeing all things Spectatorial, he held for the next four decades, until his death in 1966. When news of Wrench's acquisition became public several months later, Strachey promised the press that 'there is no risk of his altering the character of the paper or of letting it pass into unworthy hands'.[476] What is more, he added, 'there will be no change in the policy of the *Spectator*, which will continue to be independent in outlook.'[477] Writing in the paper, too, Strachey reassured his long-standing readers that he was

retiring from the control of the paper, *not* for reasons of health or through any disagreement with the *Spectator* public, but because I desire to be free from office work and to be able to devote much more time to travel and to literature rather than to the routine of journalism. The working proprietor of a newspaper cannot have the opportunity of leisure. But a proprietor who does not work must necessarily sterilize his newspaper.

As to Wrench, he added that he was handing 'him the torch without fear or hesitation – though not without trial and experiment of his powers and aspirations both at the *Spectator* and in the English-Speaking Union.'[478] In 1930, Wrench soon sold the (slight) majority of his shares to Angus Watson, a teetotaller and nonconformist Liberal, 'an austere and even Podsnapian figure'.[479] Visitors to the Norwegian Canning Museum in Stavanger will find that, as the chairman of the Newcastle-based and world-conquering Skipper Sardines, he now has a room devoted to his transformative role in that notoriously crowded industry. Watson, too, would remain on the *Spectator* board for a substantial period (until 1958), keeping a wary eye on the paper's moral fibre, editorially and commercially.

The handover from Strachey to Wrench was, in fact, more complex than the simple announcements of December 1925 had suggested. Although Wrench appointed himself 'Editor-in-Chief', he immediately promoted the paper's long-standing assistant editor to 'Editor'. JOHN (JACK) BLACK ATKINS (1871–1954) had joined the staff of *The Spectator* in 1907, having been a celebrated war correspondent and London editor for the *Manchester Guardian*. He had taken a Third in Theology at Pembroke, Cambridge, a feat that made him the first *Spectator* editor who passed through school and one of the ancient universities. When Townsend retired from leader-writing in 1908, John Buchan chose not to take up such a high-stakes post; Atkins, who had first written for the paper in 1903, made the leap instead, at the prompting of his colleague Charles Graves. The fit was good, and during phases of the Great War, and for several substantial spells thereafter, Atkins had already served as the paper's acting editor.

When he accepted Wrench's offer of the editorship, however, Atkins was quite unaware that it was being offered to him by someone elevated to the new role of 'editor-in-chief'. Once he learned of this awkward arrangement, the two men agreed a clear division of labour: he would continue as 'editor', in that he could write the chief leaders and the 'Notes of the Week'

with complete freedom; but the rest of the paper wa[s] left under the control of Wrench. Atkins carried ou[t] this circumscribed editorship with zeal and skill fo[r] twenty months.

One of his first activities was to host the first literar[y] competition in *The Spectator*'s history. Announced b[y] St Loe Strachey in December 1924, the paper offere[d] 'a prize of £5 for an original four-line epigram on "th[e] modern world".' The last of the terms for entry notec[?] with tongue not quite in cheek: 'Any epigram whic[h] mentions psycho-analysis, rejuvenation, Bolshevism[,] jazz, modern poetry or modern art will be severe[ly] handicapped, but not necessarily disqualified.' Almost a thousand entries were received, althoug[h] fifty had come from one and the same plucky Sco[t.] Reporting as judge in February 1925, Strachey note[d] that 'a surprising number of the epigrams we hav[e] printed were written by the sex which was once thoug[ht] impudent or misguided if it took to verse'.[481] Fiv[e] months later, £100 was accepted from an America[n] reader to run an essay contest on 'Unemployment: i[ts] Cause and Remedy'.[482] Competitions for readers we[re] soon established as an apparently timeless *Spectat[or]* tradition – although cut-out coupons were requir[ed] to ensure that only true purchasers of the paper we[re] entering the party. Just five years later the author M.[R.] James was serving as the rather over-qualified jud[ge] for a 'Ghost Story Competition'.[483]

In 1926, Atkins had to navigate the crisis of t[he] General Strike, which threatened to disrupt the week[ly] rhythm of *The Spectator*, itself unbroken for nigh [a] a century. With the typical printers – W. Speaig[ht] and Sons of Fetter Lane – out of action, the issue [of] 8 May had to be painfully produced in typescript a[nd] then laboriously run through a Gestetner duplicatir[g] machine. In such circumstances, it is understandab[le] that the number was reduced to eight (scarcely legib[le] pages, with no correspondence or literary matter. [The] first paragraph announced the simple aim 'to produ[ce] what the late Lord Halsbury might have called "a s[ort] of a paper" in order to preserve our continuity, to ke[ep] in touch with our readers, and to offer them sor[ne]

The Spectator

No. 5,105.]   WEEK ENDING SATURDAY, MAY 1, 1926.

PRINCIPAL CONTENTS.

IMPORTANT NOTICE TO SUBSCRIBERS

" Owing to the increase in the number of Postal Subscribers to the SPECTATOR it is necessary for notices of Changes of Address to be received by midday on Monday of each week. Notifications should be marked " Change of Address," and sent to the Subscription Department, The SPECTATOR, 13 York Street, London, W.C. 2.

The SPECTATOR is registered as a newspaper. Postage on this issue is : Inland 1d., Foreign 1½d.

NEWS OF THE WEEK

MR. CHURCHILL'S Budget, though it has a background of gloomy financial conditions, has given us much more pleasure than we expected. It is a severely disciplined Budget showing hardly a trace of Mr. Churchill's former inclination towards adventure and speculation. Moreover, it is a "national" Budget. At a great many points its structure is interwoven with great political causes from which the people in their daily work can derive nothing but benefit. It shows no favouritism to any class; it is democratic. If the Prime Minister had any lingering misgivings that the critics might have been right when they said that Mr. Churchill was a dangerous man for the Chancellorship of the Exchequer those misgivings must have been greatly relieved. The Budget admirably serves Mr. Baldwin's great purpose of putting in train a national policy which shall open a new industrial era of liberality, tolerance, comprehensiveness and consideration of one class for the other. With such a prospect we may, indeed, feel hopeful. If only the coal dispute should be settled, we could all go full steam ahead towards the happier times which we can undoubtedly make our own if we are determined to have them.

We have written about the Budget and its problems in our first two leading articles, but we must describe here some of its main points. The balance-sheet for the past financial year showed an actual revenue of £812,062,000—£11,002,000 over the estimate. The expenditure, however, owing to the coal subsidy (which cost £19,000,000), amounted to £826,100,000. This was £7,700,000 over the estimate without including the coal subsidy. If there had been no coal subsidy there would still have been a surplus of nearly five millions. As it was, the deficit to be made up out of current resources was £14,038,000. Turning to the coming year Mr. Churchill estimated the revenue, on the basis of existing taxation, at £804,700,000 and the expenditure at £812,641,000. The deficit would be £7,941,000. He then estimated that after allowing for the proceeds of the new taxation which he proposed, and for the fresh expenditure which would be possible and justifiable as the result of the new taxation, his revenue would be £824,750,000 and his expenditure £820,641,000. In other words he budgeted for a surplus of £4,109,000.

Before he came to his proposals for new taxation Mr. Churchill said that beer showed a small increase in consumption, but that spirits had again fallen no doubt as the result of the very high taxation. On the other hand, tea, cocoa, and sugar had shown " healthy compensating expansion " and the consumption of tobacco had also noticeably increased. On the whole the nation was richer now than it was a year ago. But though trade was steadily improving the basic industries remained depressed. Depression and prosperity were found side by side. " The picture," he said, " is not black nor grey ; it is piebald." The principal feature in Inland Revenue was the unexpected results of the Death Duties and the Super Tax. Last year he had reduced the Super Tax and increased the Death Duties by equal amounts. At the end of the year the Death Duties were 5½ millions below the estimate, the Super Tax 5½ millions above it.

During the past six years the diminution of the National Debt charge had been £75,000,000 a year. Fortunately all the thrift agencies had prospered in the last financial year. The receipts for the sale of Savings Certificates, for example, were £35,500,000, the increase being double that of the previous year. This is a really encouraging fact. Many of us have feared that the vast amount of Public Assistance would have a demoralising effect upon the traditional thriftiness of the nation, but though the danger visibly remains it is reassuring to know that independence and the old power of self-help are emerging handsomely from the trial. As for the return to the Gold Standard, Mr. Churchill pointed out, as he was thoroughly entitled to do, that the forebodings had already been falsified. The cost of living had declined seven points. We stood at last on a " basis of reality " and our prices were in favourable relation to those of the United States.

The Spectator

No. 5,105.]   WEEK ENDING SATURDAY, MAY 8, 1926.   PRICE 6d.

NEWS OF THE WEEK.

At last the long talk about a general strike and the assertion of the demands of labour by a "united front" has been gathered up into an act of such gravity and magnitude that no one can yet measure its significance or foresee its ending. Just as the situation is unprecedented so also is the curious form in which the Spectator appears this week. We need not apologize, our readers know only too well from their own inconvenience what our difficulties are. The General Council of the Trades Union Congress placed the printing industry high on the list of those called upon to strike in sympathy with the miners. In these circumstances it is impossible for the Spectator to be printed, and we have decided to produce what the late Lord Salisbury might have called "a sort of a paper" in order to preserve our continuity, to keep in touch with our readers and to offer them some thoughts upon the present distress.

When the General Council of the Trades Union Congress forbids men to work it challenges the existence of the Government. Thus the question before the country necessarily becomes a constitutional one. No one can prevent that from happening although it is quite true that those who are Constitutionalists in every fibre of their thought are not necessarily entirely at one with the Government on the industrial question as such. The fact remains that if Labour, in order to win, were able to make government impossible the Trades Union Congress would be the only alternative to the Government. The issue has only to be stated in this way for it to be plain that the Government must be supported in all its efforts to maintain the life, the steadiness and the peace of the nation. The Trades Union Congress could have no authority whatever to rule except the authority which belongs generally to dictators or bureaucratic autocracies, namely the right of strength or successful usurpation. It is not even certain that the General Council of the Trades Union Congress has not done violence

to its own constitution in ordering a general strike at this stage. In form the Council may have asked for some kind of sanction from its constituents, but in practice it aimed the heaviest blow at the industrial life of the nation which it is able to deliver without ascertaining the real wishes of those whom it is supposed to represent.

Our own experience can hardly be unique, and in conversations with wage earners we have come across general regret and even dismay at the order for a general strike. It is felt, very truly, that nothing can really be gained because when the discussions are resumed everybody will be worse off than before, there will be less money, less organization, and fewer opportunities for employment – all this at a time when our national fortunes were slowly but surely beginning to mend. The miners' case is not like that of men who have a fair and just hope of compelling their employers to pay more. The greater part of the mining industry is notoriously insolvent and it is impossible to make the owners hand over money which they have not got. It would be wrong and foolish to suggest that because the sympathetic strikers deplore what they are ordered to do they contemplate disloyalty to their organization. Finding themselves where they do, they will no doubt stand by their friends as their loyalty requires. But what, after all, do those who think the matter out hope from a sympathetic strike? Mr. Ramsay MacDonald once said "All my life I have been opposed to the sympathetic strike. It has no practical value; it has one certain result, a bitter and blinding reaction. Liberty is far more easily destroyed by those who abuse it than by those who oppose it".

Issues of 1 May and 8 May 1926

oughts upon the present distress.' In its last, the [lea]der 'These troubled days' gave a pointed account of [th]e rapidly changing times:

We are taking the crisis in the traditional English way and one cannot disregard even what is light-hearted and funny in these early days. It will not last long but it is very human, and a very important factor now. Nobody knows what will happen tomorrow or next week, but meanwhile into the drab lives of thousands of workers has come excitement, a sense of being in touch with great events and indeed a new purpose in life... We are generally disinclined in this country to face complicated and uncomfortable issues; it is a rational failing. But our national strength is that once the issue is inevitable we face it with common sense and courage.

Throughout his brief editorship, Atkins restored anonymity to the leading articles, thus reversing the controversial policy of previous years. Perhaps Atkins and Wrench felt this best suited their editorial compromise. Nevertheless, it was evident that pressure was routinely coming from the man above. For instance, in September and October 1926, *The Spectator* rather incongruously decided to serialise, at Wrench's behest, the autobiography of Kaiser Frederick III – though he had been dead for almost forty years.[484] That October, Atkins resigned the editorship. A private letter to Winston Churchill, his

Atkins, Wrench, Harris

long-standing friend and colleague from the Boer War, was clear enough on the matter:

> I am going to give up editing the *Spectator* shortly as I find my relations with the new principal proprietor impossible. He continually wants to interfere and he is very ignorant.[485]

Both Atkins and Wrench disguised any such disagreement in public and indeed in their respective memoirs. It is a question best left for philosophers whether a man ever was editor of *The Spectator* if, for all the claims of everyone around him that he was indeed editor of *The Spectator*, that man later denied that he ever edited *The Spectator*.[486] For our purposes it is enough to note that Atkins was in later years keen to downplay his role.

Having given up the reins, Atkins was nevertheless happy to remain the paper's chief leader-writer until 1931, when he left to edit the Anglican weekly *The Guardian*. At his leaving dinner, Wrench described Atkins, to his evident joy, as 'one of the great anonymities of Fleet Street'.[487] Perhaps he would have smiled that his editorship was until recently forgotten in the annals of *Spectator* history.

Wrench duly made the transition from 'Edito[r] in-chief' (a title only resurrected once hereafter) [to] Editor proper. Since the team around him remaine[d] unchanged, the paper's progress continued unabate[d] by 1928 it had reached its joint highest circulation eve[r] equalling the figure of 22,500, achieved in 1903 befo[re] the Tariff Reform crisis broke *The Spectator*'s stri[de]. The paper felt flush enough to indulge the sponsorsh[ip] of a sprawling collection of 1,250 'Great Poems of t[he] English Language', an American import.[488]

But the year 1928 had a greater cause for celebrati[on] than these successes: the paper's centenary. On [31] October, a lavish dinner was hosted in honour of *T[he] Spectator* at Claridge's, funded by John Astor, t[he] relatively new proprietor of *The Times*. The formidab[le] list of attendees included the Prime Minister, the Lo[rd] Chancellor, the Lord Chief Justice, along with S[ir] Ernest Rutherford, the Earl of Clarendon (chairm[an] of the BBC), Sir J.M. Barrie, John Buchan, Sir Hu[gh] Walpole and H.G. Wells – the last three *Specta[tor]* contributors. After a message of felicitation was re[ad] from the King, the Prime Minister Stanley Baldw[in] gave a speech, broadcast live to the nation's wireless s[ets] for twenty minutes. He celebrated *The Spectator* and [its] role in British society, observing that

The *Spectator* has become in our country a national institution ... a bond not only between the scattered portions of the Empire but a bond of union among all English-speaking peoples. There are a great many homes in England which would feel that some great landmark had been removed if the *Spectator* ceased to be published... We admire the *Spectator* because it has always stuck to its principles. We may not like them at times, but it has stuck to its principles, regardless of circulation, of profit, or of any other consideration. It will sink or swim with its principles... It has tried to unite the various functions of the press – the function of the watchdog, the function of the newsvendor, and the function of the critics – and to unite them in the public service and in the public service alone. The *Spectator* has never debased the currency with vulgarity or with triviality. It has never betrayed the interest of its country for sensation or for profit. These are its great traditions.[489]

Congratulations poured in from all corners of ⸠e press, which provide a good sense of the paper's ⸠nding. *The Daily Telegraph* wrote that 'with its ⸠estige unabated, [it] has established a record in the ⸠story of English periodicals of its special type'; *The ⸠ew Statesman* granted that 'of thoroughly honest ⸠d generous journalism there has never been in any ⸠untry or at any time a more conspicuous example'. ⸠e *Sphere*, though rarely a keen supporter, reflected ⸠at 'Mr Spectator has seen most of the game of ⸠man life, and has come through the experience still ⸠e gentleman, still the upright judge, still preserving ⸠ touch of the nineteenth-century blue-stocking, ⸠d (stranger still) every bit of his optimism'.[490] *The ⸠ardian* acknowledged that

there are not many newspapers of any kind or any country that can take such pride in recalling their past. In all the chief controversies of the century the 'Spectator' has taken a distinctive part... In modern times the 'Spectator' has earned public gratitude for its attention to the slum problem and its indefatigable pleading for better treatment of animals... The cause of humane slaughter, in particular, owes a great deal to its powerful championship.[491]

The Times noted that *The Spectator* was 'serious enough to be always respected and trusted, not too serious to joke or be joked about'.[492] As it happened, *The Spectator* followed *The Times* that year in taking the serious decision to secure its fortune for any centenary anniversaries to come by forming a trust, which would maintain control of at least 51 per cent of the paper's shares – thus keeping the title in the right sort of hands. Press statements declared that *The Spectator* should 'never be regarded as a mere matter of commerce, to be transferred to the highest bidder'; this new arrangement would 'eliminate as far as reasonably possible questions of personal ambition or commercial profit' and 'maintain the best traditions and political independence'.[493] This safeguarding committee initially comprised the Lord Mayor of London (later the Chairman of London County Council), the President of the Royal Society, the President of the Royal Historical Society, the President of the Law Society, the President of the Institute of Chartered Accountants, and the Chairman of the Committee of the Headmasters' Conference. In actuality, this timeless trust did not survive forty years, being disbanded permanently in 1967, when a new owner decided that life would be appreciably easier without it.

Despite this wave of well-earned celebration, and notwithstanding his Edwardian dress, Wrench was always looking forwards more than backwards. In an interview with the *Observer*, he loftily summarised the paper's goals:

the awakening of the national conscience in the question of slums, that hideous legacy resulting from the lack of vision of our fathers and grandfathers; disinterested management

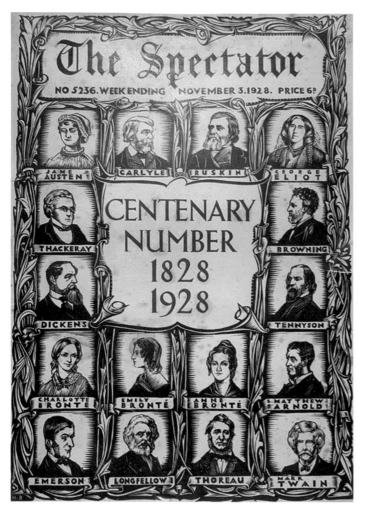

100 years in, *The Spectator* celebrates with 96 pages of articles, and 96 more of adverts

of the drink trade on lines similar to the Bratt system in Sweden; English-speaking friendship; and the more humane treatment of animals. To the League of Nations *The Spectator* has always given its wholehearted support, and in industrial affairs it advocates the sympathetic treatment of labour, on the assumption that cheap production is compatible with good wages.[494]

It is certainly true that the paper had to face up to the crisis rapidly unfolding around it, in which much of Britain had fallen into the deepest economic trouble. One of the most striking causes that inspired Wrench was the plight of a community in South Wales, where unemployment had reached 40 per cent

in 1928. Many English towns had turned to 'adopting Welsh communities, just as had happened fo France and Belgium after the Great War: Caterhan took Caerphilly, Eastbourne Rhymney, Worthin Brynmawr. Remarkably, *The Spectator* played its ow part by adopting Aberdare, near Merthyr Tydfil, wher almost one in two were unemployed. In Decembe 1928, Wrench made a direct appeal to his readers:

Only those who know South Wales can measure in their minds the full misery and piteousness of the plight into which so large a part of its population has fallen... What we have to do is to find remedies or palliatives for the appalling unemployment which has dropped like a blight upon South Wales, not to choose this moment for fixing responsibility here or there... We are all readier to relieve special cases rather than general. If we can take a personal interest in those who receive our gifts, if we know just what is being done with our money, we are stimulated to give more than we should in the usual conditions... Every £5 subscribed will keep a child from feeling really famished for the best part of three months. Please send clothes as well as money, and with the suits and dresses, the boots and shoes, the hats, any bedding that can be spared.[495]

In four days, the Aberdare Fund had receiv £2,000, in sums ranging from 2s 6d to £100, from t Empire and far beyond. After a few months, £15,0 (c. £850,000) was ready to deploy. In addition, sever tons of clothing, blankets and food were soon pi up in the York Street offices until more appropri storage could be secured in Aberdare Town H Not all readers, however, quite gauged the natu of the situation: among the gifts were silk dressi gowns, Victorian crinolines and hunting pinks. readers were keen to do more: a thousand families w individually adopted, each on a subsidy of 5s per we many travelled to the area to help promote the tra f quilting, rabbit-breeding (for fur) and afforestation.

Weekly letters were printed from the people of berdare – in Welsh as well as English. Edna Edwards, ho at the age of six remains *The Spectator*'s youngest er correspondent, wrote:

Dear Mr. Spectator, We thank you very much for the lovely toys you sent us this Christmas. We had a grand party. We had tea, brown and white bread and butter, currant and rice cake, chocolates, oranges and toys... My father has not worked for 18 months, and he is very glad that we have had such a good time in school this Christmas. When we grow we hope we shall be able to help somebody. Your grateful little friend.[496]

The anonymous 'special commissioner' based in berdare concurred: 'the way faces light up there hen the *Spectator* is mentioned ... gives proof of the during tie formed between adopters and adopted.'[497] nd so, on 26 July 1929, a deputation from Aberdare own Council arrived at the *Spectator* offices to present e silver statuette of a miner. The simple inscription, nich has been visible from the editor's desk ever since, ads 'In grateful recognition, "The greatest of these love".' Charity cannot be far behind.

It was not to York Street, however, that the Aberdare legation headed. For in March that year, *The ectator* moved once more from its premises, which d proved to be too crowded for a journal on the up. his new base, 99 Gower Street, took the magazine ay from the Strand for the first time. Although in e leafier corners of Bloomsbury, it could certainly im a lively past: it had been a brothel, notorious the press and the courts for its eccentric procuress gel Anna' – who toiled at the sharp edge of the ual occult.[498] The building, though appreciably ger, still betrayed its seedy heritage, being divided o numerous tiny cubicles. One contemporary staff mber described the rooms as 'designed either as bliettes for very minor poets or as ferret-hutches for y large ferrets.'[499]

A lasting token of thanks from Welsh colliers

Given its charitable success amid civil strife, it was appropriate that 1929 was the year when *The Spectator* first released a special 'Christmas issue'. The collection was devoted to 'outlining a better world': Lord Robert Cecil wrote on 'Anglo-American Relations', Aldous Huxley on 'Machinery, Psychology and Politics', W.R. Inge on 'Constructive Birth-Control', John Buchan on 'Conservatism and Progress', John Galsworthy on 'Animals and Birds', Mary Borden on 'How to Enjoy Being Uncomfortable' – and another ten worthies on subjects that sought to point a better way forward for the Western world under the cosh.[500] The same seasonal special also instituted a prize for the best 'short recipe' for solving the problems of humanity; given the scope of the challenge, the 5-guinea kitty seemed a little meagre. But the winning effort brimmed with so much optimism that it spilled over into verse:

Reduce the Drink: sweep all the Slums away:
  Raze Tariff walls: provide a Motor-way:
Industrialize the Dole: give Liberty
  To foster Self-respect whoe'er we be:
Safeguard the Child, and train the rising Youth
  To build the world on Brotherhood and Truth.[501]

At the other end of the spectrum – and certainly alarming to the likes of Wrench and Watson – was the following piece of blue-sky thinking: 'Kill all the women: the human race would then die out, and the world would be populated only by animals; and they, I'm sure, could not make a worse mess of it than these so-called human beings.'[502]

Trivialities aside, Wrench's great service to the paper was to push issues that transcended introspective, nationalistic concerns. From October 1930 to February 1931 he hosted a weekly debate entitled 'The Challenge to Religious Orthodoxy', where a younger writer would critique an aspect of Christianity, which would be defended by a respondent the following week. Among those posing challenges were Bertrand Russell ('Religion and Happiness'), C.E.M. Joad ('The Organized Church') and John Strachey ('Religion and Socialism').[503] Later in the decade, Harris hosted debates on 'Christianity and Communism', involving contributions from W.R. Inge ('The Christian Tradition'), Martin D'Arcy ('A Roman Catholic View') and Reinhold Niebuhr ('Social Justice').[504] Another important series of articles tackled the 'colour bar', which in Britain and several other countries prohibited non-white workers from particular areas of employment. His motivation was crystal-clear:

there is to-day no problem of greater concern to the British Commonwealth, with 400 million coloured people within its borders – over a fifth of the human race... The only policy for a world Commonwealth, which includes people of every race, colour and creed, is one of equal rights for every civilized man. No policy based on race exclusion can endure. That is not to say that

we think many of our coloured fellow-subjects are ready for Western systems of democratic government; far from it, but there must be no racial discrimination.[505]

A wide-ranging series of articles followed, from political, cultural and 'scientific' angles, covering Britain, India, South Africa, America, each preceded by the unusual disclaimer that 'The Spectator does not necessarily agree with all the views of the writers'. The discussion proceeds with some tact for its time, but Wrench reveals more than once the conviction that the differences between races are insurmountable. 'Coloured people must accept these differences, for they will never annihilate them. Let them take a nobler part than aiming at any merging with the white races as though the differences could be ignored. Let them cultivate a noble pride in their own races side by side with the white races.'[506] The primus inter pares outlook sets alarm bells ringing. More remarkable was the contribution of Paul Robeson (8 Aug. 1931), the black American singer, actor and activist, who expressed how he felt more welcome in England than in his native country. Having enrolled at London School of African Studies in 1934, Robeson later wrote for the paper an influential essay ('The Culture of the Negro', 15 June 1934) which highlighted the intellectual importance of researching the origins of West African folklore.

Wrench's international connections could occasionally land him some remarkable interviewees. While the interview with Henry Ford is striking for its timing amid a global financial crisis (29 Mar. 1930), the following year he succeeded in hosting Mahatma Gandhi at his house for a Spectator conversation. The three-hour discussion made for a three-page editorial whose core focus was India's future, and whose language trenchant. Nevertheless, Gandhi opened positively:

One of the things I wanted to do while in England was to talk to the Editor of the Spectator, because we in India appreciate very much the part the

Spectator has played in enlightening the people of Great Britain on Indian problems. I know that you may not necessarily agree with all the views I hold, but I recognize that you have repeatedly stated in the columns of the *Spectator* that the only satisfactory basis for the future relations of Great Britain and India is one of friendship, absolute equality and a recognition of the fact that the people of India must be the final arbiters of their destiny.[507]

Both parties shared the view of Townsend decades before, that an independent India, once securable, was the only viable route forward; Wrench, however, felt that British oversight would be a prerequisite to achieving total Home Rule. Eleven years later, Wrench interviewed Gandhi once more, this time at his home in India. The exchange was markedly more curt, the differences now irreconcilable: the former pushed for India's place in a British commonwealth, the latter for its own role in a global union. One of the few points Wrench accepted from his interlocutor was that 'Hitler is a scourge sent by God to punish men for their iniquities ... I have shut my mind against nothing and I am a friend of Great Britain. I always have been. I have no axe to grind. Whatever I do is out of love.'[508] Four months later, Gandhi was arrested on the orders of the British government.

The Spectator was keen to monetise itself as best possible. Issues now carried a full-page advert (for societally respectable companies) on the front, to be folded or detached from the actual paper. Several other special issues were tested out by Wrench: on finance, education, fine arts and antiques, Scotland and Ireland; a less obvious subject was 'heating and lighting', which launched in 1931 a 'Modern Home' column on interior decoration. More adventurous was the paper's decision that year – still a generation away from running its first cartoon – to host eight full-page detachable caricatures by Max Beerbohm.[509] The series was eclectic in its subjects: H.G. Wells, Lord Robert Cecil, Oswald Mosley, James Garvin, Dean Inge, Siegfried Sassoon, Philip 'Tubby' Clayton and John Masefield. All of these worthies – save the wayward Mosley – had previously written for the paper.

An indirect advantage of Wrench's editorship was his having Francis Yeats-Brown for a cousin. Here was an astounding character, who had been a leading figure in the Indian forces until the Great War; his autobiography, *Lives of a Bengal Lancer* (1930), was a best-selling ripping yarn, creating in 1935 'one of the greatest adventure films of all time'.[510] He joined the paper's staff in 1926 and soon rose to assistant editor, bringing colour and quality to the books pages – as well as a more optimistic attitude to the fast-shifting literary scene.[511] Yeats-Brown was a man who would attend Tuesday editorial conferences seated on the table in the Buddhist Lotus position; in his office, he would often be found in the *sirsa padasana*, with feet placed pensively on head. One of his greatest feats of contortion was to persuade T.E. Lawrence (of Arabia) to take up the role of reviewer. In a letter of June 1927, Lawrence outlined his terms of engagement:

D.H. Lawrence I'll be delighted to have a try at. I've read all his stuff since the *White Peacock*. Hakluyt is only a name to me. So on that you'll get the reflection of a fresh mind: if it does reflect anything. The Koran is barred. Nothing Arabian or related. Besides, it's a proper mess of a book. A mixture of Bradshaw and major prophet and police news.[512]

Lawrence went on to produce several reviews under the pseudonym of 'C(olin) D(ale)'. His own *Revolt in the Desert* (1927) in turn profited from as august a reviewer as George Bernard Shaw,[513] who had already caused a stir on the correspondence pages. When in 1925 Bishop Welldon, Dean of Durham, alleged that the anarchic forces seeking to overturn England were ideologically vague, Shaw wrote in to give his own lively definitions of capitalism, socialism and communism. While the last was 'the same as Socialism, but better English', capitalism was 'obviously no policy for a gentleman'.[514]

Wrench, it should be noted, did not actively oversee either the political or the literary side of the paper; his talents were more managerial and entrepreneurial than editorial. His dedicated staff included Atkins, continuing as chief political writer, Wilbraham Cooper, a long-standing contributor since Strachey's time, Wilson Harris, a level-headed and even-handed political commentator, E.G. Hawke, an expert on art and much besides, and Celia Simpson, literary editor – before she was dismissed for being too left-wing, a trait that instead led her to marry John Strachey. Her replacement in 1932 – when the paper's staff was rapidly reduced under the financial strain of Britain's leaving the gold standard – was Peter Fleming. The elder brother of Ian, he would go on to write a *Spectator* column with unmistakeable verve for the next forty years. 'Moth', 'Scadavy' and 'Apemantus' were among his numerous pseudonyms, but, from 1946, 'Strix' (the Latin for 'screech-owl' – a bird he once adopted for several months) was his most celebrated avatar. Fleming, in fact, was deemed such a good prospect for the paper's future that Wrench suggested he be made editor in his stead, pending the whippersnapper's return from a jaunt to Brazil in 1932. But the world is a cruel place, and Fleming came back to find not an empty editorial chair but one upon which the former political editor sat, Wilson Harris. When Atkins left *The Spectator* in 1931, Harris had become his successor as leader-writer, soon proving himself to be a safer pair of hands – and a better administrator – than the young Turk Fleming.

(Henry) Wilson Harris (1883–1955) was formally made editor on 1 October 1932. His appointment ended – for a generation, at least – the long-standing *Spectator* tradition of editor-owners: for all but eleven of its first 125 years, the paper had been edited by the man that paid the bills. Now a new – perhaps even professional – age was dawning. A Cambridge classicist (II.1, St John's), Harris was the first Cantab to take full control at the helm, although the staff during his tenure continued to be 'predominantly and defiantly Oxford'.[515] Harris had long been a journalist at the *Daily News*, and won over both Strachey and Wrench by his long-

term work with the League of Nations Union. To the further approval of the proprietors, he was a committed teetotaller and committed Quaker. The passion he had were wide-ranging: God, globalism, and the first 'e' of 'judgement'. Although the embodiment o conservative journalism, he was well known and we liked – the doyen of international journalism, bastio of the Reform Club, and occasional host of nake swimming parties. He was keen that his paper shoul be 'independent and non-party', but also that it shoul have a unified outlook overseas: 'in foreign affairs stands for the utmost development of international co operation through the League of Nations.' Harris als chose to launch a refreshingly confident slogan for th paper, 'The weekly for thinking people'.[516]

Harris was a lucid and clever writer, if unerring conventional in outlook. One frequent contributo the economist Honor Croome, waspishly noted th removing the last sentence of any article by Wilso Harris subtracted nothing from it. Edward Hodgkin, staffer, likewise described the closing coda as 'more li an amen or an embroidered full stop'.[517] But, alongsi his more stately pieces, Harris created for himself o of the most enduring and endearing *Spectator* person Each week, from October 1932 to March 1953, th figure of 'Janus' produced 'A Spectator's Notebook' a chatty survey of weekly events and timeless quibbl Its two-headed author, a spectator both forwards an backwards, often took issue with the rest of the pap and the hobby-horses ridden by the editor's straite laced *alter ego*, Mr Wilson Harris. It is telling th almost every subsequent *Spectator* editor has four it worthwhile to include, on the Janus model, such informal but elegantly expressed 'notebook'.

Irked at being so conspicuously passed over, howeve Fleming was determined to make *The Spectator* of t Thirties more lively. Wearing his first mask of 'Mot he used a column to mock the paper for its appare immutability:

thousands of readers are provided, Friday after Friday, with a fresh, clean copy of *The Spectator*, profound, witty, intensely grammatical, and always differing, however slightly, from the one they read the week before. It is the proud boast of the editorial staff that no two issues of *The Spectator* have ever been proved identical... If the same thing is said, it is said in a different way. If the same words are used, they are used of something else.[518]

That same year, Fleming teamed up with the raffish Derek Verschoyle, who used his downtime as literary editor to fire his .22 rifle at any cat visible from his window. These two *enfants terribles* of *The Spectator*, with a combined age of forty-two, produced in 1933 the first multi-authored anthology of *Spectator* articles, *Spectator's Gallery*. Advertised as 'a miscellany which is varied, informal, and not infrequently gay', it certainly showcased an impressive array of talent who had contributed to the freshened-up paper: E.M. Forster, W.B. Yeats, Rose Macaulay, John Galsworthy, Cecil Day Lewis, Vita Sackville-West, G.K. Chesterton, T.S. Eliot, Aldous Huxley, and (this time in writing) Max Beerbohm. Janus was not all-seeing: the first that Harris and his new assistant editor, R.A. Scott-James, knew of this cocksure collection was seeing it on the bookshop shelves.

Someone had their eye on the ball. In September 1932, an article appeared in *The Spectator* from 'J.E.S.' on 'The Crossword puzzle habit'. To the surprise of many – who had seen the paper worry in previous years that such puzzles were 'fast becoming one of the most anti-social influences at work among us'[519] – the article welcomed this taxing new addition to the world's daily problems:

Most popular crazes are short lived. And deservedly so: for most of them have little merit but novelty, and when that has worn off there is nothing left. So it was with diabolo, with pop-in-taw, with half a score of idle pursuits that recur to the memory. So it will be with the strange aberration of the moment which goes by the appropriately fatuous name of *Yo-yo*.

None of these things, whatever their temporary attraction, were of the stuff that endures. It is otherwise with the crossword puzzle. That has stood the test of time; it has kept its terms and taken its degree in the school of popularity; it has ceased to be a craze and become a habit.[520]

Such enthusiasm was matched by the editorial note that 'The *Spectator* will, from next week onward, provide its readers with crossword puzzles.' The country gasped, copies of the paper slipped from benumbed fingers, and – life restored to the digits – letters were fired off from all quarters. Their general thrust was as follows:

Low indeed has the *Spectator* fallen!... May I be one of the thousands of readers to protest against this vulgarizing of a paper hitherto holding a high standard?[521]

To this Harris tartly replied:

The *Spectator* is flattered at the implication that in following the example of *The Times* and the *Observer*, it is descending from a higher level to theirs.

Harris's staff was more eclectic than one might expect: alongside the standard 'left-centre' writers were some of a markedly more left-wing bent. Goronwy Rees, a socialist and part-time KGB worker, was associate editor from 1935 to 1938, and Anthony Blunt, a more committed KGB employee, was art critic between 1933 and 1938. In these confused times, readers hardly noticed. Politics aside, Harris was able to secure pieces from an impressive array of writers through the connections of Scott-James (assistant editor in 1933–5 and 1939–45), the man who first popularised the term 'modernism'.[522] Still, as a sign of its self-confidence, *The Spectator* was happy to run a parodic attack of modernist poetry from Siegfried Sassoon, which caused a flurry of spirited letters.[523]

The inter-war *Spectator* hosted a most impressive array of literary contributors: alongside Wells, Macaulay, Chesterton, Lawrence and Forster were Mervyn Peake, Evelyn Waugh, Stephen Spender, Dorothy L. Sayers and Robert Byron. On religion, we find Evelyn Underhill, Russell Barry, Spencer Leeson and C.S. Lewis; on politics, Sir Arnold Wilson, Frank Pakenham and Violet Bonham Carter; on history, G.M. Trevelyan, Hugh Trevor-Roper, E.H. Carr, A.L. Rowse and Arnold Toynbee; on the classics, Gilbert Murray, T.R. Glover and Edwyn Bevan. When faced with the death of A.E. Housman – who studiously avoided writing public-facing articles – C.M. Bowra surveyed the contribution of this titanic scholar.[524] More occasional writers included Archbishop Temple, the philosophers Jean-Paul Sartre and Reinhold Niebuhr, the statesmen Viscount Snowden and Augustine Birrell, and the veteran journalists J.A. Spender and Dilys Powell. Among the poets – who occasionally wrote articles and reviews – were Siegfried Sassoon, John Betjeman, Louis MacNeice, T.S. Eliot, Ezra Pound, John Drinkwater and C.S. Lewis. Despite *The Spectator*'s strong nationalistic feelings under any editor, W.B. Yeats was given space to argue for Ireland's retention of the picture collection of Sir Hugh Lane (23 Dec. 1916), to oppose an Irish censorship bill (29 Sep. 1928), to reflect on Ireland's rapid change ('Ireland, 1921–1931', 30 Jan. 1932), and to send in trios of politically charged songs (23 Feb. 1934, 26 May 1939).

The Spectator of the Thirties was keen to play an active part in the increasingly feverish national debate about what the future should look like. To abet the cause, a series of pocket-size 'Spectator Booklets' was released in 1934, containing topical pieces edited from the magazine. The six themes that reached print were 'Parliament or Dictatorship?', 'The Next Ten Years', 'After Death?', 'Christianity and Conduct', 'Hitler's First Year', and 'Aspects of England'. Although *The Spectator* hosted contributors from the full range of political backgrounds, under Harris it became steadily evident that, despite its turbulent Twenties, the paper was moving ever more in line with the Tory party.

In the House of Commons itself, Robert Boothby Conservative MP for Aberdeen, could casually (i incorrectly) refer in 1936 to *The Spectator* as 'one of th oldest traditional Tory newspapers in this country'.[525]

After a few years in post, Harris was evidently pleased with the progress of his paper, advertised far and wide as 'the weekly for thinking people'. When in 1934 weekly competitor, *The Week-End Review*, folded into its primary left-leaning rival, the *New Statesman an Nation*, in 1934, Harris took the opportunity to stat how things were faring. His *Spectator* was, he declared

not in the ordinary sense a commercial undertaking. Its shares are held by men and women concerned not primarily with their dividends but with the maintenance of a paper standing for certain principles, and fulfilling certain functions, in which they believe...

That the pace of life is increasing, and times of leisure diminishing, is a truism. The wireless is to some extent supplying the platform which the weekly journals have aimed at providing – though the spoken word is evanescent, as the written is not – and at the same time the competition of publications allied therewith, and enjoying a monopoly in the publication of wireless talks, is a new and far from negligible factor in the situation...

The business of the weekly is to sift and summarize the news of seven days, to discuss and comment on and explain it, and to lay before its readers views, either its own or those of qualified contributors, on subjects which hardly come within the daily papers' purview at all... There would be little satisfaction in producing *The Spectator* if it were read only by those who habitually agreed with it.[526]

But these matters of business were small fry wh set against the storm gathering on the Contine *The Spectator* was affected by the same admixtu of curiosity and scepticism at Adolf Hitler's ra ise to power. It would be an immense task to chart the shifting attitude of the paper to Germany over the Thirties and throughout the war. In the earliest stages, Adolf Hitler is viewed as a curiosity – as a case study of what tactics enthuse a populace after economic downturn. But intrigue moved to outrage when the twin realities of state oppression and anti-semitism came to light. A report in March 1933 on the 'Terror in Germany' denounced 'Fascism in its ugliest form', and reported with disgust the rumours of racist massacres.[527] The following month, Wrench himself gave first-hand evidence of the plight of the Jews under Nazism, which he had encountered on a lecture tour. Although he told audiences that he 'stood for no racial discrimination between Christian and Jew', his Germanophilia led him to infer that 'the Government would like now to drop the anti-Jewish campaign'. Such a naïve conclusion led him to the absurd position that 'the best service we can do the Jews in Germany, having expressed our disapproval of the anti-Jewish campaign, is to try and maintain an impartial attitude towards Germany.'[528] Harris, for his part, left the question open in 1934 whether Germany was indeed on the path to war.[529] From February that year, a series of eight articles on 'Germany Today' sought to anatomise and analyse the forces at work. Regrettably, the author was Powys Greenwood, who either by disposition or by profession as a German banker, viewed the rise of German militarism with wide-eyed interest.

In Britain itself, the emergence of a wave of would-be Fascists was treated as initially a mere nuisance. In early 1934, Sir Oswald Mosley and Lord Rothermere were summarily dismissed: 'the Blackshirts, like the *Daily Mail*, appeal to people unaccustomed to thinking. The average *Daily Mail* reader is a potential Blackshirt ready made.'[530] By the summer, *The Spectator* had overridden its instinctive resistance to government-led intervention, and expressed support for the public ban on wearing the Blackshirt (or any political) uniform. The problem, however, was too deep to be dissolved by stern words, and two years later the veteran Labour MP George Lansbury reported on the blight of anti-

The first report of our Special Investigator, now in Germany, appears exclusively in this week's issue.

Spectator

Times advertisement, 2 Feb. 1934

Semitism in London's East End.[531]

It would be some years before the paper settled its position on Germany. In the meantime, myriad domestic issues won lively comment. For the period 1934–7, a series of 'Marginal Comments' on matters great and small was written by various figures, such as A.L. Rowse, Llewellyn Woodward, Anthony Powell and (most successfully) Rose Macaulay. In January 1939, however, Harold Nicolson – then a National Labour MP – started an enjoyably multifarious weekly column called 'People and Things', which continued until his appointment, in May 1940, as Parliamentary Secretary to the Ministry of Information. To the delight of readers, these elegant medleys of political comment and societal reflection returned in August 1941. The column, now reclaiming the title 'Marginal Comment', lasted until 1952, and cheered many a reader weighed down by the war effort. It was not long before Nicolson was heralded as the 'outstanding essayist of the day'.[532] Here, once more, the character of the first *Spectator* was found to thrive again in the second. Two examples of Nicolson's style may suffice. In December 1943, he assessed the student outlook of recent decades:

In my own generation we were content to expose the moral fallacies of our elders and to put in their place a belief in intellectual integrity. After

the last war the young men who returned to the Universities sought to recompense themselves by all forms of self-indulgence for the hardships and dangers to which they had been exposed. They were followed by a generation of austere men and women who believed quite sinccrely in the existence of the economic man and who derived much spiritual and intellectual solace from the perfected logic of the Marxist theory. But the young people of today neither believe nor disbelieve in any theory; they have come to learn that the world is a highly intricate organism, and that most of what has been said about it is either partially or totally untrue. And since they dismiss the wisdom of the ancients as being fallacious and the advice of their immediate elders as savouring of 'propaganda', they are left naked with their own horrible but slight experience and a deep consciousness of the enormous intricacies of life.

With the tiny torches of their own knowledge they grope amid the majestic ruins of the past. I am not surprised that they should feel 'forsaken'. Yet if they can believe in no absolute theories, they can at least know that courage, truthfulness, energy, scholarship and kindness are virtues and that their opposites are vices. With their little torches they can see and illumine these great absolutes. Guided by such stable landmarks, they can find their way through the dark, wet fog which surrounds them. And in the end, I suppose, they will find warmth again, and laughter and light.[533]

In 1947, Nicolson advanced an open attitude to the removal of unnecessary clothing when weather permitted, but closed with a salutary warning about wholesale nudism:

I do not share the theory of the nudists that complete exposure offers a relief from inhibitions. Some twenty years ago I visited a nudist colony in Thuringia; it was the only occasion on which I have consciously regretted my enquiring mind; the memory of that visit remains as a scar upon my soul. Never in my life have I witnessed such ugliness, such a divestment of human dignity, such deliberately restrained self-consciousness, such stark and affected matiness, such smirking ungainliness. The whole system, so far from releasing inhibitions, was calculated to induce a physical trauma. I regretted my visit very much indeed.[534]

Although *The Spectator* had been a pioneerin journal in film criticism in the 1920s, this cutting-edg feature had been somewhat blunted under Wrench pious editorship. Realising that this was not a flash in-the-pan medium, the new literary editor Verschoyl employed the young Graham Greene, already a occasional contributor,[535] to act as the paper's fil critic. Although Greene had proposed himself after th 'dangerous third martini', he held on to the post for fiv years (1935–40), before a one-year stint as literary edito (1940–1). His reviews were strident in both cynicis and rebuke – prompting at least one libel case, and least one excrement-filled envelope. You tend not to w friends by saying Boris Karloff 'reached stardom wit the sole assistance of the make-up men', noting th when Marlene Dietrich is ambitiously cast as a youn woman 'time tells ungallantly in the muscles of th neck', and lamenting how unfortunate it is that Alfre Hitchcock 'is allowed to produce and even to write h own films'.[536] His collected criticism in the field remai fascinating, but woefully under-studied.[537]

There were other, more direct ways of appealin to the youth. As long ago as 1929, *The Spectator* ha commissioned a piece on 'The war and the young generation', which was limited to writers under thirt The first contributor was a twenty-five-year-old Evely Waugh, who thus began a forty-year association wi the paper. Keen to relaunch this idea, Harris host in 1937 twelve columns from writers aged betwe nineteen and twenty-nine. The series, 'The Voi of Under Thirty', covered politics, society, religi

...nd personal issues. It struck a chord. The collection [w]as republished as a booklet in 1937, along with two [co]untervailing *Spectator* columns on the outlook of the [ol]d guard – one by an eighty-year-old, and one by a [ni]nety-year-old.

But *The Spectator* was increasingly aware that it had [to] try harder to reach a new market. That same year, [it] hosted a special issue on how to engage the British [pe]ople. Entitled 'Reaching the Public', it had articles [fr]om Sir Kingsley Wood, the Minister of Health, on ['G]overnment Publicity', Sir Norman Angell on 'The [Pr]ess and Propaganda', Sir Arnold Wilson on 'Bias [in] Broadcasting', Graham Greene on 'Ideas in the [Ci]nema', and Dorothy L. Sayers on 'The Psychology [of] Advertising'.[58] The issue ran to an exceptional 110 [pa]ges, its bumper size being funded by seventy-two [pa]ges of advertisements, a figure surpassed only by the [ce]ntenary number of 1928. Though ever wary of selling [ou]t its character, the allure of corporate sponsorship [wa]s potent. Still, things were slowly moving in the [rig]ht direction: in the course of the 1930s, circulation rose gradually from 21,000 to a record figure of 27,000 – an achievement all the more impressive alongside the BBC's deliberate attempt to emulate the magazine by founding its own weekly (*The Listener*) in 1929, and the substantial merger of the *New Statesman* and *The Nation and Athenaeum* in 1931.

In 1936, when the Abdication crisis reached its climax, *The Spectator* was forced into direct criticism of a monarch, an attitude not seen since Rintoul's day. The founding editor would have turned in his grave on reading the breathless excitement of the preceding year's 'Silver Jubilee number' for King George V (10 May 1935). But, after months of tactful silence, as had pervaded most of the British press, a leader of 4 December intoned:

> The King of Great Britain and the Dominions is the servant of his people. His life is not his own but theirs... Nothing more is charged against him than a friendship carried to the point of unwisdom with a lady who, till the decree granted in her favour six weeks ago is made absolute, is still a married woman... But what would be a private matter for a private citizen may have grave reactions when it involves a king... Restraints on a sovereign's choice of consort become increasingly distasteful. But that the question can be regarded as one for himself alone, in which his Ministers and his people have no part, is more than can be conceded. That is the price of kingship.

One week later the inevitable announcement came. But this would be only the first of many times that *The Spectator* would find fault with the royal family's romantic assignations.

Another cataclysmic event was soon to follow. *The Spectator* masthead, a model of stability for 110 years, suddenly forwent the florid curlicues of its gothic lettering: in February 1937, the modern age left its mark on the paper's aesthetic.[59] This iconoclastic change required Harris to tread as carefully as he could:

Readers of *The Spectator* will be conscious of certain changes in typography in this week's issue. The antique letter of the title, both on the cover and on the first page of matter, has been changed, as in the case of *The Times* a few years ago, to square Roman capitals, which have a bolder effect and make the paper more easily recognisable on bookstalls and elsewhere; what was appropriate in 1828 when *The Spectator* started is not necessarily ideal in 1937... Habit goes far to determine taste, but though there may be some regular readers who will for a time feel a touch of the unfamiliar about *The Spectator*, the general opinion will, we believe, be that the paper is more attractive in its latest guise and that contents readable in the literary sense are the more readable for the form in which they are now clothed.[540]

No outraged letter made print. But more changes were to come. In 1938, *The Spectator* decided that it would try out a new-fangled device called the 'headline', thus replacing its *de rigueur* front-page title 'News of the Week' with something topical. On 16 September that year, 'A Momentous Mission' trumpeted the news of Chamberlain's appeasement efforts which led to the Munich Agreement.[541] But when, in 1943, even the definite article was removed from the masthead, readers rightly had far more important things to be worrying about. The return of 'The' to the front page would take thirty-one years; but, after its brief reprisal in 1974–6, it was then removed for another spell until 1982. Such changes are, of course, trivial, but more trivial still is the pseudo-wisdom of the advertising specialists who conjure them up.

Through his entire tenure, Harris's *Spectator* was unfailingly international in its outlook. Not only did the three-page 'News of the Week' merrily trot the globe, but it began publishing weekly columns in foreign languages. Usually written in French, or less commonly German, these appeared for most of the 1930s, even when the latter medium seemed increasingly queer. The reader of 1935 could read of 'Vacances pour les animaux' and 'Burschenherrlichkeit', 1936 'Pèlerinage' and 'Ein

The masthead evolves

Fischerei-Jubiläum', 1937 'En écoutant la radio' ar 'Shakespeare – Ein Nazi?'[542] A more direct (and perhap readable) message came from the German noveli Thomas Mann, then living in Czechoslovakia. H formidable two-part broadside 'A Warning to Europ sounded the alarm that the slow death of a share culture would lead inevitably to violence: only a 'militar humanism' could protect against war.[543] One well awa of the dangers in this period was the historian R.C. Ensor, who published an influential series of articles c the growing threat of German aggression, channellir the spirit of *Vigilans sed Aequus* thirty years earlier. Suc a serious attitude towards the simmering superpow established *The Spectator* as an increasingly importa journal for world affairs beyond the Commonwealth.

By 1938, the horrific picture was emerging wi some clarity. A reporter from Vienna, writing und the unhappy name of 'An Aryan Englishman', set out length the suffering of Jews in Austria. Of the gener populace he asked, 'How can a large group of people li lives of intense and perpetual sadism? ... for a group individuals to live lives of deliberate and lasting cruel to live in sadistic hatred of another group inside the community, and to use the language and action of th hatred, this is a phenomenon harder for the ordina man to begin to comprehend ... this is a phenomen encouraged and exploited by Fascism. Fascism extols

Fascism needs it. To resist it, we must resist Fascism.'[544] An article called 'The New Barbarism' decried 'an inhumanity so diabolical'. 'Never before in living memory, or for generations before that, has brute force divorced from every canon of morality been erected into national policy on a scale comparable with this.'[545] And yet, in what now seems editorial overreach to ensure a broad and balanced discussion, for the self-same issue Harris commissioned a piece from the journalist A.L. (Leo) Kennedy headed 'Is Hitler a Great Man?' Its uncritical answer was, 'For now, yes.'

As another global war loomed, the paper aligned with much of the press in backing Chamberlain, since 'even the most desperate attempt to save the peace was worth while'.[546] For his part, Harris argued that, if war was indeed to come, appeasement would help prepare the defence more than the offence. But, once hostilities began, the success of the Allies was the sole goal worthy of contemplation, and *The Spectator* accordingly changed gear. The spirit of Strachey's *Spectator* in the Great War was resurrected not just in this commitment to victory but also in Harris's support of state-controlled alcohol sales. Every little helped. The magazine's pages were soon playing host to the major battles of policy thrown up: in November 1939, for instance, Friedrich von Hayek offered his critique of 'Mr Keynes and War Costs'.[547]

In 1939, one of *The Spectator*'s most tangible links with the past at last retired: Robert Mackay had entered the printing staff in 1888, deep in the days of Townsend and Hutton. Described as a 'small man and very round – round everywhere possible',[548] he had cast for half a century a careful but informal eye over the paper that went to press, ensuring – insofar as he could – that its contents would not affront the Victorian sensibilities that held sway when he first joined the paper. With Mackay's exit, the past took its leave, and *The Spectator* at last started to acquire the feel of a fully twentieth-century organ.

Soon after war with Germany was declared on 3 September 1939, *The Spectator* moved to the Surrey printing works of Heinemann, at Kingswood near Walton Heath. The issue immediately following, reduced from forty-odd to twenty pages, reflected the challenging circumstances. But this *ad hoc* arrangement proved instantly unworkable – so, dismissing the very real dangers of aerial attack, *The Spectator* returned to its Gower Street garret. What is more, as a small gesture to keeping wartime spirits up, the paper launched a new series of literary competitions for book token prizes. The first, announced on 15 September 1939, was won by 'Hilary Trench' for her (his?) savvy parody of Henry James's epistolary style; in fact, Mr/s Trench was the established *Spectator* writer Graham Greene. Not long after, the third competition was won by a poem, 'The Happy Warrior', from 'DG' – initials that in fact disguised Graham Greene. The following month, the competition – on which classic work of literature one loathes and why – was won by a bulldozer demolition of Henry David Thoreau's *Walden* from the self-same Hilary Trench. Not long after, on 8 March 1940, Trench was to win again with a poem on the uncompromising subject of 'Finland'. This Greeneish dominance was indicative of the future, as he continued to subvert public competitions for decades. A particularly interesting case arose in 1980, when Competition no. 1,111 required contestants to submit an extract from an imaginary novel by Greene himself. Imagine the family gossip when the winner 'Sebastian Eleigh' emerged as Greene's brother Hugh, and the third-placed 'Katharine Onslow' turned out to be his sister Elisabeth. Poor old 'Colin Bates' was awarded no prize at all, so his puppet-master Graham Greene worked up the unsuccessful entry into the novel *The Captain and the Enemy* (1988).

In October 1940, Harris felt that it would be helpful to explain to *Spectator* readers what problems beset each issue that appeared during the Blitz:

When war broke out we, like all such journals, were faced with the prospect of loss of staff, loss of contributors, loss of advertisements, loss of revenue, loss of circulation, a severe rationing of paper... Of regular contributors – most notably Mr. Harold Nicolson – and reviewers at least 50 per cent. have become unavailable. Some have joined the Government, some the expanded Civil Service, many, of course, are in one of the fighting services; some have most deplorably gone Trappist with Chatham House at Oxford. The paper has to be produced today by a narrowed circle...

All such journals as *The Spectator* are permitted to use only one-third of their average pre-war paper consumption, and are prohibited from drawing on whatever reserves they may have been prudent enough to lay by. Since the average pre-war size of *The Spectator* was 48 pages, that would mean a reduction to no more than 16 pages if paper of the same weight and quality were still used. By substituting a much lighter and thinner paper we are able to maintain a 24-page issue, and hope to continue to do so, unsatisfactory though the expedient plainly is...

The single purpose of the staff will be to give [readers], so far as is possible under the limitations set by the present emergency, the kind of paper they have a right to look for.[549]

Throughout the war, the paper carried one leading article instead of two, four middles instead of eight, plus the essential column on military news from 'Strategicus' (the veteran war correspondent Herbert O'Neill), the charming distractions of Beach Thomas's 'Country Life', and Stephen Spender's 'Books of the Day' columns. In June 1941, paper rations forced the 'News of the Week', for so long a three-page running commentary on Everything You Needed To Know, to shrink to two pages. Still, the paper was able to carry out its primary role as in Rintoul's day – of conveying intelligence to keep a worried nation up to speed. At the same time, the correspondence pages served as a public exemplar of how the country could continue in civilised debate: high-profile letters appeared from C.S. Lewis (on the advantage of expounding Christian doctrine to laymen), George Orwell (on the perversity of the rifle bayonet), and J.R. Ackerley (on the inhumane treatment of clandestine homosexuals in Britain).[550]

Relatively powerless compared to those bearing arms,

The Spectator strove to help where it could. In 1944 for instance, it sought to raise £2,000 for a Shrine of Remembrance in St Paul's Anglican Cathedral, Valletta. Although it had suffered some damage in the Battle of Malta (1940–3), this building stood (rather like London's St Paul's) as a defiant symbol of the community's spirit. The shrine was intended 'to commemorate the men and women who died in defence of that heroic island'. The total was reached within two months and promptly put to good use. The Bishop of Gibraltar wrote to express my 'heartfelt thanks to readers of *The Spectator* for their handsome gesture of goodwill and for the substantial contribution they have made.'[552]

Despite the unutterable tragedies of the period, *The Spectator* had a good war. So central did it become as a weekly landmark in news and comment that, from 1939 to 1945, its circulation shot up by over 50 per cent, from 26,000 to 41,000. In the years that followed, the figure rose yet higher, to 53,000 in 1946–7, although 6,000 of these were bulk orders from the War Office. A surprise was in store, however: in February 1947, the paper's readership suddenly shot up to some 2.5 million. This was not the result of a sudden change in its contents; instead, for the first time in its 120-year history, *The Spectator* did not appear for two successive weeks. Because of the nationwide fuel crisis, Clement Attlee's government imposed a fortnightly ban on the appearance of weekly magazines, which suspended some 500 titles. The issues of 21 and 28 February therefore failed to drop through letterboxes. However, the daily press lent a helping hand. Although the *Observer* – which Harris had himself edited for three months in 1942 – offered the occasional chink of space in its pages, it was instead the *Daily Mail* which gifted *The Spectator* a full page on two successive Thursdays (20 and 27 Feb.). Beneath the typical *Spectator* masthead (complete with unbroken issue number) there appeared Nicolson's 'Marginal Comment', Janus' 'Notebook', a political column and a handful of book reviews. As minor compensation for the suspension, the editors of *The Spectator, New Statesman* and *Time and Tide* were summoned for colloquy on BBC radio for two successive Wednesday evenings.

Page 3 of the Daily Mail, *20 Feb. 1947*

99 Gower Street

When Harris complained of this enforced hiatus of highbrow weeklies to his fellow parliamentarian, Winston Churchill, the great man's gruff mien lightened up: 'Well, that's the first good thing I've heard of to come out of this mess.' Churchill and *The Spectator* had indeed not been on good terms for some time. Nevertheless, after receiving stout support from the paper throughout the war, he returned to reading it in the 1950s, when his son Randolph became a regular contributor. After the troubled fortnight was over, 'Janus' warmly thanked the *Daily Mail* for its hospitality:

> Nothing could be more ungrudging, or, it may be added, more efficient, than the service an historic daily has rendered to what I think may be called an historic weekly. It has been an unexpected association and to *The Spectator*, at any rate, a singularly agreeable one.[553]

From 1945 to 1950, Harris combined his editorship with being MP for the University of Cambridge. Although naturally Conservative in outlook, he stood as an Independent, thus troubling neither his *alma mater* nor the wary worthies of the Spectator Trust. But, feeling a duty to the Bright Young Things of the institution he represented, and recalling the success of his 'under-thirties' column, Harris devised an 'Undergraduate Page' to help channel the increasingly vibrant student voice. Given that Harris's columns had turned to fretting about the emergence of public condom machines,[554] the initiative was welcome. Advertisements were placed throughout university handbooks stating that any 'articles of sufficient merit contributed by undergraduates' would land 8 guineas when published. From such a simple beginning there followed 122 columns (Feb. 1949 to Oct. 1953). Successful submissions came mostly from Oxford, Cambridge and London – but several hailed from north of the border, the Continent and the United States. Unsurprisingly, these columns largely channelled the microcosmic concerns of the student press, but the initiative brought some much-needed vim to the correspondence pages, as well as being a gateway for many a future writer or politician. Among successful entrants were Norman St John-Stevas (7 Sep. 1951), Julian Critchley (28 Sep. 1951), both Julian

(6 Jan. 1950) and Giles Bullard (10 Feb. 1950), and Brian Widlake (11 Sep. 1952). The man who assessed most of the submitted manuscripts, Edward Hodgkin, later revealed that he managed to secure the winning spot for five of his cousins, something he regarded as 'a piece of nepotism which was subsequently more than justified'.[555]

In 1950 there came perhaps the first intimation that *The Spectator* was moving away from the traditional character of a weekly newspaper: special seasonal issues, for spring, summer and autumn, were produced for the calendar (as a Christmas issue had already been for three decades). However, their focus tended to be less on topical articles than on books of the season. These quarterly specials continued until the late 1960s (when they lapsed under Nigel Lawson) but have again become a typical *Spectator* feature since their resurrection in the mid-1980s. Another hint of the changing times after the war was the subtle rise in price – to 7d, 'the lowest figure economically practicable'[556] – in October 1951. Regrettably, the price of *Spectator* issues has only moved north since.

This sense of an old age giving way to something new was intensified when, in September 1950, Sir William Beach Thomas brought to a close his 'Country Life' column, written with only occasional and enforced interruptions since 1926. Many thousands of readers had been delighted and diverted by his reflections on the natural world and the humility it instils. As an encapsulation of his outlook, we can do no better than cite the last paragraph of his last column:

> The country scene is a department of art, not of science. The essential is the discovery of beauty, not of knowledge. Science comes second, and a bad second, to art. We do not listen to the nightingale in order to find out whether his song is erotic or polemic. We listen for the pleasure of the mood that the song and the scene engender.[557]

The great trio of *Spectator* sportsmen-naturalists (Cornish, Parker, Beach Thomas) thus came to their peaceful end after more than fifty years of chronicling the British countryside. 'BT' wrote two dozen books, but any randomly chosen *Spectator* column can still stand on its own merits. It is a shame that *The Spectator*'s long-standing love of nature has struggled to find proper expression in the subsequent seventy years.

One more change was to come, in December 1952, when Nicolson ended his weekly 'Marginal Comment'. When he made the surprise announcement, he was characteristically frank about his thinking:

> I am aware that many readers will suppose that I have left my post owing to some quarrel with the proprietors, editor, assistant editor, or managers of this weekly, and that the cause of this quarrel was either a profound conflict of political or theological opinion or else the offer of fat monetary payments by some one else. May I dispel such illusions? In all seriousness, I do not believe that the history of journalism can show a more shining example of amicable co-operation as that which for all these years has existed between the Editor and myself. Never once has he asked me to alter a single line of my articles; week after week he has corrected my somewhat specialised spelling and passed the typescript on to the printers without even a sigh of protest. It was not a question of agreement or disagreement: it was an instance of symbiosis... I wish to postpone the date when my friends will whisper sadly among each other that I am becoming, have in fact become, a bore. Essays of this kind must also, while suggesting habits of reflection, spring from a spontaneous impulse and an authentic mood. The moment one has to search the mind and memory for a Friday theme a sense of strain comes over one; no marginal comment should be written with an effort if it is to be authentic. People should refrain from dancing once the joints begin to creak.[558]

In a Notebook piece under the heading 'The Ideal Contributor', Janus repeated praise of Nicolson as 'unquestionably the outstanding essayist of the day', before adding that his long-standing column was always so reliable that 'it alone of all the contributions for the week's issue has gone straight to the printer unread'.[559]

Despite several incipient changes, *The Spectator* of 1953 was still very much the paper of 1925.[560] It opened with the three-page account of the week's news, the leader, Janus' Notebook, four to six 'middles' (then the vogue name for sub-leaders), a summary of the arts, correspondence, a country life column, book reviews, a financial column, before a sports column and competition added a splash of play. But this unchanged template of *The Spectator* seemed increasingly out of step as the Fifties found their feet. It would not do the trick simply to host a one-off essay by Jean-Paul Sartre, as curiously happened in 1951.[561] Once more, as in the last days of Strachey, the paper was in urgent need of new blood.

Thus, at the end of March 1953, Harris's twenty-one-year tenure finally came to its end. This was not at his own instance, but, like most with such long service behind them, he was eased out by others, much to his displeasure. The twin proprietors Wrench and Watson, themselves no spring chickens, had decided that it was time 'to give the younger men a chance'.[562] The last sentence of his (i.e. Janus') Notebook turned to Shakespeare to convey the gravity of feeling: 'Parting, Juliet said, is such sweet sorrow. I deny the adjective and double-stress the noun.' On his sacking, copious letters of condolence poured in. Anthony Eden told him that the paper's 'judgments and comments have been so balanced and fair, that a great many who follow your writings, and among them, will feel that something has been lost out of our week-ends.'[563] Although Harris was aggrieved, he remained magnanimous. After his autobiography was well reviewed by *The Spectator* in May 1954, and indeed advertised on the front page, he agreed to take up the post of regular reviewer – but his death, in January 1955, scuppered any hopes of that new relationship.

National obituaries were warm and widespread. *The Times* spoke for many in noting that Harris 'was able to give the *Spectator* a moral authority that was admired even by those who disagreed with its opinions.'[564] Scott-James recalled in *The Spectator*'s (oddly rather stinting) obituary that Harris's

> objectives were to be informed, to be frank, and to develop a firm and consistent line which was the *Spectator*'s line – and, it should be added, to be interesting and readable. His main personal interests were political, religious, ethical and, in general, practical. His views were severely grounded on common sense... Never did he cease to be primarily a journalist, devoted to the journal he served.[565]

A colleague of his final years remembered that the attitude of Harris's co-workers

> changed by a process which is perhaps most usual in the case of boys observing a headmaster as they go through their school years. It began with awe, developed into respect, and ended as a curious form of affection in which traces of the two former impressions still remained.[566]

Where, then, to find fresh energy? To keep the ship stable, the answer was from post-war staff members. Edward Hodgkin (a fellow Quaker) had joined as the number three in 1948, and in the following year Derek Hudson arrived as literary editor, after distinguished war service at *The Times*. But there was a more exciting prospect to consider: a man who had left school at fourteen, worked in a margarine factory, and then fought his way through his local college, through Oxford, through the Cabinet Office and *The Economist* – a man, indeed, who would later publish a manifesto on advertising. Here was someone going places – and *The Spectator* was ready to hitch a ride.

VI

From Paper to Magazine

1953–1975

The Spectator of 1952, a contributor later recalled, was 'a fossil paper, edited by a dodo, and circulating among a declining readership of coelocanths.'[567] Although its circulation in the preceding decade had reached its highest point ever, the paper's readership was steadily dying away – for the most part literally. It would therefore take a bold and unconventional man to shake *The Spectator* out of its pre-war format. That man turned out to be WALTER CECIL TAPLIN (1910–86). Despite leaving his school in Southampton with no qualifications, he won via night classes an exhibition to the city's university and then a scholarship to read History at The Queen's College, Oxford. After a brief spell at *The Economist*, he worked for the War Cabinet in the Central Statistical Office. Despite joining the staff of *The Spectator* in 1946 as its first 'deputy editor', he continued over subsequent years to produce material for the Information Research Department. As one who was later to edit *Accountancy* (1961–71) and *Accounting and Business Research* (1971–5), Taplin certainly knew his beans.

Full of energy, new ideas and free-market enthusiasm, he was willing and able to reshape the title. He at once appointed Iain Hamilton, who had joined the team the year before, as his deputy. But nervous proprietors tend to give with one hand and take with the other: not long after Taplin took control, he was told by Sir Angus Watson that 'no change in the present features of the paper will be made by the new Editor for a month, and then only after careful consultation.'[568] Rather than arrest any change at all, this measure presumably sought to avoid causing more superannuated readers any sudden heart troubles. The paper was to be 'opposed to Socialism, Communism, and Nationalisation.' And, lest some

iconoclastic idea emerge, 'When i[n] doubt on questions of policy, follo[w] the *Manchester Guardian*, the *Time[s]* and the *Daily Telegraph*.'[569]

An irrefutable excuse for som[e] much-needed colour was provide[d] by a special issue within the first tw[o] months of Taplin's editorship. I[n] May 1953, the paper had two joi[nt] causes for celebration: its own 125t[h] anniversary, and the coronation o[f] Queen Elizabeth II, the monarch [it] would come to revere the most. As [a] fitting sign of its enthusiasm, and i[ts] willingness to evolve, *The Spectat[or]* used this anniversary to deploy i[ts] first ever front-cover illustration, [a] full-colour crown, beneath its ow[n] boast of existing 'through eig[ht] reigns'. Contemporary covers gav[e] the *Spectator* masthead its distinctiv[e] red colour, and announced th[e] chief contents of the issue. This, [as] a specific date can exist for what [is] necessarily a gradual process, is th[e]

ISSUES FOR 8 AND 15 MAY 1953

most probable moment at which *The Spectator* transitioned from a leading newspaper to vibrant news magazine. Certainly the credit for that successful evolution lies with the editorship of Walter Taplin.

With the significant loss of Nicolson's 'Marginal Comment' and Harris's 'Janus' columns, the magazine urgently needed fresh writing. Taplin 'gave the staff a pep-talk. What could we do to liven things up, get ourselves talked about, be more influential, more sensational, and so more circulation-building, more money-making?'[70] Several solutions arose. For a start, he introduced young guns such as Kingsley Amis, Henry Fairlie, John Wain and Brian Inglis to become frequent contributors – and, in the case of the last, a future editor. The unfailingly outspoken Kenneth Tynan had already been taken on as theatre reviewer in 1951 – doubtless at the suggestion of Harris. More notably, Taplin first introduced, in October 1953, a section specifically for female contributors: under the heading *Spectatrix* there appeared a series of ten essays with titles such as 'The art of giving', 'The why-not school of fashion', and 'Make mine andante'. Defending the initiative, Taplin reported a recent dig in *The Guardian,* about 'the quiet masculine atmosphere of Gower Street'. Taplin retorted that the magazine had women among its permanent staff and regular contributors. 'We know the paper is widely read by women, and there has

SPECTATOR COMPETITION FOR SCHOOLS

The Spectator offers three prizes, each of books to the value of eight guineas, for articles to be written by boys and girls in schools in the United Kingdom. Entries should be in the form of

A Spectator Leading Article, or

A Middle Article, or

A Review Article on any book which has appeared in the past three years.

Articles, which need not be typed, should be of about 1,200 words and must reach the Spectator office (99 Gower Street, W.C.1) by December 31st, 1953. The name of the school which the entrant attends should be given at the head of the article, and envelopes should be marked "Schools." The results will be announced during January.

FIRST NOTICE OF *THE SPECTATOR*'S COMPETITION FOR SCHOOLS, 20 NOV. 1953

never been any attempt to maintain a "masculine" atmosphere in it.' This change, among others, was 'consistent with one of the oldest and most cherished traditions of the *Spectator* – that of keeping up with the times.'[71]

Another encouraging sign that Taplin was brimming with new ideas was *The Spectator*'s 'Competition for Schools', first launched that November. The contest proved to be a great success, if only for four years. Among its remarkable set of winners was Anthea Loveday Veronica Mander (later Lahr), whose 1955 winning story 'Queen of the Island' is notable for being the youngest piece of original writing published by *The Spectator*: the author was nine.[72] That same first competition also elicited an article from Tom Pulvertaft, a fourteen-year-old, on science fiction: remarkably, however, he requested that it be considered by the magazine not for the school competition but for normal publication. In the genuinely adventurous world of Taplin's *Spectator,* this was indeed possible – and it duly appeared, on 11 December 1953.

A clear statement of the new creative energy fuelling the back half of the magazine was given by an unsigned leader – the first 'literary leading article' – which opened the 'Autumn books' section of October 1954. Headed 'In the Movement', its author, the literary editor John Scott, surveyed a new wave of British writers who seemed to be at the threshold of something new: Donald Davie, Thom Gunn, John Wain, Kingsley Amis and Iris Murdoch. This was, indeed, a different world from recent *Spectator* fare, such as Laurence Housman's *The Faithful Servant,* a one-scene play about Queen Victoria receiving a McGonagall poem.[573] Scott, writing in a tone he later called 'brisk, challenging and dismissive',[574] observed that 'nothing dates literary fashions so certainly as the emergence of a new movement, and within the last year or so, signs are multiplying that such a thing is, once again, emerging.' To these new writers he gave not just a mission statement but a brand:

The Movement, as well as being anti-phoney, is anti-wet; sceptical, robust, ironic, prepared to be as comfortable as possible in a wicked, commercial, threatened world which doesn't look, anyway, as if it's going to be changed much by a couple of handfuls of young English writers.[575]

The new writers that formed The Movement in turn contributed prose and verse to the magazine's pages. Nevertheless, a *Spectator* regular such as Evelyn Waugh wrote in with the plea to 'let the young people of today get on with their work alone and be treated to the courtesy of individual attention. They are the less, not the more, interesting, if they are treated as a "Movement".'[576] Somewhat more trenchantly, Kingsley Amis wrote to a friend 'what a load of bullshit all that was'.[577] His correspondent was a similarly cynical thirty-something who had been persuaded by Scott to publish several new poems above the name of Philip Larkin.[578] Though so often mocked for being behind the literary curve, *The Spectator* now

found itself in the vanguard.

Other, admittedly older, writers gave the magazine some extra verve: J.P.W. 'Curly' Mallalieu, Labour MP for Huddersfield, wrote on sport ('Sporting Aspect(s)', 1953–4, the first such dedicated column),[579] John Betjeman on architecture ('City and Suburban', 1954–8), Nicholas Davenport on money matters ('Finance and Investment', 1953–79, taking over the multi-authored column of 'Custos'), and Sir Compton Mackenzie on all manner of things ('Sidelight', 1953–5).

The marked change in the magazine's feel was widely appreciated. *The Guardian* now noted that Taplin had 'made it more a young man's paper than it had been for years'[580] – in fact, one could quite easily say 'than ever'. Nicolson observed from the sidelines 'the interesting experiment in rejuvenation that the veteran is at present undergoing'.[581] But such a metamorphosis was soon to be jeopardised. Although he did not know it, Taplin's promotion to the editorship had been intended simply as a stop-gap until the proprietors had found a more reliable pair of political hands to steer the ship. To that end, T.E. ('Peter') Utley, a celebrated leader-writer for *The Times* since the war, was persuaded by Wrench to join *The Spectator* in the autumn of 1954. A decade younger than Taplin, at thirty-three, he was given to understand that, having learned the ropes, he would be raised to editor. Utley, in

fact, never did land the promise post: the purchase of the paper b a new owner in December 1954 pu paid to his editorial prospects.

It was the twenty-seven-year old IAN HEDWORTH JOHN LITTL GILMOUR (1926–2007) who wa being courted as the new owner liking what he saw, he formall became the proprietor of Th *Spectator* on 7 December 1954 for £75,000 (c. £1.9 million). Th outgoing owners presumably fe that they were increasingly old me in a young bucks' game. Gilmour acquisition was abetted by the fa that Sir Angus Watson mistaken supposed him to be the son of S John Gilmour Bt, Home Secreta in the 1930s. But, alas, his father w a different Gilmour baronet. Aft following in Strachey's footstep reading History at Balliol (II. he served for three years with th Grenadier Guards. Though calle to the Bar in 1952, he was more eag to busy himself in other spheres influence – journalism, politics ar society at large.

Gilmour's presence wa immediately felt, as he show a keen interest in controllir the editorial side. Taplin in tu reached the frustrated conclusi that the magazine was no long his to edit. Although his contra lasted until April 1955, he offer his resignation that November. T next day brought the announceme that Utley would serve as associa editor under a new 'acting edito Iain Hamilton, who had joined t magazine in 1953, after plying his trade on the *Daily Sketch*. Betjeman, one of Taplin's star recruits, wrote in sympathy that he was 'a jolly good editor ... for whom one was pleased and honoured to work, who had made *The Spectator* far less dull and with whom one felt secure.'[582] Charles Seaton, who had joined the magazine in 1953 with Taplin's support – first as sub-editor but soon enough as librarian, archivist and 'Lord High everything else'[583] – later spoke of Taplin as the best editor he had encountered in his forty-two years at the magazine.

By early December, the dust had settled at Gower Street: Gilmour himself was to be editor and Hamilton associate editor. Somewhat predictably, Utley's nine-month stint, in which he was rebranded as 'political advisor', was awkward, since his formal relationship to Hamilton and Gilmour was frustratingly opaque. Gilmour, it seems, vetoed Utley's editorship because he wanted the editor personally to see the paper through the press – a curiously short-sighted attitude to Utley's blindness. After the election of May 1955, Utley left Gower Street for a most distinguished career in journalism, particularly at the *Daily Telegraph*. The following year Brian Inglis joined as associate editor, becoming deputy editor on Hamilton's exit in 56: both largely had responsibility for the rear half of the magazine. Despite Taplin's transformative work at the helm, *The Spectator* could afford such political manoeuvring.

The paper's circulation was still gradually decreasing, then hovering around 37,000.

A new owner – and an editor who had no prior association at all with the magazine – allowed for a new assertion of principles. Gilmour advertised the opening leader of 1955 with the cover headline 'The Independence of *The Spectator*'. What is more, it was printed on the very first page, thus taking the place of the news summary that had opened the magazine, without fail, since its inception. It is true that, under Taplin's editorship, the two- or three-page 'News of the Week' section (now opening with its own topical headline) was steadily shrinking in size, and issued with an increasingly strong editorial steer. But Gilmour wanted the voice of his *Spectator* to pipe up as soon as the cover was lifted.[584] His manifesto was unapologetically strident:

> To apply in every field tolerant but rigorous standards of criticism and, in the process, not to forget that the reader must be entertained – that is the *Spectator*'s duty... We must now and always look for the ground on which to take our stand. In politics, at least, one broad and challenging division is evident today – the division between, on the one hand, those who believe that the future of the world depends largely on the quality and energy of individuals acting freely and, on the other, those

who believe that it rests on the power of the state to impose a rational social order. It is the first of these philosophies which the *Spectator* embraces, and it is in the light of it that the day-to-day issues of contemporary politics will be discussed.

The statement concludes by noting that the Conservatives best support this ethos for the time being, and yet giving the assurance that his paper is not 'invariably committed to supporting any party'.[585]

Gilmour was described by *The Guardian* of the day as 'a high-minded, sharp-minded, questioning young man with a rather mystical faith in the mission of the Tory party and the Church of England.'[586] Some observers expressed the hope that his magazine would 'develop lines of thought on a rather Burke-brought-up-to-date kind of Conservatism'.[587] For political comment, however, Gilmour decided to appoint for *The Spectator* the first modern political commentator – not only of the magazine but in the British press. This was the renegade Scotsman Henry Fairlie – a keen toper, incorrigible cad and instinctive iconoclast. Having joined the staff in December 1954, he succeeded over the next sixteen months in setting the mould of the well-informed and sharp-tongued columnist: his treatment of MPs – a healthy mix of admiration, suspicion and incredulity – was new in the sphere of serious journalism. Fairlie's attacks –

under the pseudonym of 'Trimmer' for their first few months – were wide-ranging and unprejudiced: it was he, for instance, who brought into the mainstream the now ubiquitous notion of 'The Establishment'. In the wake of the Burgess and Maclean spy revelations of 1955, it was Fairlie's column – prompted by Peregrine Worsthorne of the *Daily Telegraph* – which pointedly asked how such a breach of trust and power could have occurred for so long at such lofty levels of society. In doing so, he shone a lurid light on the quiet spheres of soft power:

> By the 'Establishment' I do not mean only the centres of official power – though they are certainly part of it – but rather the whole matrix of official and social relations within which power is exercised. The exercise of power in Britain (more specifically, in England) cannot be understood unless it is recognised that it is exercised socially. Anyone who has at any point been close to the exercise of power will know what I mean when I say that the 'Establishment' can be seen at work in the activities of not only the Prime Minister, the Archbishop of Canterbury and the Earl Marshal, but such lesser mortals as the chairman of the Arts Council, the director-general of the BBC, and even the editor for the *Times Literary Supplement*.[588]

The press, as well as the letters pages, went wild. But the term has been in regular (typically pejorative) use ever since. Readers rapidly realised that *The Spectator* was regaining a Rintoulian bite. Still, for all the seriousness of the observations that Fairlie made, the magazine also saw the more playful side of the world it lived in: the Christmas issue for 1955 allowed readers to try their hand at 'The Establishment Game', a double-page board-game that challenged players to scale the echelons of power 'without really doing anything'.[589] The tone can be gauged from a few randomly chosen squares:

> 18. Joins *Manchester Guardian*. Writes series of 35 articles on export of Irish donkeys to Belgium. Awarded Gold Medal of the RSPCA. +1

> 20. Translation of German verse rejected by 47 publishers. (Miss a turn.)

> 31. Holiday at Cannes with Aly Khan. Thrown out of Casino at Monte Carlo for threats against croupier. Secures £5,000 damages from Prince Rainier and Aristotle Onassis. (Move to 37.) +50

> 57. Elected to Athenaeum under Rule 2. Fellow of All Souls. Chairman of Lloyds Bank. Vice-Chairman of Arts Council. Interviewed by Richard Dimbleby. +10

The text emanated from the hand of 'Dr Aloysius C. Pepper', perhaps a veil for Gilmour himself. At any rate, this figure's subsequent send-up of 'The Movement' ('At the Poetry Reading') shows how quickly *The Spectator* could abandon its literary fancies.[590]

As another sign that *The Spectator* was shaking off some of its stuffier relations with The Establishment, Fairlie's seminal piece stood above the first political cartoon in *The Spectator*'s history. The half-page skit by 'Emmwood' (John Musgrave Wood) depicts Macmillan helplessly tied up during the Cypriot crisis and suffering a collective attack from Greece, Turkey and the Greek Cypriot separatist guerrillas EOKA.

From this point onwards, cartoons steadily became a more important part of *The Spectator*. Although their frequency has waxed and waned somewhat over subsequent editors, for many readers they have been one of the magazine's most enjoyable elements. Alongside the great names of Quentin Blake, Trog (Wally Fawkes), Gerald Scarfe, Peter Brookes, Nicholas Garland and Morten Morland, it is Michael Heath who has been the most important presence behind the magazine's cartoons and cartoonists. Having first drawn for the magazine in 1959, he has now enlivened its pages for over sixty years; for the last thirty, he has served as cartoons editor, nourishing new talent as well as humouring old. It is high time that the best

HE SPECTATOR'S FIRST POLITICAL CARTOON (EMMWOOD, 25 SEP. 1955)

pectator cartoons from the last even decades – which crop up here nd there in occasional annuals[591] were gathered into a much more mprehensive collection.

To return to Fairlie, it was nfortunate but inevitable that e fatter cheque books of Fleet reet carried away the firebrand of ower Street. By the end of June 56, he was gone, although his line occasionally ignited *Spectator* ges in subsequent years. His placement, the Conservative MP harles Curran, was manifestly a me-down, but the Suez Crisis at November forced him to duck t. This rapid exit ushered in the xt great political columnist at he *Spectator* – Bernard Levin. A aduate of the LSE before joining e Conservative weekly *Truth*, here s a fearless twenty-eight-year-old o readily accepted Gilmour's

proposal to dissect Parliament under the pseudonym 'Taper'. This was not to give him the freedom to offend – Levin could happily do that *propria persona* – but to give Gilmour the ability to sub in someone else, should the unpredictable and untested Levin not work out.

Any such doubts were wholly misplaced. Taper's first column, of 25 January 1957, showed an arrant disregard for the election of Harold Macmillan as the new prime minister:

Enthusiasm is an art; and artless indeed was the Tory welcome for Mr. Macmillan as, half-way through Question Time, he stepped stately in, the first British Prime Minister for many years with fallen arches. The cheers were little more than perfunctory... While the

dust of Suez settles slowly on the fires of the Labour Party, the Government can – must – be getting on with the job of scraping the rust off the engines and moving out of harbour.

As Levin surveyed the mixed bag of MPs (or 'fatheads' as he regularly dubbed them) in the chamber (the 'sixth ugliest building in the British Isles'), he felt no fear. He happily ridiculed the high-and-mighty: who else, at that time, could rebrand Sir Reginald Manningham-Buller, the Attorney General, as Sir Reginald Bullying-Manner? On learning that a new *Spectator* writer was being paid a lower wage than the rest of the staff, he even stormed into Gilmour's office and demanded instant action: 'You own it. Why not sell a couple of grouse moors?'[592] A few years later, while delivering a typically sharp-tongued monologue on the satirical television show *That Was The Week That Was*, he was punched in the face by Desmond Leslie in front of an audience of eleven million. Yet Levin had found in *The Spectator* a journal and editor that could not only handle him but could help him become 'the father of the modern parliamentary sketch'.[593]

A contemporary advertisement reaffirmed the magazine's newfound swagger:

The Spectator is a journal of opinion. Throughout its pages it sets out to stimulate people who think. Its readers sometimes violently disagree with its comment. That is fine. For a dull prescription of bromide would soon kill both journal and readers.[594]

Gilmour was especially keen to push his *Spectator* as an organ of libertarianism, an easier course now that Watson and Wrench had lost any power of veto. Two long-overdue causes that the magazine pressed particularly hard were the ending of capital punishment (which Harris had long fought for) and the decriminalisation of homosexuality (which was still a taboo). When the British model Ruth Ellis was hanged at Holloway, on 13 July 1955, *The Spectator* issued an outraged leader – one controversial for its time in the Tory party and the populace at large:

It is no longer a matter for surprise that Englishmen deplore bull-fighting but delight in hanging. Hanging has become the national sport. While a juicy murder trial is on, or in the period before a murderer is executed, provided that he or she has caught the public fancy owing to there being a sexual element in the crime, even Test matches are driven from the place of honour on the front pages of the popular press. Anything to do with the extinction of a fellow human being has a fascination for the people of this country...

Capital punishment is absolutely indefensible... There is no evidence whatsoever that capital punishment is more of a deterrent to murder than is imprisonment... The case against it is largely empirical; the case for it is emotional and doctrinaire. It might, therefore, have been expected that the Conservative Party, the party of empiricism, would support abolition. But in the past debate all but seventeen voted for the death penalty.[595]

The correspondence pages carried outraged responses from many readers with both feet in the past. One tartly objected that 'your leading article, with all its fictitious statement, its woeful exaggerations and its brutal innuendoes, looks suspiciously like the maudlin stuff which is the outcome of a hangover.'[596] Gilmour doubled down, issuing from *The Spectator* office a pamphlet co-written with Lord Altrincham (John Grigg) on Timothy Evans, wrongly hanged in 1950.[597] And *The Spectator*, over a succession of editors, continued to fight hard until that law at last changed in 1965.

As another mark of his 'progressive Conservatism', Gilmour also took up the cause of decriminalising homosexuality from the very start of his editorship.[598] In January 1955, *The Spectator* ran a candid autobiographical article, giving 'a biological homosexual's view'. The writer, understandably not named, objected that homosexuals were 'debarred from a permanent and publicly esteemed cohabitation with a loved and loving partner'.[599] This was a period in which the *News of the World* called homosexuality 'the evil in our midst',[600] and the *Sunday Pictorial* published a three-part series on 'evil men', which argued that this 'unnatural service' produced 'the horrors of Hitlerite corruption' in Germany, ruined classical Greece and would in turn destroy Britain.[601] In 1954, Lord Montagu of Beaulieu was imprisoned for a year for 'consensual homosexual offences' with some guests on his private estate; two friends received eighteen months. This event was only the most prominent of the thousands of criminal trials for homosexual activity brought annually in 1950s Britain. So harsh and inhumane a verdict prompted Gilmour to write a 2,500-word broadside in his own name, asserting that the trial was prejudiced by police malpractice. In order to show that most of the public was with him, he opened up the pages of *The Spectator* to frank discussion of the issue. As impassioned letters flowed in from every quarter, his magazine campaigned vigorously for a Royal Commission on the subject.

When the Wolfenden Report of 1957 made the recommendation that homosexuality be legalised in private between adults over twenty-one, most in Britain were appalled. *The Spectator*, by contrast, saw the prospect as the only truly human route forward:

Whatever feelings of revulsion homosexual actions may arouse, the law on this point is utterly irrational and illogical. It is impossible to argue that homosexual actions between consenting males are more anti-social than adultery, fornication, or homosexual actions between consenting females, none of which are crimes. Not only is the law unjust in conception, it is almost inevitably unjust in practice. Save in very exceptional circumstances a prosecution can only be brought on the evidence of one of the parties concerned, who is necessarily as guilty as the party who is prosecuted. Indeed it was a particularly unfair prosecution of this sort which was largely responsible for the setting up of the Wolfenden Committee, and it is pleasantly ironical that the actions of those concerned in that case should have led to a recommendation that the law should be changed.[603]

The open expression of such attitudes prompted widespread hostility in the press. John Gordon, the editor-in-chief of the *Sunday Express*, dubbed *The Spectator* 'the Bugger's Bugle' for having trumpeted reform so loudly. But its heels dragged throughout Macmillan's prime-ministerial terms (1957–63), the magazine remained a vocal campaigner. In 1960, three gay men used *The Spectator* to come out: the joint

letter in their names complained that homosexuality 'is often called a problem, but is only a problem because of the prevailing attitude towards it and because of the ludicrous law.'[604] Eventually, in 1967, the battle was won and the first wave of decriminalisation achieved. The magazine's support of these and other liberal causes, such as denouncing the Lord Chamberlain's censorship of the theatre and the Official Secrets Act, were not going unnoticed. In 1958, a reader and politician by the name of Michael Foot told the magazine that 'no journal in Britain has established a higher reputation than *The Spectator* for the persistent advocacy of a humane administration of the law or the reform of inhumane laws'.[605]

Gilmour continued to move *The Spectator* further into the magazine mould: in 1955, he introduced a new series of national specials, gathering writers together to discuss the present state of (parts of) the Union. The first such issue, predictably enough on Scotland, included eighteen pages of articles on Scottish affairs – by Lord Dalkeith, Sir Compton Mackenzie, Sir William Darling, Moray McLaren, Neil Gunn, and several others.[606] The following year, Gilmour added a special on Ireland to a second on Scotland; in 1957, Ulster joined the team. (An English special, however, would not appear until 2008;[607] there has never – yet – been a Welsh special.)

Although the price rose again to 9d in April 1956, readers felt that they

were getting good value for money. No one, it seemed, complained about the sudden expansion from two to three columns per page in the first issue of 1957, a space-saving innovation (and exemplified in this chapter's layout) that has remained ever since.[608] The literary scene continued to be well represented; Iris Murdoch and Patrick Leigh Fermor were occasional reviewers,[609] alongside heavyweights such as A.J. Ayer and Gilbert Ryle;[610] Osbert Lancaster wrote a skit on the road proposed through Christ Church Meadow in Oxford,[611] and four poems appeared from Ted Hughes in the summer of 1957.[612]

In that year, Peter Fleming (as Strix) wrote a piece parodying the trivial and thoughtless ways in which contemporary journalists criticised the royal family. He gave it a suitably irrelevant headline: 'Does Prince Philip cheat at Billiard Fives?' However, because of limited space on the page, the headline had to be changed at the last moment to 'Does Prince Philip cheat at Tiddlywinks?'[613] Although Prince Philip was not yet Chancellor of the University of Cambridge (1976–2011), some undergraduates were inspired to challenge him to a game of tiddlywinks to set this fresh controversy straight. Although the Prince graciously declined their invitation, he nominated that gaggle of wags The Goons to play in his stead. The match was a sell-out in the city's Guildhall, and – quite incredibly – given television coverage. An introductory message was read from the Prince:

> I wish the Cambridge team to lose and my incomparable champions to win a resounding and stereophonic victory. At one time I had hoped to join my champions but, unfortunately, while practising secretly, I pulled an important muscle in the second or tiddly joint of my winking finger.

His charges unfortunately lost – but HRH did present a trophy, 'The Silver Wink', to be awarded annually at the British Inter-University Championships. The curiosity of this episode is that, save for the intervention of a pernickety *Spec.* sub-editor, would any of it have happened?

Although now advertised as 'the weekly review of outspoken comment', *The Spectator* under Gilmour did sometimes find that such outspoken comment dropped it into painfully hot water. Indeed, much the most high-profile court case in *The Spectator*'s history arose that same year, when the Labour politicians Aneurin Bevan, Morgan Phillips and Richard Crossman sued for defamation over a *Spectator* article – 'Death in Venice' by Jenny Nicolson – which politely suggested that they seemed punch-drunk while abroad on business.[614] Her account of these grandees' tottering around the Italian Socialist Party conference noted that they 'puzzled

the Italians by their capacity to fill themselves like tanks with whisky ... the Italians were never sure if the British delegation was sober.' In the end, despite a tight-lipped apology in the magazine, the notorious Lord Chief Justice Goddard – himself pilloried in *The Spectator* about other controversial cases – found in favour of the defendants, demanding that damages of £2,500 be paid to each of them, plus £5,000 in costs (now some £200,000). The sting of this punishment sharpened when Crossman later boasted that they were indeed all sloshed – and had thus knowingly committed perjury. Forty years later, Gilmour candidly reflected:

> What our contributor said would probably not be considered defamatory today. But it was so considered 40 years ago, and we should not have printed it. Nevertheless it was true. We therefore proceeded under the naïve delusion that three leading Labour party figures, when it came to the point, would not want to commit perjury for money... But they were greedy and so opted to go to court, where by dint of incompetence on our side – quite a lot of it mine – shameless lying under oath by the plaintiffs, bending of the rules by their QC, and blatant bias by the Lord Chief Justice Goddard, whom we had recently criticised strongly on other grounds, they easily won the case.[615]

Many readers were less shocked by this indiscreet report than by the decision of Gilmour and Inglis to oppose the government on the Suez Crisis; *The Spectator* consistently denounced the Egyptian invasion as a grievous mistake and professed its complete lack of confidence in the prime minister, Sir Anthony Eden, who failed to see the direction in which the Middle East was headed. Such a sharp turn against the serving Conservative government prompted a thousand or more cancellations of subscription, and a damaging decline in established advertisers. Unperturbed, *The Spectator* ran in 1959 a devastating 10,000-word exposé by Erskine Childers of the collusion that underpinned the whole sorry episode.[616]

All in all, the turbulent events of 1957–8 had not been kind to *The Spectator*. Circulation was not improving, as new readers only took the place of those now giving it up: it was a double-edged sword to be ushering in the spirit of the Sixties ahead of Father Time. John Betjeman's much-read column on architecture ended in 1958; and the deputy editor, Brian Inglis, tried to resign that year to free up some much-needed time for his marriage, honeymoon and literary work. Aware that a change of guard was necessary, Gilmour raised the stakes by offering Inglis the editorship, a post he agreed to take up at the beginning of 1959. To amuse himself while Inglis was away, and to mark the end of his provocative tenure as editor

Gilmour devised a *Monopoly*-based board game: rather than competing for property, players fought it out as ambitious journalists-cum-politicians – à la Gilmour himself. The joke was a good one, and readers were rewarded with the gameplay, board and cards for *Spectopoly* in the issue for 26 December 1958.

BRIAN ST JOHN INGLIS (1916–93) thus became the first Irishman at the helm of *The Spectator*. He had, however, like the Ulsterman Wrench, spent much of his life outside that country, being educated at The Dragon, Shrewsbury and Magdalen, Oxford (History, First). Having served in the RAF as a squadron leader mentioned in despatches, his subsequent course was remarkably varied: he wrote for the *Irish Times*, turned out a PhD in History at University College Dublin, and went on to lecture there in Economics (1951–3). Most tellingly, his doctoral thesis, on the freedom of the press in Ireland 1784–1841 (1951), augured very well for *The Spectator*.

Inglis had been assistant, and later deputy, editor under Gilmour for the previous four years. In his own colourful account of that period,[617] he talked of himself as effectively acting editor, with only the occasional steer from Gilmour. Whether or not the latter was responsible for much of the leader-writing, it is striking that his first signed article did not appear for nine months, until August 1955. Inglis had since acquired for himself a growing public profile by presenting the BBC programme

What the Papers Say from 1956; later, after leaving *The Spectator*, he would host *All Our Yesterdays* – a celebrated documentary series on the build-up to World War II – for a decade.

The Spectator under Inglis's editorship continued its movement away from a newspaper. The 'Portrait of the Week', reduced to a single-page first-page column by the end of Gilmour's editorship, was made yet snappier. But Inglis was able to make the magazine perhaps the most influential it had ever been in calling upon the major literary figures of the day. Its appeal could hardly have been financial, as the standard rate for copy was only £10 per thousand words. Yet readers could relish Larkin on Auden (15 July 1960), Auden on Beethoven (10 Nov. 1961), Golding on Tolstoy (8 Sep. 1961), Amis on Nabokov (6 Nov. 1959) or on Waugh (27 Oct. 1961). Ian Fleming, now much more famous than his brother-columnist Peter, wrote several times, including on what he would do as prime minister (9 Oct. 1959); E.M. Forster contributed now and then, for instance on why election broadcasts should be ignored (2 Oct. 1959). Even Harold Pinter offered up a short sketch, *The Black and White* (1 July 1960).

With talent like this to call upon, *The Spectator* could raise two fingers if it fancied: when the playwright and politician William Douglas-Home wrote to complain about the arts editor Alan Brien's withering review of his comedy *Aunt Edwina*, Brien printed a curt response: 'Please stop

this dripping-water torture about your sad, soppy, dull, little play, Mr. Home. I had to sit through that out of a mistaken sense of duty – haven't I suffered enough?'[618] Among other high-class writers were Bamber Gascoigne on theatre, Isabel Quigly on film, Raymond Postgate and Elizabeth David on food, and Cyril Ray on wine. Poetry was again as rife as it had been in the 1920s, including more verse from Ted Hughes.[619]

In 1959, Inglis built on Taplin's *Spectatrix* series by introducing a new – and ground-breaking – feature: 'Roundabout', written by Katharine Whitehorn, a recruit from *Woman's Own* after Alan Brien ran out of energy and ideas. Her column – which cast 'a long, cool, very feminine look on the world'[620] – was one of the first in the national press that focused on contemporary female issues. There is no doubting that *The Spectator* had (in fact, has) always attracted a predominantly male readership, but this move to broaden its circulation seemed to find widespread favour. It was not long before other daily and weekly papers saw that they too needed to cater, without condescension, for a more diverse readership. Inglis's *Spectator* was keen to expand this new demographic, and bolstered 'Roundabout' with a domestic column called 'Consuming interest'. Written by the ambiguously gendered 'Leslie Adrien' – and primarily penned by Amy Landreth and Jean Robertson – it was pitched as a column that 'no intelligent woman (or man, for that matter) should be without'.[621]

All of this inventive evolution seemed to be working. Under the tenures of Taplin and Gilmour, from 1953 through to 1959, *The Spectator*'s circulation had hovered a little below 40,000. But Inglis's editorship managed at last to produce a steady growth every month. Over the course of 1960–2, sales grew by more than a quarter, from 38,000 to 48,000. Curiously enough, the biggest-selling issue in not just his tenure but the whole of *The Spectator*'s nineteenth- and twentieth-century history was that of 13 March 1959: not for scoop or scandal but, like the early *Spectator*, facts. It contained a twelve-page supplementary report on the pros and cons of nationalising Britain's steel industry, then an especially live question in the national debate. The 'commission' had been appointed four months earlier by *The Spectator*, to offer a steer on the question. Quite remarkably, the issue sold some 69,000 copies, 75 per cent above its typical weekly figure.

With Inglis thriving at the helm, Gilmour allowed himself – per the freedom only a proprietor could have – to write lengthier and less timely pieces. Among these was the longest single article to have appeared in *The Spectator*'s history, a 12,500-word 'think piece' on 'Franco's Spain'.[622] But there were greater trials for Inglis than finding space for such prolix contributions. In the summer of 1959, when the country

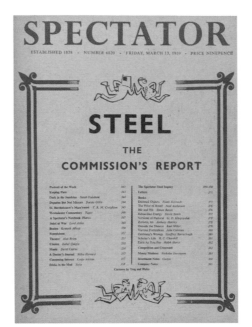

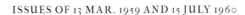

ISSUES OF 13 MAR. 1959 AND 15 JULY 1960

was struck by partial printing strikes, the magazine had to turn from the regular services of Gale and Polden – who had been printing the magazine in Aldershot since the start of 1955 – to Roffey and Clark in Croydon. After a few weeks a more convenient arrangement was struck up with Wickes and Andrews on Upper Thames Street. This emergency measure shrank the issues for 26 June and 3 July to sixteen pages, half the usual size, and wound the clock many years back in design. As a front-page notice conceded, 'We regret that some regular features will have to be suspended for the time being; others will appear fortnightly instead of weekly.'[623] Not until 14 August did the magazine regain its proper size and dress.

As the general election of October 1959 loomed, Gilmour realised that a problem was on the horizon:

not only Inglis but also Levin wa inclined to support the Libera – whose prospects of victory wer effectively zero – against th uninspiring Conservatives o Macmillan (now dubbed, eve by Gilmour, a 'quack'). Althoug Gilmour was able to steer th magazine from outright support, could not stop Taper announcing, hope that the Liberals poll well, an ... I (in a non-marginal constituenc shall vote for them... I hope, wi however little enthusiasm, th it is Mr. Gaitskell who goes to t Palace.'[624] All this was embarrassi to the aspirations of Gilmour the Tory party – especially wh the nation kept it in power. On Evelyn Waugh could rest happ who had recorded in the same p election issue his 'Aspirations a Mugwump': 'I have never vot in a parliamentary election. I sh

...ot vote this year. I shall never vote ...nless a moral or religious issue is ...nvolved (e.g., the suppression of ...atholic schools). Great Britain ... not a democracy. All authority ...manates from the Crown... I do not ...spire to advise my Sovereign in her ...hoice of servants.'[625]

An entertaining feature of the ...eriod was 'John Bull's Schooldays', ...n which the great and the good of ...ritish society reminisced about ...heir foundational experiences ...n the classroom. The occasional ...ries, running from February 1958 ... May 1961, hosted contributions ...rom Kingsley Amis, John ...etjeman, Clement Attlee, Malcolm ...Iuggeridge, Simon Raven and ...nglis himself, among others ...en to reappraise their formative ...ars.[626] Another welcome novelty ...me in the summer of 1960, when ...he Spectator serialised Evelyn ...'augh's autobiographical narrative ...burist in Africa over six issues, with ...llustrations by Quentin Blake.[627] ... was a classic example of Spectator ...ntrariness to follow this coup later ... the year with a rather lacklustre ...view of the published book, ...ncluding that Waugh 'can hardly ...said to have exerted himself in ...tting together this little volume'. ... add salt, the reviewer (South ...rican novelist Dan Jacobson) did ...ncede that it 'does make a more ...rceful impression, read between ...rd covers, than it did when ...blished serially.'[628]

...Notwithstanding Inglis's ...omotion of Bernard Levin to deputy editor in 1959, the magazine's political output was clearly weakened under his tenure. 'Taper' ceased writing regularly in October 1959, and, though Levin wrote plenty of pieces under his own name, *The Spectator* was following Westminster life with markedly less interest – and perhaps even insouciance. In 1961, the political column was again being written by a Conservative MP, now Julian Critchley, but that perspective was well balanced by fortnightly contributions from his Labour counterpart Roy Jenkins. For much of both 1960 and 1962, however, there was no political correspondent at all. It is probably not too strong to suggest that Inglis felt that this very absence gave his magazine a contrarian edge.

Meanwhile, beyond London, one of the most important of Levin's contributions was pursuing the case of 'The Prisoners of St Helena', with some 13,000 words spread over five articles of 1960–1.[629] Through detailed and trenchant argument, and some painstaking fact-finding, Levin successfully led the charge to overturn the wrongful imprisonment and arbitrary detention of three men from Bahrain: not for the first or last time was *The Spectator* quoted in Parliament to steer contemporary debate.

Under Inglis, the magazine in fact read like a proto-*Private Eye*, often finding the easiest course to be criticising all and sundry. In such an environment, Levin did not hesitate to reproduce four-letter expletives when reporting the *Lady Chatterley* trial, much to the displeasure of the Press Council.[630] When censured, Levin complained that they did not liaise with the magazine, and was outraged when they ignored these objections:

The Press Council's attitude in this matter has from the start been shabby and evasive. It had the opportunity, on the *Spectator*'s complaint, to make amends. It has not seen fit to do so, preferring further shabbiness and further evasion. It has brought itself into disrepute, and further weakened whatever slight authority over the press it may have had.[631]

These trail-blazing developments were not to everyone's taste, including the proprietor's. In the spring of 1961, Gilmour wrote an absurdly long letter to Inglis outlining how the magazine had drifted from its core ethos, becoming 'completely divorced from the political life of the country'.[632] Although circulation had risen impressively, and the magazine achieved in 1960–2 its first profit for decades, some thought it had become too raucous and too uninterested in current affairs. It had not helped that, when the energetic literary editor Karl Miller left for the *New Statesman* that year, a number of staff made the leap with him. Inglis sensed that Gilmour was keen to find a fresh editor, so when he heard the long-suspected news that the proprietor was to stand for election as a Conservative MP, he made his move first. On 2 November 1961 he announced his resignation, 'to devote more time to writing and television'.[633]

Inglis left three months later, in February 1962; the blow was intensified by Levin and several other highly prized staff joining him. On his exit he was presented with a mock-up front cover of *The Spectator*, with the three headlines that summarised his editorial outlook: 'codological' (worthy but dull articles), 'basic slag' (burdensome leading articles), and 'leave it for three months' (his preferred policy towards tedious correspondence). Inglis made sure to send a friendly but firm letter to Gilmour warning him of the real dangers ahead: 'I do not believe that you will find it possible to continue to control the *Spectator*'s policy without directing it along the lines that you, within the Party, want it to go.'[634] For his part, Inglis went on to a successful career as a television presenter, writer and paranormal researcher.

Gilmour's decision to stand for Parliament was a considerable shock to *The Spectator*'s board (on which the Wrench-Watson dioscuri still sat), its staff and its readers. In 1954, he had been bound to give the Trust his assurance that he would not become involved in politics; had he been unable to give this pledge, the purchase would not have been approved. But, in November 1962,

Gilmour at last achieved his ambition and became MP for Norfolk Central, a seat he would hold until 1974, when it was abolished; subsequently he served as MP of Chesham and Amersham until 1992. This long toil was enlivened by brief periods as Secretary of State for Defence (Jan.–Mar. 1974) and later Lord Privy Seal (1979–81) – but, when he died in 2007, much the most influential position he had held remained the proprietorship of *The Spectator*.

To find a replacement swiftly, Gilmour quite naturally turned to a former member of the magazine's editorial staff. In February 1962, IAIN BERTRAM HAMILTON (1920–86) returned as editor, having spent four years in publishing at the Hutchinson Group. A proud Scotsman who had passed from Paisley Grammar straight into the war effort, Hamilton had earned his journalistic stripes at *The Guardian* (1945–52) and *Spectator*, first as Taplin's assistant editor (1953), then Gilmour's associate editor (1954–7). Such was the owner's confidence in Hamilton, who had served briefly as acting editor in 1954, that he was appointed on a five-year contract.

On his appointment, Hamilton assured the press that the 'general line of the paper will remain unchanged; it would keep its position somewhere on the liberal wing of the Conservatives.'[635] Hamilton resurrected the weekly 'Notebook' in April 1962, which had silently – and perhaps deliberately – lapsed under Inglis two years earlier. In good

Spectator tradition, he compiled hi observations under the pseudonym of 'Starbuck', just as Gilmour – o rather anyone 'in the office who ha an axe to grind'[636] – had done unde 'Pharos'. This allowed him to fire of plenty of casual comment about th fate of the magazine, the press, an politics more broadly.

One of the early coups of Hamilton editorship was to host an excoriatin attack by F.R. Leavis on C.P. Sno and his 'Two cultures' Rede Lecture which pessimistically pitted th sciences against the humanities.[6] Aided by his well-connected deput editor Anthony Hartley, Hamilton *Spectator* was regularly able to ca upon many of the most celebrate contributors of previous years, a well as introducing to the magazin a new crop of talent. Particularl readable writers included Alan Brie Paddy Leigh Fermor, Richard We and Simon Raven. As literary edito (1962–3), Robert Conquest wro with astounding insight and learnin on the history of Europe and th crimes of Stalinist Russia. Murra Kempton, the future Pulitze winning journalist, reported ever few weeks on events in America: fro 1962 to 1970 some 150 columns cruise through the world of black activisr Vietnam and Cuba, of the Kennedy Nixon and Muhammad Ali.

In May 1962, Hamilton's *Specta* – however jaunty its tone – was se up by the schoolboy wit of a ne venture, *Private Eye*. Curiousl both titles had acquired the waggish character from Salopian

PLIN, GILMOUR, INGLIS

MILTON, MACLEOD, LAWSON N.

LE, CREIGHTON, COSGRAVE

Issue 12 of the *Eye* gleefully published a four-page mock-up of *The Spectator*: it contained a spoof contents page, absurd fragments of the leading article and notebook, a full faux-letters page, and then scurrilous scraps on arts, finance and wine. Even the magazine's pseudonyms were mocked: the *Notebook* was signed off not by 'Starbuck' but 'Ballcock'. In fact, so accurate is the mockery that it is hard to escape the conclusion that the *enfants terribles* of the *Eye* had been reading the magazine since they were in short trousers. Starbuck himself enjoined *Spectator* readers to enjoy the spoof:

> I strongly advise all who either love or loathe this paper to get hold of the current issue of *Private Eye* where the *Spectator* is sent up in pages of delectable parody. Belly-laughs are guaranteed for friends and foes alike.[638]

Either as an act of misjudged Harrisian pedantry or self-conscious Inglisian mockery, Hamilton proceeded to pick up the *Eye* on its failure to observe *The Spectator*'s precise use of commas.

As a more concerted effort to show that *The Spectator* could run with a good joke, Hamilton had the magazine's Christmas issue that year play host to the chief *Eye* wits, Christopher Booker, Willie Rushton and Richard Ingrams.[639] 'A Child's Guide to Modern Culture' was an

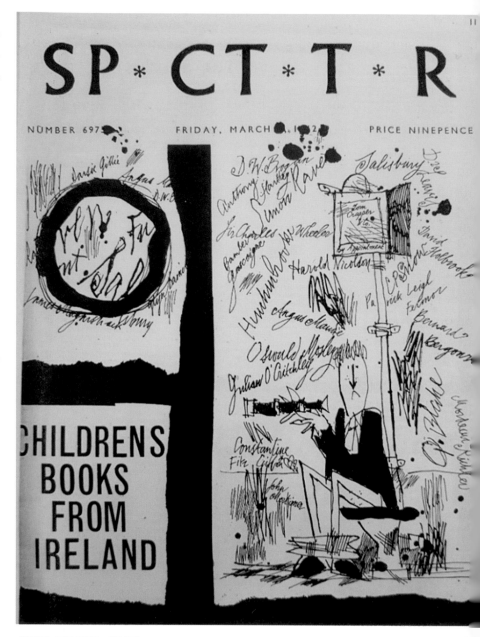

PRIVATE EYE, 1 JUNE 1962

eight-page, copiously illustrated account of not-so-highbrow Britain. There were plenty of decent jokes – including a double-page mock-genealogical spread on 'The New Establishment'. There was also an alphabetical send-up of contemporary high culture, of which a few entries convey the tone:

A is for Kingsley AIMLESS. He is a typical modern in-tele-ctual. In the olden days intellectuals were poor men with beards, who lived in the British Museum and wrote nothing but enormous books on history which sold three copies and changed the face of civilisation. No one ever heard of them until after they were dead

But Mr. Aimless is very rich and good-looking.

G is for the GUARDIAN. Today it is well-known for its endless features, the readiness of its staff to desert in all directions, and its inability to make up its mind on anything... Today its motto is 'Comment is free, but facts are expensive.'

R is for RADICALISM ... It is very fashionable these days among two sorts of people. The first are young intellectuals who know nothing about politics but want to appear vaguely progressive... The second group are politically more dangerous. They are the younger members of the Conservative Party. CLIVE BRILLIANTINE, the staff of the SPECTATOR, etc., who claim to be Radicals in order to disguise the fact that they prefer society to remain just as it is.

Although not truly radical in politics, readers of Hamilton's *Spectator* will have smiled to read Constantine Fitzgibbon belittling the Profumo scandal. Describing 'all this chatter about the sexual habits of politicians' as 'pseudo-news', he concluded with a flourish: 'Men of ability ought to run our democracy for us, and provided that they do so honestly and efficiently, it matters not a fig what their private life may [be]'.[40]

The appearance of the 7,000th number of *The Spectator*, on 24 August 1962, gave Hamilton the opportunity to state his own beliefs about the magazine's role in the contemporary world:

Now, as in 1828, there is urgent need for independent and well-informed comment on the events of the day. It is this need that the *Spectator* tries to supply. Our independence does not mean that we avoid political commitments, but rather that the direction of our policy is determined by what we believe to be the national interest. We wish to inform as well as to amuse our readers, and we do not see why these tasks should be incompatible. Our comment aims to be as constructive as possible and as critical as is necessary. The *Spectator* has always welcomed dissenting opinions and radical views, avoiding dull uniformity and setting store by hard fact and good writing.

But Hamilton would have little time to advance this mission. Although he gave a sharp and self-confident feel to the magazine, its circulation was still falling rapidly: those who had turned to *The Spectator* for its sense of fun now found it sobering up and drifting back to politics – serious Conservative politics at that. Within twelve months of his tenure the circulation fell by 11,000 (almost a quarter) to its pre-war level of 37,000; although

the termination of a discounted American subscription scheme accounted for 4,000 of these, things were rapidly heading in the wrong direction. Genuine panic about the paper's future perhaps prompted its increase in price to one shilling in October 1962, a sum *The Spectator* had not demanded since 1835.

Still, it was both a great surprise and a great misfortune in October 1963 for Hamilton to learn of his sudden sacking via an out-of-the-blue call from the *Evening Standard*. Hamilton suspected that Gilmour's anxiety reflected a plan to sell the magazine; he had not cottoned on that his own dismissal could be an alternative route out of the bind. The subsequent chaos of his exit, and the controversial appointment of an established Conservative MP in his stead, thrust *The Spectator* under national, and unfavourable, scrutiny. Gilmour aside, the staff were swift to rally round Hamilton. Their public statement, printed across the national press, expressed their desire

to make a vehement protest at the shabby treatment meted out by the proprietor to Mr. Iain Hamilton, who has enjoyed our full confidence as editor. The fact that he and some of the directors of *The Spectator* were not informed of the change of editorship until it was published in the press speaks for itself. Nor has Mr. Gilmour explained his action to the staff. We believe strongly that *The Spectator*, with its long and honourable history of independent opinion, should not be tossed about at the whim of the proprietor or lose its independence by identification with a narrow political faction.[641]

Others agreed, not least Hamilton's predecessor, Brian Inglis, who told the press that his successor 'had been disgracefully treated';[642] he promptly resigned from the magazine's board, to which he had been appointed on his own resignation the previous year. The journalistic trade declared itself appalled. Gerald Barry, a long-serving director of the *New Statesman*, pontificated to *The Times*:

I doubt whether in the whole history of Fleet Street (and I can claim in this matter a personal experience not wholly dissimilar) has a proprietor behaved to an editor in this way.[643]

The Free Press Society offered to purchase *The Spectator*, giving a commitment that they would not honour Macleod's appointment. In the end, Gilmour's will prevailed. Hamilton naturally rejected the insulting offer of being demoted to deputy editor and took the magazine to court, duly winning £12,500 for loss of office. Hartley, his deputy, held the editorial reins throughout November, and then promptly followed him out of the door.

The furore about *The Spectator*'s peremptory dealings was soon increased considerably by the

" *. . . Mr. Iain Macleod (who if he was in the business would be the greatest political journalist of them all) puts the matter succinctly . . . "*

(Anthony Howard, New Statesman, 12th October, 1962)

. . . meanwhile

IAIN MACLEOD
IS EDITING THE
SPECTATOR
OUT TODAY 1/-

ADVERTISEMENT, DEC. 1963

identity of the man airlifted in as editor. For this was none other than IAIN NORMAN MACLEOD (1913–70), who had recently resigned from the Tory Cabinet on refusing to serve under Macmillan's successor, Sir Alec Douglas-Home. Although he did not take up the post until December 1963, the news spilled into the public domain at the end of October. The second Yorkshireman to steer *The Spectator*, Macleod had been educated at Fettes and Caius College, Cambridge (History, II.2); his subsequent training for the Bar was permanently interrupted by the war. Although wounded in France in 1940 he was later involved in the D-Day Landings. A high-flying and high-stakes bridge player in his younger years, he was naturally drawn to the great game of politics. The subsequent eighteen years saw him shimmy up that greasy pole, first as

an MP, then subsequently Ministe of Health, Minister of Labou and National Service, Secretar of State of the Colonies, and at las the triple-bill of Chancellor of th Duchy of Lancaster, Leader of th House of Commons and Chair c the Conservative Party. But hi principles – and paradoxically h ambition – now prompted him t take a back seat. His only experienc in journalism was writing on brid for *The Times*.

Although Macleod called himse a Tory-Radical, he was someone c undeniable and unshakeable par connections. Yes, a generatio beforehand, Harris had indee combined the editorship with fi years in Parliament, but he had serve throughout as an Independen While Macleod had boldly le the Cabinet, he continued life an MP, and his Tory ambitio had certainly not faded to blac Gilmour's choice to appoint hi made as early as August, sure contravened the magazine's trus protected independence. It was surprise that the firebrand Lev used *That Was The Week That W* to mock his former employe However, for all its troubl beginnings – which includ plastering a last-minute stick across his first (and Christma cover starkly announcing 'T Death of Kennedy'[644] – Macleo editorship soon showed its quali An early move was to bring in t prodigiously talented J.W.M. (Joh Thompson from the *Standar* deputy editor. And, to the relief of many, Macleod showed his respect for the inventive editorship of Inglis by providing a sequel to the earlier series 'John Bull's Schooldays': he successfully encouraged worthies of the day to reflect on their entry into paid work. Among the twenty contributors to 'John Bull's First Job' were John Betjeman (schoolmaster, 29 Nov. 1963), Clement Attlee (the bar, 13 Dec. 1963), Virginia Cowles (antiques shop, 21 Feb. 1964) and John Le Carré (department store, 27 Nov. 1964).

Another early coup was to recruit Randolph Churchill to write the magazine's first dedicated column on the press. Over the fifty years that followed, *The Spectator* would host a series of spiky media correspondents: Christopher Booker, John Walls, Bill Grundy, Paul Johnson and Stephen Glover. Macleod also made his own media move: readers gasped agog when, on 25 April 1965, *The Spectator* suddenly appeared on that arriviste medium of television. In the thirty-second slot, Macleod told readers from behind his office desk that if viewers were interested in public affairs or politics, they should be reading *The Spectator*. Its generous pitch was that, if anyone sent a letter to him at Gower Street, he would dispatch a copy of the magazine *gratis*.[645]

Macleod, a colleague recalled, had a natural feeling for journalism and went about the job with wholly pompous zest'.[646] The boardroom under his tenure was described by a staff member of twenty-five years

as 'a haven of tranquillity and efficiency'.[647] Although fond of a drink, Macleod was less given to small talk; it is unclear whether it was for social or professional reasons that he stopped the weekly editorial conference. Although many of the regular writers were less illustrious than those that Inglis and Hamilton had attracted in previous years, the core team of David Watt on politics, Malcolm Rutherford on foreign affairs, David Rees on literature and Randolph Churchill on the media produced robust and intelligent coverage every week. If Gilmour's editorship had popularised the word 'Establishment', and Hamilton's the insult 'pseud', Macleod's dread phrase was 'nanny state'. In that spirit, he knew it was essential to allow a free hand in the magazine's politics: Watt recalled that his editor was 'fantastically generous in allowing me to express views which he regarded as dangerously heterodox'.[648] This impression was intensified by his replacing Watt in October 1964 with Alan Watkins, an avowed Socialist – like his colleagues Nicholas Davenport and Jean Robertson. Occasional contributions came from Labour politicians such as Roy Hattersley, Desmond Donnelly and George Brown.

Macleod took especial pains to bolster the foreign coverage of the magazine; some of his own most important contributions concerned Africa, a subject to which he had been devoted since serving as an unusually liberal-minded Secretary

of State for the Colonies (1959–61). To mark the twentieth anniversary of D-Day, Macleod published his own vivid recollections, alongside those of General Leo Freiherr Geyr von Schweppenburg, Commander-in-Chief of Panzergroup West.[649] To the approval of many, Macleod introduced a chess column and restored a crossword to the magazine, which (as with other things) had gone missing under Inglis;[650] both have remained ever since. The crossword was later to be pushed to new levels of difficulty during the ten-year tenure of 'Jac' (J.A. Caesar, 1971–81), who transformed a relatively straightforward (and unsigned) puzzle into one of the nation's great thematic cryptic crosswords. He has since been followed by a talented team of cruciverbalist riddlers: Mass, Dumpynose, Doc, Columba, Lavatch, Ascot, Smokey, Pabulum and the delightfully named Mr Magoo.

Macleod had editorial flair. Indeed, the most explosive single issue in the magazine's long history was an early number of his invention. Douglas-Home's succession to Macmillan had surprised many, in both the Conservative party itself and the press at large. Under the guise of a book review – of Randolph Churchill's rather biased and incomplete account of this episode[651] – Macleod, writing as both Tory MP and scoop-savvy editor, revealed the inner workings of the party in astounding detail. The story was run as the cover piece with the uncompromising headline, 'What happened'. His article exposed how Supermac and his 'magic circle' had conspired both to block the most obvious successor – Rab Butler – and to usher in the old-school-ties candidate, Old Etonian Douglas-Home. This rip-roaring piece has since been described as 'the most celebrated article in British magazine history'.[652] Understandably, the issue flew off the stands, comfortably selling some 65,000 copies.[653] Readers were gripped, if aghast. The letters page for the following issue carried a diverse array of responses. One telegram was kept in capitals: 'WHAT A NASTY LITTLE BIT OF WORK YOU ARE STOP FIRST NOTICED YOUR EYES AT THE BLACKPOOL CONFERENCE ON TELEVISION STOP THANK GOD YOU'RE NOT PRIME MINISTER = HERBERT GREENE.'[654] Some corners of the national press could not prevent themselves from noting a certain irony in *The Spectator*'s criticising ruthless decisions about leadership. JAK, the *Evening Standard*'s cartoonist, ran a picture the morning after which showed Macmillan popping his head into Douglas-Home's office with a simple request: 'Get Iain Hamilton to do a story on how the editor of *The Spectator* was chosen!'[655]

When the next general election fell, in October 1964, it was impossible for the editor to be 'a mere spectator'. Aware of the conflict of interest, Macleod took up an offhand joke by Robert Conquest, and renamed his weekly column 'A Participant's Notebook'.[656] In the end, the victory of Harold Wilson, first Labour PM

ISSUE OF 17 JAN. 1964

for thirteen years, freed the editor to criticise the government of the day in traditional Spectatorial fashion.

When, in the following January, Winston Churchill breathed his last, *The Spectator*'s political cartoonist Roy Dewar sombrely depicted a cigar left to burn out, above the heading 'Britain without Churchill'.[657] Macleod's leader, always keen to

look forward as well as backward reflected on the difficulties th Britain's post-war policy h presented for entry into Europe.

One of the last long-standi connections with *The Spectat* of old stood down in 1965: t managing director, H.S. ('Berti Janes had joined the staff in 19 appointed by Strachey as the fi advertising manager, a sector he soon revolutionised at Wrench's behest. The Toryfication of *The Spectator* continued, by the appointment of a new managing director, George Hutchinson. 'Are we to have', Inglis complained to *The Guardian*,

as the owner of the 'Spectator', Ian Gilmour – Conservative MP and PPS to Quintin Hogg, Lord President of the Council – as editor, Iain Macleod, Conservative MP and still, it must be assumed, a strong contender for high ministerial office in the not-too-distant future; and as managing director George Hutchinson, for some years high in the counsels of the Conservative Party?[658]

The Spectator Trust – which in 1965 consisted of the chairmen of the London County Council and the Headmasters' Conference, and the presidents of the Royal Historical Society, the Law Society, and the Institute of Chartered Accountants – was unconvinced by the direction of travel. Two of its former presidents – Victor Mishcon and Frederick Lawssop – said they would never have supported Gilmour's acquisition of the magazine if they had known he would become an MP. But, despite their misgivings, there was no mechanism to force a change of proprietorial control. As it happened, however, this particular worry soon resolved itself.

On his appointment as Shadow Chancellor in November 1965 at the instance of the new Tory leader Edward Heath, Macleod tendered his resignation, leaving office at the end of the year. Tragically, his subsequent political career was not to last long: one month after the Conservatives were returned to power in 1970, and thus one month into his service as Chancellor, Macleod died of a heart attack, aged fifty-six. The press and the nation were united in mourning the passing of a unique figure, one who as Colonial Secretary had earned the rebuke of Lord Salisbury for being 'too clever by half'.[659] all agreed that Macleod's considerable promise was cruelly cut short. Quite what he would have achieved in 1970s Britain is open to debate; perhaps, too, he still had more to give to *The Spectator*, for in him (as his deputy editor fondly recorded) 'the journalist and the politician were indistinguishable'.[660]

Gilmour was forced once more to cast about for a new editor – the sixth under his tenure – who was prepared to fill increasingly big shoes. A good appointment was sorely needed, as Macleod had managed only to pause the decline in sales. Gilmour first offered the post to William Rees-Mogg of *The Times*, who, after politely declining, rapidly rose to that newspaper's editorship. Although he carefully considered the prospect of Macleod's deputy, John Thompson, he decided instead to bring in a man very swiftly on the up: NIGEL LAWSON (b. 1932). Fiercely ambitious and frighteningly clever, Lawson was the embodiment of a young man in a hurry. After a high-flying career at Westminster and Christ Church (PPE, First), he joined the editorial staff of the *Financial Times*. In 1960, he became City Editor at the *Sunday Telegraph*, a post he later gave up to serve as a special adviser to Douglas-Home, newly installed as prime minister. It is one of those quirks of history that one *Spectator* editor entered journalism so as to avoid working with Douglas-Home, whereas his successor had left that field to do exactly that. It is another remarkable quirk that both later ended up being in charge of the nation's purse-strings.

With the continued support of Thompson as deputy editor, Lawson swiftly made *The Spectator* more serious in look and outlook. In particular, the magazine became appreciably more political than it had been under Taplin, Gilmour, Inglis, Hamilton – and even Macleod. He 'sought to give the paper a distinctive political voice, perhaps best described as British Gaullism laced with economic liberalism.'[661] Among Lawson's chief political battles were fighting for justice for the people of Biafra, who had seceded from Nigeria in 1967 and thereby faced atrocious suffering, and opposing military action in Vietnam, despite intense pressure from the United States. The paper soon gained a strong campaigning voice that it had lost since Gilmour's early years.

Surprisingly or not, this sharpening up of the paper's political

ISSUES FOR 29 JAN. 1965, 22 OCT. 1965, 8 JULY 1966 AND 17 MAR. 1967

position did not translate into an increased circulation from where Macleod had left it. In fact, in the five years from 1965 to 1970, sales were set to drop by a further 40 per cent, from 37,000 to some 22,000. Wider factors were in play here than the character of the magazine *per se*. In particular, the 1960s was the decade that saw the transformative rise of the Sunday papers, which were moving increasingly into new territory: the *Sunday Times* introduced a full-colour magazine supplement in 1962, followed by the *Observer* in 1964; in 1961, the *Sunday Telegraph* also entered this increasingly crowded field. These intelligent, wide-ranging and well-resourced weekly magazines suddenly started to trouble the self-assurance of established titles. *The Spectator* was stuck between being an expensive weekly news journal and a politically focused magazine review, all the while being threatened by the growth of televisual media.

In March 1967, perhaps to challenge the Sunday papers more directly, Lawson restored to *The Spectator* the appearance of a weekly newspaper. Most strikingly, for the first time in the magazine's history the leading article was moved on to the front page. Here was a clear and concerted pushback against the relaxed magazine aesthetic of recent years. In due course a second leader emerged to follow it, restricting the 'Portrait of the Week' to a miserly three paragraphs.

As the debate about entering the European Common Market heated up, Lawson steered *The Spectator* on a confidently pro-European course. This was entirely in line with his long-standing beliefs: as he later recorded, 'I had been a believer in closer European unity ever since my days as an undergraduate at Oxford in the early 1950s.'[662] This fervour was not naturally in line with the magazine's readership, or owner. What is more, Lawson fell out with Gilmour by supporting currency devaluation – and by

running stridently *ad homine[m]* attacks against the incumben[t] Labour prime minister, Harol[d] Wilson (1964–70), the proprietor['s] parliamentary colleague.

Aided by the energetic Hilar[y] Spurling as literary editor, *T[he] Spectator* continued to draw upo[n] an impressive array of talent from t[he] great and the good: Kingsley Ami[s], Evelyn Waugh, Graham Greene an[d] Gabriel García Márquez, the last [of] whom contributed a short 'Tuesda[y] Story' in 1967.[663] In 1968, Nan[cy] Mitford also filed a much-circulate[d] diary piece (in two instalments) [on] the Paris riots of 1968, written fro[m] a rather rarefied angle: 'I've g[ot] masses of champagne and no miner[al] water, so if the tap gives out Ma[rk] and I will be permanently drun[k]. What a picture.'[664]

Lawson's relationship wi[th] Gilmour was somewhat unhapp[y;] they were, he has recalled more th[an] once, 'not soulmates'. Gilmour, [for] his part, confided his regret at n[ot] appointing John Thompson. A[s] elling sign of the growing distance between editor and proprietor, and of how Gilmour frequently chose to operate unilaterally behind the scenes, the news that he planned to sell *The Spectator* reached Lawson only when a colleague spotted a suspicious-looking advert in the *Financial Times* (as below). The claim that it was 'In need of revitalisation' was, in a financial sense, by no means untrue: *The Spectator* was losing some £20,000 each year, and Gilmour could not keep the magazine afloat indefinitely. It would also free his hand politically, he was learning, if he could let *The Spectator* sail free. Rumours were rife about possible purchasers, with Richard Lamb, the writer and aspirant Liberal politician, among the chief prospects. George Hutchinson approached Harold Macmillan, in the hope that Macmillan's would put in a bid, but the offer was politely turned down. Lawson himself, who tried and failed to put together a consortium for the acquisition, said

that he would accept any proprietor with a 'reasonable, middle-of-the-road approach to politics... One wouldn't want a Communist who was going to turn *The Spectator* into a weekly edition of the *Morning Star.*[665] In the end, the successful purchaser was a comparative unknown, the thirty-nine-year-old industrialist Harold ('Harry') Creighton, Chairman of the Glasgow-based Scottish Machine Tool Corporation, who had spent time smelting tin on the other side of the planet. The sale price was kept under wraps – and was apparently not the highest sum offered – but seems to have been near-identical to Gilmour's purchase price of £75,000.

Creighton explained to the press that he bought *The Spectator* 'because I believe in independent journals, independent of groups and combines', before adding the critical and commendable observation that 'the only really independent paper is a profitable one'.[666] He also expressed the desire to increase coverage of

money matters, as *The Spectator* first had in the 1920s, in order to attract a wider readership in the City and the (rapidly growing) university sector. In the magazine, Creighton (or a spokesperson?) told readers that, 'When genuinely independent journals are so few, it follows that those which have successfully maintained that quality have an extra importance thrust upon them. *The Spectator* recognises this, and accepts the responsibilities it implies.'[667]

Creighton was a rough-and-ready figure in the journalistic world – a world in which he had no prior experience. He was known to boast that he could derive whatever he required from books simply by reading the notes on the dust-jacket. Somewhat predictably, Lawson's relationship with Creighton was distinctly worse than with Gilmour: not only did the editor take care to avoid running into the new owner, but Lawson soon felt compelled to invoke a clause in his contract to protect himself from proprietorial influence. A telling anecdote survives from the late 1960s, when some nocturnal intruders to the *Spectator* offices on Gower Street had fitted the safe with gelignite in the frustrated hope of blowing it up. When the dangerous remnants were discovered the following day, the staff promptly evacuated the building. Only when the realisation dawned that Creighton had been left in the boardroom with his close circle did George Hutchinson reveal with a smirk, 'I didn't think they'd

FINANCIAL TIMES ADVERTISEMENT, 3 FEB. 1967

want to be disturbed.'[668] Hutchinson would later describe Creighton in *The Spectator* as 'not without aptitude, albeit of a somewhat slapdash, capricious sort.'[669] Certainly his repeated attempts to follow in Gilmour's footsteps by becoming a Conservative candidate were unsuccessful. His no-nonsense attitude to committee governance was encapsulated by his decision soon after acquiring *The Spectator* to dissolve the Trust designed to oversee the magazine's ownership – the very body that had approved his acquisition. Although one may regret that the project of policing *Spectator* ownership lasted barely forty years, Gilmour's tenure had in fact shown it to be unfit for purpose.

Other changes were afoot. In 1967, the ever-readable Alan Watkins abandoned his political column to ply his trade at the *New Statesman*, which was at the historical height of its powers (at some 90,000 weekly sales). Lawson failed to persuade Christopher Booker to take up the post, and then surprised almost everyone in appointing Auberon (Bron) Waugh, son of Evelyn – a man who proudly admitted that he knew 'practically nothing about politics'.[670] Still, he was a man with such self-confidence and wit that the column almost wrote itself, steered by his golden rule that almost no one wants to read about politics. Another significant arrival at the same time was Christopher Fildes, who started to provide a 'City Diary': he thus joined Nicholas Davenport, whose

twenty-six years of service he would outrun by a further thirteen.[671] When these two new recruits arrived, a pointed notice circulated the office:

LIBEL. Mr Christopher Fildes and Mr Auberon Waugh have today joined the staff of *The Spectator*. As from today, *The Spectator* is no longer insured against libel. Gatley's *Libel and Slander* (sixth and seventh edition) may be consulted in my office.

—Nigel Lawson, Editor

Among other regulars that Lawson secured were two very different thirty-somethings: Andreas Whittam-Smith, a future co-founder of *The Independent*, and Roy Hattersley, Labour MP for Birmingham Sparkbrook and protégé of the long-standing *Spectator* contributor Roy Jenkins. The magazine was happy to spar on all fronts.

1968 was a year of change: it saw the end of coal-mining in the Black Country and the cotton trade in Manchester, and the arrival of the M1 motorway, the first decimal coins, and the Isle of Wight festival. Amid this hubbub came Enoch Powell's infamous 'Rivers of Blood' speech, delivered in Birmingham on 20 April. This was an interesting test case for Lawson's *Spectator*, and indeed Waugh's political column. The leader dismissed the rhetoric in no uncertain terms as

a nonsense and dangerous nonsense. Dangerous because the politics of hatred – and hatred is what this sort of talk is bound to arouse – is always dangerous, whether it is the class hatred of the Marxist socialist or the race hatred of the quasi-fascist. Mr Powell is no fascist (not even quasi-), but his speech has been welcomed by those who are; he is a Christian, yet the emotion his speech has sanctified is that of hate ... his speech last weekend is one that he will live to regret ever having made.

Waugh, concurring that Powell wa[s] unlikely to be a eugenicist or on[e] seeking inhumanely to quarantin[e] immigrant communities, criticise[d] him instead for appealing to th[e] people over and above the part[y] structure: 'he apparently do[es] not know how to behave like [a] gentleman.'[672]

1968 was also the year of stude[nt] riots – the event that brought th[e] F-word to *The Spectator*'s pages. But readers were thrown a ve[ry] strange curveball when they m[et] the headline 'Student Stirs: [a] Document'. This was not quite t[he] breakthrough text it suggested. [A]s habituated as subscribers were [to] reactionary views and archaisi[ng] prose, this new 'document' actua[lly] channelled an impossibly bizar[re] voice. For this was the first lette[r of] Mercurius Oxoniensis ('the Oxfo[rd] Messenger'), a port-swilling, boo[k-] loving, arch-conservative do[n] writing from centuries past. In expression and outlook, Mercurius wrote as a curious chimera, part Anthony Wood, part John Aubrey, both men of letters in the late seventeenth century.

Mercurius' pen was first stirred to action by the 'fanatiques' great demonstration' in London' of October 1968, when students set about the collective business of overthrowing the British Establishment. Fomented by the established rabble-rouser Tariq Ali, and the President of the National Union of Students, that 'sturdy peasant' Jack Straw, a spirit of unrest was spreading across university campuses. By November, it had reached Oxford, especially the lefter-than-thou students of Balliol and Nuffield College. Mercurius peered from his ivory tower and dismissed the brouhaha with patrician disdain: these were mere games of the naïve youth, who were following the fashion of American students rather than pushing a fully formed and freshly forged political agenda. Nuffield had become 'peopled with neoterick tub-preachers, who dignify themselves with sesquipedalian names, as cephologists, sociologists, etc.: anglice: agitators'; Balliol had become little other than an extroverted privy-house'. In addition, he looked with horror at his colleagues, who seemed happier to let their principles slide in order not to cause a fuss: ''tis easier for college drones to buzz with the hive and make a virtue of their harmony than by independency, to change the

tune and be thought excentrique.'[674]

And thus began a series of tart, truculent letters addressed to a fellow scholar, Mercurius Londiniensis (supposedly a professor at the LSE). Somehow, however, the missives kept reaching the hands of Lawson, then charged with editing that 'weekly intelligencer' *The Spectator.* Although manifestly ridiculous in form and expression, each letter packed a fierce counter-cultural punch against the way the world was moving. Mercurius stood firm against most modernising prospects on the horizon – the introduction of a new 'Human Sciences' school, the building of a Zoology Tower 'like a gigantique stone beanstalk', the end of single-sex colleges – and served as a remarkably well-informed source of gossip on Oxford issues: a road proposed to cut through Christ Church Meadow, unsound candidates for the deanship of Christ Church or the wardenship of Wadham. The prospect of a 'national student strike', by contrast, was received with mirth: 'O noble prospect! O blessed freedom for us poor college mokes, tied fast to the treadmill of lectures, tutorials, examinations! O liberty, sweet liberty!'[675]

Mercurius railed against the expanding and clogging bureaucracy of higher education, as well as the misplaced self-certainty of academics instructing the public. In particular, he mocked the notion of the 'Elect' – academics who sign communal letters in the press in the quaint belief that their signature should and

would weigh particularly heavy with the nation.

A sense of his principled, if old-school, ideals can be discerned from his defence of Latin as an entry requirement to Oxford. The field-guide to those seeking change ('Progress') is still of some use to the academic observer:

First, there are the Moderns: that is, the Sociologists, Oeconomists and Chop-logicians, whose whole science (as they maintain) needs no solid bottom of knowledge to grow upon, nor no roots in Antiquity to nourish it, all their learning being set out in a few slim books writ in the last ten years, in English (of a kind), and bound in paper; so that by their means a man can, without exerting himself, become master of all modern learning and obtain an office in Broadcasting House and tell us all what we should think on all great problems. Secondly, there are the Friends of Progress and Equality, who cry out against this university as opening its doors only to such as have been bred up in good schools, and know something, which is a badge of privilege, whereas true liberty requires that we should be equally hospitable to those who come from bad schools and know nothing at all. Finally, here as elsewhere, there are always the With-it crew, who, having themselves gained a good education, must needs atone for that guilt (as they conceive it), and show themselves to be morally untainted by it, by running with the other two classes and crying up modernity and ignorance as true innocence; of which party I could name one or two, not unknown in the world, but forbear, honoris causa.[676]

'Mercurius' inspired Junius-like fascination about his true identity, as the letters manifestly came from someone at the very heart of high-society gossip. The Oxford historian Hugh Trevor-Roper fiercely denied involvement when suggestions came his way, but eagerly proffered the names of colleagues as their true author. When the first tranche of letters was published (by Harvard University Press) in 1970, it was Trevor-Roper who reviewed them for *The Spectator*:

No one seems to know who Mercurius is. Many of my colleagues have come under suspicion... Others maintain that Mercurius is a syndicate, like Homer. This view is said to be received as orthodox in Christ Church: which for me is a strong argument that it is true. As one who has himself been suspected ... I am naturally as anxious as anyone to detect and neutralise the real culprit.

In fact, PHS – the mischievous diary of that 'silly London gazette' *The Times* – heard tell in March 1970 that none other than Trevor-Roper himself was Mercurius.[677] Such tittle-tattle apparently emanated from the champion gossip-monger Auberon Waugh, recently fired from the magazine (see below). That assertion was stoutly rebuffed by Mercurius, who dismissed Waugh and Rees-Mogg for 'this exquisite new piece of folly',[678] and by Editor Lawson, who told *The Times* that 'while it is indeed true that Professor Trevor-Roper writes for the *Spectator* from time to time, he does so under his own name.' The closing sentence tartly rebuked PHS for speaking chummily of 'my old acquaintance Mercurius Oxoniensis': 'That, too, is false: the true Mercurius is not an old acquaintance of PHS.'[679] To complete the revenge, *The Spectator*'s press column, written by Bill Grundy, duly revealed the names of the five men behind PHS.[680] But the truth, in fact, was irrevocably out.

Now that his mask had slipped, Trevor-Roper's effrontery became all the balder. His colleagues at Oriel understandably felt aggrieved: Christopher Seton-Watson wrote as 'Porcus-Piscis Orielensis' ('the Pigfish of Oriel') to complain about Mercurius' 'grotesque fantasies and vulgar abuse'.[681] Trevor-Roper was duly hauled in front of the Provost, Kenneth Turpin, who asked: 'Are you, or are you not, Mercurius Oxoniensis?' After a careful pause, Trevor-Roper responded, 'You asked me for a straight answer, and the straight answer is no.'

Most readers instead enjoyed the fun, laughing at or with Mercurius as per their taste. After all, *The Spectator* never claimed to be a safe space. The letters continued to crop up sporadically until 1973, by which point the thrill of student unrest had fossilised into folk memory. When Trevor-Roper was ennobled in 1979, Nigel Lawson helpfully suggested 'The Baron Mercurius' as the most appropriate title. But it was not to be. And as to those original protesters, both – oddly enough – would end up appearing in *The Spectator*, whether reviewing restaurants or offering interviews as pillars of the Modern Establishment.[682] Yes, Mercurius would have liked that one.

In the summer of 1969, Lawson moved the leading article back to page 2 inside the magazine, duly freeing up the front page for the striking caricatures of Richard Willson. The look of a newspaper was thus set aside for good.[683] Still, the magazine retained an ancient title's high ideals of proper practice. In February 1970, Bron Waugh took umbrage at an article on Catholicism and celibacy written by his rambunctious *Spectator* rival George Gale, who had started writing a weekly column 'Viewpoint' on all manner of things the previous October. Encouraged by his colleagues, Waugh surreptitiously changed the contents page as he saw it through the press, rebranding poor George as 'Lunchtime O'Gale'. This name of course echoed *Private Eye*'s ever-sozzled journalist *Lunchtime O'Booze*, not itself modelled on Ga

CONTENTS PAGE, 14 FEB. 1970

whose bibulosity was instead covered by his appearance as 'George G. Ale'). This tongue-in-cheek tweak reached print without anyone noticing.

Lawson felt the only appropriate response was to fire Waugh, who was shocked at the abrupt dismissal. He lamented to the *Observer* that 'what I intended as a small office joke has suddenly become a subject of public scrutiny', counting it a sad feature of the world that 'the weeklies take themselves too seriously'.[684] Waugh soon sued the magazine successfully for six months' compensation. Flush from victory, he even wrote to the Houses of Parliament, petitioning the Serjeant-at-Arms for *The Spectator*'s press gallery ticket to be transferred to him as the new political correspondent of *Private Eye*. The latter journal, he emphasised, had twice *The Spectator*'s circulation and (he claimed) markedly more interest in politics.

Lawson's own political interests, at any rate, were made manifest in June 1970, when he unsuccessfully contested the seat of Eton and Slough – the first shaky steps in his long career as a Conservative politician. To help focus his mind on that exacting task, Creighton spontaneously handed him his

notice, and that was that. Over four and a half years Lawson had restored *The Spectator* to its classic role as a serious and thoughtful campaigner, with a strong interest in – and appreciable influence on – current affairs. But the climate was challenging for serious weeklies, and the circulation had steadily decreased to below 30,000. Bron Waugh, one of the writers whose long career at the magazine Lawson had started, later wrote that he 'was a good journalist and is a great loss to journalism'.[685] The gain to Conservative politics was more substantial, including six years' transformational service as Chancellor of the Exchequer under Margaret Thatcher.

For the three-month period that followed – from mid-June to mid-September – the deputy editor John Thompson served as acting editor. In the weeks that he took his holiday, the acting acting editor was the wide-ranging man of letters Anthony Lejeune. In fact, Thompson had at last been offered the editorship itself, but tellingly found it a more prudent course to refuse Creighton's offer. He later confided, 'It wasn't that I didn't like Harry Creighton, I just couldn't see myself working with him.'[686] A call soon came from

Lord Hartwell, editor-in-chief of the *Telegraphs,* signing him up as political correspondent for the Sunday title. Six years later, he began a ten-year stint as editor of that quondam *Spectator* rival.

The editorship of *The Spectator* remained an embarrassingly open question. The post was dangled before all manner of prospects: Colin Welch, deputy editor of the *Daily Telegraph*; Peregrine Worsthorne, deputy editor of the *Sunday Telegraph*; Bernard Levin, once its spikiest columnist; Anthony Lejeune, who had sampled a taste of the position; and Enoch Powell, then rumbling in frustration at the state of Conservatism under Heath. Yet none of these felt moved to take the post on – probably because of who posed the question. Perhaps closest to accepting was Levin, about which the national press frequently gossiped, but his stipulation that Christopher Booker (a long-standing *Spectator* columnist) become his literary editor was turned down – doubtless on the prompting of the Cambridge don quite happily holding that fort, Maurice Cowling.

While the frantic search for a new editor continued, Thompson maintained a steady ship, although Fleming wrote his final 'Strix' column that June. A fresh challenge emerged when, for the first week in *The Spectator*'s history, no issue could appear at all: because of inescapable printers' strikes, the contents for 4 July were instead rolled into the issue of 11 July, which bore the laconic editorial comment, 'we apologise to readers for this departure from the normal pattern.' The ever-stoic *Spectator* reader was doubtless braced for this minor deviation from the clockwork frequency of the previous 142 years.

To the surprise of many, Creighton's eventual appointee, in September 1970, was a journalist who had spent most of his time at a tabloid desk. GEORGE STAFFORD GALE (1927–90) had certainly been around the block: after taking the leap from Newcastle Grammar to Peterhouse, Cambridge (History, First), he eventually ended up at *The Guardian*. From 1955 to 1967 he was special and foreign correspondent for the *Daily Express*, a post he followed with two lively years at the *Daily Mirror*. Although he was a very talented writer – and had almost become the magazine's political columnist in 1957 – he was not an obvious editor for *The Spectator* of 1970. But Creighton had been impressed by his 'Viewpoint' column, on which Lawson had let him loose since October 1969. Perhaps Gale's recreations in *Who's Who* – 'looking, brooding, disputing, writing poetry, roasting beef' – provided sufficient reassurance to those who felt uneasy.

More importantly, Gale was well known to members of the 'Peterhouse New Right' who had started to gather around the magazine. Maurice Cowling, a Fellow of that college, had become literary editor earlier in 1970, and Patrick Cosgrave, who took

his PhD there, had been writing as assistant editor on politics with increasing regularity; other regular writers from this stable included Sir Denis Brogan, Colin Welch and Perry Worsthorne. This cabal of Libertarian High Tories, colloquially dubbed the 'Peterhouse Mafia', were all keen supporters of Enoch Powell – who continued to contribute regularly to *The Spectator*.[687] The group was somewhat out of step with Gale's own Liberal politics; it was completely at odds with the political editor active under Thompson, the socialist Peter Paterson, who was soon removed from the post. Nevertheless, it was characteristic of Gale's editorial flair (or flippancy) to replace him in December 1970 with another socialist, Hugh Macpherson: the choice had the advantage of recruiting a staunch ally in opposing the Common Market, on which fraught topic Gale reversed Lawson's enthusiasm. Contributions from other figures on the Left were frequent enough, with Frank Field, then Director of the Child Action Poverty Group, beginning his long association with the pages of *The Spectator*.

To promote the much more vocal Conservative elements of the magazine there were Gale's leader, a multi-authored 'Notebook', and the twin columns of 'A Conservative' (i.e. Cowling) and 'A Senior Conservative' (i.e., somewhat misleadingly, Cosgrave). In addition, the magazine included two contributions that

gave a more playful – and tabloid influenced – account of politics: th Marxist *Daily Mirror* journalis Sally Vincent wrote parliamentar sketches, and 'Tom Puzzle' (i.e. Hug Macpherson, later John Grose wrote 'Corridors', *The Spectator* first Westminster gossip column. A its own concession to changing time in February 1971, the price leapt fro imperial (2s) to metric modernit (10p) – and a week in advance of th dreaded Decimal Day.

As suggested by the appointme of Michael Wynn-Jones as assistar editor from the ill-starred *Mirr Magazine* (1969–70), Gale *Spectator* became much chattier style, and soon differed marked from Lawson's tenure in both tor and content. Wynn-Jones introduce a number of lifestyle colum alongside a resurrected Count Life: City Life, Travelling Lif The Good Life and Sporting Li Many of these gave a fresh and live feel to the magazine; it is telling th the back pages of the magazine ha reflected some of these innovatio ever since.

In the front half, Gale started experiment with ways of enliveni its inherited format. No long seeing quite what purpose t 'Portrait of the Week' served, he fi had Wynn-Jones sign off a person 'Portrait of a week';[688] after a cou of months it moved to an ult depersonalised 'Diary of the Yea which amounted to nothing mc than a gazette-like record of t main business of each calendar day

By October 1971, it was squeezed beneath the contents on the opening page;[690] come March 1972, Gale – and perhaps his readers – no longer felt invested in this increasingly small and compacted feature, and [it] was unceremoniously dropped.[691] And so a feature that had conveyed the week's news without pause for 44 years was allowed to lapse in silence; ironically, this break with a sacrosanct tradition occurred in the very issue where Gale celebrated the magazine's 7,500th number.[692]

But Gale preferred to get stuck into the fray: one of the most irrepressible aspects of his character was a willingness to scrap with politicians, journalists and celebrities. As one colleague conceded, 'Gale loved a fight. He liked causing trouble.'[693] Dowling recalled that he 'was a journalist and a character who simply projected himself and his opinions and prejudices on the public. The radio show [which he later hosted for LBC] was a demonstration of personality and so was *The Spectator*.'[694] Whatever long-standing readers thought of Gale himself, they knew his magazine was going to provoke and entertain.

In political terms, Gale's hard-line opposition to Europe was the sharpest deviation from Lawson's *Spectator*. He was proud to maintain the magazine's tradition of putting principle ahead of profit: although the readership continued to decline with a rapidity similar to that of recent years, *The Spectator* pursued its campaign against the

COVER BY FRANK WHITFORD, 17 APR. 1971

Common Market with a martyr's resolve. Despite the tension, the magazine was content to maintain its general support of the Tories: 'except on the issue of principle raised by the European question, *The Spectator* broadly supports the present administration and the Conservative Party.'[695] However, it was simultaneously committed to attacking its *bête noire*, Ted Heath. The Prime Minister, it declared in his second year, 'has become in short a religious fanatic' about joining Europe: 'he is possessed as by a devil.'[696]

But, as ever with *The Spectator*, politics formed only a small part of the weekly offering. The back of the magazine could still call upon an impressive array of contributors: both Kingsley and Martin Amis regularly wrote and reviewed, as did Terry Eagleton, Roger Scruton, Bron Waugh, Hugh Trevor-Roper, Nancy Mitford, Shiva Naipaul, Glubb Pasha, Paddy Leigh Fermor, John Casey and Freya Stark. Rodney Milnes began reviewing opera, a column he would control magisterially for the next twenty years.

Yet the magazine's coverage of contemporary culture was unparalleled in having its finger on the pulse. A young Duncan Fallowell landed himself a job as pop critic by telling Gale that no other writer was under forty: although as a recent History graduate from Magdalen, Oxford, he seemed par for the course, this was a man who knew his way around psychedelic drugs, was a habitué of the burgeoning festival scene, and – to the delight of Harry Creighton – a friend of the iconoclastic transsexual April Ashley. His column foresaw the multimedia genius of Bowie, lauded the 'balletic, beautiful, bizarre ... androgynous teenager' who fronts the Rolling Stones, and lamented – when forced to endure Slade – that 'the country's most popular group should be so terribly bad'.[697] But one of the most talked-about features was the 'From the Underground' column, written by the renegade film-maker and rock-music apparatchik Tony Palmer, then in his late twenties. In August 1971,

though, one such article caused the biggest single fall in *The Spectator*'s circulation since the American Civil War, prompting one subscription cancellation for every word it contained. The article, 'Princess Anne and the facts of life', began with the matter-of-fact enquiry, 'Has Princess Anne had sex?'[698] This question Palmer proceeded to explore with sarcastic fascination:

I have been passionate about her for well over a year. After all, she's rich, well-connected, and provided she keeps her mouth shut, not unattractive ... it's possible that she does listen to pop music, that she does know about the underground, that she has heard of the hippies and that she has had sex – or, at least, knows what it's all about...

I would like to be reassured that sexy Anne Elizabeth Alice Louise is not going to have every last drop of humanity squeezed out of her by all those boring escorts ... there's something seriously wrong with the upbringing of any young person these days, whether royal or not, whose education consists of being made to suffer the imprisonment of a girls' private school followed by the round of private dances and private supper parties and private visits to the theatre and private escorts, as if that way of life and that alone is relevant to anything happening to Britain in 1971. It is not.

Gale was on holiday when thi impish salvo appeared; but Wynn Jones, as acting editor, had give it the green light, even though Cowling, as literary editor strongly opposed its appearance He promptly resigned, disclaiming via the correspondence pages an responsibility for its appearance His outrage was widely shared, a may be gauged from some letter printed:

'This is a wicked and shameful attack on an innocent girl who cannot defend herself. It is also an indirect attack on the Queen and the Royal family... You should be ashamed of yourself for publishing such rubbish. I challenge you to give publicity to this letter.'

'If Tony Palmer feels that he is entitled to know the details of Princess Anne's sex life, he should ask her the next time she appears in public. I feel certain that he would then get the slap in the face which he deserves.'

'Tony Palmer must go or your readers will. Or do you like having to eat crow in issue after issue because of the incompetence of this very stupid young man? The only alternative is to get a sub-editor who knows how to wield an effective blue pencil.'

'This style of writing is more appropriate to a sleazy girlie magazine than to *The Spectator*. Journals of opinion are necessary in a free society and I think that *The Spectator* is the best that we have. However, it is not inexpensive and so regular readers have the right to expect that it will not become *cheap*.'

'The inexpressible vulgarity of Tony Palmer's article on Princess Anne is certainly not beyond belief but will be incredible to many when read in the columns of a paper of the quality of *The Spectator. Facile descensus averni.* You have sunk; and you will find it hard perhaps to rise again.'

'Tony Palmer's intentions towards Princess Anne are certainly a sort of treason, and therefore probably punishable by death ... but I hope you will stand up to those readers whose idea of freedom of the press is a freedom limited by their own tastes and prejudices, and continue to publish a column of nonconformity, dissent, sedition, indecency, disrespect, and downright bad taste.'[699]

The column certainly catalysed the magazine's fall in circulation; in fact, it would take nearly a decade for sales to return to the level when Palmer's article hit the news-stands. It was not, however, the future of the monarchy but of Europe that proved to be much the most defining issue for the magazine in the early 1970s. As a leader put it in February 1971:

The SPECTATOR is not in two minds. Its position is unequivocal. It has been for some time, and remains, opposed to any attempt to join the European Economic Community. It stands fast on the principle of preserving the national identity and the national will insofar as these are created by, and create, our institutions and law and language, and are expressed in the unsophisticated but popularly understood concept of sovereignty.[700]

Lest anyone doubt the magazine's sincerity, in May that year a front cover ominously depicted John Bull swinging from the European gallows.[701]

Given the gravity and intensity of this argument, Gale sought to provide a counterpoint via some lighter features. In November 1970, Juliette Harrison introduced a column of racing tips entitled 'Juliette's Weekly Frolic'; although she lost her initial stake of £100 within the year, she broke ground as the nation's first female tipster. In 1972, Gale sourced some fresh – and cheap – writing for the magazine: following Taplin's lead twenty years earlier, he hosted '*The Spectator*'s Schools Writing Competition'.[702] In subsequent years, the magazine tried the middling compromise of a 'Sixth-Form Prize', which was at once more competitive and more readable: how many other prizes have been shared between two schoolgirls, one from Darlington, one from Montevideo?[703] But despite these and other efforts, nothing could arrest the slide of sales. Embarrassed about how things were playing out, Creighton used his proprietorial powers to block sales figures being recorded by the Audit Bureau of Circulations.

The attempt, in January 1973, to add urgency to *The Spectator* by bringing the leading article once more on to the front page was ineffectual.[704] If anything, the increasingly narrow focus upon Europe was a turn-off on the news-stand. By April, the crisis was reaching tipping-point: Bron Waugh (restored as chief novel-reviewer) left for the *Standard*, and Christopher Hudson, the capable but short-lived literary editor, was made redundant. Although there were ten or so folk in the advertising team, Gale's team was thus reduced to only three editorial staff: Patrick Cosgrave as associate editor, Kenneth Hurren as literary, arts and production editor, and Charles Seaton as sub-editor, librarian, and countless other things behind the scenes. So keen was he for talent that, in June 1973, Gale appointed as literary editor the twenty-three-year-old Patrick Ackroyd – who sealed the deal by confessing to a marked partiality to drink. (As one *Spectator* contributor since that period recalls, the amount of alcohol the team drank 'would float a fleet'.)[705] Although he had never published anything in the magazine, the move was inspired: Ackroyd at once brought fresh energy and ideas to the back half of the magazine – until 1979, when he shifted media to become a splendidly individualistic cinema critic.

With the budget only able to stretch to £10 (or, exceptionally, £15) per article, the stable of *Spectator* writers was steadily dwindling. One long-standing contributor, Christopher Booker, told readers of the *Daily Telegraph* in 1973 that *The Spectator* was on its way out: stuck 'midway between Anarchic Reaction and Boring Triviality', it had become moribund:

> The portals of 99 Gower Street unmistakably bear that contemporary equivalent of the plague cross, the mysterious initials which are allegedly scribbled by doctors over the terminal patient's temperature chart – NTBR, or 'Not to be resuscitated.'[706]

Cost-cutting measures were enforced with increasing urgency. The magazine started to appear curiously early in the week – drifting from Thursday to Tuesday – to limit office hours, and less attention was given to its physical make-up. Typographically it was a scrappy affair, over which poor Rintoul would have shed a poignant tear. Advertisements were becoming increasingly desperate: the rear

regularly hosted the 'Spectator Hotel Guide', where backs were mutually and conspicuously scratched. More alarmingly, the classified pages were starting to become appreciably bluer, with massage parlours and mysterious group gatherings finding a place alongside lonely hearts messages. Messrs Watson, Wrench and Janes would have fainted in a collective heap. Yet more shocking among Creighton's mooted money-saving ruses was to purchase a derelict cinema in Tring (which he did) and to replace it with an office block for *The Spectator*; it remains one of the great public services of Hertfordshire County Council to have overturned this dread plan, thus keeping the magazine at the heart of the city it has never left.

Creighton's most extreme strategy for minimising expenditure was to save on the cost of the editor's salary by taking on that job himself. Thus in September 1973, quite out of the blue, Gale was paid £5,000 to head elsewhere and allow HAROLD DIGBY FITZGERALD CREIGHTON (1927–2003) to become – as he liked to say – 'editor by purchase'. Contemporaries muttered that Creighton, never an active journalist, wanted to be editor only because it would guarantee him inclusion in *Who's Who*. His new colleagues told the *Observer* that 'he took over the *Spectator* more to enhance his own standing than to put across any particular, pre-conceived ideas.' The paper added, rather sniffily, 'He is 42, likes fast cars, admires pretty women and

enjoys nightclubs.'[707] He was als[o] passionate about stemming th[e] magazine's considerable losses [and], by being the nominal edito[r] could repurpose Patrick Cosgrave a[s] effective editor beneath him, albe[it] without the typical salary that suc[h] a role should command.

In practice, Creighton had n[o] direct role in editing the magazine beyond commissioning his friend th[e] harmonica-wizard Larry Adler t[o] write regularly. Rather, as one sta[ff] member recalled, he was a 'necessar[y] burden that had to be carried'.[?] Cosgrave, who shared his anti-EE[C] and pro-Israel convictions, seems [to] have been trusted with a free han[d,] later recalling that he never had [a] moment's trouble with Harry';[?] only once, in the first general electio[n] of 1974, did the 'editor' overrule t[he] acting editor. The annals of *T[he] Spectator*, then, should also inclu[de] PATRICK JOHN FRANCIS COSGRA[VE] (1941–2001) as an editor. Irish-bor[n] like Inglis, Cosgrave had passe[d] through University College Dubl[in] (History, First), before moving [to] Cambridge to take his PhD – on th[e] policy of Sir Edward Grey towar[ds] the Balkans in World War I. It w[as] perhaps his supervisor, the histori[an] and long-standing *Spectator* writ[er] Herbert Butterfield, who fi[rst] steered Cosgrave to the magazi[ne.] Cosgrave later acknowledged th[at] he had been 'the greatest influen[ce] on my life I can define'.[710]

Cosgrave had become politi[cal] editor in 1971, and rose to depu[ty] editor in 1972. Thereafter, his li[ne] with the world of politics steadily grew stronger. In particular, he became ever closer to Margaret Thatcher as her star stealthily but steadily rose. Two issues of July 1972 carried his 3,000-word interview with the sparky minister; the focus was schools, given her ministerial brief as Secretary of State for Education. But some answers ranged more widely:

It is a very easy process to teach a child to question anything. It is much more difficult to teach them to question with a view to coming to a positive belief at the end of it, and if you are not careful, by a quite ordinary process of mental cross examination, you can cast doubt on anything. But really, you can't live a very constructive life on doubts. You have got to believe in something quite positive.[711]

Under Cosgrave's (effective) editorship, The Spectator became the most active cheerleader for Thatcher's prospects as Conservative leader – and, of course, as the nation's first female PM. She was, at the time, a frequent guest at Gower Street – the very building where Sir Richard body first heard the idea of her leadership. By contrast, Cosgrave's vitriol towards Heath was unbridled. In 1974, he spoke for many in the Conservative party by lamenting the refusal of its most unsuccessful and unlikeable leader this century to bow to the manifest wishes of his voters, and depart for Broadstairs or wherever with an odd shred or two of dignity.[712] Nor did he shrink from acknowledging, 'I have been accused before of using excessively violent language about this morbidly pathetic creature.'[713] Cosgrave was acutely aware of his pugnacity, and knew that his castigations rankled with much of his readership. But, in June 1973, he sought to make such internecine disputes a strength of the magazine by moving the ever-feistier letters pages to stand as its opening section, on the second and third pages proper.

By the general election of February 1974, so disgusted had The Spectator become with Ted Heath and his pro-EEC stance that Cosgrave wrote a leader advising readers to vote for Wilson (another Gower Street guest) and bring Labour back into power. Only as a result of Creighton's unwelcome but understandable influence as proprietor was the piece rewritten just before publication. Still, the article gave no encouragement to vote Tory, instead proffering good reasons for abstention or alternative voting.[714] By the time of that year's second election, in October, The Spectator declared openly that 'anti-Marketeers must vote Labour', a party 'now certain to offer the electorate an open choice on whether or not Britain should remain within the European Economic Community'.[715] Principle over party was, as ever, the order of the day. The Tory-voting faithful, meanwhile, gave up on the magazine's abuse of Heath – and its admission of Sir Oswald Mosley to the review pages.[716]

It was natural, though, that Labour proto-Brexiteers contributed actively to the Cosgrave-Creighton Spectator, including MPs such as Frank Field, Eric Heffer and Leo Abse. Anthony Wedgwood Benn's strident letter to dissuade his constituents from joining the Common Market was published in full only by The Spectator in the national press.[717] In fact, the magazine came to be a haven for any journalists who felt constrained by the title that employed them: George Clark of The Times and Gordon Tether ('Lombard') of the Financial Times turned to the magazine to publish anti-European pieces. What is more, the Gower Street offices gave up space to host the Get Britain Out and National Referendum Campaign teams. As the vote on EEC membership approached in 1975, The Spectator solemnly declared the referendum to be 'the greatest decision that people have had to make this century'.[718] To give academic weight to its regularly rehearsed free-trade arguments, the magazine even hosted an eight-page article by William Pickles, Lecturer at the LSE, on why Britain should do without Europe.[719] The piece, 'Your rights and the Market', was widely reproduced in papers of all political stripes.

All of this effort, of course, was frustrated by the outcome: the nation voted two-to-one to stay in the Common Market. When, in 1975, the campaign was lost, and so decidedly, Cosgrave used the front-

ISSUES FOR 12 OCT. 1974, 8 MAR. 1975, AND 7 JUNE 1975

page leader to note sombrely, 'there's a good deal of work ahead for those in charge of our affairs, but for an objective observer it is impossible not to be profoundly gloomy.'[720] *The Spectator* was not to throw away its principles, and over the next five decades it would have plenty more to say on the European Question.

Creighton's energies – financial and emotional – were flagging in the wake of the European debate. He therefore announced his intention to sell the magazine in June 1975. After sifting through various prospects, including Sir William Barnetson, the owner of *Punch*, Creighton chose to sell to another surprise figure. Step forward the thirty-six-year-old Henry Keswick, recently installed as chairman of the Hong Kong conglomerate Jardine Matheson. The sale price, agreed on 1 August

1975, was for the third time the sum of £75,000 (c. £650,000), although the press reported a figure as low as £30,000. It is an astounding fact that Keswick, purchasing *The Spectator* almost 150 years after it was founded, would become the first owner who did not also hold the post of editor.[721]

There was some serious work to be done. The European campaign, the worn-out hobby horse of Gale and Cosgrave, had let circulation drop dangerously low, halving over five years. For the first time since the nineteenth century, *The Spectator* was now barely reaching five figures: the estimated circulation of 11,000 may have included copies that were not actively purchased. Keen to sell the crisis as an opportunity for fresh innovation, a former managing editor wrote in the magazine that

there is, I believe, a durable if not permanent minority who like and value good writing, considered, unhurried argument and sound information presented at substantial length when occasion requires, free from irrelevance and invested with the independent expert authority frequently encountered among their contributors.[722]

Keswick, the new owner, eviden[t] agreed with these sentimen[ts]. And to achieve them he made t[he] call of employing a man who ([in] good *Spectator* tradition) had nev[er] actually edited anything before.

VII

Spectator Redivivus

1975–1995

Things, it has to be said, did not look good in 1975. *The Spectator*'s long-sought *cause célèbre* – of removing Britain from the Common Market – was lost. The Conservatives were out of power and looked likely to be for some time. The serious weekly magazines of the day were, without exception, losing circulation. And yet *The Spectator*'s new owner had zero experience of the press. Since the only journalist he knew was a family friend from their days at Eton and Cambridge, Keswick installed his man at the helm of his newly acquired title. To save the magazine in such circumstances, and in so hostile a climate, required nothing short of a miracle.

The man tasked with delivering that miracle was the thirty-five-year-old ALEXANDER SURTEES CHANCELLOR (1940–2017). After a conventional route through Eton and Trinity Hall, Cambridge (unclassified in German, then an ordinary in History), he had spent ten years at Reuters News Agency (where his father was been general manager), followed by a year of scriptwriting at ITN. Not only was he inexperienced in the twin tasks of editing and management, but he was hardly a natural fit for a political weekly. As Chancellor himself recalled, 'I wasn't a particularly political animal. I hadn't been close to British politics, having spent seven years abroad.'[723] Like many a *Spectator* editor, he had also never voted Conservative.

Chancellor's first weeks were frenetic: Creighton had not just sold up the magazine but also its Gower Street home for the last forty-six years – along with many other paintings, prints and books that had accreted over *The Spectator*'s history. But, well connected with the well-heeled, Keswick heard after a few frantic days that his friend

To Convey Intelligence

56 DOUGHTY STREET, AS SPECTATED BY HEATH

Anthony Blond was selling up the premises of his publishing firm – at 56 Doughty Street, half a mile east. The townhouse was, for all the upheaval, fundamentally similar to the Gower Street building, although without quite as colourful a history: it had been owned – and lovingly decorated – by the carver and modeller Laurence Turner. It was also just four doors down from Dickens's house, which the Rintoul family had occasionally visited.

In his first (unsigned) 'Notebook', Chancellor acknowledged the need for evolution, albeit of a most gentle kind:

> There will, of course, be changes in *The Spectator*, but they will be introduced gradually. One reason is that we are confronted by urgent practical problems, such as the need to move from our traditional home in Gower Street within the next ten days. But a more important reason is our awareness of the great traditions we have inherited. We are opposed to change for change's sake. Our aim is to improve the paper without fundamentally changing its character. That is why we invite you, our readers, to offer your suggestions.[724]

This being *The Spectator*, every reader had an opinion. The first printed came from Lord Shinwell, who seemed to want to recreate the institution in which he sat:

I suggest that exposure of Government and Opposition errors of judgement and their defects, and maybe their occasional quality would be useful. To this I would add more on the financial page; short articles by financial experts on financial trends, on investments, occasional articles by trade union leaders clarifying the concept of collective bargaining, views on legal enforcement of industrial agreements; in short giving the Trade Union movement some space to explain themselves… What *The Spectator* needs, I say this with respect, is a wider range about ideas, trends, and above all dialogues, bringing in various political and other personalities, as controversial as possible. Readers are interested in controversy, apart from views expressed by the paper itself.

The literary features are excellent and I have no suggestion to make in this respect. I hope you don't mind my butting in.[725]

It was fair play to lend an ear: the writer was ninety, alive before Strachey had first joined the paper, an MP under his subsequent editorship, financial secretary to the War Office when the Aberdare delegation visited Gower Street in 1929, responsible as Minister of Fuel for *The Spectator*'s temporary sojourn in the *Daily Mail* in 1947, Secretary of State for War when Harris combined his editorship with a term as MP, and a long-standing observer of the paper's steady transformation into a magazine. It is hard to think of a more well-informed *Spectator* subscriber.

The second set of suggestions came from Sir Arthur Driver, a reader of almost forty years, since 1938:

I have always regarded its proper function to be the presentation to its readers of fair and balanced views as to the problems of our time, and not the pursuance of a policy without, or at any rate with little, consideration of the arguments that there may be against it, and that is why, during the months preceding the Referendum, I became so increasingly exasperated by its obsession with the anti-Common Market cause, that I was on the point of giving up the paper when I heard that its ownership was about to change hands… My suggestion, therefore, in response to your invitation is that *The Spectator* should under its new direction revert to what I consider to be its proper role namely that of 'a Looker-on'.[726]

Other suggestions were simp good writing – which mea ushering out some of the 'regula fewer diary features; the return o front-page leader; across-the-boa improvement of the magazin appearance; more articles bas upon real-life experience; more heavyweight political writers.

Despite the flurry of suggestions, the change of address, and the loss of Creighton, Gale and other occasional writers, *The Spectator* was able to preserve its core of continuity. Crucially, among its skeletal staff Chancellor successfully retained one man who formed the unbroken backbone of the magazine in its post-Harris era. This was Charles Seaton, who had first arrived under Taplin's editorship in 1953, turning his back permanently on the travails of the secondary-school classroom. From his first weeks as sub-editor, Seaton – by virtue of his broad learning and meticulous research – became the go-to man for *Spectator* queries of all and sundry. Already by 1957, Peter Fleming (as 'Strix') observed that he was

like a well-trained hawk. You fly him at facts as you fly a hawk at game. He knows a great many facts already; but no one in his position can have at his finger-tips the answers to all the questions he is liable to be asked by his colleagues, or even a rough idea of the fields of knowledge which the questions are liable to cover. His duty is not to parade facts which are already on the strength, but to go out into no man's land and bring back a prisoner... A bright, predatory gleam comes into the eyes of such men when you ask them apologetically on

which day of the week the Battle of Bannockburn was fought, whence the Isle of Purbeck got its title to insularity, or in what year the Martini-Henry was taken into service in the British Army.[727]

Another early editor dubbed Seaton 'a fountain of knowledge, and one who never failed to remind the rest of us that we were but human'.[728] Here, indeed, was an 'amazingly loyal, long-serving and long-suffering servant of the paper'.[729]

Seaton's responsibilities involved the compilation of the six-monthly index to *The Spectator*, then separately issued. Such an index had been published from the very start of the journal (i.e. first appearing at the beginning of 1829), and was provided as a free supplement for its first century.[730] But under Seaton this index reached its fullest and most engaging form. This major undertaking required him every Thursday to work methodically through the new magazine and produce index cards for future inspection. His accuracy in this largely thankless task remains formidable. Although Seaton sub-edited much of the magazine, he gave particular attention to the finance column, the competition, the crossword and the chess column. For the last, he would always play out the problem on a little board to check that the moves were correctly printed. *The Spectator's* long-standing chess correspondent

Raymond Keene (1977–2019) recalled Seaton's sterling service as his copy-editor:

Perhaps he had not realised that the articles would be coming from all over the planet, often with extremely tight deadlines. In one world championship match, which finished unexpectedly early, Charles virtually had to write the article himself based on a couple of grunts from me on a telephone line from St Petersburg. His diligence was extraordinary and I thought he would go on forever.[731]

But it was for the competition, run by 'Jaspistos' (the poet, translator and proofreader James Michie) from 1979, that Seaton had particular affection. Each week readers were tested on impossibly abstruse or absurdly contrary literary subjects; within a few years, Joanna Lumley had more than enough material to edit an anthology of winning entries which still sparkles as a collection.[732] On one occasion, Jaspistos somehow lost the entire clutch of entries and was forced to substitute a winning poem of his own. When (as often) Michie was away from the column and the country, Seaton would set and judge the competition under his own name, something he had in fact first done under the editorship of Nigel Lawson.

One colleague of ten years recalls Seaton as a man of 'stoical outlook' who 'spoke quietly and economically' and 'persevered against adversity'.[733] Perhaps this was clear enough from the quatrain ('Demande et Réponse') he contributed in his first few weeks at the magazine:

'Old man! old man sitting at the
    window,
What do you see?'
'I am looking at a world that is
    breaking apart,
And it has no heart.'[734]

Although one editor described him as 'eternal',[735] *The Spectator* could profit from only forty-two years of service. Seaton's only other appearance in the front half of the magazine came in the 'Portrait of the Week' for 1 April 1995: 'Charles Seaton, for many years librarian at *The Spectator*, died, aged 84; he worked to the end.' If anyone has ever been in the position to have known everything worth knowing about *The Spectator*, Charles Seaton was that man.[736] In a better-ordered world, he would have written this book.

Patrick Cosgrave also continued to keep his bubble-bursting nib busy at *The Spectator* after the twin exit of Gale and Creighton, despite his growing links with Thatcher and her immediate team. Still, during these early months of Chancellor's editorship, *The Spectator* was becoming palpably less political. Some readers soon felt betrayed: a Cambridge undergraduate (Magdalene) fired off a letter in January 1976:

Wake up 'Spectator'! The danger lights are flashing and the fight is on, but *The Spectator* is becoming respectable and even boring. No longer does one have to hide one's weekly copy under the table at Young Conservative Committee Meetings, no longer is it considered a vile aberration to admit to reading it. In its present state, the idea of *The Spectator* taking up a 'cause' of any sort is swiftly diminishing... The editorials, once the lifeblood of the paper, are now dull and turgid: compromising rather than incisive...Without Patrick Cosgrave, one would almost despair.[737]

Bad news was to follow. Although Cosgrave continued to write the magazine's political column for another nine months, by May 1976 he had to abandon it through a conflict of interest: as senior adviser to the Leader of the Opposition, he was just too close to power to play the critic. Since Chancellor could not cover politics himself, he at first struggled to find an adequate replacement in this essential post. The columns of his successor, the counter-cultural historian John Grigg, proved to be disappointingly bet-hedging, or unduly drab: he was more comfortable in writing broad sweeps of narrative – often broader than British affairs – than dissecting the weekly cut-and-thrust of politics that readers expected. Chancellor soon sought help elsewhere: Gale

briefly returned to write the weekly leader, typically of a political bent until, in September 1977, Ferdinand Mount joined as the political correspondent. Having honed his craft at the *Daily Sketch* and *Daily Mail*, Mount held the post with astounding verve and vigour for the next five years. Graham Greene congratulated Chancellor on this coup: 'Surely Ferdinand Mount is the best parliamentary journalist since Taper. On the whole I think he was better than Taper was.'[738]

Although Mount was close to the political fray, and would later advise Margaret Thatcher at Downing Street, Chancellor's *Spectator* was no straightforwardly Tory organ. As a sign that it could not sustain Cosgrave's hero-worship, Thatcher's electoral victory in 1979 was followed by a devastating assessment from Germaine Greer: the new PM lacked feminine feeling, was devoid of personality, and – compared to the great stateswomen of the past – was 'a Head Schoolgirl talking down interruptions in Assembly'.[739]

After six months in post, and having re-established the paper's traditional appearance on Thursdays, Chancellor felt brave enough to impose upon readers a much-needed redesign of the magazine. Under Creighton's thrifty proprietorship, it had become a gallimaufry, confusingly ordered and amateurishly presented: certainly the quality of its appearance was out of step with the ambition of its contents. As one correspondent wrote to Chancellor in his first months, 'The present typography does not fully reflect the character of the paper'.[740] In February 1976, therefore, *Spectator* appeared, once more flaunting its freedom from the traditional definite article. It also made the long-desired transition from continuous pagination – spread over a six-month 'volume' – to issue-specific page numbers. After a four-year absence 'The Week', written on the traditional Spectatorial model, was restored to page 2; the letters page was moved back from Cosgrave's ear-baiting front pages to a more traditional position in the middle. What more, the magazine, strangely square in shape during the early seventies, was transformed to its current small tabloid size. The leader was given additional prominence by being brought (for the third time) to the front cover, thus restoring the intellectual self-confidence of Lawson's *Spectator*. But Chancellor was no Lawson – and *The Spectator* was very definitely a magazine. And so, a year later in February 1977, it retreated once more to page 3, where it has remained ever since. Regrettably, 'The Week' – despite the editor's noble act of resuscitation – was once more dropped without comment, replaced instead with the more lucrative fodder of a full-page advertisement.

Abetted by what can only be called 'Chancellorial charm',[741] and steadied by his cool and experienced deputy editor George Hutchinson, Chancellor was able to secure an exciting host of new writers, most of whom would have been loath to write for *The Spectator* under the forthright editorships of Gale and Creighton-Cosgrave. His most regular columnist was Auberon Waugh, who in January 1976 began writing a weekly column under the pointed banner of 'Another Voice'.[742] Always outspoken, yet always gracefully expressed, these medleys of cultural grandstanding and political mischief-making proved to be a considerable fillip for Chancellor's *Spectator*. The column would in fact continue for twenty years, supported by three more editors, until February 1996.

Other regular writers included Patrick Marnham, Christopher Booker and Richard West. Marnham was a regular contributor of the 'Notebook', before settling down to the 'Postscript' column, which playfully read between the lines of current affairs.[743] Booker, a founding father of *Private Eye*, was astounding in the variety of his contributions – on art, science, literature, sport, religion, manners, sex. West was blessed with an aquiline eye, allowing him to penetrate areas and aspects of society that others glibly ignored. All three shed valuable light on what the nation would do well to think harder about – before such things vanished from the world entirely. Roy Kerridge was another unusual writer, exploring the marginalised and under-documented communities in Britain, typically by wandering there with bag and biro and striking up conversations. His relaxed, almost naïve style is unfailingly readable and reliably eye-opening.

This multifarious crowd – many of whom were regular *Eye* contributors – was bolstered elsewhere in the magazine by Paul Johnson on the press, John McEwen on art, Geoffrey Wheatcroft on literature and Richard Ingrams on television. The last (another *Eye* founder) was a particularly inspired choice: ever dismissive of the unmerited self-obsession of TV personalities, Ingrams was a caustic critic of what he watched. Readers of his partial dissection of a *Question Time* episode were unsurprised to learn the following week that he was forced to hear the programme through a hotel wall in Hay-on-Wye and reconstruct the events as best he could.[744] The arts enjoyed wide and outspoken coverage, including from readers: in 1976 an 'Open Art Essay' competition sought 'to encourage clarity of thought and expression in writing about the arts'; the prize of £1,000 was won by an article on Constable by a young English don at Christ Church, Oxford.[745]

Among other frequent contributors were Gavin Stamp, A.N. Wilson, Germaine Greer, Christopher Hitchens, Craig Brown and Shiva Naipaul, whose inimitable wanders through Africa and beyond were given ample space for the telling. Older figures also returned to the paper to critique the course of the country, such as Brian Inglis, Alan Watkins, Peter Paterson,

Enoch Powell, W.F. Deedes and T.E. Utley. Although *The Spectator* still could not pay well, the freedom and frisson of its pages exerted a sufficient pull. As Marnham, then literary editor, noted:

> It is a cliché to say that good journalism depends on the absence of proprietorial (or political) interference. In the case of the *Spectator* it has also depended on the absence of editorial interference ... many journalists have, happily, succumbed to the temptation to submit a routine report to a wealthier publication and reserve their best work for the *Spectator*.[746]

Regular reviewers who signed up to Chancellor's *Spectator* included George Axelrod, P.J. Kavanagh, Diana Quick and Piers Paul Read; the old Oxford adversaries, A.L. Rowse and Hugh Trevor-Roper, continued their long and distinguished service. Alastair Forbes, the social gadfly whom everyone and no one knew, became a notoriously loud-mouthed and long-winded reviewer, especially on high-society gossip. After trenchant criticism of her intellectual prowess, Dame Rebecca West sued speculatively but successfully for libel. Although Chancellor more than once printed apologies for Forbes's words, he was content to give him full rein. Remarkably, after the furore over Princess Anne seven years earlier, Forbes condemned the 'spoiled rank-pulling' of her 'ill-educated, ill-informed and sullen' aunt, Princess Margaret.[747]

A certain Jeffrey Bernard, already a notorious man-about-town on the London scene, began reviewing television in January 1976 but soon moved to writing an 'End Piece' that embraced racing and gambling. Not long after, Taki (Panagiotis Theodoracopulos), a globe-trotting, club-touring playboy, started writing for *The Spectator* on Greek politics.[748] Such were the lofty circles in which he moved that, the following year, he began filing a weekly column under the heading of 'High Life'.[749] As Taki has recalled of these early columns:

> Jet-setters did not read *The Spectator*... Politicians, literary people, Oxford and Cambridge dons, and clubmen did, but not jet-setters. So I invented the quintessential English jet-set couple, Mark and Lola Winters, based on Martin and Nona Summers, a real twosome I ran into everywhere I went. I began chronicling their life. The trick worked. The story of their egregious social climbing made the rounds after gossip columnists picked it up and people from all walks of life started to read the column.[750]

Over the last five decades Taki has given his view on the world, unfiltered, unfettered, and by no means unchallenged. It surprises some that his *Spectator* column has attracted lawsuits only seven times. Even when he was detained at Her Majesty's Pleasure for three months in 1985 – for possession of a notoriously more-ish powder – Taki remained on the payroll: a dinner was held in his honour before he went to prison.[751] Just as Rintoul did not baulk at supporting jailbirds, so was the editor Charles Moore happy to explain to Perry Worsthorne, sceptical member of the Spectator board: 'If Taki were our religious correspondent, I would have fired him on the spot. But as he is our high life correspondent, we expect him to be high at times.'[752]

At the other end of the spectrum was Jeffrey Bernard's colourful, often hazy, recollections of nights and days as a barfly in the sawdust strewn pubs and down-and-out clubs of Soho. It was thus an inspired suggestion of the managing editor Simon Courtauld, that from August 1978 his column be paired with Taki's 'High Life' and christened as the counterpoint 'Low Life'. The names stuck – except once when Bernard enjoyed gambling success, Taki the public lash, and the two switched position.[754] Bernard (for a handy £100 a column) set alight the magazine's rear pages for the next two decades, and acquired with each piece ever more devoted followers. Only he could think to circumnavigate the logistical nightmare of losing his driving licence by writing and posting a letter to himself every day: the guarantee rrival of the postman at his remote cottage each morning secured him a lift to the pub in town. Another Bernardian classic was the famous race he and his betting pals hosted between Keir Hardie and George Lansbury. To make the contest competitive, Hardie was retarded by a set of kitchen-scale weights sellotaped to his legs, while Lansbury was given a hit of Dexedrine. After several failed re-runs, the much-backed Lansbury finally won, and at such a pace that he 'tried to crash out of the flat through the letterbox'.[755] Both competitors – the brace of cats owned by Caspar John – survived his sorry debacle. His Low Life/High Life partnership with Taki – a Townsend-Hutton union of world-weary wisdom – would last until 1997, when there eventually came the much-feared and much-regretted death of Jeff.[756]

Well-versed in overseas media through his formative years abroad, Chancellor was quick to employ a bevy of foreign correspondents: most issues ran at least four pieces on foreign affairs, with some stretching to six. The eclectic team included Murray Sayle in Japan, Charles Glass in Beirut (later kidnapped by Hezbollah), Xan Smiley in Africa, Sam White in Paris, Andrew Brown in Sweden, Timothy Garton Ash in Eastern Europe, and – most polemically of all – Nicholas von Hoffman and Christopher Hitchens in Washington. Roger Cooper regularly filed pieces from the Middle East, which was to be the

primary cause of his imprisonment – in solitary confinement – from 1985 to 1990. Although Chancellor's *Spectator* allowed diverse opinions to spill on to its pages, two general trends were discernible: an anti-American snobbery, and an anti-Zionist scepticism, neither of which positions has aged well in print.

Gradually, *The Spectator* was turning its thirty-year slide into sure-footed progress: although for his first three years the magazine's circulation floated below 13,000, in 1979 it leapt up to 17,000, and would remain in the high teens until 1984. While these sales figures look rather small beer compared with any other decade of *The Spectator* between the 1930s and the modern day, Chancellor's achievement was nothing short of saving the magazine. He successfully arrested a steep drop in circulation – no mean feat in the 1970s – and established a growing and increasingly committed readership. All the more impressively, he did this without sacrificing any of the character and quality that had defined the post-war *Spectator*.

Perhaps subscribers were simply enjoying a slice of the fun that the staff were having. Throughout Chancellor's tenure an industrial drink culture prevailed at *The Spectator*. Of course, since the puritanical Harris had left the post in 1953, the magazine had become increasingly lively as a place for convivial drinking. When on Gower Street, the staff almost

treated the Marlborough Arms as a second office; on Doughty Street, the Duke of York was almost a second home, before Creighton started the institution of afternoon-long Thursday lunches.[757] But in Chancellor's day the drink flowed more freely than ever. Kingsley Amis, when trying to finish a book that required use of *The Spectator*'s archives, recorded in 1977 that

the chief problem with the *Spec* side is not getting arseholed whenever I go there. Just as I got back from their pub [the Duke of York] at 4.35 the other afternoon, six of them came into the boardroom where I had been trying to read back numbers and each opened a bottle of wine. I don't know how they bring the paper out.[758]

Geoffrey Wheatcroft (literary editor, 1977–81) has given a memorable assessment of the working week, toasted religiously by Thursday's famously bibulous lunches. These were laid on by Jennifer Paterson (later one of the 'Two Fat Ladies'), who served as *Spectator* cook for eleven years (1977–88). (She was eventually fired for hurling coffee cups from the top window of Doughty Street because the 'ghastly, vulgar people in advertising' were spoiling her kitchen.) Wheatcroft recalled that

Thursday was something of a *dies non* [which saw] some of the most entertaining lunches ever given. They certainly had an ecumenical cast of guests. One week Jennifer cooked for Enoch Powell (whose hair she ruffled, going 'coochie coo'), the next for Eric Heffer. Alger Hiss was followed by Spiro Agnew. The last-named is engraved on the memory of all those who were there: the other guest was Barry Humphries, who left the room towards the end of the meal, reappearing as Dame Edna. Agnew had seen a thing or two, but even he was taken aback.[759]

Wheatcroft went on to summarise Chancellor's *Spectator* as 'the most extraordinary magazine in London – not just a publication, but an institution, an unusually convivial club or permanent party.' It was hard to gauge the staff's levels of sobriety when *The Spectator* played the *New Statesman* at (human) chess in June 1977: each paper was represented by their own Grand Master – Raymond Keene and Tony Miles respectively – and co-opted their staff members in fancy dress to represent the chess pieces. The baffled crowd gathered on Lincoln's Inn Fields was disappointed to see the game eventually limp to a draw.

In 1978, a far greater party was due, when *The Spectator* at last reached the milestone of 150 years. The achievement was widely celebrated, albeit without the prime minister broadcasting a celebratory speech to the nation, as had happened in 1928.

The Times – that is, William Rees-Mogg – gave over a leader to mark the occasion:

The *Spectator*, having quite recently been a very bad magazine, is at present a very good one. For that Mr Alexander Chancellor, its still new Editor, and Mr Henry Keswick, its still new proprietor, deserve much praise... The *Spectator* now plays an important part in the most interesting intellectual movement of our times. Just as the *New Statesman* was the leading intellectual magazine of the movement to collectivism in the 1930s and 1940s, so now the *Spectator* is the leading intellectual magazine of the movement away from collectivism in the 1970s.[760]

A *Daily Telegraph* leader toasted the anniversary by declaring *The Spectator* to be 'the best weekly in the country'. It continued, 'Witty, sometimes irreverent, literate, no stranger to bad taste, *The Spectator* is above all else fun.'[761]

To mark the achievement, *The Spectator* issued a ninety-six-page anniversary issue, which revisited the magazine's history and pondered its future. Chancellor's leader, appropriately enough, showed something of the spirit of Rintoul and Townsend in lamenting that 'the genius of the English people has atrophied'.[762] Nicholas Davenport, the magazine's city correspondent

for a quarter-century, took th[e] opportunity to reflect on his career. In particular, he recorded with gratitude that, despite his politic[s] being decidedly to the left, the nin[e] editors under whom he had writte[n] never requested so much as the change of a word. He also took th[e] opportunity to re-assert his neo[-] Keynesian principles, especiall[y] the long-held belief that the 'onl[y] alternative to communism' was '[a] mixed capitalism shared betwee[n] managers and workers'.[763] To fun[d] the expense of so grand an issue – th[e] first ever to have a glossy cover – it wa[s] replete with congratulatory advert[s]. Some of these were necessaril[y] rather playful, such as *The Tribune*['s] provocative remark that '150 year[s] is a long time to fight for a lo[st] cause'.[764] In addition, a splendi[d] party – naturally dubbed a 'ball' b[y] the press – was held at the Lyceu[m] only a hundred yards from where T[he] *Spectator* had first taken root.

All of this was moving th[e] magazine in the right directio[n:] the figures for the first half [of] 1979 showed the sharpest rise i[n] circulation of the twentieth centur[y,] up a quarter in six months, to 17,00[0.] Amid the troubles of Britain in t[he] late Seventies, readers revelled [in] the relaxed, eclectic and adventuro[us] *Spectator* of Chancellor's tenure. T[his] was a fair reflection of the man: [as] friends later recalled, he was 'bless[ed] with an in-built boredom detecto[r]' and 'realised that articles are ther[e,] above all, to be read'.[765] His editor[ial] nous and nose were excellent, ev[en]

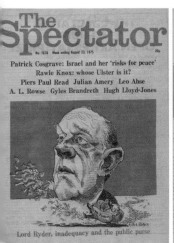  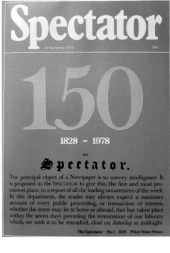 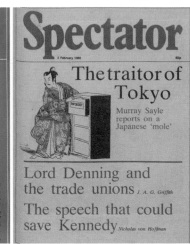

ISSUES OF 23 AUG. 1975, 14 FEB. 1976, 23 SEP. 1978, AND 2 FEB. 1980

though, like Macleod, he never held a regular editorial meeting – at Doughty Street, the Duke of York or anywhere else. When the magazine later celebrated its 8,000th issue in 1981, Chancellor confessed to readers of his 'Notebook' that the paper does tend to edit itself… is the writers who collectively give the paper its identity without much assistance from the editor.'[766] Even the end of his tenure, he repeated is no-policy policy:

The good thing about the *Spectator*, as I think I have discovered, is that unlike most papers it actually benefits from a lack of editorial direction of the sort implied by the word 'policy'… The main difference between the *Spectator* and most other papers is that the *Spectator* has scarcely any writing journalists on its staff. Its pages are filled by free-ance writers, some of whom have regular columns and others

of whom pop up when they feel they have something interesting to say. The paper does not offer them serious financial incentives. They are drawn to it as a haven in which freedom of expression suffers from a minimum of restrictions and taboos.[767]

The effect of Chancellor's magazine on his successor, for one, was transformative:

when I first read Alexander Chancellor's *Spectator* when I was at university, it was a bit like 'On First Looking into Chapman's Homer': I recognised at once an exhilarating air of freedom. That is the best thing about *The Spectator*.[768]

The magazine was even a haven for other papers. Between November 1978 and November 1979, when *The Times* could not appear due to printers' strikes, *The Spectator* served

as one of the primary condu its for charting that dispute and giving voice to displaced parties. As a *Times* and *Spectator* reader wrote to the newspaper soon after its longed-for re-emergence:

This excellent little weekly has been a great source of comfort to many of us who have missed *The Times* so badly. Besides chronicling the ups and downs of your suspension comprehensively, it has regularly printed work by several of your correspondents at home and abroad. More importantly, perhaps, it has had the unique honour of printing one of your crosswords.[769]

It was indeed a rare honour for *The Spectator* to host that iconic puzzle, on 25 August 1979.

In the same year, however, the magazine found itself in unusually hot water. In an unprecedented move, the issue of 28 April 1979 had to be recalled from newsagents because of Bron Waugh's 'Another Voice' column. He had included within the piece his General Election address as the candidate for 'The Dog Lovers' Party' in the constituency of North Devon. During the course of this speech, he observed that:

> it is one thing to observe the polite convention that a man is innocent until proven guilty. It is quite another thing to take a man who has been publicly accused of crimes which would bring him into the cordial dislike of all right-minded citizens and dog-lovers, and treat him as a hero.

The reference – as Waugh went on to make explicit – was to Jeremy Thorpe, then that constituency's Liberal MP, who was due to stand trial at the Old Bailey for historical homosexual activity (from the early 1960s). On the ground that Waugh's remarks could unduly influence the jury, Thorpe successfully obtained an injunction for the magazine to be withdrawn from sale during the weekend. To *The Spectator*'s genuine shock, Waugh's remarks fell flat, and the jury acquitted Thorpe.

In 1981, however, Waugh moved to safer ground by writing the magazine's 'Portrait of the Week' – restoring once more this essential contextual framework to *The Spectator*.[770] He was the first of many to hold this post of laconic chronicler: Patrick Marnham (1982), Simon Courtauld (1982–4), Andrew Gimson (1984–7), Michael Trend (1987–9), Ross Clark (1989–90), Kate Ehrman (1991–2), and – most enduringly and endearingly – Christopher Howse (1992–), the modern master of this lapidary art form. Since April 1985, when Heath was promoted to cartoons editor by Moore, a mischievously topical tableau has provided a vivid visual counterpoint to the Portrait below.

In 1981, *The Spectator* changed hands once again. Henry Keswick had concluded that, despite his enthusiastic support for the magazine, it was imprudent to plough funds into it indefinitely. For all Chancellor's sterling work in boosting circulation, it was still losing £300,000 per annum. On hearing that the magazine was for sale, Sir James Goldsmith, a long-standing adversary of both *The Spectator* and *Private Eye*, tried to secure the title, hoping to merge it with his flagging magazine *Now!* (1979–81) and expunge its name from the world permanently. Keswick shuddered at the prospect and instead sold the magazine to a genuine Spectatophile, John Gordon ('Algy') Cluff. Appropriately enough for a weekly whose future was unknowable, they had first broached the topic in John Aspinall's gaming club. The sum, agreed in March and exchanged on St George's Day 1981, was £160,000 (c. £600,000).

Cluff, a former Grenadier Guardsman, had since become an oil tycoon and was still very much on the up. Although he, once more, came from outside the journalistic world, his interests lay in fostering the spirit of the magazine, not in the cold lucre of financial return. *The Spectator*, he told reporters, 'has always been very much part of my life. It is an excellent read, it is a radical magazine and I think it is rather a romantic notion to own something like that.' He was quick to make clear, however, that he had neither the time nor the desire to implement changes: 'I work 10 hours a day on this oil company, so it would be difficult for me to have very much influence, anyway.'[771] Despite the genuine enthusiasm, he later confessed that owning *The Spectator* proved to be 'a very difficult distraction. It was losing money hand over fist. I had to keep it going and was costing me £1m a year.'[772]

For his part, Chancellor was grateful:

> there are mysteries which no wise man should probe, and the motives of *Spectator* proprietors are one such mystery. What matters to the *Spectator*'s journalists is not only that they should enjoy the security which, in present circumstances, only a rich proprietor can give them, but that they should be required to offer nothing in exchange other than the best of their abilities and their own honest judgment of what is interesting entertaining or true.[773]

The relationship was friendly, if at times frustrating. Over the next three years, Chancellor was keen to display his autonomy: when he received an insightful article on Hong Kong's future, it was perhaps the author's identity that led him to print it instead as a letter above the name 'J.G. Cluff'.[774] Whether because or in spite of this fresh proprietorial energy, Chancellor took the remarkable step in June 1981 of dropping the magazine's leading article, and replacing it with the recently resurrected 'Portrait'. No longer, it seemed, was *The Spectator* to have a collective voice to speak over and above the merry dissent of the individuals it hosted. This was indeed a major change: ever since the late 1930s, one particular – and almost always anonymous – article had been promoted above all others as *The Spectator*'s take on the week that was or will be. In the comfier surroundings of his 'Notebook' column, Chancellor was candid about his decision:

Its disappearance is a consequence of my unease about the leading article as a journalistic form. For a start, there is no such thing — in this paper at least — as a collective opinion; there is a variety of opinions of which the leading article has, in effect, been only one, dignified by anonymity and served up in larger type. This form of presentation implies an authority which we would not always like to presume, it demands a certainty of opinion which may not necessarily be present, and it casts us as preachers rather than spectators. In this column, I hope, it should be possible to put forward opinions in a manner both more flexible and less presumptuous.[775]

Rather understandably, this iconoclastic change was not well received in all quarters. The following issue carried a letter expressing 'utter dismay':

What a shame, sir, that you have smothered one of your paper's great assets. Bring it back and stop being so wet, otherwise your spinelessness will fast make the *Spectator* indistinguishable from its ugly sister in Great Turnstile WC1.[776]

But the staff of the *New Statesman* had little time to react, as the *Spectator* leader returned in triumph in October 1982, given fresh purpose after the political drama of the Falklands War. An accompanying editorial note was gracious in defeat:

We have found it difficult to fill the gap left on this page in a manner satisfying to our readers, and we have decided on reflection that the leading article does have a point. At the least, it helps to concentrate the mind each week on a particular issue.[777]

Among the various figures charged with leader-writing, which Chancellor always delegated, was the young Charles Moore. Chancellor instead filed his 'Notebook' – a random gathering of four or five observations on all manner of affairs. The tone was very much in the tradition of Janus and his successors, although he needed no recourse to a pseudonym. Even though he often complained about the difficulty of turning up ideas, Chancellor was built for the medium: the column was routinely bashed out on Wednesday morning, i.e. on press day itself. To remember this when reading a randomly chosen Notebook is to be amazed. An anthology is sorely needed.

It is true that the Falklands crisis, spanning April to June 1982, re-energised the magazine's political engagement. But not necessarily in a way that pleased all readers: a cover piece by Ferdinand Mount, which called for a cease-fire after the sinking of the *Belgrano*, led to a number of outraged cancellations of subscription.[778] Kingsley Amis was one such, complaining to Philip Larkin that 'that sodding fool Ferdy Mount ... has called for an unconditional cease-fire before trooping off to advise Mrs T at no. 10'.[779] Since Mount was indeed on the verge of becoming Thatcher's spad, this was a particularly bold move. The *Mirror* mockingly claimed that the PM had 'recruited a traitor'.[780] For many, Mount's aversion to full-blown conflict showed sound intuition about how the world was changing; to others, including *Spectator* contributors such as the military historian John Keegan (writing as 'Patrick Desmond') and Max Hastings (reporting from the war zone), the time was ripe for decisive action.

One of the main boons of Cluff's acquisition was the appointment of James Knox as business manager in October 1981. Knox had written to ask for a post, and *The Spectator* was in a position to put him to good – and novel – use. Swiftly gauging the limiting factors, Cluff changed the magazine's distributors, lowered the costs of production, and – through the wonder-working strategies of Knox – very quickly doubled its advertising revenue. *The Spectator* at last gave some serious attention to its appearance, and thus its appeal on the news-stand: it became glossy in May 1982, and the cover's confused clutter of headlines and images was tidied up, typically combining one larger headline with a sharp-penned cartoon from John Springs or Nicholas Garland.

In addition, a new company – The Spectator (1828) Ltd – was formed in 1982, a protective aegis that had not been raised since 1967. Under Cluff as its chairman were the Conservative MP Dennis Walters, the businessman Charles Letts and the journalist Ludovic Kennedy. Over the subsequent twenty-two years, the board would have a rolling team of members, including the politicians Francis

ADVERTISEMENT, OCT. 1982

Maude and Norman Tebbit, the former chairman of British Airways Lord King of Wartnaby, the former chairman of British American Tobacco Sir Patrick Sheehy, the chairman of BTR Sir Owen Green, the publisher André Deutsch, the *Spectator* contributors Ferdinand Mount, Peregrine Worsthorne, Christopher Fildes, and the future publisher Kimberly Fortier; non-executive members were the future proprietor Conrad Black and his wife Barbara Amiel, along with future chief executives of the Telegraph Group, Daniel Colson and Jeremy Deedes. It is clear enough that the board was populated more with a view to bringing together interesting people than interested parties. As one editor recalls, 'Its duties were minimal, its dinners long.'[781]

One further sign of the magazine's new-found vim came in 1982, when Chancellor ushered in a wave of large-scale, multi-week competitions. The first, 'The Great Spectator Treasure Hunt', posed a series of twelve fiendish clues (set by Christopher Booker) over three months. Rather bizarrely, the first prize was 'an oil painting of a Moroccan interior – "Habiba" by Sir John Lavery – valued at £3,000'.[782] In 1983, the stakes were raised: 'The Great Spectator Car Chase Competition' required readers to answer a curious medley of questions (set by Jeffrey Bernard, Kingsley Amis, Richard Ingrams, Sir Alec Guinness, Malcolm Muggeridge and Michael Heath in the hope of winning a yellow 193 Daimler limousine, owned – if rarely driven – by Cluff. *The Times* of 2 October 1983 carried eight separate adverts to promote the contest and the magazine, presumably a record.

Although circulation was steadily improving, boosted by the sterling efforts of sales manager Suki Phipps, the financial situation was never comfortable. Cluff later recalled that he and Knox 'worked like Trojans to get the banks off our backs – could easily have disappeared.' The dogged persistence of these two men was essential to the magazine's remarkable resurrection under Chancellor. To keep money coming in, any idea was considered – save for an unconscionably steep rise in cover price. In early 1984, for instance, *The Spectator* decided that it was out of step with the world of fast cars and barking yuppies. It therefore made its first – and last – foray into

SPECIAL SPECTATOR T-SHIRTS
Featuring a Heath cartoon

ANOTHER IDIOT WITH WRITING ON HIS TEE SHIRT

The Spectator

Finest quality white US made T-shirts
Only £5.50 inc p+p

Send cheques (made out to The Spectator) to: Spectator T-shirts,
56 Doughty St, London WC1N 2LL.
Please state size: S, M, L, XL, and enclose name & address.

HE SPECTATOR DIPS A TOE INTO
*A*SHION (1984)

...shion by advertising a 'special ...pectator T-shirt'. Well aware that ...is promotional move would hardly ...ign with the magazine's character, ...e shirt bore a Heath cartoon of ...me young'un with a mohican, ...mself in a T-shirt, which read ...nother idiot with writing on his ...e shirt'. Sales figures are unknown ...r this bold experiment in meta-...shion – but it served as the garment ...' choice for a *Spectator* deputy editor ...en he headed under cover on a ...ub 18–30 jaunt to Majorca.[784]

...Still, it came as a surprise to ...any when, on 1 February 1984, ...hancellor was formally dismissed, ...ter almost nine years in post and ...er 450 issues to his name. The ...mplest explanation for this decision ...s Chancellor's own dismissal the ...evious year of the literary editor, ...N. Wilson, who had run the books

pages to much acclaim since 1981. Although Wilson had successfully recruited the likes of Philip Larkin and Anita Brookner, he had a playful streak: in June 1983, he had mischievously abridged a review by Bel Mooney (of a biography about the journalist and quondam *Spectator* contributor G.H. Lewes). The result was that criticisms of Lewes ('pushy, conceited, vulgar, over-energetic') replaced Mooney's praise of Clive James ('lively, a polymath') to read as outright mockery of him.[785] Cluff, *inter alios*, was amused by the joke but displeased by the outcome: he generously subsidised Wilson's two-year trip to Russia for his biography of Tolstoy.

Another, more substantial factor was that Chancellor had been distracted from his editorial duties throughout 1983, and spent several weeks away from the magazine. What is more, Cluff was hearing reports from a Doughty Street observer that the working day for the editor and his staff was becoming uncommonly short: Chancellor later confessed to taking a sleep on the sofa each afternoon. When his sudden dismissal came, a trio of veteran contributors said that they would leave with him: Ferdy Mount, Bron Waugh and Richard Ingrams. Even though all three later returned to write for the magazine (perhaps since they did not receive the £25,000 severance package that Cluff generously offered Chancellor), this collective protest manifested their respect for Chancellor's *Spectator*.

The new literary editor replacing Waugh was no less a figure than John Gross, 'the best-read man in Britain'.[786] But his tenure of the post was more remarkable for its brevity: having commissioned one review, Gross was signed up within days by the *New York Times*, and that was that. Marnham, another old hand, held the post for six months before Mount returned to the fold.

Although somewhat shocked at being sacked, Chancellor went straight on to edit *Time and Tide* (1984–6), while Courtauld (with a severance payment of £20,000) departed to edit *The Field*. But Chancellor would keep on giving as an editor: he founded and edited *The Independent Magazine* (1988–92), oversaw the *Sunday Telegraph Magazine* (1995), and had a fine spell at the helm of *The Oldie* (2014–17). As well as writing regularly for *The Guardian* and the *Daily Telegraph*, in March 2012 he began a fortnightly 'Long Life' column for *The Spectator*, which was one of the warmest and wisest features the magazine has hosted. It ran until his death, aged

JASON FORD'S CARICATURE OF
CHANCELLOR FOR HIS 'LONG LIFE'
COLUMN

seventy-seven, in January 2017.

A staff member who joined at the close of Chancellor's editorial tenure remembered the magazine as 'daring, anarchic and slightly amateurish'.[787] A later successor noted admiringly that, 'with few resources, he made it the repository of fine writing'.[788] Taki expressed his admiration that 'Alexander must have been the first ever editor to run a major weekly by moving about in a leisurely manner and operating at a congenial, pre-digital pace.'[789] His deputy editor affectionately recalled his 'endearing personality, his diffidence and his mastery of the art of gentle persuasion';[790] his successor was certain that it was Chancellor who 'restored *The Spectator*'s greatness'.[791]

It is true that Chancellor, as such, was irreplaceable – and yet he urgently needed replacing. Cluff tapped up Germaine Greer, who had written occasional pieces on books, television and Thatcher, and then Richard Ingrams, but neither was keen. In fact, the man for the job was already installed at Doughty Street, and (as Chancellor reminded Cluff) had been given to understand that he was next in line. In March 1984, CHARLES HILLARY MOORE (1956–) was duly appointed, albeit at a terrifically young age: at twenty-seven and five months, he was almost the youngest editor in *The Spectator*'s history – only a whisker older than John Scott, who took up the reins in 1858, aged twenty-seven and two months. After Eton

and Trinity College, Cambridge (English and History, II.1), Moore headed promptly to the *Telegraph*'s 'Peterborough' column. Very soon he was writing the paper's leaders. His first piece for *The Spectator* – which made the cover – appeared in May 1982.[792] In October 1983, he was appointed as assistant editor and writer of the political column, taking over from the rather hit-and-miss Colin Welch, Mount's replacement the previous year.

Moore first entered *The Spectator* with a stipulation in his contract that said he would become co-editor with Chancellor after six months in post. However, on seeing quickly enough that this would be impracticable, he let this clause lapse. In March 1984, though, when the editorial chair became vacant, Moore was the obvious choice. But the press were intrigued by this staunchly principled young buck who seemed to encapsulate the collected wisdom and critical world-view of many decades past. When his succession was announced, he made clear that good writing would matter above all else in his *Spectator*: 'If people want information they buy *The Economist*. What I like is people who have something amusing or illuminating to say.'[793]

Like the great majority of his predecessors, Moore was not a member of the Conservative party but an 'independent Tory'. Nevertheless, those Tory beliefs were to become the hallmark of the magazine in the coming years,

which soon forged a more consisten[t] – if still complex and diverse – attitude towards Britain in th[e] Eighties. By the end of the decade *The Spectator* was unquestionabl[y] the leading intellectual journal o[f] the political right.

Since Courtauld had left wit[h] Chancellor, Moore brought i[n] as deputy editor a sharp-minde[d] acquaintance from Cambridge[,] Andrew Gimson. Other potentia[l] changes in the staff were stymie[d] by the financial troubles Moor[e] inherited: even the Doughty Stre[et] building leaked, and working [at] a desk gave no sure protectio[n] from raindrops. Knox and Clu[ff] still strove to keep the busines[s] financially, not literally, afloat: th[ey] 'wore their trousers out at the kne[e] going from bank to bank' for fund[s] until the Drummonds Branch [of] the Royal Bank of Scotland at la[st] offered some support.[794] Wit[h] budgets so constrained, it prove[d a] convenient cost-cutting measu[re] for Moore to continue writing t[he] political column. Alongside thi[s] he contributed a page of 'Note[s]' – which followed the *Spectat[or]* notebook model by covering curre[nt] affairs, the magazine's contents a[nd] anything else that seemed wor[th] talking about. The leading articl[e –] also the editor's responsibility – th[at] struggled for its own *raison d'êt[re]* and was quietly removed for a seco[nd] time in five years.[795]

Aware that his editorship wou[ld] need to strike the right balance in [its] political content, Moore's first su[

column (headed 'A non-manifesto') argued that 'The Spectator ought not to disdain politics, though it should not go on and on about it.'[796] Throughout Moore's tenure, the magazine remained closely engaged with the affairs of the Thatcher government, abandoning the cool reserve that had characterised much of the political comment under Chancellor. However, Moore never gave his magazine over to uncritical support of the Conservatives' leader or policies, and Thatcher never chose to use its pages. In particular, although it had been relatively quiet on the European Question under Chancellor, The Spectator was strongly opposed to the Single European Act of 1986; when in 1988 Thatcher voiced her scepticism towards the Bruges-based College of Europe, she channelled only a fraction of the magazine's principled objections. The Chancellor of the Exchequer, Nigel Lawson (1983–9), could be trusted to be a careful reader of the magazine he once edited, while Jock Bruce-Gardyne, who had recently been a Conservative MP and Economic Secretary to the Treasury, had now begun filing first-rate copy on financial matters.

When Moore took up the editorship, the most common advice he received – as most editors do – was 'Don't change anything'. Yet a good Spectator editor must take this with a few salutary pinches of salt. In his very first issue, Moore therefore introduced the 'Diary' – a weekly column by a rolling cast of figures, whether employed, admired, or humoured by the magazine. Originally diarists filed copy for a month – the first trio were the bankable Spectator stalwarts A.N. Wilson, Alan Watkins and Peregrine Worsthorne – but it soon became a weekly free-for-all. A huge variety of writers appeared throughout Moore's tenure: Deborah Devonshire, John Mortimer, Woodrow Wyatt, Mary Soames, John Osborne, Jennifer Paterson, Barry Humphries, David Hare, Nirad Chaudhuri and P.D. James appeared alongside Spectator regulars. Former editors also had their say, such as Brian Inglis, Alexander Chancellor – and even Moore himself, when his 'Notes' ceased to appear.[797] Set against the deep-pocketed national dailies, Moore acknowledged that 'the editor of The Spectator, by comparison, is a beggar'.[798] Still, he succeeded in encouraging first-rate writers to offer the magazine their liveliest material. Among several famous signings was Nigella Lawson (daughter of Nigel), who began her no-nonsense restaurant reviews in 1984. That same year, Ursula Buchan (granddaughter of John) began a monthly column on gardening: over the next twenty-six years her green fingers ranged far and wide, from the great aristocratic gardens to the state of the wicket at Trent Bridge.

It was in one of the earliest Diary columns that The Spectator was explicitly united with the 'Young Fogeys' movement of the mid-1980s. The aesthetic – for some a distant memory, for others a tantalisingly elusive ambition – will always be associated with the magazine, where it was first given currency by Alan Watkins. Although the phrase 'young fogey' had first appeared a century earlier,[799] and had been deployed in The Spectator a generation beforehand by Alan Brien,[800] Watkins gave it fresh clarity and colour:

It is always agreeable to write for the Spectator, turn up at its offices or meet its contributors and staff on licensed premises. But it does tend to attract a class of person that can be called the Young Fogey. I owe the term to Mr Terence Kilmartin, though he may not be its inventor. I have nothing against the Young Fogey. He is libertarian but not liberal. He is conservative but has no time for Mrs Margaret Thatcher and considers Mr Neil Kinnock the most personally attractive of the present party leaders. He is a scholar of Evelyn Waugh. He tends to be coolly religious, either RC or C of E. He dislikes modern architecture. He makes a great fuss about the old Prayer Book, grammar, syntax and punctuation. He laments the difficulty of purchasing good bread, Cheddar cheese, kippers and sausages – though not beer, because the cause of good beer has been taken over by boring men with beards from the Campaign for Real Ale. He enjoys walking and travelling by train. He thinks the *Times* is not what it was and prefers the *Daily Telegraph*. He likes the *Observer* (particularly Dr C.C. O'Brien) more than the *Sunday Times*, which stands for most things the Young Fogey detests. Mr A.N. Wilson is a Young Fogey. So is Dr John Casey. So, now I come to count them, are most of my friends. I am something of a Middle-aged Fogey myself. I shall have to watch it. The causes are mostly good but can become tedious to others if pressed too often and too hard.[801]

One of these primary causes was the Church – not a topic that had enjoyed much coverage in the *Spectator* of the last three decades. An Anglo-Catholic streak did start to influence much of the reporting – a streak that has not disappeared since. While many readers admired the serious treatment of spiritual matters, others were wary: one correspondent announced that the 'conversion of the *Spectator* into a Vatican house journal continues apace'. Although he was then not yet a Catholic, Moore's *Spectator* was manifestly high church: it was under his editorship that the Prince of Wales (an occasional lunch guest at Doughty Street) presented the prizes for a 'Thomas Cranmer School Prize' on the Archbishop's quincentenary in 1989: entrants

had to recite collects from the Book of Common Prayer. Poets, actors and writers joined the Archbishop of York and Andrew Lloyd Webber as judges.[802]

The Young Fogey movement was more a social than a religious matter. Bron Waugh recalled that Moore's appointment 'brought with it a host of young men in pin-striped suits with loud voices and double-barrelled names which I never learned'.[803] And, while the raucous lunches continued at Doughty Street, the attendance of the future monarch rather changed the tone. Inspired by this genuine social phenomenon, Suzanne Lowry published in the following year *The Young Fogey Handbook*, which duly gave pride of place to *The Spectator*'s editor, placing him with A.N. Wilson and Gavin Stamp as 'the perfect YF triptych' – although Giles Auty, Moore's staunchly anti-modernist art critic, would have been close at hand to admire that tableau. The magazine, it added, 'has long been the *Boy's Own Paper* of the radical Right'.[804] Although Stamp had started his architectural commentary under Chancellor, and from 1978 to 2017 wrote (as 'Piloti') the 'Nooks and Corners' column for *Private Eye*, he was at his most expansive and expressive in his regular contributions to *The Spectator*. It was he who headed the magazine's successful campaign to save Sir Giles Scott's red telephone box from destruction, if not widespread decommission, by culture-blind BT mandarins.[805] Readers were rewarded

for their sterling efforts in 1987 wit the chance to win their own 'Jubilee K6 box – by providing their mos lurid horror story of dealing wit British Telecom.[806] Entries natural flooded in.

Moore retained Chancellor' active crop of contributors statione abroad. Early in his editorship, h appointed Timothy Garton Asl active in Eastern Europe, as *Th Spectator*'s first foreign edito Garton Ash played a very significar role in spreading Western nev via the clandestine distributio of the magazine (funded by U subscribers), in the dying days o Communism. His 1989 dispatcl reporting first-hand on the Velve Revolution in Czechoslovaki is one of many ground-breakir reports from the East.[807] In fact, revealing were the articles from h six-year tenure that the magazir won a file in the records of the Sta – as 'Spekta'.[808] When Hitcher and von Hoffman stopped writir from Washington, Ambrose Evar Pritchard took up that important lir of correspondence, though testir the post to extremes by regular filing from far-flung corners Latin America.

In October 1984, Moore – association with Lloyds Bank launched a 'Young Writers' prize find the best young journalists a writers in schools and universities' thus fusing the competitions Harris and Taplin. (Cannily, t competition was advertised alongs a half-price subscription option

THE MAN IN THE STREET PAYS £52 FOR JUST £39.50 YOU CAN HAVE IT DELIVERED TO YOUR DOOR

irrent students.) The first prize as £500, along with (willy-nilly) 100 for the winner's university or hool. Moore thus created a direct ute for setting the best young riting before the growing family Spectator readers. More than 200 tries for the two categories flooded , ranging over the Ethiopian mine, the miners' strike, the onomies of Britain, Ireland, land and Nigeria, feminism, hill-lking, ghosts and goats. Moore's low judges were Gimson, his puty, Christopher Fildes, and – circumstances required – Iain veedie, press officer for Lloyds. e winning school entry, 'In Care' Noeleen Gorman, elicited a ter to *The Spectator* saying that it s 'perhaps one of the best articles u have published in the last 12 nths'.[810] Few school pupils can

have received such high praise in the national press – and none from Graham Greene. The following year, the cash prize was replaced with a flight to Hong Kong. In 1986, it was augmented by association with the *Sunday Telegraph* (then still a rival title): the winning article was to be published in either of these journals (the winner's choice) and a total of six further articles would be commissioned and paid for, three in each; furthermore, the winner would enjoy a return flight to New York, Los Angeles, Hong Kong or Lusaka, taking with them £500 in cash. The joint winners were D.S. O'Connor (on joining the army) and Jason Goodwin (on travel), beating a young Radek Sikorski to third.[811] Perhaps revealingly, in 1987 the prize was reduced to only one further article being automatically commissioned. In 1988, no doubt owing to the presence of Perry Worsthorne and Derwent May on the panel, no entry from the large field was deemed truly worthy of the first prize; but the winner of the 'second prize' is now a successful writer.[812] Finally, in 1989, the last year of this admirable competition, the victor was a future star of the *Spectator* constellation, Ross Clark.

As a sign of its newly concerted political engagement, in December 1984 the magazine launched its first 'Parliamentarian of the Year' award. The Orkney-based Highland Park Whisky, which sponsored the event at the prompting of Knox, had suggested a debating competition,

but Moore intuited a neater gap in the market. The contest (since funded by Zurich Financial Services, Threadneedle and Benenden) has become a very successful – and very jolly – fixture in the calendar, especially once it moved from a lunch. As per *The Spectator*'s creed, merit is accorded without slavish subservience to any one given party: perhaps winning this award is the only thing that unites Douglas Hurd (1990), Gordon Brown (1997), Tony Benn (2000), Douglas Carswell (2009) and Ruth Davidson (2017)?

In 1984, Cluff found (as previous proprietors had) that the annual losses were too substantial to sustain: 1983 was considered a good year because it kept that figure below £150,000. In January 1985, he concluded that he had 'neither the time nor the money ... to fulfil my duties to the shareholders (and myself) and *The Spectator*',[813] and sold the magazine. As a sign of the changing times, the buyer was now a professional publishing firm, albeit on the other side of the planet: John Fairfax Ltd of Australia. The purchase price was £815,000 (c. £3 million): an eightfold return over three years showed what sterling work had been done. Most useful to the magazine was the commitment to pay off its alarming overdraft of £300,000. As editor, Moore was given assurances that *The Spectator*'s fourteen staff members would retain their jobs, and that there was 'no plan, or wish, to change the magazine's editorial policy, a dedication to fine writing, quirky opinions, and right-of-centre political views.'[814] Fairfax immediately offered £250,000 to spearhead a promotional campaign, including a subscriptions drive in America. Knox was rebranded as 'publisher', and a team of five descended upon Doughty Street to oversee advertising and sales.

With change in the air, Moore felt it was time to brave a change in the magazine's appearance:

It took me more than a year to pluck up the courage to change the magazine's design and to introduce colour covers. When I did so, I was vilified by almost everyone whose taste I respected, yet these changes, perhaps more than anything else, produced a dramatic improvement in *The Spectator*'s fortunes. Most readers now believe, I hope, that the present design has come down from time immemorial.[815]

This redesign, of April 1985, orchestrated by Alan Brew, at last gave the magazine glossy pages inside. It also opened the floodgates for coloured advertising: one positive spin-off of this was the concomitant introduction of colour illustrations and cartoons, bringing to a close 157 years of monochromatic uniformity. It could now be only a quaint archaism to call *The Spectator*, as the editor did and does, a 'paper'. The new design also introduced the first full page of contents, a list that had previously been compacted here and there; more importantly, it finally created space for the much-needed reintroduction of a leading article, which emerged seamlessly from Moore's 'Notes'.[816] *The Guardian* observed with some relief that 'only in the last few weeks has there been any concession to modern ideas on the layout that makes even great writing easy to read'.[817] *Spectator* readers, however, were quite another matter:

Your new layout is ugly, loud and a waste of paper. I do not think it will help to sell your magazine unless your new target audience is philistine cretins. Did you pick this trick up from the *American Spectator*?[818]

So steamed one letter (from an American reader). Another chided:

There have indeed been design changes. What on earth is the purpose of all those vertical lines between columns? Is it scaffolding, are your contributors being caged, or is there some new Euro-regulation we should know about? The last time I saw so many boxes was in the *Beano*.[819]

Such an outcry led Moore to scale back the changes a little in the following issue, according to the tried-and-tested *Spectator* method of change: two steps forward, one step back.

From September 1985, colour covers were introduced to the magazine. With a crisper design, stronger headlines and full-cove[r] cartoons from Garland, Brookes, Springs and occasionally Nich[olas] Harris, the magazine was now in [a] position to promote cover storie[s] properly and see them picked up an[d] pursued by the daily press.

Fairfax swiftly propelled *The Spectator* into new gears of self-promotion. Most strikingly, o[n] 15 April 1985, the advertiseme[nt] break for Channel 4 News reveale[d] an armchaired Kingsley Ami[s] enjoying a read: he was, in fac[t] leafing through an early copy o[f] Moore's *Spectator*,[820] picking ou[t] for the camera pieces of particula[r] quality. Soon satisfied with his rap[id] perusal, he gave a Del Monte-esqu[e] stamp of approval: 'Now *that's* wh[at] I call good writing.' It is a sign of th[e] diversity *The Spectator* openly foste[rs] that, only a couple of months earli[er] Amis had written to the magazi[ne] to rebuke its use of English ([as] 'infamous');[821] what is more, he ha[d] cancelled his subscription two yea[rs] prior to that because of its ambivale[nt] handling of the Falklands War. Th[e] ex-editor Chancellor, now serving [as] Moore's television critic, record[ed] the memorable event:

My re-introduction to the joy[s] of television after a three-wee[k] absence took place last week i[n] the offices of the *Spectator*... A reverential hush fell in th[e] editor's office when, half wa[y] through the evening news o[n] Channel 4, Mr Kingsley Ami[s]

ARTICLES FOR 20 APR. (PRE-CHANGE), 27 APR. (CHANGE PROPER), 4 MAY (CHANGE LITE) 1985

appeared on the television screen to tell the world what an excellent paper the *Spectator* is. Leafing magisterially through a copy of the magazine, pointing out its various attractions, he came to rest on a passage comparing the life of H.G. Wells to a bicycle ride... I devoutly hope that this campaign will at least double the *Spectator*'s circulation which is, as we all know, much lower than it deserves to be. But even [if] it doesn't, the fact that the advertisement was broadcast at all is a little victory for a point of principle. Not long ago we were gratuitously advised by the Independent Broadcasting Authority that we would not be allowed to advertise on television even if we wanted to because, in effect, the IBA regarded the *Spectator* as a vehicle for political propaganda. It was pleasing to witness the end of this ridiculous taboo, which has never applied to any of the national dailies, whatever political propaganda they may peddle.[822]

A second advert followed soon after, filmed outside Doughty Street at twilight. The campaign seemed to pay off: although it cost £10,000 (not including the wine Amis consumed), the readership over the subsequent year rose by over 6,000 (some 30 per cent). Over the first three years, in fact, subscriptions tripled, half of which were from abroad; over five years, the magazine's total sales doubled to 36,000 – and have stayed above that mark ever since.

The magazine was able to expand to an unprecedented size, with many issues extending from thirty-two to forty-eight pages and far beyond. Moore also felt that he had a sufficiently solid footing to re-introduce specially themed issues, just as Gilmour had done in the 1950s, building upon the tentative experiments of Wrench in the 1920s. Not only did he issue a number of Scottish specials but there were others on Japan, London, Fine Arts, Fashion and the Edinburgh Festival. As further proof of his enduring festive spirit, he opened both 1989 and 1990 with a special 'New Year Issue' to follow the Christmas Doubles.

In 1985, Mark Amory and Christopher Howse joined *The Spectator* as literary and production editors respectively. Both men soon became essential threads in the *Spectator* fabric. Amory, who had already served as a caustic theatre critic since 1981, brought valuable stability to a post that had changed hands with alarming frequency in earlier years: from 1970 to 1985 one woman, and then eleven men, held the position. Amory also proved to be remarkably well and widely connected. To the great benefit of *The Spectator*, he continued in post for twenty-nine years, until 2014, thus providing the lifeblood for the back of the magazine throughout six (very different) editors. Among the regular reviewers he secured for Moore's *Spectator* were Richard Cobb, Hugh Trevor-Roper, Paddy Leigh Fermor, Max Hastings and C.H. Sisson. Barbara Cartland, however, filed only a single, gushing review.[823] Amory later recalled that 'almost everyone wrote best when off their familiar subjects. My favourite review was by Roy Jenkins, on croquet.'[824] On his retirement he said,

I have always hated people who say that it has been a privilege to be allowed do their job and am not keen on those who remember how much they used to laugh, but it has been and we did. I wouldn't have stayed so long if I didn't like it, would I? It seems safe to admit now that I would not have lasted a week without Clare Asquith as deputy editor.

The unflappable and indispensable Asquith, happily enough, was following in the footsteps of her great-grandfather and grandfather – Herbert and Raymond – in working for *The Spectator*, and writing occasional leaders. She has continued to provide flair and feeling to the literary pages, which have steadily become the most beautiful section inside the magazine.

Howse, meanwhile, fast became the linchpin for rolling out an attractive and accurate magazine each week; for many, he became a new oracular source of arcane facts and abstruse trivia, to complement the slowly fading powers of Seaton. It was only natural that he should take on the role of 'Portrait' artist, decocting, crystallising and reconstructing the morsels that matter from the week that was. Now thirty-three years on, and with only one unhappy hiatus, Howse's 'Portrait of the Week' (modestly signed 'CSH') is the essential – and essentially readable – agenda-setting backdrop for the magazine's contents that follow. Before the millennium was out, he was heralded for having 'perfected the art, providing a list of often incongruous items that amuse and inform at the same time'.[825] Howse himself added that 'interesting news keeps well – like good wine. After all, there's nothing more fascinating than the old newspapers you find under the carpet.'[826] Predictably enough, he also fell into the role of resident Christmas quiz-setter, a task that he still discharges to the joy of *Spectator* readers – a joy that soon gives way to frustration. Although he ceased working in *The Spectator* offices in 1992, he has since run the column, as well as filing a second weekly piece on language, albeit under a name more elusive and illusive than mere initials.

In 1985, Kingsley Amis, who had done so much in the preceding years to promote the magazine among the public, offered up a spirited salvo against the woes of the world beyond *The Spectator*. The topic was what he took to be the motto of government and business: 'Sod the public'. His A–Z romp through the ills of the age was an Old-and-Young-Fogey delight:

COUNTIES: Changing the names and boundaries of half the counties in Great Britain and abolishing others is an effective way of sodding the citizenry not only on a large scale but for a long time, until all those who remember the old ones are dead, in fact.

HOTELS (British): No other institutions quite touch these in their single-minded devotion to the interests of those who work in them and indifference to those of the idiots who use them.

PUBS: Any pub redesigned internally in the last ten years or so is likely to be uninhabitable. (I leave out the question of music, which is a case of the staff sodding the customers.)[827]

Three years later, an even more depressed follow-up emerged – one for *The Spectator*'s arch-parodist Craig Brown to mock Amis

Eeyoreish lamentations.[828] Brown's character – Wallace Arnold – was a pastiche of an earnest-but-boring *Spectator* subscriber, whose faux-archaic pomposity was designed to grate on the reader: the 'Afore Ye Go' column, commissioned in 1988, lasted until July 1991, when Arnold followed Brown to *The Independent on Sunday*. For one curious week, 'Afore We Go' appeared from the pen of the Editor Moore.[829] A more sustained series of a similar, if gentler, bent arrived in 1986, when Moore introduced an instantly popular column 'Home Life' – on domestic, country and community affairs – by 'Alice Thomas Ellis'. This was the long-standing *nom de plume* of Anna Haycraft, the razor-sharp writer and wife of Colin, vibrant owner of Duckworth Books. For a portion of *Spectator* readers, Ellis's columns were, along with Bernard's 'Low Life' musings, the most readable aspect of the magazine. One future columnist wrote that she and Bernard

can stand comparison with the greatest double-acts of history – Moët et Chandon, Jennings and Darbishire, Hillard and Botting – though 'Ellis and Bernard' do sound rather like a pair of 19th-C. body-snatchers. All Miss Ellis does is cast an incredulous and alarmingly frank eye over a world that seems congenitally incapable of behaving as any ordinary, sensible, unbiased housewife and mother would expect it to.[830]

In the same year, 1986, *The Spectator*'s circulation passed 30,000 and finally overtook its major twentieth-century rival, the *New Statesman*. Founded in 1913, this bastion of the Left had merged in 1931 with *The Nation and Athenaeum*, after those two titles had themselves merged in 1921. It grew steadily under the editorship of Kingsley Martin (1931–60), overtaking *The Spectator* at pace in the mid-1930s.

It reached its peak circulation of 93,000 when John Freeman (1960–5) handed the post over to Paul Johnson (1965–70). From those heady days, its sales fell steadily, and sometimes sharply. Johnson himself soon swung to the right in politics and settled in 1981 as a regular writer at *The Spectator*, where he was perhaps reminded of his former days by the regular appearance of fellow contributors Kingsley (and) Martin (Amis). In 1977, 'the Staggers' – as the *Statesman* is known for its roller-coaster fortunes – saw its sales drop below 40,000, and by the mid-eighties to 27,000. Although it merged with *New Society* (founded 1962) in 1988, its circulation would fall to below 20,000 in the early Nineties. Its current sales in 2020 hover around 35,000, although this figure contains the lowest percentage of active purchasers among the serious weeklies, below 70 per cent. There is some history here: when *The Spectator* first appeared in

1828, *The Athenaeum* was a serious rival; the lifeblood, if not the politics, of that organ survived via its mergers detailed above. The weekly renewal of that rivalry is one of the healthiest features of Britain's socio-political debate.

To commemorate a long-standing *Spectator* contributor under Chancellor and Moore, Shiva Naipaul – who died in 1985 at the appallingly young age of forty – a prize was launched for 'the writer best able to describe a visit to a foreign place or people. It is not for travel writing in the conventional sense, but for the most acute and profound observation of cultures and/or scenes evidently alien to the writer.'[831] The judges for the first prize (of £1,000 in 1987) were Martin Amis, Gillon Aitken (Naipaul's literary agent), Chancellor and Moore. The winner, with an eye-opening piece on Saudi Arabia, was an aspiring novelist named Hilary Mantel – who duly became *The Spectator*'s film critic for the next four years; the man leaving that post, Peter Ackroyd, closed by recording his two major achievements in harness: 'I am proud never to have used the word "movie", and of never having had a quotation from one of my reviews used to adorn a cinema advertisement.'[832] The Shiva Naipaul Prize continued for the next twenty-five years, putting a feather in the cap of writers such as William T. Vollmann (1989), Miranda France (1996), John Gimlette (1997), Mary Wakefield (2000) and Clarissa Tan (2007), whose success led to her becoming a regular writer and staff member for *The Spectator* before her own tragically young death, in 2014, aged forty-two.

When Gimson resigned the deputy editorship in 1987 for a most exciting prospect, the newly founded *Independent*, Nigel Lawson's son Dominic was lured from the *Financial Times* to take up the post, from which he filed many a story that thrust the magazine's name into the national news. In 1987, Noel Malcolm – another acquaintance from Moore's Cambridge days and then a Fellow of Gonville & Caius – replaced Mount as political correspondent. To this post he brought for the next four years a keen eye for detail and an astoundingly capacious view of history – British and beyond.

But a sign that Moore's *Spectator* kept a wary eye on the fast-changing world – and that even Young Fogeys could own a Walkman – came with the appointment of Marcus Berkmann that year as a monthly correspondent on pop music. Brother to a DJ who would found the Ministry of Sound, Marcus had ventured to submit three sample pieces, which were almost certain to be lost in the pile of unsolicited manuscripts. But the editor's secretary, Jenny Naipaul, widow of Shiva, happened to stumble across them while recovering in hospital, and arranged for Berkmann to meet Moore. A few reviews followed – but when Naipaul went on to become arts editor, Berkmann was given a monthly column; although he was not immersed in the ever-evolving scene as Fallowell had been, his range of recall and self-deprecating humour made the column a cherished long-player. It ran almost thirty years – a musical period of purple patches and arid deserts – before he at last hung up his headphones in 2016.

More entertaining initiatives were in store: with the assistance of his wife Caroline, Moore resurrected some of Chancellor's more ambitious competitions. These included 'The Spectator Game of Consequences' (1985–6), 'The Spectator Twin Town Treasure Hunt' (1987), and 'The Great Spectator £1,000 Wine Competition' (1990), where the winner received twelve vintage wines selected by Bron Waugh, the fantastically opinionated but good-humoured co-ordinator of The Spectator Wine Club, which he launched in 1982. The runners-up instead won tickets to a curious new show playing at the Apollo Theatre in London. The play was Keith Waterhouse's *Jeffrey Bernard is Unwell*, a title drawn from the frequent (and euphemistic) apology on the *Spectator* contents page that caused many a heart to sink. Although Bernard was impossible to cast – a contemporary profile said 'he is 57, but looks 97'[833] – Peter O'Toole was thought to be the best bet for carrying off the barfly at the Coach and Horses pub. The play – which is really a skilfully woven cento of 'Low Life' columns – has been revived and run many times

PECTATOR PROMOTION, 1987

ith Tom Conti later following in he stumbling footsteps of O'Toole. Meanwhile, there had been hanges at Fairfax: aided by the idicrously large loan of half a billion ounds, Warwick Fairfax, from 1987 iccessor to his father, had bought ontrol of the whole company from is half-brother, the chairman imes. When the whole edifice arted to crumble, 'young Warwick' t it be known that *The Spectator* as for sale. The indefatigable istralian Malcolm Turnbull, later at country's Prime Minister, made nove to buy it for the omnivorous edia tycoon Kerry Packer. When at prospect fell through, he fered it to another member of e species, Rupert Murdoch – hough it was in no sense his to sell. ter the approach had been made, February 1988, Moore turned

Murdoch down in no uncertain terms. His letter set out the various problems calmly and methodically, and began uncompromisingly: 'Most of our contributors and many of our readers would be horrified at the idea of your buying *The Spectator*. They believe you are autocratic and have a bad effect on journalism of quality.'[834] To his credit, Murdoch had confessed that he did not want to take it on if the staff were against him – and against him they were.

Aware of the looming sale, Robert Maxwell and a 'mystery financier' expressed an interest;[835] even Cluff was considering the possibility of buying the title back. Meanwhile, Andrew Knight, chief executive of the Telegraph group (a subsidiary of Hollinger International), had intimated at the Tory party conference in October 1987 that Conrad Black would be open to acquiring it. As prospects looked bleak with the current owners, Moore later made a formal approach; the response was hearteningly positive, and Black purchased the title via Hollinger for £2.5 million (c. £65 million) on 6 April 1988. The timing proved to be extremely lucky, as two years later Fairfax suddenly went bust – and *The Spectator* could have collapsed with it. In the magazine, Knight promised that, since *The Spectator* thrived on autonomy, the new owners would be 'able to continue this independence'. Moore in return expressed his confidence that 'the Telegraph Group ... is the right owner for us'.[836]

As it turned out, Moore's *Spectator* was now able to profit from a close relationship with its newfound stablemate, the *Telegraph*, where he wrote a weekly 'View from Doughty Street' column to promote each magazine's contents. He nevertheless continued to write a weekly column for the *Daily Express*, a post he had taken up in 1987. His focus, however, remained unswervingly with *The Spectator*, where things were progressing well. In 1988, he was pleased to learn by survey that three-quarters of *Spectator* subscribers read three-quarters of *The Spectator* – a statistic that any editor would greet with an approving nod.[837]

Good writing was as much a hallmark of Moore's editorship as it was of Chancellor's, but it was often combined with a more energetic and earnest response to current affairs. Among the most engaging and widely circulated pieces of the period were Nicholas Coleridge on the 'New Young Rich',[838] Dominic Lawson's exposure of the UK as the lead importer of toxic waste,[839] Colin Welch on the horrors of the D-Day Landings,[840] Gavin Stamp on the intellectual transience of post-modernism,[841] T.E. Utley on the nonsensical neologism 'Thatcherism',[842] Ferdy Mount on how anarchism is merely a route to totalitarianism,[843] Timothy Garton Ash on the fall of the Berlin Wall,[844] Jock Bruce-Gardyne on his forthcoming death through cancer,[845] and Freddie Ayer on the bicentenary of the French

Revolution – his last article.[846] It was first-rate writing of this kind that caused circulation to leap, spiking in the first half of 1989 at 40,000, a figure that had last been seen in the early 1960s.

Long-standing readers were finding Moore's *Spectator* very much to their tastes. In October 1989, a remarkable letter arrived from Hilda Reddich of Rugby:

I am 88 and my sight is poor so I can no longer read *The Spectator* with any care, so I am not renewing my sub. But I feel I must say 'thank you' for so many happy years. I first read my father's copy at the age of 18 [i.e. in 1919 under Strachey]. In those days *The Spectator* cost 6d, always spelt 'judgement' with an 'e', declined to publish adverts for alcoholic drinks, specialised in letters from country rectors who had heard the first cuckoo, and also it had never heard of sex! I should like to suggest that you do not stoop to vulgarity, even though some readers may like it. With many thanks – it will be strange not to have your paper dropping through the letter box in various parts of the country, and with all good wishes for the future.[847]

Conrad Black was an energetic force as the head of the Telegraph Group. Although he would occasionally flex his proprietorial muscles – with notorious letters printed without further comment in the correspondence pages of his titles – he was for the most part a benevolent patron. Moore and he did not have a close relationship, perhaps because (like several editors before him) Moore felt it important not to fraternise excessively with an owner of other journals. In January 1990, he admitted in the Diary that

This ownership has been beneficial to *The Spectator* in every respect except one: it has been awkward when we have wanted to write about the affairs of the *Daily Telegraph* or the *Sunday Telegraph*.[848]

Moore went on to express his regret at the treatment of Andrew Knight, who had recently been replaced as chief executive of the Telegraph Group by Black himself. He proceeded to critique the epistolary style of Black – 'like some huge mediaeval siege engine' – before noting that his 'bark is worse than his bite'. A letter, naturally enough, followed from Black:

Almost any stylistic critique is fair comment, and there is probably some merit in this one, but must Mr Moore react to every subject involving the *Daily Telegraph* like a bantam rooster who feels his independence is threatened? He would do better to congratulate himself on having sought and found for *The Spectator* a proprietor who responds so equally to the minor irritations, such as this one, that *The Spectator* inflicts upon that person who ultimately, and more or less uncomplainingly, pays *The Spectator*'s losses and endures Mr Moore's occasional condescensions.[849]

Moore's resignation followe[d] shortly after, in February 199[0]. His exit was known privately fro[m] the preceding autumn, howeve[r,] which doubtless afforded him a free hand in his teasing of Black. At th[e] end of March 1990, on completin[g] precisely six years in the post, he le[ft] the magazine to take on the roles o[f] deputy editor of the *Daily Telegrap[h]* and – more exactly – of father t[o] new-born twins. Two years later h[e] was editing the *Sunday Telegraph*, an[d] five years later doing the same back a[t] its daily sibling.

The Spectator was in vastly bett[er] health than when Moore arrive[d:] over his tenure circulation ha[d] doubled from 18,000 to 36,000. Wh[at] is more, as *The Independent* note[d,] 'under the editorship of Charl[es] Moore, the magazine has becom[e] an increasingly fashionable ar[d] unpredictable read'.[850] Although [it] had made a financial loss each ye[ar] (decreasing from £450,000 in 19[to £250,000 in 1989), spirits we[re] buoyant about its future prospec[ts,] as Dominic Lawson told the pape[r:] 'If there wasn't public sympathy f[or] a magazine like ours, we would ha[ve] folded some time between 1828 a[nd] now.'[851] Moore himself confess[ed] in the *Sunday Telegraph* that 'one cannot avoid being conscious of an apparently embarrassing contradiction; a magazine which generally defends the operation of the free market could not survive for three months in that market unaided.' But there followed the charming addition, 'Actually this contradiction does not embarrass me.'[852] In such circumstances, the price of *The Spectator* had increased steadily in recent decades, at first to balance out a falling circulation, but then to match an increasingly large and lavish product – all on the wave of high levels of inflation. The cost of two shillings in 1970 had become 40p by 1980, and £1.40 by 1990. The price would continue to rise at a similar rate: in 2000, the magazine cost £2.20, in 2010 £3.20, and now – in 2020 – it is approaching the full fiver at £4.75.

The transition to the new editor was the simplest process it had been since the accession of Strachey: the deputy editor was made the editor proper. To the long-standing *Spectator* reader, the name was reassuringly familiar for DOMINIC RALPH CAMDEN LAWSON (1956–) was the first dynastic editor. Just as it took 104 years and ten Roman emperors for a son to succeed his biological father, so it took 162 years and twenty-two editors for *The Spectator* to see a son do the same. (The closest hope hitherto had come with Strachey, who later gave up on his son's prospects because of his evidently Left-wing politics.) Like his father, too, Lawson took a degree in

PPE at Christ Church (II.1) after a prize-winning career at Westminster (to where he transferred from Eton). But he was drawn more to journalism than to politics, and had successful spells at the BBC and the *Financial Times*. Lawson recalled that he left his well-paid job at the latter 'because nobody at dinner parties had read what I had written', whereas *Spectator* contributors 'write for love, or for attention, and not the money'.[853] From his arrival as the magazine's deputy editor in 1987, he had become a regular writer on an admirably broad range of topics; what is more, his ability to elicit telling responses from big-name interviewees (notably Michael Heseltine and Chris Patten)[854] augured well for the future. Moore (born the same year) soon decided that he was his natural successor. Whether or not the CV of his father commended the appointment, Lawson had more than demonstrated his suitability for the post.

Having been three years at the editor's side, Lawson inherited a magazine he knew to be in good shape. Nevertheless, market research reported that a quarter of *Spectator* readers felt that there was too much sport in the magazine. There was, in fact, none, save for the occasional nod towards cricket culture. So, ever the contrarian, Lawson rapidly introduced such a column, from the *Guardian* stalwart Frank Keating. But he designedly made no change to the general form and appearance of *The Spectator*, which had been steadily and successfully refined

by Moore. The only change was to list the contents in order of their pagination, for which rationalising gesture readers were grateful.

Politically, however, the magazine continued along similar lines: its editor and city editor continued to oppose the UK's joining the European Exchange Rate Mechanism (despite its support from father and former colleague respectively), but that battle was lost in 1990. Two years later, when Black Wednesday brought our rapid exit, *The Spectator*'s pages were mixed with joy and anger. Simon Heffer's devastating account of John Major's statesmanship ('A Vacuum of Policy and Leadership', 26 Sep. 1992) set the tone for the rest of his uninspiring term as prime minister. Lawson's leader for the 1992 general election nevertheless defended Major *faute de mieux*. If the Conservatives could not win a majority,

not even the British people at their most petulant deserve the prospect of falling victim to some deal between the two least intelligent and least principled opposition leaders in modern British politics, which might sacrifice the only stable electoral system in Europe to the fashionable whim of constitutional reform. Proportional representation is not the answer to hung parliaments. It is the only known way to guarantee them. For all its recent errors of judgment, the

Conservative Party is still the only party pledged to maintain a political system which is – still – the envy of the world.[855]

It was sentiments like these, presumably, that helped bring the Tories the surprise outcome of a fourth consecutive term in office. Nevertheless, that term was going to see *The Spectator* drift farther from the dwindling and introspective prospects of the Tories, and on occasion towards what one could fairly dub proto-Blairism.

Lawson's predominant passions were chess, cricket and controversy. All three found a place in his magazine, especially the last. He made *The Spectator* more provocative than it had ever been; perhaps never had it been more talked about, in the press if not necessarily the pub. His taste – and knack – for eliciting exposés was quickly in evidence. In his first four months, he had published the Queen Mother's informal table talk (via A.N. Wilson),[856] Nicholas Ridley's supposedly off-record comparison of the German Chancellor Helmut Kohl to Herr Hitler (via Lawson),[857] and Lord Denning's private conviction that the Birmingham Six and Guildford Four were guilty men who deserved to be hanged (via A.N. Wilson once more).[858] And thus, in four months, *The Spectator* caused outrage in the royal household, the sacking of the Secretary of Trade, and the sullying of the reputation of one of Britain's most celebrated judges.

The leaking of royal conversations caused uproar among the great and the good. Nicholas Soames fired off a letter rebuking Lawson for his editorial decision: 'You, Sir, have condoned this deceit by printing such gossip and in so doing have greatly diminished the high reputation of your newspaper.'[859] Woodrow Wyatt, the host of the party in question, took a similar tack: 'your publication of the deceitfully obtained and stolen "interview" was a greater gross impropriety than A.N. Wilson's.'[860] For his part, Wilson would later recall of these two episodes that, regarding the Queen Mother, he behaved 'like a cad' but 'censored the right-wing stuff' that was 'not repeatable'. The Denning affair, by contrast, was 'one of the most nightmarish weeks of my life ... interviews are not really my sort of thing. I seldom read them, and I've only ever interviewed a handful of people in my life.'[861] The impact of the Ridley affair was felt widely, with 5,000 extra copies being printed after the magazine sold out for the first time since 1964. Even the Prime Minister felt aggrieved, rebuking Black for allowing his magazine to oust her Cabinet colleague. But it was Lawson who decided to print Ridley's remark that 'you might just as well give [UK sovereignty] to Adolf Hitler, frankly'; and it was Lawson who ran Garland's cover image, where Kohl sports Hitlerian hair and moustache – added impishly by a paintbrush-wielding Ridley.

Yet these characters were the inevitable casualties of a concerted and far broader campaign to get the magazine more widely discussed. Lawson knew that he was ruffling many a feather in the *Telegraph* eyrie when he tried to sell the Ridley story to *The Times*, thus costing his sister paper £5,000 to retain the rights. A good sense of how *The Spectator* was striving to compete with the Sunday papers for scoops is given simply by some of the (larger-than-ever) cover headlines: 'Blacklash', 'Gotcha!', 'Pffftt!', and even 'Read all about it'.[862] On the strength of his initial seven months in post, Lawson won the accolade of 'Editor of the Year'.

Although there was plenty of negative comment about *The Spectator*'s behaving in a rather infra dig manner, these scoops had only a positive effect on circulation. In the first half-year, it rose by 3,000 (8 per cent), the largest rise the magazine would see in the Nineties. Doubtless the collapse of both *The Listener*, the BBC's in-house magazine, in 1991, and the tired jokester *Punch* the following year had helped bolster *Spectator* subscriptions. Nevertheless, the established title had to fend off the glossy glamour of a new British genre, the men's magazine: the British offshoots of *GQ* (1988–) and *Esquire* (1991–) appealed to at least part of *The Spectator*'s male readership, even if the same would not be true of the iconoclastic lads' mag *Loaded* (1994–2015).

Wholly undeterred by murmuring discontent, Lawson continued

Dominic Lawson meets Nicholas Ridley

Speaking for England

A.N. Wilson
Why I tell royal tales

Vicki Woods
The joy of sects

FERDINAND MOUNT
ON CONSERVATISM

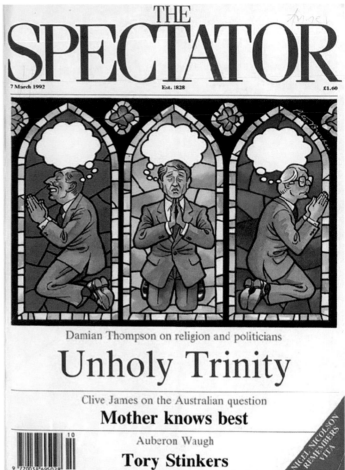

Damian Thompson on religion and politicians

Unholy Trinity

Clive James on the Australian question
Mother knows best

Auberon Waugh
Tory Stinkers

NIGEL NICOLSON
REMEMBERS
VITA

SUES OF 14 JULY 1990 AND 7 MAR. 1992

---

nd and field controversial stories. 1992 article by Hugh Massingberd eighed up the consequences of iana's separation from Charles, rofiting from the sort of inside nowledge that can only come to an litor whose wife was her personal iend.[863] Although the piece was ritten before that announcement me, the scoop instantly lost its lash: on the day it went to press, e Prime Minister reported some haste to the House of ommons that same news.[864] A more ntroversial article emerged in 94, when Amity Shlaes, a leader-iter at the *Wall Street Journal*,

published something that would have struggled to reach print in her native country: in the wake of the Long Island Rail Road murders, she expressed the fear that the non-black community of New York felt about subsequent reprisals.[865] Although carefully researched and expressed, it caused outrage in America, and her fellow colleagues petitioned to have her sacked.

A more notorious example of these incipient episodes in outrage culture was William Cash's no-holds-barred assertion that Hollywood was the fiefdom of a Jewish cabal.[866] The claim elicited cries of outrage from

the great worthies of Tinsel Town. One letter conveyed the collective complaint of Kevin Costner, Tom Cruise, Kirk Douglas, Charlton Heston, Barbra Streisand and Steven Spielberg: 'Far from being the thought-provoking discourse usually found in your magazine, this appeal to the worst kind of "group think" also crosses the line into very dangerous territory.'[867] Closer to home – and the bone – was Alasdair Palmer's exposé of *The Guardian*'s literary editor (and *Spectator* contributor under Macleod) Richard Gott. Strong evidence emerged that Gott had accepted all-expenses-paid trips abroad from the KGB – although *The Spectator*'s legal team worried that the insurance would not stump up if it went to court.[868] Despite Gott's claim that the trips were part of 'a hugely enjoyable joke', he was promptly fired from *The Guardian*.[869] Deeply embarrassed, the paper has kept a wary eye on *The Spectator* ever since.

Curiously enough, however, it would later emerge that Lawson's *Spectator* had itself come into contact with the intelligence services. Three stories in 1994 by 'Kenneth Roberts' filed from Sarajevo were probably the work of an MI6 intelligence officer.[870] Lawson thus seems to have given cover to at least one agent active abroad, who was in turn able to file articles from far-flung corners. These allegations had indeed emerged from a rather rum source – Richard Tomlinson, a former MI6 officer later jailed for breaching the Official Secrets Act. But it was *The Spectator* itself – when edited by Boris Johnson – that later publicised this link with Lawson, trailing on its cover the question 'Who was Smallbrow?' The answer it gave was that this was the MI6 codename of Lawson – a man who did indeed occasionally visit the SIS Building. But, for a magazine that employed Blunt and published Philby, whatever Lawson's direct knowledge of UK intelligence operatives, the story seems relatively small beer.

Black, in the meantime, continued to be a vigilant, and vocal, proprietor. A letter of prodigious length (two full columns) arrived in October 1991 to slap Lawson's wrists for his magazine's supposedly anti-American sentiments:

I caution you against reversion to the old *Spectator* practice of mere anti-Americanism, whether of the back-biting left, clutching their Marx and Laski, or of the disgruntled high Tory Imperialist right, wistfully fingering the later volumes of Arthur Bryant... It is not normally the duty of the proprietor to distinguish between intelligent controversy and bile.[871]

A few years later, Black fired off a 1,000-word letter rebuking Ferdy Mount for his castigation of British Catholicism. Lawson simply ran it as an article, under the heading 'Ridiculous, Febrile, Lurid, Ludicrous'.[872] Such missives were sufferable, however, especially since Black chose not to have *The Spectator* follow the rest of the Telegraph Group in moving to Canary Wharf; for this all in Doughty Street were supremely grateful. In fact, one year later, Black was magnanimous enough to confess that some of his earlier criticism had been misjudged:

While I continue to believe that President Bush's conduct of foreign policy was quite successful and that the articles about the Reichmanns and Lord Carrington were unnecessarily snide, subsequent events demonstrate that Stephen Robinson was not mistaken in taking the Democratic quest for the Presidency seriously and Edward Whitley, the author of the Canary Wharf piece, was essentially correct in his financial prognosis for Canary Wharf.[873]

I would like to retract those aspects of my letter of 12 October [1991, as above] and apologise to Mr Robinson and Mr Whitley for them.[874]

Lawson's growing circulation was aided not only by his skill in producing and selling stories, but by the gung-ho tactics of Luis Dominguez, who succeeded James Knox as the magazine's publisher-cum-manager in 1990–6. Having spent twenty years at the *New Yorker*, he well knew the value of high-end advertising, even if these brands were far removed from the tastes of *Spectator* subscribers. Over Lawson's tenure, he increased the advertising content to fill a quarter of the magazine (thus tripling its revenue) and successfully syndicated its contents abroad. One immediate advantage for readers was that the magazine could grow to a larger size than ever, regularly of seventy-two pages or more. What is more, *The Spectator* was now visible in all quarters: on posters, on the radio, on the Tube, on Concorde – as much *Spectatus* as *Spectator*. Sometimes the push for sales went too far, as shown by a letter the editor received from

Graham Greene. The esteemed author warmly thanked *The Spectator* for the promotional offer of four free issues but expressed his sincere regret that he could not take it up by dint of having died four years earlier.[875] The irrepressible subscription drives of Dominguez had, it seemed, provoked the subsequent occupant of Greene's house in Antibes to stem the flow of promotional bumf.

Lawson was proud of his outspoken team of writers, launching a poster campaign that gathered their faces above the words 'Politically incorrect'. So confident, in fact, was the magazine of its writing and brand that, for the years 1990–5, *The Spectator* produced (at Dominguez's instance) a hardback annual of the preceding year's best writing. Each volume opened with a laudatory introduction, from the likes of John Osborne, Keith Waterhouse and P. D. James. Of Lawson's *Spectator*, Waterhouse suggested that it could be encapsulated by the one-word epigraph 'civilised', adding the claim that 'you can identify any *Spectator* reader one minute into any casual conversation'. James described it as 'a weekly therapeutic antidote of sanity, eccentricity, good writing and, above all, a blessed absence of that silliness which is the mark of our unfortunate era.' Yes, she acknowledged, *The Spectator* 'may occasionally irritate or provoke, but never bores. No one has ever cast it aside with the comment, "Nothing worth reading this week."'[876]

In addition to many of the rolling cast assembled by Moore, Lawson was able to persuade an array of celebrity types to open up their Diary: Jilly Cooper, Alec Guinness, Stephen Fry, Joan Collins, Robert Harris, John Osborne, Frederic Raphael, Keith Waterhouse, Matthew Parris, William Dalrymple, Julie Burchill and – to some raised eyebrows – Ruby Wax. To get more bang for his buck, these submissions were often commissioned as fortnightly pairs, not weekly one-offs – with the pointed exception of Jonathan Dimbleby.[877] Despite the views of their immediate advisers, diarists eagerly accepted the challenge of filling so prominent a page. Osborne, for instance, used the introduction to the 1994 *Spectator* annual to recall his agent's sceptical belief that 'to write for a small fee for a publication with a modest circulation was a waste of my time and his own cut would not cover a bottle of supermarket claret.' Osborne added that it was 'useless to point out that it would be most likely read by the great, the good and the literate ... *The Spectator* is the only publication I know which rarely produces a dud issue.'[878]

Charles Moore retained a connection with *The Spectator* by alternating with Bron Waugh under the 'Another Voice' banner, which gave both writers free rein to cover whatever came their way. Paul Johnson, by contrast, was steered away from his weekly criticism of the overreach and underperformance of the media world: since Lawson himself surveyed this field with an unremitting eye, Johnson was encouraged to use his new billing ('And Another Thing' from Sep. 1991) to write about matters beyond the fourth estate. Garton Ash had returned to academia in 1990, leaving the post of foreign editor to be taken up by the Dutch-born Ian Buruma, whose coverage of the Far East was particularly strong. A year later, Noel Malcolm took up the reins, passing on his politics column to the sharp-suited and sharper-penned Simon Heffer.

Two further turns of the wheel were to come under Lawson. The redoubtable American Anne Applebaum arrived from *The Economist* in late 1992, persuaded to become foreign editor by Lawson's proof that his magazine had been more correct on the ERM; she specialised in stories on America, Eastern Europe and Russia, and informed her convictions on the present with rich historical wisdom. Under the pseudonymous cloak of 'Veronica Lodge', she also contributed two defences of the notorious journalist Darius Guppy, adding the confession that watching pornography is plain boring.[879] In 1994, when Heffer left to become deputy editor of the *Daily Telegraph*, she was promoted to deputy editor, and during Lawson's holiday leave she became the first woman to steer the ship for 150 years, i.e. since the occasional stints of Rintoul's daughter. At the same time, a thirty-year-old Boris Johnson returned from Brussels to be the political columnist, on what the outgoing Heffer tartly

THE EARLY NINETIES (COVER OF *SPECTATOR* ANNUAL, 1992)

called a 'youth opportunities exchange scheme'.[880] For seventeen months (July 1994–Nov. 1995) Johnson wrote from the as-yet-uninvested position of mere spectator.

In the back of the magazine, too, Lawson chose to make changes. After a couple of years in post, he brought to an end Zenga Longmore's 'New Life' column, which had begun in the last year of Moore's tenure. Its author was a woman of wide-ranging skills – acting, singing, illustration and writing – whose father was Nigerian and mother Danish-Russian. Her accounts of raising a young child in Brixton were charming, if not obviously worthy of weekly updates. In its stead he commissioned Nigel Nicolson, son of the inimitable Harold, to write for

the next three years a 'Long Life' column – which, for the author, was enjoying its eighth decade. For five months in 1995, the Glaswegian novelist Carole Morin gave in 'Half Life' colourful expression to the episodes of everyday existence – randomly punctuated by 'Betty the Maid'. A rather stranger column was 'Office Life' by 'Holly Budd', which catalogued the chaos of the professional workplace for seven months (Oct. 1994–Apr. 1995): this was the parodic creation of Alan Judd (i.e. Alan Petty), then active in the intelligence services, who was given the green light to use his daily experience for comic fodder. In 1994, that unmovable bulwark of Blairism, Alastair Campbell, filed unimpressed interviews with

Conservative politicians (David Evans, David Hunt, Marcus Fox Virginia Bottomley), and ventured a political column on what Labour should be doing better.[881]

Many other talented writers joined the team. Alasdair Palmer (employed in broadsheet language as 'home affairs editor') and Rebecca Nicolson (likewise as 'features editor') both wrote and commissioned first-rate copy. The magazine profited greatly from the veteran BBC broadcaster John Simpson, who filed on-the-ground accounts of the first Gulf War and the Bosnian War (often delivered by cassette tape). Willing also to write on television and other topics, Simpson was appointed as one of two 'associate editors'. The other Martin Vander Weyer, had spent fifteen years as an investment banker at Schroders and Barclays, and contributed several pieces primarily on the business world. More notoriously, his cover-piece exposing the cynical financial wrangling over Thatcher's memoirs caused quite a stir in the political and publishing world, doubly so when syndicated in *The Independent on Sunday*.[882] The American financial writer Michael Lewis provided frequent reviews and occasional articles: his account of his experience working at Salomon Brothers on Wall Street, before its corrupt dealings were exposed in 1991, or his review of Donald Trump's *Surviving at the Top* (1990) were more prescient than anyone could guess.[883] Also on the finance front, Margareta Pagano secured n 1991 a revealing interview with he rapacious industrialist Lord Hanson, who had recently failed to cquire ICI, thereby setting in train ts split.[884]

Lawson showed excellent instinct or establishing new columns. In 992, 'Dot Wordsworth' – a female ame chosen by Christopher Howse o give the appearance of a healthier ender balance – began writing a Mind Your Language' (initially Mind Your English') column. lthough it began with restricted pace and scope, it soon became he splendidly learned survey of anguage, literature and lore that has ontinued in full strength into the urrent *Spectator*. In 1994–5, another ig beast of Fleet Street, Simon enkins, began a general column lled 'Centre Point', and has been a gular contributor ever since. More ft-field was the arrival, at the start Lawson's editorship, of Theodore alrymple (viz. Anthony Daniels). his remarkable doctor, who had iled in Africa, the East End and e prison service, was a major coup: harles Moore had already published me pieces from 'A.M. Daniels' and dward Theberton' in the 1980s, e only author he ever printed on e basis of unsolicited articles. nder Lawson, Dalrymple started riting on health and medicine with sarming honesty: the column (first lled 'If Symptoms Persist', later econd Opinion', 'Medicine and tters' and 'Global Warning') ran almost twenty years, until finally ssing away in 2009.

As per *Spectator* tradition, Ian Hislop, then the editor of *Private Eye*, wrote on television; the sharp-tongued Rupert Christiansen took over the opera box occupied for the last two decades by Milnes. Film was briefly handled by Vanessa Letts, who took over from Mantel in 1992, before Mark Steyn began his devastating critiques the following year, culminating in his immortal sentence of 2003: '*Love Actually* is crap actually'. Steyn soon started writing feature articles on the world and its faults, as viewed from his uncompromising Canadian perspective. Similarly hard truths were to come from Mary Killen, who began her 'Dear Mary' columns in 1991. Almost thirty years on, these showcase every week the most astounding queries – and most measured responses – on etiquette, customs and the quandaries of quotidian life.[885] Nigella Lawson – who had started writing for the magazine three years before her brother arrived – continued to write regularly, and ruthlessly, on restaurants.

All of this made the difference. In 1992, *The Spectator* shocked the world and its staff by turning its first profit for thirty years: although it was only the small sum of £10,000, the feat had not been achieved since Inglis's editorship. Seaton sombrely noted: 'Very bad news. They'll expect us to do it always now.'[886] Lawson, too, advised against Dominguez's suggestion that the success be publicised, lest contributors start

asking for more competitive fees.[887] But the following year's profit, of £230,000, was an all-time record, and too big a light to be buried beneath bushel. Since this point, *The Spectator* has stayed, for the most part, in the black without making much fuss. Although it has proved hard to tread a careful line between maximising advertising revenue and leaving readers to read unhampered, no mis-step or misjudgment has taken long to correct.

For all its daring, Lawson's *Spectator* was sometimes unwittingly traditional. In September 1993, a new series (commissioned by Simon Heffer) began with writers sketching a county close to their heart; Simon Courtauld kicked off proceedings with Cornwall. Over the next eighteen months contributors included Hugh Massingberd (Lincolnshire), John Simpson (Suffolk), Enoch Powell (Staffordshire), Ross Clark (Cambridgeshire), Martin Vander Weyer (N. Yorks) and Nigel Nicolson (Kent). In fact, a similar survey had been carried out exhaustively, if prosaically, by the Townsend-Hutton *Spectator* in 1866–70.[888]

One of Lawson's great strengths lay in curating pieces that challenged you to read them: John Patten (then in his first week as Education Secretary) on the importance of believing in heaven and hell,[889] Charles Moore on the distracting power of baldness,[890] John Casey on the priggishness of Cambridge undergraduates,[891] Noel Malcolm on the societal blight of 'Geographical Correctness',[892] and Enoch Powell on Shakespeare.[893] Even the letters page had its novelties, such as the fabricated biography of Tiddles, Admiral Nelson's cat,[894] a fact that soon embedded itself – via the *Nelson Society Journal* – in the minds of imaginative but unwary scholars of naval history.[895] Much the most stirring piece of Lawson's tenure, however, was one of his last, in June 1995, on the birth of his youngest child Domenica, who has Down's Syndrome.[896] A letter the following week said that it surely 'must rank as the most moving article that you have ever published'.[897]

In January 1995, the press could cry that '*The Spectator* has probably never been so famous in all its 167 years as it is under Dominic Lawson'. This is improbable, but the circulation was indeed at its highest for thirty-five years. Operating profits were then the highest ever, at £250,000, with a quarter of revenue coming from advertising. But after five years of Lawson's editorship, the patience of some long-standing *Spectator* devotees was wearing thin. Sex had been a frequently recurrent subject: articles included Martin Harris on married couples' sexual appetites, Tabitha Troughton on her masquerade as a sexual escort, and Boris Johnson on the difficulties of getting Japanese pornography in Britain.[898] But the camel's back was broken for many by an article – 'A Sense of Mounting Excitement' – on the erotic appeal of horses.[899]

SPEAKING THE LANGUAGE OF STUDENTS (ADVERTISEMENT, 1994)

The author, features editor Rebecca Nicolson, argued that for women riding was inevitably infused with a sexual energy. As a representative of the more traditional reader, and a veteran of the *Spectator*'s security council, Perry Worsthorne led the protest: the fuss brought about his dismissal as a board member, eliciting the lament that 'Britain's erstwhile leading intellectual journal, which at any rate used to be the staple weekend reading of the more serious-minded clergy', had sunk to publishing 'distasteful tosh'.[900] Later that year, he complained further that 'Lawson argued it was improper for me, a director of the company, to criticise one of its products... For all its striking achievements, *The Spectator* cannot be said to stretch the mind.'[901]

The time was perhaps ripe for Lawson to move on to a larger team and far larger audience. But he continued to tweak the title

throughout his last months in post. On 1 April 1995, a bridge column at last appeared in the magazine, a feature that was overseen by the star player Andrew Robson for five years, before Susanna Gross, literary editor of the *Mail on Sunday*, took over; in 2008, she began sharing the column with the philanthropist Janet de Botton. On a far grander scale was the launch in March 199[?] of the Spectator Lecture, sponsored by Allied Dunbar, for which the first speaker was the new leader of the Labour Party. The reproduction of this lecture in the magazine was thus the first appearance of the byline 'Tony Blair';[902] 'Anthony Blair', however, had already written two rather drab pieces for Chancellor *Spectator*, on contemporary legal wrangles (a third submission had been spiked).[903] The Spectator Lecturers maintained a high bar: the future Prime Minister was followed by the incumbent Prime Minister, John Major, who was himself followed by the successor to both, Gordon Brown.[904] The series understandably failed to continue thereafter.

Just before Lawson moved on, Kingsley Amis made his final contribution to *The Spectator*, for which he had first written forty-one years ago, under Taplin.[?] His letter – the last that survives from his life – sought to defend English idiom, castigating Br[?] Waugh for following the clause 'we had anything to communicate with 'but we don't' instead of 'b[?]

THE SPECTATOR

5 October 1994   Est. 1828   £1.80

Boris Johnson witnesses the fate of the party faithful

The old guard

Roy Greenslade meets the editor of the News of the World

'I totally believe in the monarchy'

Nigella Lawson experiences

Nicole Farhi's fiasco

OFFICE LIFE: HOLLY BUDD'S NEW COLUMN

70038 695042

BORIS JOHNSON'S FIRST COVER STORY AS POLITICAL CORRESPONDENT (15 OCT. 1994)

and for.'[906] Over the course of his five-year editorship, circulation of the magazine grew by a third, from 36,000 to 47,000. The magazine's finances had been turned around: when he took up the post, it was losing £250,000 per annum, and when he left, it was making that amount. Lawson had proved himself ready to take on a national newspaper, so Black reshuffled the pack, moving Lawson on to edit his sister title, the *Sunday Telegraph*, while Moore took up the reins at the *Daily Telegraph*.

Against all the doom-laden predictions of demise in the previous generation, disaster had been averted. Three men – Chancellor, Moore and Lawson – under four indulgent proprietors – Keswick, Cluff, Fairfax and Black – aided by two enterprising business managers – Knox and Dominguez – had with labour, love and luck transformed a magazine whose sales were plummeting headlong into four-figure obscurity into one that was at once on the pulse and on the rise. And so, in twenty years, a rarefied and somewhat political weekly had increased its circulation fourfold. Where next?

haven't'. After setting out other [cau]ses of the regrettable influence of [A]merican English – such as 'tidbit' [an]d 'chickadee' – he ended with the [wa]spish remark that following 'don't' [wi]th 'have' 'is easier for monoglot [im]migrants'. One struggles to think [of] another correspondence page [wh]ere such precise details could [ca]use such passion.

In his final contribution as editor, fittingly to the Diary column, Lawson pointedly wrote, 'The emotion I feel at leaving 56 Doughty Street, after eight idyllic years, is a profound sense of loss. And that, in turn, has told me what I never sufficiently appreciated during my time here: that *The Spectator*'s staff and readers are delights to work with

Making the News

1995–2020

To find a new editor, Black turned to the writers he knew, and what he knew well was the Telegraph Group. Among these, there was a man who combined staunch Conservatism, journalistic irreverence and an ever-ready wit. In October 1995, then, **FRANK ROBERT JOHNSON** (1943–2006), deputy editor of the *Sunday Telegraph*, was announced as *The Spectator*'s new editor, a post he took up at the start of November. Like many of his predecessors, from Rintoul onwards, Johnson had not trodden the establishment route through university. Instead, having left school with one O-Level (in Commercial Studies), he took a bus to Fleet Street, entered the first set of offices he saw, and asked for a job. Thus his journalistic career began in 1959 with a brief spell as messenger boy for the *Sunday Express*. Before long, his talent for writing and his impish sense of humour helped him work his way up through various local papers – and those not so local, such as the *North-West Evening Mail* of Barrow-in-Furness (1965–6). For most of the 1970s, he had been a political writer for the *Daily Telegraph*, before working at *The Times* and the *Sunday Telegraph*, straddling a brief spell at Goldsmith's ill-fated *Now!* magazine. Setting aside the *sub rosa*

editorship of Atkins,[907] Johnson (at fifty-two) remains the only editor who has taken up the *Spectator* reins aged over fifty.

Although he had written now and again for the magazine – first in the early days of Chancellor's editorship, with a piece on the directionless Liberals[908] – Johnson had not been closely involved with its more recent fortunes. His appointment therefore raised some eyebrows – and set rumours running that his close friendship with Barbara Amiel, the wife of Conrad Black, explained the surprising elevation. A number of his other colleagues had been regarded as front-runners for the post, most especially the magazine's recent deputy editor, *Telegraph* columnist Simon Heffer. On hearing that he had been passed over as both *Spectator* and *Telegraph* editor, Heffer promptly left the Telegraph Building and the Telegraph Group to join the *Daily Mail* – whose editor, Paul Dacre, had just been persuaded not to jump ship to the *Telegraph*. The long-standing chairman of the *Spectator* board later described Heffer ruefully as 'one of the best editors we never had'.[909] Some felt that even Johnson himself was disappointed with the outcome of Black's reshuffle, in which he had hoped to become editor of either *Telegraph*. His friend Stephen

Glover disagreed: 'One of the joys of *Th Spectator* is that it doesn't have all th crap that bores Frank – stuff about fashio and soft features – which you've got t have in a newspaper… Frank's more i the entertainment business than Charle Moore or Dominic Lawson.'[910] He wa certainly a man who enjoyed life – and th freedoms afforded by bachelordom.

Lawson, always a step ahead in th journalistic game, had taken with hi all of the *Spectator* articles that we cued to appear. Having to think on h feet to fill his first issue (of 4 Nov. 199 Johnson decided to make clear to a readers the change at the tiller. The Dia of the infamous diarist Alan Clark (a occasional reviewer) took a remarkab personal swipe at the outgoing editor its opening paragraph:

How lovely to be invited to write fo *The Spectator* again. Now that the loathsome sneering features, pastil glistening, of its former editor pee slit-eyedly out at the reader from the op ed page in the *Sunday Telegraph* I may occasionally be granted this the most eclectic of all privileges i journalism.[911]

Lawson, among others, detected more than a whiff of anti-Semitism. Aghast correspondence arrived post-haste, including a letter from Black, condemning the 'outrageous comments' and reassuring all that 'the publication of those offensive and tasteless reflections was an oversight for which the editor has spontaneously expressed regret to his predecessor.'[912] Clark too later confessed his surprise at getting these lines through: 'I can't believe Frank actually put that paragraph in!'[913] It seems that the text in question was a private note added on the submitted copy: Johnson, mischievously or mistakenly, had worked it in as the opening paragraph.[914]

In his first leader, Johnson set out his plan to make the magazine a space for open dissent: 'New editors are often accused of simply bringing in their friends. I have. But, in a break with this tradition I have also tried to bring in my enemies.' To make the point, the first issue also contained a rather supercilious piece from the veteran political journalist Ed Pearce, entitled 'Why I dislike The Spectator'. The magazine, readers were told, suffers from 'overdone dandyism': anachronism is the name of The Spectator game', combined with 'brutish Europhobia' and 'snob-flecked malice towards the Prime Minister'. It was, indeed, a curious commission.

Commentators were quick to declare that Johnson was 'the first person of working-class origin … to edit The Spectator'.[915] This perhaps seemed credible, but could not be true: Walter Taplin was a case in point, but the magazine's founding editor epitomised the route from a staunchly working-class background into the heart of journalism. Johnson himself was ready

to remind others of his unconventional *cursus honorum*, and used to say 'PPE is the degree you get by reading the papers'.[916] Alan Watkins told *The Guardian* that the new editor was 'not seduced by snobbery or love of power, so much as glamour. He regards himself as a sort of Balzacian or Stendhalian hero – the young man who conquers London by storm and is invited to all the best dinner tables.'[917] The contributors to Johnson's Diary soon revealed those wide-ranging society contacts. Alongside many diarists from the Moore-Lawson stable, and the predictable roll-call of Tory politicians, he introduced a number of media personalities (Anna Ford, Trevor McDonald, John Humphrys, Rory Bremner) as well as some more outspoken journalists (A.A. Gill, Peter Hitchens, William Rees-Mogg, Andrew Neil), all spiced up with the occasional reappearance of Alan Clark. For all the reader knew, Johnson was spending long evenings in such company, lurking between the lines of their weekly reflections.

Those who knew the provocative and sometimes flippant character of Johnson's journalistic career were interested to see how he would handle the unique challenge posed by *Spectator* leaders. Most would have been surprised to find that his solution – apparently recommended by Stephen Glover – was not just to write in his usual style but to sign them off with his own name. Whether, like Chancellor, he felt uncomfortable in speaking on behalf of the personified but depersonalised *Spectator*, whether he had no strong political homilies to preach each week, or whether he had no wish to reinvent his distinctive prose style, this novel practice lasted for ten months. Johnson also followed Moore's initial

habit of using some of the space available on page 3 to add a second, pseudo-leader, which operated more like an editor's notebook commenting on the magazine's features. This bet-hedging arrangement did not please all: one correspondent wrote in to say '*The Spectator* is not an opera buffa and one hopes that you will not trivialise it… By the way, you are too famous to need to sign your leaders, and I am surprised that you wanted to sign the last one.'[918] In August 1996, Johnson's name quietly disappeared. Thereafter, Edward Heathcoat-Amory (nephew of David, the Conservative MP, second cousin of Mark, the long-serving literary editor) joined as an assistant editor and became a regular leader-writer, although he – and several other divers hands – were content to work behind the traditional veil of anonymity.

On Lawson's exit, two of his editorial staff, Alasdair Palmer and Rebecca Nicolson, had followed him to the *Sunday Telegraph*. Other changes rapidly followed: Boris Johnson gave up the political column to become chief political correspondent at the *Daily Telegraph*. And Anne Applebaum, the recently installed deputy editor, soon left for the *Evening Standard*, presaging that an era of instability was afoot. There was thus a pressing need for Johnson to recruit some new talent just to keep the magazine's wheels turning. He duly brought in the twenty-nine-year-old foreign correspondent for *The Times*, Anne McElvoy, who had written on and off for *The Spectator* since 1990. To take command of the politics column he called into action Bruce Anderson, who had occasionally – but always

Johnson (F.), Johnson (B.), d'Ancona, Nelson

memorably – performed this role for Moore when correspondents were away from the magazine. The appointment was ingenious at a time of growing political consensus around the New Labour mission: Anderson, as one of the sharpest political minds of the modern *Spectator*, could cut through the group-think with a stroke of his trenchant nib. Although he is now typically pictured with bottle at hand, it was he who was clear-headed enough to tip John Major as a future Tory leader in 1987, see that William Hague was headed for the same post when Welsh Secretary in 1995, and promote the prospects of David Cameron in 2003 before anyone else in the national press. But his political nous is secondary to his laconic wordsmithery: only a handful of *Spectator* writers past and present can challenge Anderson in knocking out diamond-cut and rapier-sharp epigraphs in a four-word subordinate clause.

Johnson's other significant appointment was Petronella Wyatt (daughter of Woodrow), introduced from the *Sunday Telegraph* as associate editor and first charged with alternating a fortnightly piece with Waugh's 'Another Voice' – by

now an unbroken *Spectator* institution for almost twenty years. Wyatt, then twenty-seven, was already fêted as 'The Forces' Sweetheart of right-wing journalism';[919] the young age of her and McElvoy led a contemporary observer to remark that '*The Spectator* seems oddly reluctant to employ anyone in their thirties and forties.'[920] Wyatt had first been thrust upon *Spectator* readers in 1988, as the subject of a wide-eyed piece headed 'In praise of Petronella'.[921] Its author was Taki, who had been sent into a reverie by her strictures against pop music in the *Sunday Telegraph*. The magazine had to wait another four years for her own byline to appear, beneath the knowing title 'In praise of summer pudding'.[922] Not everyone was convinced by Johnson's bold call: a contemporary report in the press alleged that 'Everyone seems to lament his appointment of Petronella Wyatt … to alternate as a columnist with Auberon Waugh, because she is so limply punching above her weight.'[923] For his own part, Waugh chose to end the column three months later – but his reasons were rather cruder than the awkward clash of journalistic styles:

Last time I left *The Spectator*, in 1973, it might have been for the idealistic reason that I thought it had no business to be so boring about Europe. But I have been writing the 'Another voice' column for 20 years, and my only reason for leaving it now is greed for money. That is all the New Conservatism has to teach, and I have learned the lesson too well.[924]

Waugh was quietly replaced wi[th] Matthew Parris, a long-standing columni[st] at *The Times*, and occasional contribut[or] to *The Spectator*, especially when Sim[on] Heffer took his holidays. Parris has fil[ed] fortnightly ever since (although t[he] question-begging title 'Another Voice' w[as] dropped as a header in 2010); he continu[es] to chart the ebb and flow of political a[nd] social causes, now with earnest optimis[m] now with pejoristic scepticism, especia[lly] on the Brexit aftermath. Although o[f] Conservative bent, his particular streng[th] is firmly in the broad-brush liber[al] traditions of *The Spectator*.

From Johnson's first issue, the politi[cal] editor of the BBC, Robin Oakley, beg[an] his weekly racing column 'The Tu[rf] which later became a fortnightly dose of good humour and sense; if his ease of expression is matched by an ease of pin-sticking, Oakley must be the wealthiest columnist in Britain. In January 1996, indulging somewhat his own obsessions, Johnson resurrected the *Spectator* tradition of having a press commentator. His appointment was the admirably outspoken Stephen Glover, a co-founder of *The Independent* and frequent *Spectator* contributor. His weekly 'Media Studies' column soon became one of the most clever and controversial corners of journalistic criticism, fast forging friends as well as enemies – until, nine years down the line, it found itself spiked for good. Other innovations came unprompted. In February 1996, a classics lecturer at the University of Newcastle wrote a piece on the unjustly overlooked similarities between Ancient Greek literature and Newcastle United's vacillating fortunes on the football pitch.[925] Its author was the sparkling and sparky Peter Jones, who won by this piece the column which first appeared a fortnight later.[926] *Ancient and Modern*, juxtaposing modern absurdities with ancient doctrine, still proves to be a weekly *Spectator* fixture – a veritable keepsake, or κτῆμα ἐς ἀεί – more than a thousand pieces on.

Despite these fine acquisitions, not all observers were confident about the direction in which *The Spectator* was heading. For all its increasingly diverse columns, one staff member leaked that the magazine 'lacks focus. The features were sharper under Dominic Lawson.' Another simply said that it was 'no bloody good'.[927] A. N. Wilson was moved to lament how the magazine had changed from Lawson to Johnson:

When *Punch* died in April 1992, there was in existence a weekly magazine that was in every way sharper, funnier and more interesting, namely *The Spectator*. Now that *The Spectator* has mysteriously died on its feet and become, by general and sad consent, totally unreadable, there is a gap in the market.[928]

Yet even these critics could hardly have braced themselves for a remarkable piece unveiled in the Christmas issue of 1996. It was an interview about European policy and Conservatism. Nothing to surprise there, but it was the first *Spectator* political interview conducted with a globally famous pop group – for the Spice Girls were then at the height of their powers. The deft dialogue of Simon Sebag Montefiore somehow elicited the most astounding soundbites from so tightly managed a quintet:

'We are true Thatcherites.'
'We are desperately worried about the slide to a single currency.'
'The single currency is an outrage… The Euro-bureaucrats are destroying every bit of national identity and individuality.'[929]

The sound of journalistic jaws hitting the ground was serenaded by a nation scratching its head. The Spices Ginger and Posh were, it seemed, hard-line anti-EU Conservatives. When Geri Halliwell 'argued the Eurosceptic case with passionate pride', she was said to resemble 'nothing less than a leggy, pouting, pneumatically Eurosceptic John Redwood'. Alas, such strident

politics did not translate into pop – and the mooted concept album on the Lisbon Treaty never landed. As some consolation, this *Spectator* Christmas issue achieved sales of 60,000 – a third more than its typical circulation.

Luis Dominguez, the hot-shot publisher who turbo-charged Lawson's success, was replaced in 1996 by another American, who proved to be even more go-getting. Kimberly Fortier (*née* Solomon, and from 2001 Quinn) had studied British political and social history at Vassar, before starting a master's degree at Oxford. The lure of journalism led her to abandon academia and head for the offices of Condé Nast. A decade later, she found berth at *The Spectator*. Her objectives were clear: the magazine needed to make more money, and to do so it needed to be more efficient in its day-to-day operations. To show the earth-shattering gravity of her commitment, she restricted the staff's access to the Doughty Street drinks cabinet. Rather worryingly, she also expressed the desire for the parent company to purchase its essential counterweight, the *New Statesman*. Her ten-year tenure – soon enough marked by the addition of her name to the *Spectator*'s contents page[930] – was destined to be turbulent. Her decision to terminate the compilation of the biannual *Spectator* index in mid-1998, issued as a vital reference aid for 170 years, was a telling sign of things to come.

Times, inevitably, were changing. The last 'Low Life' column by Jeffrey Bernard appeared on 23 August 1997. His final pieces, written from Middlesex Hospital, gave a profound insight into the mind of man when the end draws nigh amid such surgically and emotionally sterile surroundings. Even in these trying times, however, Bernard found solace in humour and past escapades: it was he who, when asked by one doctor why he drank so much, answered, 'To stop myself jogging.'[931] His last column, weighing up whether or not to end his dialysis treatment, acknowledged that to do so would be like 'a man tied to a post opposite a firing squad: the squad pull their triggers and the prisoner stands there watching the bullets coming rather slowly towards him for three weeks or more.'[932] He chose to face the squad, and died, aged sixty-five, on 4 September – a death lost in the profound public mourning for Princess Diana. At his funeral, Chancellor recalled that

> Jeff not merely led the life of total self-indulgence of which millions live in fascinated fear and envy. He let them know precisely what this kind of life was like and told them in merciless detail how terrible the consequences could be of devoting a life exclusively to the pleasures of drink, sex and gambling… But because he was so brilliant and so funny, so brave and so astonishingly honest, he gradually acquired special status as the middle class's one officially tolerated moral reprobate. Even the doctors, whose every instruction he flouted and whom he lambasted to the end, came to regard him not only as a fascinating medical phenomenon but as a person deserving of special indulgence and care… Just as much as anybody else who has died in recent days, he, too, is literally irreplaceable.[933]

His biographer attributed Bernard's popularity to his being a case study in the antithesis of Thatcherite Britain:

> At a time when a Big Nanny Prime Minister was urging the nation to be sober, thrifty and hardworking, Bernard was famous for being precisely the opposite. He had never taken out a mortgage, insurance policy or pension or paid a penny in alimony to any of his four ex-wives. He was, in effect, the ultimate example of political incorrectness, a devil-may-care rebel who personified the naughty, irresponsible side of our natures. If Mrs Thatcher represented the lion in the British national character, Jeff Bernard was the unicorn.[934]

Johnson gave over the leader to lament *The Spectator*'s loss. Under the heading 'The Missing Voice' he told readers that '"Low Life" dies with the writer who graced it.'[935] None could have predicted that, a few years hence, a worthy successor would spontaneously emerge to write under so lowly and lofty a banner.

Throughout Johnson's tenure, *The Spectator*'s atmosphere – in print and in person – was eminently affable, cool-headed and chatty; Johnson himself revealed the curious desire to make the magazine 'frothy'.[936] An outside observer of his editorial conferences gives a colourful account of proceedings:

> The word 'office' hardly describes the large, ramshackle room, somewhere between the waiting-room of a private dentist and the study of a Christ Church literature don. The carpet is ancient, the drop-leaf table covered in magazines is battered, the sofas have seen better days, the chairs come from a variety of Terence Rattigan plays. The editor's desk is a colossal affair, an awesome barricade the size of a small tank.

The core team – Johnson, Anderson, Wyatt, Heffer, Amory and Heath, aided by the frequent presence of the erstwhile *Spectator* political editor Alan Watkins – are depicted in quick-fire brainstorming and playful banter. The meeting ended, order is at once restored:

> The sun streams into the garden. *The Spectator* family are at peace with the world. Disgusted with Tories but devoted to Toryism, ready to put up with Labour provided they're not too 'bossy', they may not find the world as 'perfick' as Pop Larkin [from *The Darling Buds of May*]; but in their sofa-strewn, donnish, Doughty Street capsule, it will never be less than perfectly agreeable.[937]

As a counterpoint to this congenial calm, Michael Heath – the 'doyen of cartoonists', by this point with almost forty Spectator, years to his name – is vividly sketched. The 'épateur of modern style excesses' wears 'a spectacular black frockcoat like a Trollopian bishop on holiday' – as well as 'a look of fathomless contempt'. However unstructured, Johnson used such group gatherings as his primary means of running the magazine; often after fifteen minutes, he followed a long-standing *Spectator* tradition of suggesting that the team head to the pub. A previous editor recalled that 'organisation bored and depressed him. He tended not to answer letters or attend meetings.'[939] Certainly his handling of the *Spectator* board was notorious for its disdain: the chairman, Algy Cluff, once called a meeting short because Johnson seemed anxious to attend an engagement elsewhere, only later to find the editor eating *tout seul* across the road at Wilton's.

Johnson did, however, have the all-important knack of finding and engaging a talented team of columnists, many of whom have stayed the course of time. Alongside Oakley, Parris, Jenkins and Jones, Mark Steyn wrote provocatively over a wide range of subjects, especially on America. In 1997, Sir Perry Worsthorne left the Lawson-controlled *Sunday Telegraph* to return to the Lawson-free *Spectator*: his fortnightly – and forthrightly expressed – column, 'As I was saying', thus advertised the resumption of normal service. In March 1996, Leanda de Lisle began a weekly piece entitled 'Country Life', a name that suggested the sensitive and stoic nature notes that had appeared from Cornish, Parker and Beach Thomas in decades past. It was instead an account of social life in the country, which did the rounds until 2001. More significantly, in September 1997, Johnson himself began a fortnightly column under the title 'Shared Opinion'. His first piece opened with a splendid account of the regrettably common social vice of 'Johnsonism' – assuming that everyone with that surname is, if not related, fundamentally the same sort of person.

Mark Amory continued to work his gentle magic on the literary pages, though Johnson took the assignation of

political books under his remit. Under the new arts editor, Elisabeth (Liz) Anderson, fresh energy was given to various fields with the vim one would expect from the partner of Bernard Levin. The artist, collector and critic Andrew Lambirth arrived in 2002 to dispense a masterly column on all manner of pictorial art over the next dozen years. And for the first time, a dedicated dance column appeared, showing the deft footwork of a genuine expert on Italian and English ballet, Giannandrea Poesio. Although he began as an unknown name – with the Director of the Royal Opera House positing in the *Spectator* Diary that it was a pseudonym for Johnson himself[940] – over the next twenty years Poesio's column established him as a leading critic in world ballet. Michael Tanner, the Cambridge-based philosopher, replaced Christiansen as opera critic, a role he has since played wittily and waspishly for a quarter of a century. Simon Hoggart took the seat of Hislop to tackle television, a role he shared with the irrepressibly eruptive James Delingpole, who has controlled the remote since 2002. The ex-but anti-BBC reporter Michael Vestey arrived for a ten-year spell of rigorous radio reviewing, a post Kate Chisholm has since taken up to great acclaim after Vestey's death in 2006. Restaurants, no longer able to profit from regular visits by Nigella Lawson, fell under the purview of the barrister David Fingleton and the journalist Alice Thomson, whose fresh and inventive (if London-centric) insights attracted a keen following.

The letters pages remained lively, especially when Sir Edward Heath turned his wrath on *The Spectator* that had once

vilified him so much as PM, for claiming that he opposed a new royal yacht:

There is no excuse for Bruce Anderson's characteristic personal abuse… Mr Anderson accuses me of disloyalty to the Queen and to the Most Noble Order of the Garter of which I am proud to be a member. Had he listened to what I actually said on this subject, he would know that I most certainly did, and said, nothing which could have embarrassed Her Majesty, or any member of the royal family, in any way. I am so informing Her Majesty.[941]

In other weeks, one could encounter the Dowager Marchioness of Reading expressing her idiosyncratic view on football hooliganism at the 1998 World Cup:

Sir: I would like to join with Alan Clark's recent remarks defending the English soccer fans in France. We are a nation of yobs. Without that characteristic how did we colonise the world? And our fame as fighters is second to none. Now that we don't have a war, what's wrong with a good punch-up?[942]

– or A.A. Gill responding with gusto to the jibes of Taki:

Sir: Might I impose on the hospitality of your correspondence column to pass a message to Taki: Go fuck yourself, you smelly dago lesbian.[943]

Johnson was predictably hands-off in the task of editing the magazine, and

Issues of 24 Aug. 1996, 18 Jan. 1997, 11 Oct. 1997 and 15 Aug. 1998

particularly uninterested in its aesthetics. Perhaps, reasonably enough, he felt that he had been delivered a sufficiently attractive object from Moore via Lawson. The layout of his *Spectator* differs in almost no way from that of his predecessors, save for the regular deployment of some spectacularly ugly front-page cartoons. These are from the hand of Jonathan Wateridge, whose stock in trade was inflated heads.

Another move that caused some alarm with long-standing readers was Johnson's ban on poetry in the magazine – save for the entertaining, if circumscribed, humour of James Michie's 'Clerihew Corner'. While poetry had become rarer over the course of Lawson's editorship, no explanation was given for this strange culling of the Muses. Those who knew Johnson, however, were aware that his dislike of poetry came a close second to his loathing of sport. An editor with narrowing interests is rarely a good thing.

The overall political thrust of *The Spectator* was deemed by some to be flagging, or at least lagging behind the time. Johnson was a relatively old-school

Tory, and had little desire to engage seriously with the inexorable rise of New Labour. His deputy editor recalls how he reassured his 'nonplussed lunch guests a week before the 1997 election that the Conservatives would still win' – rather than receive their lowest post-war share of the vote.[944] The surge of New Labour and the landslide victory of Tony Blair soon prompted something of an identity crisis for *Spectator* staff. Michael Heath rapidly responded by inventing his devastating 'Blairs' cartoon strip (which in 2007 gave way, no less witheringly, to 'Flash Gordon'). For his part, Johnson at last saw the pressing need to look up-to-speed with the dominant political force of the day, even if that meant wheeling in paid-up, flag-waving Cool Britannia types. As he explained, 'I looked for some new contributors who broadly supported The Project – the Blairites' slightly sinister name for their larger design – but who could be readable about it.'[945] In came Siôn Simon, who oversaw media relations for the 1997 Labour campaign, and Derek Draper, adviser to Peter Mandelson –

then on the verge of being exposed as pa[rt] of the Lobbygate scandal. And Blair['s] sister-in-law, Lauren Booth, offered u[p] a mordant Diary piece that Decembe[r.] Readers were divided: one wrote to sa[y,] apparently without tongue in chee[k,] that the column was 'the best since Jil[ly] Cooper', while another demanded that th[e] editor 'not allow the lady near the Diary [or] elsewhere – ever again.'[946] Unimpresse[d] by all of this, deputy editor McElvoy ma[de] her excuses and left to become executiv[e] editor of *The Independent* in Janua[ry] 1998. Wyatt was hurriedly promoted [to] the deputy editorship, an appointment th[at] compounded the shock.

In the early days of Blair, Johns[on] managed to achieve three royal cou[ps] – of a very different kind from those [of] Lawson's magazine. In 1997, the Duche[ss] of York wrote the Diary.[947] It bega[n] 'Time.' – and went on to cover gol[f] photo-shoots for Weightwatchers, a[nd] the express desire that horses could ta[lk.] It was syndicated around the world, th[us] making global the name of her Italian h[ost] and future paramour, Count Gaddo de[

erardesca. When challenged about
e piece's bizarre content and syntax,
nson explained that it was no parody:
ke all great writers there are depths of
aning. You have Proust, Dostoevsky …
gie.'[948] In fact, the piece was a surprising
mission because *The Spectator* had
o years earlier hosted the view of Lord
arteris of Amisfield: 'Quite simply,
e Duchess of York is a vulgarian. She is
lgar, vulgar, vulgar, and that is that.'[949]
There was another royal in the fray:
e Duchess's Diary appeared in the
me mid-August issue whose front
ver depicted Dodi Fayed aboard his
cht *Jonikal*, with Princess Diana as
r figurehead (the first cover to appear
m the Wateridge imaginarium). Taki's
ece inside contained the mini-scoop
at Diana – a *Spectator* reader – had
ughed off the possibility of marrying
r lover. The timing of all of this proved
be supremely tragic, two weeks before
e death of both. The third coup was to
ing to *The Spectator* the only piece
a monarch-to-be: in August 1998,
e Prince of Wales wrote an article on
chitecture, entitled 'Why I'm modern
t not modern'.[950] Again, the author's
tes on this score had been challenged
The Spectator earlier in the decade.[951]
ch royal connections endure: given the
current appearance of the magazine
press photographs of the twenty-first
ntury, it is fair to assume that *The
ectator* is still widely read throughout
e Windsor family – at least beyond
ogmore House.

The rest of the world, however, was
oving on, and the magazine needed to
ep a closer eye on it. *The Spectator* at
t came to broach the Internet with a low-
profile launch in July 1998, combined with
the magazine's 170th anniversary summer
party. The small-scale website (www.
spectator.co.uk) carried comparatively
little content, beyond uploading some
features of the weekly magazine: for
anyone with access to a print issue, there
was certainly no cause to head online.
Johnson's announcement of the launch
was less than enthusiastic, reminding
readers that there is

no substitute for the versatility of the
printed page. *The Spectator*, unlike
most televisions and computers, can
accompany its reader on country
walks, on Virgin trains, in short
to many places where modern
technology has yet to reach. We do
not guarantee that, at some time in
the future, *The Spectator* television
channel will not bring Paul Johnson
and Matthew Parris to your small
screen. But we do promise that the
magazine itself will continue to be
available, as now, on paper, to read
and keep.[952]

Long may that promise hold.

For all the concessions to the fast-
approaching millennium, dissatisfaction
continued to bubble away that the
magazine was not active enough in public
debate. Although most issues of Johnson's
tenure dealt with fresh developments in
policy, very few succeeded in setting or
steering the agenda in a way comparable
to previous decades. Simultaneously, his
magazine was reporting less frequently
on affairs abroad: the wide-ranging reach
under Chancellor, Moore and Lawson
had rapidly retreated. *The Spectator* was
starting to become a mere spectator,
without an obvious stake in the emergent
issues of an increasingly self-assured
Parliament. The need for new blood to give
The Spectator fresh purpose was clearly
conveyed to the press by an unnamed
Spectator writer:

Under Charles Moore and Dominic
Lawson the paper had real power in
Westminster, fuelling the rifts in the
Tory party over Europe, but politics
have changed and *The Spectator* has
been left behind. Circulation is okay,
but the magazine itself is editorially
lacklustre.[953]

Peter Wilby, the new editor of the *New
Statesman* and therefore inevitably
conflicted in interest, said, '*The Spectator*
is a shadow of its former self. It is out of
touch and not interesting enough.'[954]
Another anonymous figure lamented that
the magazine 'seemed to be carping, rather
than getting involved in a critical debate.
That needs to change.'[955]

The owner was also growing a little
impatient. When, in July 1999, Mark
Steyn's cover piece seemed to make light
of the Kennedy family's many tragedies,
Black joined many more respectful
readers in taking offence. One letter told
the editor that the headline ('The Kennedy
Assassination of Women') 'demeans you';
another, '*you* should know better.'[956] At
any rate, that month the announcement
came that Johnson was to be replaced.
Black later suggested that the change was
inevitable and a long time coming: 'Frank
didn't do anything.'[957]

Nevertheless, Johnson's tenure of nearly
four years had kept up circulation, which

stabilised after the steady growth of the previous two decades: at the end of 1995, *The Spectator* sold 48,200 copies; by mid-1999, the figure was 47,800. Taking the news on the chin, he remarked that it was 'not the end of an era, only the end of an aria.' Keen to develop the metaphor, his publisher Fortier said that his magazine was 'like Mozart, delicate and nuanced'. Regarding the incoming editor she saw a pointed contrast in tone: 'Now we will have Beethoven.'[958]

Johnson's closest friends felt that he regained a sense of freedom in the post he resumed – of Parliamentary sketch-writer for the *Daily Telegraph*. But just seven years later, in 2006, he died almost in harness, culled by cancer at sixty-three. As a sign of his anger at how his time at *The Spectator* panned out, he often noted that his disease began the day he was fired. Praise was abundant and sincere. His successor as editor asserted that 'there are very few journalists who can claim to have invented a whole genre, which is what he did with the modern parliamentary sketch... He was the master of that particular genre.'[959] He did indeed combine the cynical clarity of Bernard Levin with an uncanny ability to uncover politicians' unwitting idiosyncrasies. His main love, however, was journalism. A predecessor in post admiringly recalled:

He was astonishingly well-read in the works of dead as well as living journalists. He loved the lore and language and tricks of newspapers, the low just as much as the high. It distressed him when others were less appreciative. You could almost say that he loved newspapers too much, and

Cover images for 4 July 1998 (170th anniversary issue) and 24 July 1999

therefore sometimes found the reality of working for them upsetting.[960]

The question of who should succeed him would have thrilled Johnson as dinner-party banter. But it needed answering only by Conrad Black. Happily, as he later recalled, the decision was easy: 'There was no doubt the star in waiting, the man to make the *Spectator* a household name, was Boris.'[961] The announcement was made in July. To the relief of many, this new incumbent was a long-standing *Spectator* writer. And those guilty of Johnsonism felt a mixture of elation and anxiety, when Frank was replaced by **(ALEXANDER) BORIS DE PFEFFEL JOHNSON** (1964–). An Eton Colleger, scholarship-holder at Balliol, Oxford (Lit. Hum., II.1), and President of the Oxford Union (Trinity 1986), Johnson had subsequently earned his stripes as *The Spectator*'s political correspondent in Lawson's last years (1994–5). After a short but self-sabotaged spell at *The Times*, Johnson had risen over twelve years at the *Daily Telegraph* from European cub reporter to chief political columnist; no one was better placed t[o] lead the magazine forward into mor[e] robust scrutiny of the shiny edifice of Ne[w] Labour. He had steadily drifted closer t[o] the theatre of Conservative politics, an[d] was still plotting a route into the Hous[e] of Commons, having failed in his fir[st] optimistic push to turn Clwyd Sout[h] blue in 1997. For those who remembere[d] a column from his spell as political edit[or] – 'No money. No power. No sex. Who['d] become a Conservative MP today?' – th[e] ambition seemed rather half-hearted.[962]

Although his first two weeks in po[st] were spent on paternity leave, Johnson['s] arrival created a buzz. There wa[s] genuine excitement that a raucous an[d] rambunctious era of *Spectator* provocati[on] was due to return – perhaps a combinati[on] of Lawson junior's forthrightness wi[th] Inglis's devil-may-care bluster? But fe[w] could predict quite how talked-abo[ut] the magazine – in print and in perso[n] – would become. For a start, not all we[re] entirely convinced about how careful t[he] incoming editor would be at the helm; o[ne] of Johnson's close associates described t[he] appointment as 'like entrusting a Ming vase to an ape'.[963] Crucially, this was the opinion of not just his future biographer but a former deputy editor of *The Spectator*, Andrew Gimson, who knew full well what the magazine required to succeed. For all Johnson's undoubted talent, would he have both the commitment and the energy to steer the ship successfully?

A long-serving staff member set out the problems that Johnson inherited from his namesake's *Spectator*, which was 'too comment-driven and not agenda-setting enough… The covers weren't up to it… People weren't picking it up on the newsstands which is the real key to whether a product is doing well.'[964] Simon Courtauld – a man intimately familiar with the character of the post-war *Spectator* – felt that Johnson's *Spectator* had fallen out of balance: 'Frank had too much politics in the magazine which made it rather dry. I always found myself turning past the politics to the arts which are excellent.'[965] But the new editor was hearteningly confident about where he would be directing the magazine:

In the glutinous consensus of New Britain, *The Spectator* is a refuge for logic, fun and good writing. It challenges the orthodoxy, whatever that happens to be. It will continue to set the political agenda, and to debunk it.[966]

He also showed a sound awareness of how diverse the magazine's amalgam of contributors had been and would be: *The Spectator* is a training ground for prime Ministers, Chancellors of the Exchequer, innumerable peers of the realm and a wide assortment of drunks and deadbeats.'[967] Curiously or not, it was the speaker of these words who later trailblazed the first of these future career paths. While still on leave, Johnson was pushing *The Spectator* hard and wide, telling *The Independent*:

Every week, for a paltry outlay, the reader is treated to what, at its best, is a pyrotechnical display of groundbreaking, story-breaking, cutting-edge journalism… We are more relevant than ever. We represent an 88-page palliative, a relief, a refreshment from the ghastly treacly consensus of New Britain. We are a refuge, an oasis.[968]

That refuge and oasis needed protecting. Despite the formidable powers of his no-nonsense secretary, Ann Sindall (whom he had brought from the *Daily Telegraph*), Dan Colson – the cool-headed Canadian who managed the Telegraph Group – felt he should bring in as deputy editor Stuart Reid, then comment editor at *The Independent on Sunday*. Reid was by no means the obvious first choice as Johnson's right-hand man. He had worked briefly at the *Catholic Herald*, before a long stint as comment editor at the *Sunday Telegraph*, where he had struggled with Johnson's notoriously last-minute-or-later submissions. The decision, however, was inspired: over the next seven years Reid proved to be an essential First Mate to steady the ship when the seas became unseasonably choppy. In fact, for many weeks here and there, he could only be described as Captain. Or so it seemed. Rather amusingly, Reid later recalled of his appointment:

They got me completely wrong. I'm just as irresponsible as Boris but I lack his courage. I have actually urged caution and been utterly delighted when he went ahead anyhow.[969]

Despite his professionalism, Reid did indeed play the proper role of a deputy editor: to challenge and provoke both the editor and the magazine without having to bear editorial responsibility. At any rate, if the new editor was a gamble, it quickly paid off. Within his first year, Johnson raised circulation by 7,500 (15 per cent), taking the magazine not just beyond 50,000 copies but to a higher figure than it had ever achieved. What is more, it was making around £1m in annual profit, and reaching a broader readership than it had enjoyed for a long time – perhaps ever.

Johnson had already made his name in journalism as a provocative and witty columnist, with an inimitable mastery of recondite verbiage – a feature he defended against sub-editors' tinkering by filing copy fifty words short and with no fat to trim. Keen to deploy writers with a similarly outspoken style, he recruited in December 1999 Toby Young and Jeremy Clarke to write a column in alternating weeks headed 'No Life'. Young had been an acquaintance of Johnson's at Oxford (PPE, Brasenose) and had since made waves, first by co-founding the short-tempered and short-lived *Modern Review* (1991–5) with Julie Burchill and Cosmo Landesman, and then by spending three chaotic years at *Vanity Fair*. Clarke, by contrast, was brought into the *Spectator* fold through his association with Stuart Reid at *The Independent on Sunday*, where his first piece in the national press

– on ferrets and ferret-fanciers – had appeared.[970] Reid knew Clarke to be a wildly entertaining boon companion, and a lively storyteller to boot. Although he knew nothing of Jeff Bernard and his writing, it emerged that Clarke's own musings on women, winos and worldly woes – through the haze of drugs, drink and depression – were in the genuine and unaffected tradition of 'Low Life'. In July 2001, he was therefore entrusted with the venerable mantle of *The Spectator*'s second 'Low Life' correspondent, which he was to serve up the following year as a weekly remedy to quotidian boredom. Twenty years on, his column is thriving, and soon to outlast its founder's. Through his candour and clarity of thought, Clarke has become – much like his predecessor – one of the first-read and last-forgotten elements of the magazine.

Johnson clearly possessed the core skills of attracting readable writers, spurring them to entertain and challenge, and selling to the public the sense of a collective *Spectator* spirit. By contrast, the traditional Thursday-morning conference was not a time when the coming issue was planned out in meticulous detail. Instead, it gave the opportunity to pitch outlandish ideas and exchange outrageous jokes – many unprintable even in *The Spectator*. But Johnson showed in these boisterous gatherings the peculiar knack of spotting stories that would fly, delegating with confidence, and affording contributors a free hand. So long as the writing was up to it, the result would be a page-turner. Although hands-off, this leadership style won him both loyalty and trust. Peter Oborne, newly appointed as

The Spectator's first website

political editor, found that he was free to write with the minimal steer: 'we would speak once a week for about a minute, and in that minute you covered the whole ground.'[971] In the same spirit, and perhaps as a concession to his sudden defenestration, Frank Johnson was able to continue his far-roaming 'Shared Opinion' column, which continued unbroken until his death in 2006.

But in May 2001 an article appeared defending the BBC against the charge of political bias, especially in regard to its Europhilia. Here was the editor of the *Today* programme advertising the diversity of his team's party-political sympathies.[972] Ten months later, a peanut-prompted panic in the airline industry elicited a second article from Rod Liddle, this time appreciably more caustic. Having left the BBC in October 2002, he started writing regularly for *The Spectator*, and was rapidly scooped up as an associate editor. His column, first called 'Thought for the day' (a pointed nod), was later rebranded as 'Liddle Britain'. Somewhat unconventionally for the magazine, Liddle

is a Middlesbrough-raised, Millwall-supporting, Old-Labour-loving firebrand. But, as well as usurping Taki's mantle as *The Spectator*'s most controversial columnist in its twenty-first-century guise, he has proved to be unquestionably the most successful. At times bravely, at times rashly, he has subjected himself to the live experiment of establishing where and when the written word can and cannot be policed by others. Without lofty abstraction or empty theorising, he sets out in plain prose his principles, and indeed prejudices, however distasteful to the panjandrums of modern Britain. As one fascinated by where the dividing line is between the acceptable and the unprintable, he has inevitably overstepped the mark more than once over the last two decades.[973]

Indicative of Johnson's live-and-let-live philosophy was his commissioning Ross Clark to begin the weekly column 'Banner Wagon'. Filed from January 2000, this was a short and snappy summary of how personal freedoms were steadily being eroded by government intrusion. Clark had plenty of material, and more ground to cover: in November 2003, the column evolved into 'Globophia', challenging international resistance against globalisation and free trade. Finally, in January 2005, he unspun the absurd Panglossian claims of governmental press releases ('Everybody Benefits'), exposing the double-speak and logical flaws that corrupt public debate. The series ended that April, presumably overwhelmed by the ever-increasing supply of material to ridicule. Happily, however, Clark has remained an uncompromisingly honest and principled voice for *The Spectator*, in page and online, on money and on liberty ver since. He has served as a most trusted dviser to Mr Spectator as he surveys the wenty-first century.

As a man with friends in high places, ohnson was able to persuade Nicholas oames, grandson of Winston and nephew f Randolph Churchill, to take over the nonthly 'wine club' column from Bron Vaugh. But, after nine months' expert upping (Feb.–Nov. 2000), it soon emerged at touring cellars and draining bottles ere not obviously compatible with life s a serving MP – at least not so publicly. hus, after a brief and sobering hiatus, imon Hoggart, political sketch-writer r *The Guardian*, took over in March 001. When a member of the *Spectator* ard expressed the worry that high-level enophilia would now be entrusted to a ommunist, Fortier gave the reassurance at 'he won't write only about red wine'.[974] ver the next thirteen years, Hoggart vingly polished that column into a gem the genre, until his untimely death. Since nuary 2014, Jonathan Ray – who has en drinks columnist for almost every blication under the sun – has shared his ng-tested tastes with *Spectator* bibbers.

Meanwhile, Johnson's own calendar s proving increasingly hectic. In 2000, r instance, it was perfectly in character r the man to be simultaneously test-iving a Jaguar XKR-R (for his regular) motoring column) while composing peech, due to be given half an hour rlier to Marlborough College's ector Society (founded to discuss his agazine).[975] But he could still find time reach out to old enemies: the continued ipathy between the *New Statesman* d *The Spectator*, left at an awkward lemate in the 1977 chess match,[976]

was briefly resolved by a cricket match, in Crouch End on 2 July 2000, when *The Spectator* won by a wicket. The Staggers, in an act of charity or chutzpah, declared at 195–4. The fixture has not been renewed, leaving the magazine to content itself with matches at Althorp, where Earl Spencer's XI competed against a team chock-full of Johnsons.

A more controversial development that month, however, was the realisation of Johnson's long-standing political ambitions: he was selected as the Conservative candidate for Henley-on-Thames to succeed Michael Heseltine (1974–2001). Although there were some 200 applicants, and Johnson's entry papers arrived a week late, his public persona already had momentum, bolstered by a brace of idiosyncratic appearances on *Have I Got News For You*. The papers – and indeed *The Spectator*'s board – supposed that this near-certain prospect of professional politicking would bring a swift end to his editorship. The *Evening Standard* was typical in its self-assured declaration that 'as soon as a general election is called, he will vacate the editorial chair.'[977] Such talk swiftly shifted into fevered debate about his probable successors; the four names dominating the debate were Matthew d'Ancona, the young deputy editor of the *Sunday Telegraph*, Cristina Odone, deputy editor of the *New Statesman*, Stephen Glover, sometime editor (and founder) of *The Independent on Sunday*, and Alice Thomson, assistant editor of the *Telegraph*. Other names alleged to be in play included Michael Gove, Sarah Sands, Emma Soames, Simon Heffer and Rod Liddle. But all such talk proved to be idle: notwithstanding the

press excitement, Johnson deftly deferred the precise point of his resignation so long that he ended up remaining in post as *Spectator* editor for another four and a half years. As he confessed in the subsequent electoral campaign of 2001, the process temporarily distracted him from journalism: 'We're off. With a glint in his eye Stuart Reid, deputy editor, seizes the reins at the *Spectator*. My *Telegraph* column is prorogued.'[978] While Colson sternly warned Johnson that *The Spectator* was not to be treated like 'some magazine on pig-farming in Wales',[979] Black, as proprietor, saw that a favourable wind could be blowing, and seemed willing to see how things fell out. In the end, Johnson won the seat and won more readers to his magazine. As Black later recalled, 'I thought it was wrong in principle for someone to be both an MP and editor of a political magazine. And I think it's still wrong. But having said that, I think he's incredibly independent.'[980] Johnson was only too happy to keep his various balls in the air.

As an eclectic editor, Johnson proved to be astoundingly persuasive in bringing to *The Spectator* a more international and publicly visible cast of Diary writers. Alongside a lively crop of journalists and Tory grandees were various political outliers (Jonathan Aitken, Alastair Campbell, George Galloway) and cultural curiosos (Tim Rice, Nicky Haslam, Ulrika Jonsson and Barbara Amiel, a.k.a. Mrs Conrad Black). There is, it may be observed, something of the Oxbridge High Table Feast in the eagerness with which modern *Spectator* editors have sought to out-celebrity their predecessors in the Diarists that they can corral to write – and

Johnson's successors would only raise the game. But these guest contributions, after the occasional fourth or fifth edit, did add some external colour to a magazine that was broadening its range.

Johnson himself knew that this was only part of the broader picture: as one colleague recorded, 'Frank tended to get scoops by getting Joan Collins in to write the diary, but Boris is more in the old school.'[981] Although he would often declare 'Scoops are us!', Johnson was frequently frustrated in his speculations. Andrew Gimson, brought in as foreign editor (unpaid, and with no requirement to go abroad), gives an atmospheric picture of the *modus operandi*: 'There was a slightly brutish desire to "get" Blair, but brutishness is one of the traditions of our free press; and Blair would have been an amazing scalp.'[982] For instance, the magazine put great effort into researching the story that the PM had punctuated his prime-ministerial service with a pheasant shoot. Jeremy Clarke was sent to sniff out evidence in Devon but – after a number of false leads and tight-lipped rebuffs – the story got nowhere.

The sport of needling Blair – who had gamely followed tradition in hosting the newly appointed editor at Downing Street – could occasionally draw blood. In April 2002, Oborne published the story that the PM had tried to wangle a more high-profile role in the state funeral for the Queen Mother.[983] Alastair Campbell, the No. 10 attack dog, promptly headed to the Press Complaints Commission and demanded an apology from *The Spectator*. But the magazine stood its ground and, when the emerging evidence looked set to damage the government, Campbell

coyly retracted his objection. Flush with a victory of sorts, Johnson triumphantly wrote, 'When we first broke the story, they demanded a correction, an apology, and the payment of a sum of damages. They have now put their tanks into reverse in the most hilarious way.'[984]

A less clear-cut case emerged when Elton John took exception to an article of June 2000 by Cardinal Thomas Winning, which adopted a predictably dogmatic position on homosexuality.[985] In his letter, Sir Elton was 'astonished to be told by Cardinal Winning that my sexuality is not good for me… As a cardinal and presumably a celibate and solitary individual, how can he possibly be in a position to judge?' He ended on a tone of stout optimism:

Britain has proved itself to be a more tolerant and open-minded place to live. Gone is the out-dated and ill-informed notion that homosexuality is a question of choice. The reality is that homosexuals have no choice – we are born that way and no amount of hectoring or hypnosis can make us change.[986]

These sentiments, in fact, resonate precisely with those first advanced in the national press half a century earlier, by *The Spectator* of 1954 and beyond.

One widely appreciated innovation of Johnson's *Spectator* was the prudent restoration, in September 2000, of poetry to its pages. Although verse had been banned by his predecessor, Johnson already felt the time was ripe to rekindle the British muse. His leader, 'Proper Poems', explained the pragmatic thinking behind the decision: 'the reason no one reads

poetry any more, of course, is that none o it is any bloody good.' He therefore calle for change – albeit spectating backwards not forwards:

As of this issue, *The Spectator* is reversing its anti-poetry policy. From today we have a new poetry editor. His name is Lloyd Evans. He has a beard. He knows his stuff. He has performed in pubs, but he knows the difference between a tribrach and a molossus, a sapphic and an alcaic. We will be looking for poems that are well made, and that show decorum. They need not rhyme (Virgil didn't) but they must scan and have an argument, in the old-fashioned sense: a theme.

We share the general assumption that poetry has decayed because people think they can simply pour it forth in profuse strains of unpremeditated art; which leads to profuse reams of unbelievable bilge… We make no promises: if nothing any good comes in, nothing will be published. But we hope that anyone reading this, who has a good poem in him or her, will knock it out and send it in. It is time for our generation to think of posterity.[987]

For the magazine that had played h to Tennyson, Swinburne, Hardy, Lark Plath and Hughes, such grandstandi was reasonable. But, quite inevitably fierce row emerged in the letters pages subsequent weeks, chiefly between t quondam beat poet Michael Horovitz, w claimed that all the best modern verse v without metre, and Philip Hensher ('ch book reviewer' for *The Spectator* eve month since 1994), who countered that the best poetry *tout court* is mostly metrical.

Readers were enthused, poetasters grafted, and plenty reached print. Eight months later, Evans assessed how the experiment had fared:

'Bung us your verses,' we asked. And blimey, how you bunged. They flew in from every corner of the globe. Sonnets, ballads, satires, laments, ditties and dithyrambs, roundels and rants. In the first week a bloated parcel was dumped on the doorstep each morning, but as the onslaught gathered strength the Royal Mail had to drive round to the office in a special lorry piled high with trussed sacks.

It was a lonely sojourn through a wilderness of tosh… About a third of the submissions were written in 'free verse' or, as I prefer to think of it, 'hobbled prose'. It amazes me that anyone still bothers with this alphabetti spaghetti. Craftsmanship is one of the essential qualities of poetry, and the opportunity to display skill and ingenuity within an ordered scheme of rhythm and rhyme is the poet's great adventure, his great fulfilment.[988]

Wherever one stands on this hoary question, a much more eclectic range of verse has appeared in the magazine in subsequent years, deftly and delicately edited by (the award-winning poet) Hugo Williams since 2007.

The modern world was transcending modernism. In July 2001, *The Spectator* launched its website with Toby Young at the helm, who had been the magazine's first 'online editor' since October 2000.

Young saw that specifically commissioned writing was needed to add independent value to the piecemeal content reproduced from the magazine: he intended the site to be a lively hub of irreverent blogging and comment, a chattier and snappier companion to its print counterpart. At the launch party, he quipped that a more apt name would be *The Spiketator*, since he sought to publish the sort of stories that would not pass the editorial gates – and legal hurdles – of the magazine proper. The die was cast and the adventurous spirit of the online *Spectator* launched.

The website certainly succeeded in bagging scoops and getting them talked about. One early online columnist, Aidan Hartley, wrote regularly from Kenya under the billing 'Wild Life: a great white hunter takes aim at a few sacred cows in contemporary Africa'. Alongside his farming expertise, Hartley had a keen nose for stories. When, in July 2001, Prince William unwittingly shot an ibis while staying with his girlfriend Jecca Craig on Mt Kenya, the news broke on the *Spectator* website. In fact, the story appeared in the national press a little earlier, since Young had sought publicity by leaking it to *The Times*, and Fortier had spiked the original piece on the *Spectator* website without consultation. Her reasoning – to pre-empt any libel suit from the Windsors – did not go down well with the editors. Hartley's subsequent scoops included Rowan Atkinson's successfully landing a plane when the engine failed, and a lion's nearly eating Glenn Close while he rode in the Maasai Mara. After a one-off column in the magazine in November 2000, 'Wild Life' became

from March 2002 a monthly affair, often filed from impossibly rough and remote locations throughout Africa. On one occasion, Hartley, inconvenienced by an IED explosion in Somalia, had to dictate the copy via satellite phone to his wife in Kenya, who got it to print via the ambidextrous Lucy Vickery.[989]

The world came to a standstill on September 11, 2001, when Al-Qaeda co-ordinated plane hijackings to fell the Twin Towers and penetrate the Pentagon, killing 3,000 people. Arriving late to the office, Johnson learned of the tragedy from his assembled fellow staff. Two days later Heath's cover for the magazine depicted the Statue of Liberty, silhouetted in front of apocalyptic clouds.[990] Its question 'What Next?' was immediately answered: 'The West must fight back.' That case was argued by Matthew Bishop (of *The Economist*), along with *Spectator* regulars Mark Steyn, Bruce Anderson, Peter Oborne and Stephen Glover. The leader, doubtless written by Johnson, opened by declaring that

There is no moral difference between the destruction in America and a bomb in a fish-and-chip shop in the Shankill Road. In intention, the two sets of actions are the same: to cause death and terror. Nor will the havoc in New York mean, as some of the coverage seems to suggest, the end of the world as we know it. The markets will reopen. Capitalism will go on. America will remain the planet's pre-eminent power…

On one point it was particularly unequivocal:

America is not to blame for the carnage. The culprits are the terrorists, and those states who actively or passively support them.[991]

Having drawn the line in the sand, *The Spectator* forthrightly supported military action, first in Afghanistan and then (more controversially) in Iraq. For Johnson, it was his regret at opposing the Kosovo War (1998–9) that spurred him to back boots on the ground. This choice made, the magazine's support of this Second Gulf War was sincere, if carefully qualified. A leader of September 2002 argued that the goal

> should be severely circumscribed. It is to remove Saddam and to destroy his regime, not to bring about democracy in Iraq, a task greater than that of Sisyphus. The only thing that should be required of the new Iraqi regime is that it should not endanger the peace of the world. The message sent by America, then, should be clear and unambiguous: dictators are to be removed not because they are dictators, but because they threaten American interests and international peace. Naïve domestic little dictators can be safely left to their own devices, and to the wrath of their own people.[992]

However, when Johnson commissioned and published a Diary piece from George Galloway that challenged the legitimacy of war in Iraq, Anderson felt compelled to give up his post as 'editor-at-large' (*honoris causa*).[993] In actuality, the *Spectator* staff were divided on the issue: both the deputy editor Stuart Reid and

his future replacement Mary Wakefield attended the Stop the War march of February 2003. In the years to come, when the evidence – or lack of it – rubbished the government's claims about Saddam Hussein's arms capabilities, Johnson's *Spectator* started to tone down and delimit its support. From the start of 2003, the dogged BBC journalist Andrew Gilligan filed several pieces from Iraq, before delving deep into the spin on both sides of the Atlantic. In June, a long article ('A Conspiracy Theory Too Far') demolished the government's desperate attempts to lay blame on anti-Blair 'rogue elements' in the intelligence services.[994] The preceding month Gilligan had made the bombshell allegation on Radio 4 that the government had doctored the dossier; a few weeks later, weapons expert David Kelly was found dead. A *Spectator* leader headed 'The Enemies of Truth' defended Gilligan's brave and unflagging journalism, which had unwittingly brought Kelly into the public eye:

> To those who attack Gilligan, *The Spectator* asks this: are you in favour of truth, or of the suppression of truth in a sandstorm of obfuscation? It is dismaying to read in the *Daily Telegraph*, normally a model of logic, continual attacks on Mr Gilligan's motives.

Instead, here was

> simply a journalist who in the course of his diligent researches came across highly credible witnesses who believed that No. 10 did ramp up, flam up, soup up, big up, rev up aspects of

the data it was given, to maximise political impact.[995]

Johnson's hand is unmistakeable – which gives the rebuke of the *Telegraph* ye greater bite. For its part, *The Spectato*. closed the year by hosting a 'Save Andrew Gilligan' dinner. A more pointed method o attack was the cover piece of the following summer, headed 'Impeach Blair Now' Wateridge's cartoon depicted the Prim Minister in the dock, awaiting convictio 'for high crimes and misdemeanours'.[996]

Despite the geopolitical turbulence Johnson was an editor keen to keep hi options open in Britain. At times this coul make for a chaotic editorship. One day i June 2002, for instance, he found himse triple-booked for lunch with Conra Black, Charles Moore and Iain Dunca Smith – his bosses at *The Spectator*, th *Daily Telegraph* and the Conservativ Party – all doubtless wanting to hav rather incongruent conversations. In fac Johnson seems to have relished creatir such conflicts of interest: just before th Tory conference in October 2002, l happily ran a cover piece by Oborne – 'Yo time is running out, Iain' – which argue that the Conservative Party was in cha under Duncan Smith, and that he shou be turfed out sooner rather than later. To officials were sharply divided: one sai 'For a sitting Tory MP to publish an artic in a magazine that he edits portraying t leader as a failure is unforgivable'; anoth countered that 'the leader [IDS] may or make matters worse by taking on Boris'. To muddy the waters further, for go measure, *The Spectator* cheekily chose its 'Parliamentarian of the Year' one To Blair – although Johnson arrived too late

194

10,000 NOT O

he staff meeting to control that decision.

Given the increasing demands on his time, Johnson shared the duty of leader-writing with several staff, including Stuart Reid, Simon Heffer and Andrew Gimson. When pressed on what, if any, editorial policy steered the magazine, Johnson answered that he would 'only run pieces if they are interesting'[998] – a Chancelloresque outlook that saw the eighty-seven-year-old Eric Hobsbawm tackle Roy Kerridge's take on blues and rap, or Tony Benn give a potted sketch of those who, unlike him, had become post-war prime ministers.[999] As Johnson rather pointedly told *The Guardian*:

One of the pleasures of working for *The Spectator* is that nobody would ever be so discourteous as to ask you your politics, but if you have something unusual, unexpected, entertaining or startling to say, then you're in.[1000]

The Spectator thrived on the motto 'firm but unfair' – a creed that encouraged outspoken and confident writing, even if it could not find favour with all. Johnson nevertheless had a very high conception of his duties towards his readership:

You are a Time Lord, and your readers expect you to take them to all parts of the human experience, and to remember that the Bible and Homer are far more interesting and important, *sub specie aeternitatis*, than the price of oil or Tory prospects. You will be told that the magazine is elitist, and you should take that as a compliment. Every society has been run by an elite,

and every elite needs elucidation. Every industry or profession needs an angel at the top of their Christmas tree, and in the case of journalism, you hold that angel in your hands.

The angel wobbled when, in early 2003, Johnson fell out with his predecessor – a major upset for the Johnsonist conspiracy theorists. Boris pulled up Frank, his long-standing colleague at the *Daily Telegraph*, for writing a Parliamentary sketch without actually being in the House of Commons.[1001] Frank in turn alleged that Boris was not pulling his weight in either his political or journalistic capacities: he dubbed him 'the so-called Member of Parliament for Henley' and added (somewhat illogically and ambiguously) that 'he's in the chamber so much he's probably neglecting his duties as Editor of *The Spectator*. And I should know.'[1002] These charges resonated elsewhere. The Labour MP Ian Lucas taunted Johnson in the Commons for looking at his watch: 'Clearly, he wants to go and put *The Spectator* to bed.'[1003] Some felt the magazine was losing focus as a result: Andreas Whittam Smith, co-founder of *The Independent*, and in his thirties an occasional *Spectator* writer, granted that Johnson was 'a brilliant commentator' but

from the readers' point of view, there is no evidence that anybody is in charge… *The Spectator* doesn't want to change anything. It doesn't carry a flag for any cause. It is just there, unchanging, an authentic expression of the conservative temperament, but at its core, empty.[1004]

Rumours even circulated that Johnson was manoeuvring to become a *Telegraph* editor; some even said that he agreed in principle to edit the *Daily Telegraph*, so long as he could stay in politics until the next general election – a prospect that neither Black nor Moore could brook.

Despite the chatter and distraction, *The Spectator* did have fish to fry, as it campaigned actively for a referendum on EU membership. Johnson was particularly irked by the proposals for changing and mandating the European Constitution in the wake of the Nice Treaty of 2001. One editorial, characteristically headed 'Referendum est', argued that the proposed constitutional obligation for EU nations

is like herding squirrels. It is about as meaningful as giving a family of drunks a washing-up rota, and telling them they have a constitutional duty to follow it… There is only one way this kind of change in our institutions can possibly be ratified, if the government is so foolish as to agree it, and that is through a referendum. Article 1 speaks of the 'will of the people and the states of Europe to build a common future.' Let us therefore hear the will of the people.[1005]

Although that effort came to naught, it was a reminder that, as in the blustery days of Gale, *The Spectator* was keen to let the nation reconsider the European Question.

Johnson was at the height of his editorial powers when, in 2003, *The Spectator* celebrated its 175th anniversary.[1006] A 130-page, self-standing anthology of the magazine's highlights was produced for the occasion, under the savvy editorship of the business correspondent Martin Vander Weyer. To fund such a lavish volume (priced at £4.95), sponsorship was sought from the Diamond Trading Company, whose name duly appeared on every page. Johnson's upbeat editorial noted:

It is part of the genius of *The Spectator* that its writers continue in the belief that they are communicating with a smallish and, in general, highly educated readership. If there is one literary virtue that this encourages, it is frankness. There is no publication in any language – and I say this without fear of contradiction – where distinguished writers, of all persuasions and none, will show such uninhibited candour about themselves, politics, sex, food, art and death.[1007]

When the magazine's actual anniversary week came, in early July, Johnson shared with the press a simile that would have chimed particularly well with the *Spectator* faithful:

As a cricket ball is passed through the outfield, each player buffing it on his shirt before passing it on, so over the past 175 years *The Spectator* has been diligently buffed by the assorted buffers who have made up its college of editors… You could call them a buffer zone.[1008]

An anniversary party was thrown, which *The Times* described in no uncertain terms as 'debauched'.[1009] There are perhaps better words for a do that saw the Labour grandees Peter Mandelson, David Blunkett and Robin Cook receive trinkets

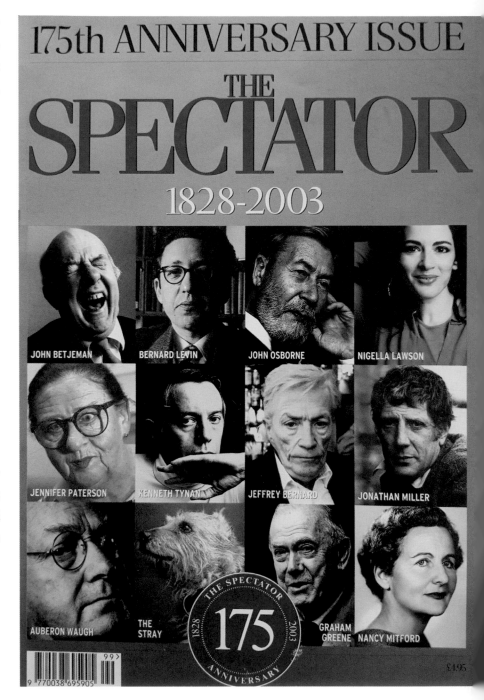

The 175th Anniversary Anthology

from the Diamond Trading Company. As Johnson was happy to acknowledge, 'It's the height of vulgarity.'[1010]

With such frequent and favourable press coverage, and with Johnson as a gift to the marketing department, circulation continued to rise, reaching the dizzy heights of 60,000 in 2004. Mark Amo[ry] still working literary wonders in t[he] back of the magazine, voiced Seaton[ian] scepticism about such large figures [— 'I] remember when our circulation w[as] 14,000, and *everybody* read it.'[1011] T[he] view reflected the remark of Bron Wau[gh]

Issues of 16 Oct. 1999, 18 May 2002, 1 Mar. 2003 and 24 Jan. 2004

who pooh-poohed the growth by asserting that 'there are only nineteen thousand agreeable people in Britain and they all read *The Spectator* already.'[1012]

In November 2003, Johnson's political career took another step forward when he became Vice-chairman of the Tory Party, newly under the leadership of Michael Howard. Within the month, Howard was pleased to receive the career-defining accolade of *Spectator* Parliamentarian of the Year. Onwards Johnson marched, appointed in May 2004 Shadow Minister for the Arts, for which the back of his magazine formed an unbeatable CV. Such privileged access to Westminster duly helped bring stories to the magazine.

June 2004, for instance, a crisis was caused by the unguarded chatter of Jonathan Powell, Blair's chief of staff, with a fellow parliamentarian: while their bikes waited at Westminster traffic lights, he told Johnson that Gordon Brown (the Chancellor on the rise) would never become PM. Oborne duly built his 'pol col' round this apparent insight into the strife that Labour had to come.[1013]

Although the magazine's layout preserved the general appearance set by previous editors, the cover started to run full-page illustrations in 2000, which became regular the following year. With occasional appearances from Steve Bell, hammer of *The Guardian*, alongside Wateridge and Garland, the magazine stood out more than ever on the news-stands. Among the more memorable images from Johnson's tenure are Ken Livingstone as a rampaging lizard ('King Con'), William Hague as a pro-European Napoleon ('Blair Will Bounce Us In'), Tony Blair in the dress of Diana ('Princess Tony'), a Caucasian mother pushing a jihadist in her buggy ('How Britain Breeds Terrorists'), Rupert Murdoch as a kangaroo with Blair the joey ('The Man Who Runs Britain'), Michael Howard as a vampiric bat ('The Tories' Secret Weapon'), and a naked Michael Portillo peeing on to the Conservative torch ('What's the Point of the Tory Party?').[1014] Other visual surprises were in store. The issue for 28 June 2003, for example, was a triumph of Kimberley Quinn's powers of persuasion: every single advertisement

space, including the several classified pages at the back, was replaced with blank space, save for a small and subtle Mercedes logo. It began with an editorial letter from Johnson, relating how a reader of the magazine had complained of being 'overwhelmed by the sheer luxury of the merchandise' advertised. He went on to suggest that 'For those who feel like scribbling on their copy, it is a unique opportunity for marginalia. For the many who have unsuccessfully submitted articles, here, at last, is the chance to write your own in the space provided.' This note was followed, of course, by an advert for the 'new Mercedes-Benz CLK-Class Cabriolet', which launched an ill-conceived competition to 'nominate your favourite open-air space in the UK'. Anyhow, although a fair wodge of money must have changed hands, this remains the most aesthetically striking issue in *Spectator* history.

A more lasting innovation came that year in the form of a new weekly gossip column ('The Spectator's Notes'), written now by 'William Boot', now 'Questing Vole'. Behind these Waughian names was Sam Leith, an astoundingly active figure at the *Telegraph*, who had propelled himself into the ether by frenetic activity in the *Peterborough* playpen. In May 2004, Charles Moore took over the column under the same heading, although it proved vastly different in character. This weekly notebook at once set itself in the tradition that stretches back not just to Moore's own editorial 'Notes' but to Harris's 'Janus' columns. It has continued unbroken ever since – except for those spells when Moore took refuge to work up his three-volume biography of Margaret Thatcher.[1015] His musings, on the timely and the timeless, in fact approximate even more closely to the eighteenth century: their casual mixture of conversational comment with literary, historical and religious learning conveys much of the spirit of Addison, Steele and their raffish circle under Queen Anne.

For all the fine work at the magazine, all was not well in the upper echelons. In 2003, Conrad Black became involved in criminal and civil lawsuits about his management of Hollinger Inc. On hearing that the company was considering selling the Telegraph Media Group, *The Spectator*'s chairman, Algy Cluff, explored the possibility of buying the magazine out of the group, an idea keenly supported by Johnson. Although this soon proved to be a non-starter, there was considerable commercial interest in acquiring the Telegraph Media Group's suite of titles. Potential bidders included Richard Desmond's Express Newspapers, the Daily Mail and General Trust, the Berlin-based Axel Springer, Condé Nast, and various private investors. But in January 2004 it was Sirs David and Frederick Barclay, co-owners of Press Holdings, who agreed a sale price for the

Telegraph titles. At first the figure was a mouth-drying £260 million; after six months of legal wrangling with Hollinger, and pressure from other rival bidders, it was eventually driven up to the eye-watering sum of £665 million.

Who, it may fairly be asked, has both the pockets and the passion to spend two thirds of a billion pounds on a couple of print titles on the British political right? The Barclay brothers, twins among ten children to Scottish parents, had made their fortune from the bottom up and on their own terms: through confectionery, property, hotelry, shipping, and – like Rintoul – the press. Sir David has called his success an example of 'what can be achieved in this country from whatever background or education or humble beginnings'.[1016] Described by an acquaintance as 'working-class Tories', they may fairly be assumed to be long-standing *Spectator* readers. Alongside the many family members who have helped manage the business, Aidan Barclay, Sir David's eldest son, oversees the day-to-day operation of the Telegraph Group. Given the Barclay brothers' long history of philanthropy (the cause of their knighthoods in 2000), the traditionally loss-making magazine was perhaps deemed a most worthy cause for their charitable support.

The Spectator was quick to respond to this change of ownership, however slowly the legal wheels turned. In January 2004, a remarkable article appeared from the Oborne stable arraigning Black's crumbling empire and outlining his steady downfall. Although the general account revealed some grudging sympathy, it contrived to mention Black's 'hairy knuckles and paddle-like hands', 'murky

business origins', 'stolidity, clumsiness and provincialism', and 'fondness for ceremony and dressing up', before repeating the hotly contested claim that he was 'London's biggest bore'.[1017] Black's record as proprietor was not, he alleged, totally white. As a response to an owner who had indulged the magazine's foibles and peccadilloes over fifteen years, and overseen a 70 per cent circulation increase, this seemed a low blow.

One significant change under the new ownership was the dissolution of the Spectator board in late 2004, after twenty-two years of paternal oversight. These quarterly meetings, largely based in the Cavendish Room at Brooks's (one of Cluff's many clubs), were treated with different levels of attentiveness by different editors. Johnson, in particular, was sorry to lose the support of Cluff, who ensured that his salary was not reduced to a more realistic *pro rata* sum. From Cluff's perspective, this sudden end was bittersweet: when he joined the board, the magazine's losses were the same as its profits when he was dismissed – some £1.5 million. With the protective carapace removed, in mid-November 2004, *The Spectator* moved under the aegis of the editor-in-chief of Press Holdings, Andrew Neil.

As a Scotch creation, *The Spectator* had maintained a strong thread of Scottish control over its two centuries. Neil, like the fourteenth editor Iain Hamilton, was forged in Paisley Grammar; like the future editor Fraser Nelson, he was a graduate of the University of Glasgow (MA in Politics and Economics), where he was a prominent figure in journalism, politics and the theatre. Neil had started reading *The Spectator* as a teenager successfully siphoning off a copy from his paper round in Glenburn. After a decade at *The Economist*, reaching the post of UK editor, he was appointed to edit the *Sunday Times* – then *sede vacante* after the Hitler Diaries scandal. Over his eleven years in post, Neil was always hunting the scoop, most notably in uncovering Israel's nuclear programme. He gained plaudits for its principled opposition to the poll tax, advocacy for victims of the thalidomide scandal, and defence of press freedom, but was condemned for its conviction that HIV did not cause AIDS. In fact, it was Neil's own commitment to privileging stories over loyalties that abruptly curtailed his editorship, when the paper's reports of corruption in Malaysia seemed to jeopardise Rupert Murdoch's acquisition of a television franchise there. Through his association with Murdoch, who had acquired Times Newspapers in 1981, Neil became a founding chairman of Sky TV, whose disruptive and provocative presence he helped launch.

Since 1996, he had served as the editorial overseer of the Press Holdings group, which then contained the *Scotsman* (1817–), the (*Sunday*) *Business* (1996–2008) and the *European* (1990–8). Neil had written for *The Spectator* on and off since 1997, despite being provocatively profiled by the magazine in Moore's day.[1018] Beyond the world of print, Neil was becoming an increasingly well-known figure across Britain through his hosting of the BBC's weekly politics review *This Week* (2003–19), and its ever-vigilant partners *Daily Politics* (2003–18) and *Sunday Politics* (2012–18). Fortunately, notwithstanding some serious missteps

by BBC muckamucks, his maximum detail, minimum nonsense interviews have been broadcast to the nation on the weekly *Andrew Neil Show* (2019–) and in the critical run-up to general elections.

As overseer of Spectatorial fortunes, Neil soon found that he had his work cut out. In October 2004, a leader appeared on the grim murder of the Iraqi hostage Ken Bigley. Its opening paragraph contended that holding a minute's silence before a football international between England and Wales 'emphasised the mawkish sentimentality of a society that has become hooked on grief and likes to wallow in a sense of vicarious victimhood'.[1019] Although this had been a legitimate complaint of *The Spectator* for many years (and more recently reappeared in Roger Alton's sports column),[1020] the article noted that 'there had been a two-minute silence for Mr Bigley that same morning in Liverpool, according him the same respect offered annually to the million-and-a-half British servicemen who have died for their country since 1914.' After discussing the genuine tragedy, *The Spectator* made the case that Liverpool, in particular, had a propensity for self-pity:

A combination of economic misfortune – its docks were, fundamentally, on the wrong side of England when Britain entered what is now the European Union – and an excessive predilection for welfarism have created a peculiar, and deeply unattractive, psyche among many Liverpudlians. They see themselves whenever possible as victims, and resent their victim status; yet at the same time they wallow in it.

Before returning to the politics of the Iraq War, the leader harangued Liverpudlians for their response to the Hillsborough tragedy of 1989 – ignoring (the piece alleged) 'the part played in the disaster by drunken fans at the back of the crowd who mindlessly tried to fight their way into the ground'. Not only had this canard been dismissed after formal investigation, but the 96 Hillsborough casualties were woefully underestimated as 'more than 50'.

The furore that this rather incoherent and unhappy piece caused was inevitable – even though most of the angriest protesters knew it only via selective and provocative quotations. (Mercifully, Reid had managed to remove some of the more trenchant criticisms of Bigley.) Since the actual author – Simon Heffer – was lost in the anonymity of the magazine's collective voice, and since his noble offer to claim the piece as his own was rejected, Johnson himself was duty-bound to bear the brunt as the editor. Within two days he publicly apologised for the errors of fact, but clarified the broader point:

I think the article was perhaps a little too trenchantly expressed but we were trying to make a point about sentimentality and risk and people's evaluation of risk these days. We certainly intended no insult to the people of Liverpool and as far as any offence was taken I'm very, very sorry.[1021]

In the following *Spectator* he wrote that the piece had been 'sloppy' and contained 'tasteless inaccuracies'.[1022] But this was not enough for a politician in post, not least a Tory shadow minister and vice-chairman. The party leader who had gifted these positions, Michael Howard, forced Johnson to make a pilgrimage to Liverpool to apologise to its residents in person. To the veteran commentator Alan Watkins, this was an outrageous demand upon a journalist: having cited the *Spectator* careers of Gilmour, Macleod and Lawson, he asked, 'Who … does this pipsqueak think he is, issuing orders to the editor of a great journal?'[1023] The result of what Johnson soon dubbed 'Operation Scousegrovel' was inevitable and unenlightening: he was chased around town and mercilessly pilloried at every turn. Nevertheless, the staff were surprised to see the magazine's sales in the area spike, prompting the classic Johnsonian quip, 'The quality of Mersey is not strained.' And, at least for a while, Howard's beloved Liverpool FC had to endure the chant from rival fans, 'There's only one Boris Johnson!'

The year 2004 had further upsets in store. A number of *liaisons amoureuses* found fervid coverage in the press – most notably that between the magazine's publisher Kimberly Quinn (recently remarried) and David Blunkett, then Labour's Home Secretary. Blunkett had already revealed his own affiliations in June 2004: 'I always read *The Spectator.* It's infuriatingly good.'[1024] But the news – in part turned up by Dominic Lawson's *Sunday Telegraph* – that Blunkett had fast-tracked a visa application for Quinn's Filipino nanny, and that their three-year affair was manifested in a two-year-old child, prompted Blunkett to resign that December.[1025] Such ample material led in the following year to Martin Witts's *David Blunkett: The Musical*, and the Channel

4 satire *A Very Social Secretary* – both replete with *Spectator* references. Quinn nevertheless fought through the storm, and remained at the magazine for another two years, before she left the building (and the contents page) for good.

The tabloids had more to splash – that editor Johnson was having an affair with the previous deputy editor, Petronella Wyatt. Nothing of public interest there. But, in November 2004, Johnson fell foul of party elders for denying the truth of these allegations as an 'inverted pyramid of piffle' – a word, as some remarked, not very far removed from Pfeffel.[1026] Howard, perhaps more out of a mistaken sense of Tory polling than ministerial candour, sacked Johnson as Shadow Arts Minister. Just two days earlier, this very man had spoken at the Spectator Parliamentarian of the Year Awards, an opportunity that allowed for some merry *double entendre*:

These are *The Spectator*'s awards and *The Spectator* is an incomparable magazine. There is nothing like *The Spectator* for stirring up and stimulating political controversy. Indeed, in all senses of the word it could best be described as political Viagra. And I must take this opportunity of congratulating Boris on the tremendous enthusiasm with which you have approached your various front-bench duties. I had no idea when I appointed you as shadow minister for culture, media and sport that you would take to the task with quite such aplomb. You were keen to make your mark with the city of culture. You wanted the people of Liverpool to get to know you better.

And you succeeded beyond my wildest dreams in achieving that objective… All I can say, Boris, is you're doing your front-bench job absolutely superbly: keep it up!

Soon after the laughs subsided, Johnson was exiled once more to the back-benches. As he told the press while peering through a friend's letterbox, 'I am now going to have a stiff drink.' Stephen Glover, the magazine's increasingly reflexive media commentator, gave a positive spin on Howard's decision, calling it 'by far and away the best thing he has done since becoming Tory leader'. Johnson had, he explained, now 'been freed from his chains'.[1027]

The newspapers, of course, were enthralled with these events, and the magazine was soon being dubbed 'The Sextator'. In February 2005, a one-hour BBC documentary charted these colourful events under the rather leading title *The Spectator Affair*. The film interspersed a chronicle of how the media revealed these various trysts with more general contributions from Johnson and four previous editors (the Lawson, Chancellor and Moore) – as well as Black, the previous proprietor. Johnson expressed bewilderment at the tittle-tattle. 'We live a life of almost embarrassing monastic seclusion and contemplation. It is no exaggeration to say that we are capable of arguing for three hours about Anselm's ontological argument.'[1028] When asked about his own part in the merry-go-round, Rod Liddle joked that 'it is the raw excitement of the magazine that causes sexual intercourse to take place at every opportunity… Perhaps it's the magazine's tradition of libertarianism.'[1029] 'One would

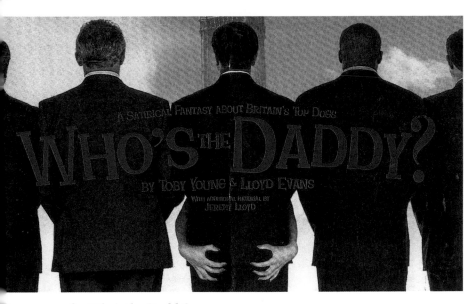

Programme for *Who's the Daddy?*

urn up for editorial meetings,' he would ater recall, 'to find naked men swinging rom the light fittings and fruity well-bred itten-faced females with their ankles ehind their ears.'[1030] Well, it is true enough at Liddle met his second wife behind the *pectator* welcome desk.[1031]

Given all this excitement in the press (if ot necessarily the public), the magazine as more talked about than ever: in 004, Johnson and *The Spectator* were entioned thrice as often in the British ress as in each of the previous three ears.[1032] But there was still more to be id. If some critics thought that the BBC ocumentary had gone rather easy on the litor, perhaps in exchange for permission film so much material in the Doughty reet offices, they were soon to be satisfied om another quarter. Ever open to arguing ith itself, *The Spectator* now saw two of staff produce a play on these sundry andals: *Who's the Daddy?*, written by e puckish theatre critics Toby Young and oyd Evans. Originally intended to be a it performed at the *Spectator*'s summer

party in 2005, it ended up playing to a sell-out crowd for six weeks at the King's Head Theatre in Islington (guide-dogs allowed). Although it inevitably required some tweaking on legal advice, this was a farce of full-blown proportions, set in *The Spectator*'s offices (and cupboards).[1033] Sheridan Morley, himself ousted as the magazine's theatre critic by these two playwrights, professed himself shocked at the spectacle: 'it is rather like buying a copy of *Private Eye* and finding that inside the cover it is entirely filled with pages from *Playboy*.'[1034]

At the time, Young confessed, 'It's sweet revenge for me. Kimberly took me to lunch, plied me with alcohol, but did not make a pass. I have been smarting ever since.'[1035] He reasoned, too, that '*The Spectator* is portrayed in a very favourable light as a chaotic haven of bohemian self-indulgence and aristocratic broad-mindedness. It would be totally out of character for Boris to sack us. *The Spectator* has a long and distinguished tradition of tolerating dissent.'[1036] His

optimism was well founded. For his part, Johnson tartly remarked, 'I don't know whether I'll have time to catch it before it closes … I'm sure it will be a thoroughly good lark. Ha, ha, ha.'[1037] But the editor's tolerance did not extend to green-lighting the play for a follow-on run in the West End. Incidentally, Petronella Wyatt's 'Singular Life' column (its name since October 1998) came to a quiet end in February 2005.

Given this exhausting turmoil, Andrew Neil reassured Radio 4, 'I think we are looking forward to a period of quiet.'[1038] In November 2004, he became chief executive of *The Spectator*; not only did this separate the magazine editorially from the Telegraph Group, but it made Neil the direct line-manager of Johnson. The two men soon reached a gentleman's agreement that, should Johnson return to a position in the Tory shadow cabinet, he would stand down from the editorship. Neil explained at the time, '*The Spectator* is a right-leaning magazine, but it is not the propaganda arm of the Tory party. The Editor must be free to take whatever editorial line they see fit. You can do that as a Tory MP but not as a front-bencher.'[1039] It is indeed true that, for the pre-war *Spectator*, such competing loyalties and conflicting interests would have been utterly unsustainable. Post-war events, however, had already turned up a serving Tory MP, one of the two editors who went on to be Chancellor of the Exchequer. In the meantime, Neil said, 'I think the more time the Editor spends in Doughty Street editing the magazine and the less we see of him in the newspapers, the better.'[1040] A sound, if optimistic, hope: six months later Neil was still wary of Johnson's magazine:

'I love the quirkiness and the humour, but we also have to inject some intellectual rigour… The *Spectator* is "work in progress" – it has to get dragged into the 21st century.'[1041]

Meanwhile, doubtless inspired by the likes of Disraeli and Churchill in previous centuries, Johnson published a novel in 2004. Yet, unlike *Sybil* or *Savrola*, *Seventy-Two Virgins* was a comic piece. When Douglas Hurd reviewed the work for *The Spectator*, he joined most in supposing the lead character – an ambitious Tory MP concerned to stop his private indiscretions from appearing in the press – not to be an entirely *ex nihilo* fiction. Although all smiled at his female assistant being called Cameron, none matched Hurd's clairvoyance in describing the author as 'the next prime minister but three'.[1042] The book's plot, however, of an Islamist suicide-bomb attack by four northerners in central London, was far more eerily prescient. The London attacks of 7 July 2005 killed fifty-two. Even *The Spectator*, whose office was not far from the Tavistock Square bus explosion, nor far above the Piccadilly Line Tube bomb, was profoundly shaken, and the editor's plan still to host the summer party that evening naturally fell flat.

There were, of course, difficulties afoot, even without Johnson on the shadow cabinet bench. The magazine had become uncommonly open about its support of the Conservatives. In April 2005, as the general election approached, Johnson matched the leading article ('Vote Tory') with a splash on *The Spectator* website that declared, 'Vote Tory! Vote Often! Any member of the Spectator staff caught voting Liberal Democrat will be dealt with severely.'[1043] Victory did not come, but the magazine continued to provide an avowedly partisan platform for rising talent in the party. In July 2005, for instance, it hosted a piece by Theresa May, then an MP angling for action, about (curiously enough) the need to reform the procedure for electing new Tory leaders.[1044]

Despite its open politicking, Johnson was keen to leaven any flat analysis with humour: as he explained to *The Independent*, 'most people find politics unbelievably dull, so I don't see any particular vice in trying to sugar the pill with a few jokes.'[1045] When pressed on what his envisaged *Spectator* reader looked like, he prudently eschewed 'any kind of psychometric profile':

He or she could be anyone who likes to be provoked in their journalism and likes good writing… I could not say that the Spectator reader has the mouth of Marilyn Monroe, the mind of Einstein, and the legs of, errm, Kermit the Frog. Just people who like the feel of something civilised and different.[1046]

In February 2005, Stephen Glover resigned from his 'Media Studies' column, after nine years of energetic and insightful criticism. The cause was his piece on recent job losses at the *Daily Telegraph* being spiked by Johnson – because, Glover suspected, it made negative remarks about the sister-in-law title. Johnson countered that the article's real problem was its recommendation that cuts be made to staff rather than in other *Telegraph* departments. 'Why', he asked the press, 'should I put a piece in our pages that advocated the sacking of people who

I've worked with?'[1047] In addition, he said that Murdoch MacLennan, managing director of the Telegraph Media Group, felt the piece contained a crucial factual error in the stated profits of the *Telegraph*. As the disagreement wore on in a number of newspaper columns, Johnson became more riled with Glover:

If he thinks that writing about the *Telegraph* is any sign of independence or machismo he must be joking. What would be true courage would be if he ever summoned up the gumption to attack the *Daily Mail* or comment on the management of the *Mail* and Dacre, or the bestial approach of the *Mail* to some stories. But he doesn't… Media columns are an opportunity for journalists to settle scores, pursue hobby horses and sit in judgment over everybody else in their profession… The talk of impartiality is phooey.[1048]

It was a similar attitude that also led him to mock his predecessor Frank Johnson for never daring to mock his editor-in-chief: 'I think Frank's a wimp. You big girl's blouse, Frank. Chuck in some Andrew Neil jokes.'[1049] For his part, Glover soon found a post at *The Independent*, and a role for the next five years as *Spectator* sniper-in-chief. Yet there seemed, after a while, to be an amnesty: in October 2005, Glover was re-employed as *The Spectator*'s (monthly) media columnist – only to be sacked again after two columns, the latter of which shone lurid light on the long-rumbling conflict between two *Spectator* big beasts, Bruce Anderson and Simon Heffer.[1050] Not for another seven years would Glover write again for the magazine, but in November

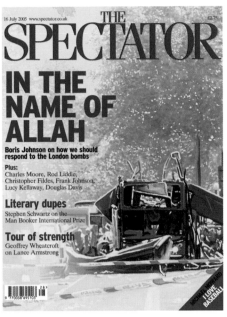

ssues of 9 July, 16 July and 24 Sep. 2005

---

012 he did at last return, with a piece on reedom of speech.[1051]

Despite – or because of – its controversial punk, *The Spectator* was enjoying an unprecedently wide readership, and with considerable amusement. Johnson later recalled that, amid all the staff scandals, not a single reader got in touch to complain.'[1052] Dylan Jones, editor of *GQ*, told *The Guardian* that its 'contrary nature makes it a magazine you can't possibly not pick up.'[1053] The quondam rebels Mick Jagger and Pete Townsend could not resist taking out a subscription, nor Michael Wolff praising the magazine in *Vanity Fair* as 'the world's most literate, funny, snobby, bitchy, and readable journal of opinion'.[1054] There was a feeling, however, that *The Spectator* was not publishing the sort of in-depth investigative pieces that had caused such a stir in the days of Dominic Lawson. While Gilligan's articles in 2003 and 2004 were hard-hitting dispatches, and Johnson's five-page, tag-team interview

with Nicholas Farrell of the Italian prime minister Silvio Berlusconi (6 Sep. 2003) made waves around the Mediterranean, these were relatively anomalous. But when Johnson was pressed by Neil for more journalistic scoops, he acted quickly, publishing a three-page, 3,200-word article under the running header 'Investigation'. Its title certainly caught the eye: 'How to live forever'. Such a billing by the author, Johnson himself, must have hooked many a reader; but he soon baffled them by devoting the entirety of the piece to the Roman lyric poet Horace, his aristocratic patron Maecenas, and the Emperor Augustus. It is a fine piece, and those at least who had entered the magazine's 'Classics Cup' competitions for Greek and Latin composition in 2004–5 were rapt.[1055] This was the sort of provocation in which Johnson revelled: writing with flair on a topic that matched the expectations of neither proprietor nor subscriber. Another came in October 2005, when he took the

surprising step across the floor by writing a diary piece for the *New Statesman*.[1056]

In December 2005, the crux moment came: with the selection of David Cameron as the new Conservative leader, Johnson was eventually appointed as the shadow minister for higher education. Such a post practically made his position at *The Spectator* untenable under Neil's *nouveau régime*. Certainly, if he wished to make a serious impact in Parliament, the demanding and unrelenting requirements of editing *The Spectator* would be too much: one role would scupper the success of the other. Accordingly, Johnson was, as he put it, 'gathered to the Valhalla of ex-*Spectator* editors'.[1057] He agreed to remain in post until the end of the year to see through the Christmas special – a valedictory issue that managed to sell a third more copies than in the previous year.[1058] When the announcement was made, he summed up his editorial tenure with tongue characteristically in cheek:

For the last six and a half years we have had more fun than seems altogether proper. When Conrad Black gave me the editorship in the summer of 1999, he said he wanted the magazine to be more talked about. I believe we have discharged that obligation beyond his wildest dreams. We have won all sorts of prizes. We have broken all sorts of stories.

But he reserved his warmest thanks for his staff and writers:

For most of my time here I have been propelled by their talents, as a fat German tourist may be transported by superior alpinists to the summit of Everest. I am completely confident that they will continue to expand and improve the oldest, best and best-written magazine in the English language.[1059]

In a lower-key interview, he confessed that he had felt he should move on since the summer of 2004: 'by the end you're starting to hit the ball back with exactly the same shot you used last year and the year before.'[1060] He also acknowledged the tensions of his post: 'what I have tested to destruction … is the idea that you can be on the front bench and edit a national magazine, which imposes its own self-censorship. I tried to ride both horses, but I got bumped off the shadow arts thing… It's been incredibly kind of Conrad Black and the Barclays to allow a Conservative MP to edit a national magazine for a very long time.' At his farewell speech to staff, he confessed that he had 'a terrible feeling that I'm going to dissolve into great

floods of blubbing sentimentality, and that would not be true to the traditions of the *Spectator*.'[1061] His last sentence in post was, 'I'm shattered. Shattered.'[1062]

Voices in the national press felt that *The Spectator*, however entertaining a read, had not yet fully found its form for the twenty-first century. Cristina Odone, once touted as a potential editor, said that under Johnson

all too often the magazine was frivolous to the point of vacuity and you had to turn to the (ever more frequent) travel advertorials before you ran into a fact or a figure. There was no inkling, ever, that in Notting Hill a group of young Tories were plotting the seismic political changes that would free the Conservatives from their dated and unsympathetic image. *The Spectator* that under Charles Moore and Dominic Lawson had flourished as a high Tory coven, where ideas were thrashed out and positions debated in advance of Tory central office, was no more. Johnson's political vision was coherent – an anti-European, pro-American, pro-market Conservatism; the problem was that he wasn't around enough to stamp his vision on the magazine.

Other commentators were unsure about whether the magazine was modern or outmoded, class-obsessed or meritocratic, Conservative or anarchic. *The Independent* at the time felt that

for many, *The Spectator* is redolent of claret, double-breasted suits and fogeyish men from Eton, Harrow,

Oxford and Cambridge. Despite his recruitment of less crusty figures such as Liddle and Andrew Gilligan, Johnson himself embodied this tradition. His editorship was made on the playing fields of Eton even if he did embrace pedal-cycling as a commuter fashion. He nudged *The Spectator* into the present but never risked alienating it from the classical tradition set by his eminent predecessors.[1063]

'For many' frames this as the vague an amorphous feeling of those who did no read the magazine but did recognis Johnson from *Have I Got News For Yo* In actuality, the magazine was amiabl irreverent, and often very funny indee – not least in the withering restaura reviews of Deborah Ross (fortnightl April 2000–Oct. 2006). It was als 'Unashamedly Elitist' (as adver declared), but only in expecting readers approach its pages with both an inform and an interested outlook.

As an editor, Johnson was manifest popular and inspiring: he brought a ne found confidence to the *Spectator* bran and invited writers to challenge the read and themselves. His deputy editor Re was crucial to that process: Johnson, recalled, was not a 'conscientious, for filling, tradition-observing editor … a thank God for that.'[1064] 'If Stuart was t workhorse,' one long-standing contribut reflected, 'then Boris was the plumed hor the dressage.'[1065] But Reid – who seems have lost his temper with Johnson only on in five years – always maintained that it w 'absolutely Boris's magazine … Boris di lot of the work and I had a lot of fun.'[1066]

his PA Ann 'be-all-and-Sindall' observed, He edited *The Spectator* on a knife edge. He couldn't do it otherwise.'[1067] For his part, Black weighed up these lively years with typical pragmatism: 'Boris's performance was outrageous, but the chief criterion is what's good for the *Spectator*, and Boris was a good thing for the *Spectator*.'[1068] A *Spectator* contributor for more than thirty years later called Johnson 'one of the most inspired editors the *Spectator* magazine has had'.[1069]

Despite the frantic frivolity, Johnson's *Spectator* landed many pieces of substance: on the shortcomings of the British education system (Philip Hensher, 17 Feb. 2001), the collapse of British masculinity (Michael Gove, 11 Aug. 2001), the crisis facing Anglicanism (Peter Hitchens, 9 Aug. 2003), the global aspirations of Islam (Anthony Browne, 24 July 2004), the growing societal taboos of public speech (Simon Heffer, 30 Oct. 2004), 'Goodbye England' on the hunting ban (Boris Johnson and Peter Oborne, 19 Feb. 2005), and a 'race and culture special' on British children being 'divided at birth' (Boris Johnson et al., 24 Sep. 2005). In 2000, Johnson had hosted a live and fiery debate on Irish republicanism between Ronan Bennett (a staunch republican) and Sean O'Callaghan, former IRA terrorist who had recanted his extremism (publ. 7 Oct. 2000).

Although sorry to leave Doughty Street, Johnson was not done with *The Spectator*. He has been a frequent contributor ever since, with plenty of cover pieces both by and about him. Four years later, the magazine would issue a supplement to assess his career as Mayor of London one year in. A decade later, he was appearing on the cover of *The Spectator* more often

than not. Perhaps this was mere piety to a former editor; perhaps it reflected the fact that, for the second time in the magazine's history, a former *Spectator* employee had become prime minister. For a title that had spent its entire history mocking the leading (wo)men of the day, Johnson now had to face the music as the most spectated figure of all. It is a sign of the man's allegiances not only that he later composed the winning entry to the 'President Erdogan Offensive Poetry Competition'[1070] but also that he has become the first prime minister to pen a *Spectator* article while in post.[1071] In an age of transferable skills, running a weekly periodical must do much to help constructing and inspiring the weekly meeting of Cabinet. *The Spectator* thus congratulated itself by crowning Johnson 'Parliamentarian of the Year' in January 2020. Johnson responded in kind by calling it 'the greatest magazine in the English language' – but the most striking segment of the acceptance video came from Dilyn, his dog, who announced that he devoured the magazine 'from cover to cover', which he proceeded literally to do.

With Johnson's long-mooted exit at last confirmed, there was no clarity about who would follow in his footsteps. The press was rife with rumours for what proved to be a three-month hiatus. During that interregnum, the long-serving deputy editor and leader-writer Stuart Reid acted as editor, overseeing a fine crop of issues – including a 'Rude Britannia' special.[1072] None of this was done lightly: as he later told the press, '*The Spectator* is given to us in trust. It is more than just a product and more than just a brand.'[1073] That commitment was bolstered during Reid's caretakership by launching the first digital version of the

magazine, via Exact Editions, who hosted a perfect page mock-up of it.[1074] Three years later, once the writing on the wall came into focus, this format was launched as an iPhone app, fitting the magazine firmly in the palm of the hand.

Meanwhile, the magazine's presence online was steadily growing, providing a near-autonomous companion piece to the print magazine's weekly voice. The online editor, Dominic Cummings (then based at *The Business*), was overseeing a successful rolling blog on current affairs (*Spectator Xtra*) and a provocative news digest (*Spectator Live!*). In February 2006, it was the latter of these that published something at once innocuous and dangerous: a cartoon of the prophet Muhammad with a bomb in his turban.[1075] This image, drawn by the Danish septuagenarian Kurt Westergaard and reproduced from the newspaper *Jyllands-Posten*, had on its original publication received widespread protests from the Muslim world, prompting the withdrawal of the Libyan, Saudi Arabian and Syrian ambassadors from Denmark. The picture linked to a *Guardian* story about which European newspapers had run the cartoon, and in so doing made *The Spectator* the first UK publication to show the image – and indeed the last.[1076] The caption lamented that 'Britain's comic political class cannot even control Islamic terrorists when they finally lock a few up in prison.' Cummings, a staunch believer in press freedom, was able to operate independently of Johnson and Reid, not least when based up at the family farm in County Durham. Neil, who had encouraged Cummings to make the website better known, summarily ordered the removal of the image before the afternoon was out. One staff member recalled that Cummings 'didn't work in the actual office but one of his first actions was to publish the forbidden cartoons of the prophet Mohammad that were causing a stir at the time. We, who did have to work in the *Spectator* office, were all furious "thinking this lunatic was trying to get us blown up by Islamists".'[1077] That did not come to pass – but, reader, that same staff member married him five years later. Not long after, Cummings promptly resigned his post, which was placed in the less pugilistic hands of the well-connected gossipmonger Matthew Bell. Come 2019, Cummings was reunited with his erstwhile Spectator colleague, as Johnson's chief adviser in Downing Street.

In the meantime, Neil set about finding a replacement who could continue – if not necessarily build on – the momentum of Johnson's riotous tenure. In a perfect world, this would be someone who had the freedom both to throw themselves wholeheartedly into the job and to assess the socio-political scene without formal party ties. The magazine, Neil said, needed 'a little bit less froth' – recalling the very thing that Frank Johnson had sought out[1078] – 'and a bit more seriousness.' This could be achieved, he said, by 'marginal balancing – a tweak'.[1079] To the more superannuated reader, Neil's desire to firm up Johnson's *Spectator* would have been reminiscent of Iain Gilmour's move, in 1961, to rework Brian Inglis's *Spectator*, despite the impressive circulations won by both.[1080]

The press was cock-a-hoop in its speculation: everyone had an opinion, and almost everyone seemed to have put in for the post. After excited talk about Michael Portillo and Rod Liddle died down, the

names given serious consideration were Geordie Greig, editor of *Tatler*, Simon Heffer, associate editor of the *Telegraph*, Quentin Letts, sketch-writer for the *Daily Mail*, John Micklethwait, US editor of *The Economist*, Peter Oborne, political editor of *The Spectator*, Iain Martin, editor of *Scotland on Sunday*, Martin Vander Weyer, long-standing city correspondent, Ross Clark, stalwart *Spectator* contributor, and Matthew d'Ancona, deputy editor of the *Sunday Telegraph*; Stuart Reid, then indeed acting editor of *The Spectator*, chose not to apply. All were intriguing prospects. The ex-editor of the *New Statesman*, Peter Wilby, wrote rather mischievously in the *Evening Standard* that 'The Spectator needs somebody eccentric, even slightly crazed,' before adding that the perceived front runner, Matthew d'Ancona, 'is too sane.'[1081] Neil, by contrast, was clear that because 'The Spectator is a great success story it will not be destroyed by unnecessary radicalism.'[1082] Radicalism, of course, is a slippery term.

Before the announcement of the incoming editor was made in February, Neil introduced two new recruits to the magazine. Press Holdings' sale of the *Scotsman* to Johnston Press in December 2005 brought two of its staff south of the border: Iain Martin and Fraser Nelson. Martin headed to the *Daily Telegraph*; Nelson, along with Allister Heath, deputy editor of *The Business*, entered the *Spectator* fold as associate editors. In times past, 'associate editor' was tantamount to 'deputy editor' of the magazine; in the hierarchy of the twenty-first-century *Spectator*, however, this was the lowest rung of paid editorial staff. Although Heath was soon back editing *The Business*

(2007–8), before becoming editor of *City AM* (2008–14) and the *Sunday Telegraph* (2017–), Nelson was due to bed down and become an integral organ in the body Spectatorial.

By mid-February 2006, the new editor was selected after an exacting interview with Andrew Neil (and, in some cases, Aidan Barclay): Letts, Vander Weyer and Micklethwait came close. But the winner was revealed to be the very man who had been touted to succeed Johnson five years earlier: **MATTHEW D'ANCONA** (1968–). An outstandingly clever cove who followed a First in History at Magdalen, Oxford, with a prize fellowship at All Souls, d'Ancona is one of the few public figures actually to have earned their nickname 'two brains'. His academic credentials – including research on medieval sin – placed him in the high-minded *Spectator* tradition of Hutton and Moore. But his interests ranged beyond cloisters and the clergy, and from his early twenties he became feverishly engaged in journalism, including a four-year stint at *The Times*, where he became assistant editor at the age of twenty-six. In 1996, not long after his fellowship lapsed, he joined the *Sunday Telegraph* and soon became deputy editor, a post he held with much acclaim. D'Ancona had won the reputation of being an excellent researcher, a polished writer and – relatively rare in the industry, the saying goes – a thoroughly nice chap. When news of his appointment broke, Neil wrote that he

combines the requisite political gravitas and insight with the wit and originality that the post requires. The list of candidates was the strongest I have ever seen for an editorship; many were well qualified for the job. But we concluded that Matthew was the best qualified to build on the superb legacy of Boris Johnson.[1083]

D'Ancona's first manifesto for the magazine was clear and cogent:

Under my editorship, I want *The Spectator* to adapt its fine traditions as a source of superb writing, news exclusives and wit to a new and exciting political landscape. It will be modern, free-thinking and indispensable.[1084]

He soon clarified that it would be 'indispensable'

as a treasure trove of information. Not arid facts, but nuggets of opinions and things you would never have imagined… Using the magazine to promulgate a world view is not what we are about at all. It's not a stick of rock, it's a pick and mix. It should be full of diversity… What I want is fine writing that is witty and engaging. I've no ambitions to turn the magazine into *Newsweek* or *Time*, but nonetheless it's extremely important to be on top of what's happening.[1085]

Neil was in agreement about the benefits of divergent opinion, but keen on establishing a more serious backbone:

The appetite is there for serious political commentary, but with excellent book reviews, great arts coverage, interesting, provocative and often funny columns intermixed.

If the world didn't want some serious commentary, the *Economist* wouldn't be selling a million copies.[1086]

Given his substantial spell at *The Economist*, and his formative relationship with Alastair Burnet (editor, 1965–74), Neil had learned much from the model of this magazine, which reached seven-figure sales in 2005. Since he had also overseen the introduction of the multi-section *Sunday Times*, he could plot a route forward that widened the appeal of the magazine while preserving its core identity.

D'Ancona was not without his own politics, but they were tied up in a complex web: that he was the son of a distinguished civil servant – who played two seasons of football for Newcastle – told one little; but his personal friendship with Gordon Brown and marriage to David Miliband's political adviser pointed in a rather different direction from his declaration that he was 'clearly right of centre, an Atlanticist, pretty hawkish'.[1087] At any rate, the magazine did indeed return to its earlier position of supporting the cause of the Iraq War. Despite his rightward slant, however, d'Ancona was keen to stress that he had no desire 'to be the in-house magazine of the Conservative Party. I want to surf the Cameron wave, not be part of it.'[1088] Although he had impeccable journalistic credentials, and was comfortable on the High Table circuit, d'Ancona moved in different circles from many of his predecessors: like four of the previous five editors – and four of the last five proprietors – he had been a member of the Beefsteak Club, but he had resigned from this traditional corner of Clubland in 2004.[1089]

Since he readily self-identified as a 'film

maniac', it was appropriate that the cover of d'Ancona's first issue, of 11 March 2006, bore a *Godfather*-themed cover, alongside the headline 'The Loneliness of Don Tony'. Attentive readers perhaps recalled that d'Ancona's first article for *The Spectator*, a cover piece some seven years earlier, had been on the important contribution of Mickey Mouse and other Disney characters to Western culture.[1090] This opening issue had some other surprises. One was a new 'Deep Thought' section, which for its first contribution carried a 3,000-word piece by Nigel Lawson on the quasi-religious zeal of the Green lobby. The section did not reappear.

The staff of *The Spectator* was largely the same as under Johnson, with the addition of Nelson and Heath. Crucially, Reid continued to provide a stabilising effect as deputy editor. Within a couple of months, however, d'Ancona had appointed five contributing editors (i.e. non-stipendiary associates): Anne Applebaum, Matthew Norman, David Rennie, Jemima Lewis and Peter Oborne. All had contributed to *The Spectator* before, but Norman, Rennie and Lewis have not done so since 2006. Oborne promptly decided to leave his post as political correspondent, heading for the *Daily Mail* that April, where he spent two long spells (2006–10, 2015–19), straddling five years at the *Daily Telegraph* (2010–15). To the admiration of many, and the shock of some, Oborne has put principle ahead of paper, resigning whenever he has come to dislike what he sees. His replacement at *The Spectator* surprised many, since the mantle fell on the freshly recruited associate editor Fraser Nelson. d'Ancona's editorial instincts here were excellent: Nelson's next three years in that post proved to be a great success for the magazine and a stepping-stone to things beyond. Like many contributors, Nelson supplemented his salary by a column in a national newspaper – or in his case two: from October 2006 to February 2008 he played the political Poseidon, wielding a trident of columns in *The Spectator*, *The Business* and the *News of the World* ('Nelson's Column', a.k.a. 'Nelson's Mandela' and 'Nelson's Gollum'). After the separate collapses of the last two titles, Nelson became a columnist at the *Daily Telegraph*, where he has remained a weekly fixture since.

In order to keep the financial side of the magazine healthy, Neil brought in the publisher David Hanger from *The Economist* in a 'loosely consultative role'.[1091] The idea was to formulate a five-year plan for growth, but one staff writer whispered to *The Guardian* that it also was a ruse to 'breathe down Kimberly Quinn's neck'.[1092] The chairman's own ambitions were certainly high-reaching – including the publicly declared hope of surpassing 100,000 in sales. This figure proved to be a little too punchy, but circulation did rise in 2006, to 62,700 (or some 75,000 for the Audit Bureau of Circulation). To foster further success, d'Ancona was given the freedom to expand the magazine. The seventy-two-page format often expanded to eighty, eighty-eight or ninety-six pages, although most of this growth came in the form of print advertisements: the inclusion of a 'luxury goods special' swelled the issue of 4 November 2006 to the record proportion of 112 pages.

One of the earliest decisions of d'Ancona's editorship was one of the strangest. This was to end the 'Portrait of the Week' news digest that introduced each issue. He told the press that the feature 'has had a long and glorious reign but I felt it was time to move it off into retirement'.[1093] Perhaps he felt that the steady rise of the hebdomadal news amalgam *The Week* (1995–) made it difficult for this section to be realistically competitive; perhaps he felt that, in the burgeoning markets of twenty-four-hour news, the Internet and ever-smarter phones, such a summary had become an unusual anachronism. Whatever the thinking, this was a grave editorial mistake, as previous perpetrators of the cull (Gale and Chancellor) had rapidly realised. For *The Spectator* had always sought to present its readers with a summary of the current affairs that mattered – to distil the dizzying array of events, facts and figures into something not just digestible but more-ish. To anyone picking up the magazine who had no sense of what was happening in the world, this summary grounded them and foreshadowed the unpredictably varied contents that followed. Such a decoction of the week's news had been prepared with skill, and seasoned with learning and humour, for almost two centuries, juxtaposing the grave and the grim with the quaint and the ridiculous. But, in a flash, that long-holding and much-admired cord was cut. *Spectator* readers received no explanation.

In its stead, d'Ancona introduced the 'Diary of a Notting Hill Nobody'. Under the guise of 'Tamzin Lightwater', Melissa Kite began satirically chronicling the vapid world of the 'Cameroons' and their wannabe clinger-ons. So well-informed was this anonymous writer that some supposed Sam Cameron or Frances Osborne was leaking from Downing Street. Senior figures in Conservative Central Office pressured the editor for information – but lips were sealed. The series ran from d'Ancona's first issue until shortly after the Conservative victory at the 2010 general election; when the *Evening Standard*'s 'Londoner' column revealed Kite as the author, she promptly killed off Tamzin.[1094] Meanwhile, since October 2007, she has agonisingly been surveying the grinding gripes of 'Real Life', which moved from a fortnightly to weekly billing in November 2009.

Throughout his tenure, d'Ancona recruited a wide range of new Diary writers. More so than in previous decades, these contributors came from popular quarters of the public domain: among the more recognisable faces were Piers Morgan, Emily Maitlis, Louis Theroux, Jimmy Carr, Charlie Higson, Michael Atherton, and HRH Princess Michael of Kent. Both Boris Johnson and Peter Oborne were also willing and able to return to the fray.

To give some zest to d'Ancona's *Spectator*, a 'Champagne for the Brain' advertising campaign was launched in May 2006 around London, on taxis and the Tube. Quinn told *The Independent*:

Champagne is potent and effervescent, just like *The Spectator*, which is light, witty and clever but with a real kick. Our ad agency … identified who should be reading it and wasn't. There will be another campaign this autumn backed by a £200,000 media spend. This is a generic branding exercise which ran in some newspapers and in

Advertisements, 2006 (Walford Wilkie)

taxis, and added a couple of thousand copies on to sales at the news-stand.[1095]

However cringe-inducing, this was an important initiative in what was a dangerous time for *The Spectator* and its fellow serious weeklies. Revenues for digital and display advertising were starting the fall from which they would not recover; the sale price of issues was at the upper end of what the public was prepared to swallow; printing and distribution costs were continuing to rise. Readers, too, were starting to turn elsewhere: almost every print title in the country would never sell so many copies again. Magazine editors were panicking across the sector, unsure of which baskets to fill with eggs, and uncertain, too, of which eggs would even hatch.

It was partly for editorial but primarily for commercial reasons that a weekly lifestyle section was introduced to the magazine that same month. This included a four-page business section (edited by

Vander Weyer) and a three-page luxury goods section called 'You've Earned It' (edited by Sarah Standing). Despite some fine writing from A.A. Gill, Nicholas Coleridge and Geordie Greig, the somewhat presumptuous title of the latter was soon mocked by *Spectator* staff as 'You've Inherited It'. Before long it was formally renamed 'Style and Travel'. Glover was quick to heckle from *The Independent*: 'Surely one of the main attractions of *The Spectator* has been that, virtually alone in the British Press, it did not have such a section.'[1096] Glover was doubtless still smarting from d'Ancona's decision not to reinstate a media column: as the latter had told the press, 'Our pages are precious and I do not think the internal wranglings of our trade are high on the list of *Spectator* readers' priorities.'[1097]

Some were worried. Cristina Odone wrote in *The Guardian* of the delicate balance that needed preserving at *The Spectator*. The piece, polemically headed 'How to make friends and alienate readers',

channelled a number of contemporary views about where the magazine was heading:

The Spectator was where fine writing trumped a famous name, and where you found solace from the absurdities of political correctness and the excesses of vulgar consumerism. Include in the mix one too many pedestrian pieces by a celebrity, or one too many advertorials, and you risk upsetting the fragile ecosystem… Pages of obvious product placement, glossy ads and brochure photographs threaten to turn *The Spectator* into a dentist's waiting-room read. The counter-intuitive eccentricities of the weekly do remain – Charles Moore, Rod Liddle, Matthew Parris and the Johnsons, Frank and Paul; but they now seem like havens which the reader can only reach after thrashing about in a sea of price tags and 'for sale' signs.[1098]

Meanwhile, Quinn broadcast that 'the head of a company will always read *The Spectator* – we want the new hedge fund managers, the guys coming down the pike.'[1099] Neil, too, shared the belief that the readership could expand among the wealthy, but the correlation between high salary and high literary interest is notoriously imperfect.

Perhaps because of a change in the environment, perhaps by mere coincidence, not every writer in the *Spectator* stable chose to stay. Along with Oborne, Christopher Fildes left in April 2006, thus ending twenty-three years' devotion to his wide-ranging financial column 'City and Suburban', unfailingly written with seemingly effortless elegance and enlivened by a series of fabricated 'special correspondents' (such as I.K. Gricer on railways, Captain Threadneedle on racing, and a Jumbo Speedbird on aviation). But his replacement was ready in the wings: since September 2005, the even-handed and good-humoured Martin Vander Weyer, a long-standing contributor, had been alternating his column 'Any Other Business' with Fildes; Vander Weyer successfully followed in the tradition established by Davenport more than fifty years earlier, of turning out interesting and independently minded copy, which at last won him a weekly berth in 2010.

In late 2006 James Michie died, and thus *The Spectator* lost not just the great competition-setter 'Jaspistos' but a proofreader worthy of the palm. Tributes from all quarters were warm and wistful. Boris Johnson said that he 'was plainly a man of great gifts. His headlines were lapidary, and swiftly produced... Michie gave every appearance of a consummate lack of ambition, but he has left his *monumentum aere perennius*.'[1100] Moore recalled that he 'was not pedantic, but he was exact. Enoch Powell said of A.E. Housman that "It was a big mind that chose to live in a small room" – there was something of that in James. The small room that is *The Spectator* benefited hugely.'[1101] His funeral, at the Chelsea Arts Club, was described by one *Spectator* writer as 'a last gasp of geriatric literary bohemia, one of the most memorable parties I've ever attended.'[1102] In April 2007, Lucy Vickery, previously an occasional correspondent for the magazine on 'Hot Property', took over the setting and

judging of the competition, and has proved to be a very worthy successor in providing this essential condiment at the *Spectator* table – even if Cobra lager no longer forms part of the weekly prize.

Yet d'Ancona was able to bring a broad array of new writers to *The Spectator*. In October 2006, the veteran journalist and literary critic Allan Massie began a column on 'Life and Letters'; this learned and provocative survey of books and the literary world continued to much acclaim for the next six years. Less obvious a recruit arrived the following September: Alex James, the bassist of the Britpop mercenaries Blur. Appointed an associate editor, he began – from his Cotswolds estate – a fortnightly column entitled 'Slow Life'. This series, which garnered mixed feedback and failed to find a consistent rhythm, nevertheless continued until January 2010. Also in September 2007, Toby Young began a weekly 'Status Anxiety' column on all manner of societal woes and worries; it is still going strong, albeit with the significant rebranding in January 2018 'No sacred cows', after a Twitterstorm led to Young's enforced resignation from the new universities regulator, the Office for Students. From April 2009, Sarah Standing started offering a witty and wide-ranging look at the day-to-day travails of modern life ('Standing Room'): it enjoyed a six-month stint before being stood down by a new arrival.

One writer who had continued the magazine's spirit over five previous editors was Taki; as a reflection of *The Spectator*'s support of writers who express themselves openly but lawfully, d'Ancona continued to host 'High Life'. Although ever popular with readers, Taki kept editors on their

toes. Both Johnsons had in fact braved the storm more than once: three years earlier, he had declared that 'Britain is being mugged by black hoodlums' and that 'West Indians were allowed to immigrate after the war, multiply like flies, and then the great state apparatus took over the care of their multiplications.' Liddle, hardly a shrinking violet, recorded in *The Spectator* his disapproval of this 'inaccurate and ... pretty foul' piece.[1103] In 1997, Taki had defended the 'clean German army' a brave soldiers free from the taint of Hitler' Nazism,[1104] and described Puerto Rican marching in New York as 'a bunch of semi savages' that were 'fat, squat, ugly, dusky dirty and unbelievably loud'.[1105] Three years on, he handled the hot potato of racial stereotypes: 'Race is more than skin deep no ifs or buts about it. On average, Oriental are slower to mature, less randy, and have larger brains and higher IQ score Blacks are at the other pole, and whites fall somewhere in the middle, although close to the Orientals than the blacks.' He went on to explain that black athletes can run faster because of the narrower hips they possess, compared to those races that need wider hips to birth bigger-brained children. As it happens, these were not Taki's own assertions but a near-verbatim crib from the controversial psychologist J. Philippe Rushton's *Race, Evolution, and Behavior* (1995). Necessarily, the piece caused the editor, Boris Johnson, to apologise for publication at the time of his election to the London mayoralty.

Taki was preternaturally aware that his writing was on the edge. When criticised the behaviour of American athletes at the Sydney Olympics in 2000 he clarified, 'I do not, of course, have racist bone in my body, if racism means disliking someone because of the colour of their skin.'[1106] As he later acknowledged, 'I am not at all racist, although I do sound like one at times.'[1107] This nuanced position has typically found acceptance from editor and reader alike. But when, in 2001, Taki acknowledged himself to be one of the *soi-disant* anti-Semites for daring to protest about [Israeli] soldiers shooting at kids',[1108] the proprietor Conrad Black weighed in on the attack: 'It is hard to imagine that a person with whom you are friendly and have had many memorably agreeable times is a racist who wishes and incites violence against innocent people because of their ethnicity or religion.'[1109] He proceeded to defend the right of his writers to 'dislike individuals and whole nationalities and ethnic groups … if they do so rationally, are not legally defamatory, and if they are within the bounds of civilised taste. Our publications will never be hounded into politically correct avoidance of any forceful opinion touching ethnicity, sectarianism, gender or sexual orientation.' But, he continued, 'Taki's reflections were indefensible … irrational and an offence to civilised taste'. Uniquely, the following issue's correspondence filled two pages under the one heading 'Conrad Black v. Taki'. Most correspondents denounced his provocative simplifications, though Ian Gilmour and Naim Attallah were critical of the proprietor's heavy-handed response.[1110] All of this certainly kept the pulse of readers up, who continued through d'Ancona and beyond to relish Taki's readiness to thumb his nose at both vaunted celebrity and sacred shibboleth.

Of his new recruits one would prove to transformational. Early in d'Ancona's tenure he ran as the cover piece an article by a twenty-five-year-old assistant editor of the Washington-based *Foreign Policy* named James Forsyth, an Englishman then earning his stripes abroad.[1111] Fortuitously, this proved to be the beginning of a relationship that would shape and steer the modern *Spectator*. In February 2007, Forsyth was signed up to replace Matthew Bell as online editor, who headed to the *Evening Standard*'s Londoner's Diary. This he filled with *Spectator* gossip for several months, having not been removed from the staff's email circulars. Forsyth meanwhile was faced with a project requiring serious renewal: although the site had been reprinting articles from the magazine, and syndicating *Telegraph* columns from d'Ancona, Johnson and Moore, it was not yet a major player in the political blogosphere, having lost steam after Cummings's exit. But it was clear that both the opportunity and the energy for change were now at hand. In May 2007, d'Ancona launched the website's biggest ever initiative: 'Coffee House'. The name was pointedly chosen: as an always-live political blog on ever-changing current affairs in Westminster and beyond, it sought to channel the chatter and gossip of the original *Spectator* that caused such mischief in the coffee and chocolate houses of Queen Anne's London. As d'Ancona stated, perhaps with some ambiguity about the relationship between the two titles, 'We want to try and recreate online the milieu and edginess of the eighteenth-century coffee house world that the *Spectator* actually emerged from.'[1112]

Just as Rintoul drew upon the character and cultural kudos of the Addison-Steele *Spectator*, so did the new site reach back into history again, rechannelling not just the well-informed banter of Addison and Steele but also the ready debate of Rintoul's paper. The branding proved to be astoundingly successful: almost no newspaper or weekly journal in Britain has managed to forge an active but distinctive blog online that enjoys an independent existence from its print counterpart. For his (increasingly expanding) part, Forsyth worked like a colony of caffeine-fuelled beavers, and did not take a day's holiday in his first eighteen months. In the earliest days, two bloggers were appointed to chronicle the issues of the day: Stephen Pollard, the biographer of David Blunkett, and Clive Davis, arts journalist for *The Times*. Within a year of such frenzied activity, the site was already being spoken of as 'one of the best examples of rolling political comment' and 'a prime example of cross-fertilisation between print and the web'.[1113] Star bloggers alongside Pollard and Davis included Melanie Phillips, Fraser Nelson, Martin Bright and – naturally enough – James Forsyth himself.

In February 2007, after a year of rumbling rumours about such a move, *The Spectator* changed premises, leaving behind Bloomsbury for its first entrance into Westminster proper. Although Boris Johnson had bid his staff chain themselves to the railings if they were threatened with removal, in reality they had no choice. Compared to the ramshackle townhouse of 56 Doughty Street, however, the five floors of 22 Old Queen Street, which overlooked Birdcage Walk to the rear, were a rather luxurious prospect. Explaining the shift southwards, d'Ancona said, 'We are an expanding title and we need proper modern offices. The new building is right

Coffee House, May 2007 and Nov. 2019

by Parliament which I think is a good thing for a magazine that writes about politics.'[1114] Nor was the building without historical interest: what is now *The Spectator*'s boardroom was once the space where Sir Edward Elgar premiered several of his pieces to the building's enterprising owner, Frankie Schuster. Aware of the significant effect buildings can have upon his staff, Neil transformed the basement into a splendid subterranean cavern watched over by shelves of all *Spectators* past. As with the move from Gower Street in 1975, however, several objects and records intrinsic to the magazine's history failed to reappear in the new premises.[1115]

In July 2007, the front cover proclaimed that the broadcaster Emily Maitlis had joined *The Spectator*, as both a columnist and contributing editor.[1116] She filed a fine Diary piece that week – but by the following issue had left the post. The reason

was to be found in BBC equivocation: Peter Horrocks, head of TV news at the BBC, approved Maitlis's position, on the basis that it would appear to balance out the general Leftist lean of high-profile employees. On seeing the announcement, John Kampfner, editor of the *New Statesman* and perhaps recipient of recurrent refusals from BBC contributors, harangued Horrocks to demand restitution. He in turn referred the dispute upwards to Helen Boaden, the director of BBC News, who demanded that Maitlis stop formally associating with a – or, perhaps, this – political weekly. Within seven days the post was forcibly given up. D'Ancona's reaction, by contrast, was unequivocal: 'I'm furious that the BBC seems to have gone to the Vicky Pollard school of management – yeah but, no but, yeah.' Maitlis has since contributed to the magazine now and then – and is doubtless still a keen reader.

In May 2008, Andrew Neil becam[e] chairman of Press Holdings. As a result, th[e] commercial side of *The Spectator*'s activi[ties] moved under the aegis of a new managi[ng] director, Ben Greenish, who replaced Pa[ul] Woolfenden. Neil had already decided [to] implement a suggestion from Woolfende[n] namely to rebrand a paper in the Pre[ss] Holdings stable with the *Spectator* nam[e]. Founded in 1996 as an alternative to t[he] *Financial Times*, the *Sunday Business* ha[d] been relaunched in 1998 but was struggli[ng] to maintain growth in the mid-2000s. [In] 2006 it evolved into a weekly magazi[ne] (*The Business*), but stiff competition ke[pt] its sales around the 15,000 mark. Given t[he] overlap in ownership and staff writers, t[he] *Spectator* team were encouraged to gi[ve] of their best to keep *The Business* goi[ng]. After it ceased operation as a month[ly] magazine in February 2008, Neil there[fore] created a new magazine under the hyb[rid] title *Spectator Business*, hoping to tailor the content for an audience that read and trusted *The Spectator*. Vander Weyer was the natural choice as editor, assisted by Lucinda Baring; subsequently Janice Warman (from *MoneyWeek*) and Laura Staples (from *Money Observer*) joined the team. Since the magazine contained its own lifestyle section ('Connoisseur'), content of this kind was scaled down in *The Spectator* proper. Although some writers, such as Matthew Lynn and Elliot Wilson, were regular *Spectator* contributors, there was in practice very little overlap of content between the two titles. The magazine – first monthly, later quarterly – was notionally available for sale (at £4.95) but was primarily circulated *gratis* throughout the City and business communities, or via purchased lists. It lasted seventeen issues in an infamously difficult financial climate, before the team were permanently stood down in June 2010.[1117]

The year 2008 allowed the magazine to mark its 180th anniversary, releasing a companion anniversary anthology to Johnson's of 2003. This volume – propped up by Barclays Wealth sponsorship – again enjoyed the attentive editorship of Vander Weyer. In addition, the magazine's own anniversary number, the issue of 28 June 2008, presented readers with their 'own piece of history' – a full-size, sixteen-page replica of the first issue of the 1828 *Spectator*. This was a genuine curioso – albeit gifted without any further comment or context.[1118]

Although *The Spectator* was now manifestly a title that had got to grips with the twenty-first century and its myriad technological advances, some glitches still emerged from the changing tools of the

22 Old Queen Street

time. The first issue of 2008, for instance, printed one article that stopped mid-sentence halfway through, reproduced another piece twice on consecutive pages, and failed even to contain the article by Michael Gove advertised on the cover. This sloppy mistake in production served as a reminder not to lose sight of the small and simple. Since d'Ancona was on holiday, it was Reid who had to carry the can: under pressure from above, the editor announced the resignation of his deputy at the end of the month. D'Ancona nevertheless warmly praised Reid's sterling service over nine years, the longest stint in the role: 'No tribute can do full justice to his contribution to this magazine, its culture, its morale and its traditions of civilised excellence.'[1119]

After Reid had found sanctuary at the *Catholic Herald*, he was replaced by Mary Wakefield, who had joined *The Spectator* as assistant editor in 2001. Descended from the same Westmorland Quaker family as Edward Gibbon Wakefield,[1120]

she had already shown a similar verve and reformist drive in her writings. An earlier winner of the Shiva Naipaul prize (2000), and a survivor of a long-term road-trip with Bruce Anderson in the States, Wakefield had become a brave and inventive writer, with a native instinct for the subjects that would or should matter to the nation in months and years to come.

Happily enough, soon after this editorial mishap, *The Spectator* recruited the peerless Rory Sutherland, Vice Chairman of Ogilvy, to write as 'The Wiki Man'. Trained as a classicist but let loose on the world of advertising, he packaged up lateral and left-field thoughts on technology, management and human irrationality. Another addition to the team that year was Roger Alton, the former *Observer* and *Independent* editor, who in February introduced a good-humoured and wide-ranging fortnightly sports column.

In October 2008, *The Spectator* established itself – albeit in less geographically massive terms than Rintoul had[1121] – on the other side of the planet by the launch of *Spectator Australia*. The magazine mostly reproduced the UK *Spectator*, but replaced much of the political and British-news-specific content with the addition of twelve Australian-focused pages, bolstered by its own cover and editorial. The launch issue depicted a kangaroo grinning alongside the headline 'Only 180 Years Late!'; the leader likewise acknowledged the pro-Australian advocacy of Rintoul's paper, which 'smoothed Australia's transition from a rum-drenched scattering of military barracks to the rich, sophisticated, if arid, cornucopia of 2008'.[1122] Its first editor, Oscar Humphries (son of

 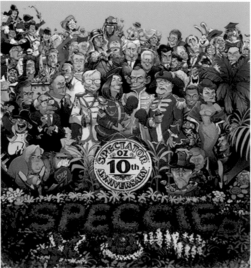

Spectator Australia, 15 and 8 Sep. 2018 (tenth anniversary issue)

Barry, and already one of d'Ancona's contributing editors), chose to be based in London. Given that *The Spectator* then sold some 4,000 copies in Australasia, the hope was that this natural base of readers could help spur further growth, and eventually support a fully Australian-produced magazine. D'Ancona heralded this as 'but Phase Two of a programme of world domination… Next stop Spectator Mars.'[1123] In fact, Neil was briefing the press about his plan (since abandoned) to launch a *Spectator India*. Over its first dozen years – and trio of editors (Tom Switzer followed Humphries in 2009 before Rowan Dean took over in 2014) – it has maintained a keen and committed readership, but has not yet quite broken into a five-figure circulation.

As d'Ancona's editorship progressed, *The Spectator* was increasingly ranging into new – and rather surprising – territory. Such a case was provided by the Christmas issue of 2008, which emulated Sebag Montefiore's notorious exchange with the Spice Girls by interviewing a chart-topping figure from the world of pop: Lily Allen. D'Ancona reported to readers – to whom the name may have been a novelty – that she looked 'more like a Jane Austen heroine than a party queen' and put 'a napkin over her face in embarrassment when I compliment her on her new album'.[1124] For some *Spectator* readers, this was a triumph of the magazine's expanding reach; for others, it was unconscionable.

In March 2009, Paul Johnson resigned from the magazine, having written a column – to many an 'inimitable weekly essay'[1125] – in almost every issue for twenty-eight years, predominantly under the title 'And Another Thing'. Their subject had moved from the quirks of the media world to the totality of the human condition. His reason was the editor's request that he halve his output to a fortnightly column. D'Ancona's was that, with budgets constrained, his fee was too high for a weekly billing. Although Johnson wrote a courteous letter to explain his decision to go, he simultaneously told the press, 'I'm not sad about leaving – I

don't regret it at all.'[1126] From his eyrie at *The Independent*, Glover was all too ready to assess the affair:

> He was a treasure who should never have been let go. Presumably he was considered a bit too highbrow for the new, hip, dumbed-down *Spectator*. That would be nonsense, of course. Mr Johnson has never written a boring sentence in his life. One might have thought that Mr d'Ancona, a former Fellow of All Souls and supposedly an intellectual, would have died in a ditch to retain such a man, but he did not… Along with Peregrine Worsthorne, he should be placed in that part of the Pantheon reserved for columnists of quite advanced years who were struck down by lesser men while still in their prime.[1127]

D'Ancona, for all his intelligence an[d] charm, could sometimes seem a close[d] book, much as he was a closed-door edit[or.] A genuinely puzzling decision was h[is] appointment of the ex-Python agitator Joh[n] Cleese as a contributing editor. In Marc[h] 2009, he produced his first piece in th[at] post – an at-times ironic, at-times snark[y] account of how he disagreed with *T[he] Spectator* – which also doubled up as h[is] last.[1128] In April, James Delingpole starte[d] a spiky fortnightly column, having lo[ng] been the magazine's television critic, a r[ole] he has alternated with James Walton sin[ce] 2014. A grander initiative began that sa[me] month, when Stephen Fry gave the fi[rst] Inaugural Spectator Lecture (unconnect[ed] with the self-defeatingly august Alli[ed] Dunbar affairs of the late Nineties),[1129] at t[he] Royal Geographical Society. Sponsor[ed]

10,000 NOT OU[T]

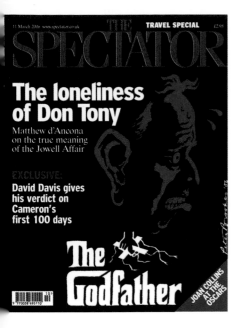

ssues of 11 Mar. and 30 Dec. 2006 and 19 Apr. 2008

y Continental Airlines, the lecture lauded he prospect of living in America, and was oon reprinted as a *Spectator* insert. In '010, the magazine hosted a second lecture n the series, given by Kevin Spacey on the mportance of philanthropy in the arts. .egrettably, the series has since retreated ermanently into the wings.

D'Ancona's *Spectator* devoted ncommon energy to the production of n astounding array of supplements, most f which were funded by bouncingly ıger advertisers. These inserts covered vast, almost bizarre range. Among such igh-end but low-relevance inserts were onnoisseur's guides' on the cricket orld cup (24 Feb. 2007), James Bond pons. Aston Martin, 11 Nov. 2006) and hristmas gifts (2 Dec. 2006). There were so a dozen or so supplements on all and ndry: gardening (28 Apr. 2007), making e most of time on Virgin Trains (spons. irgin Trains, 18 Nov. 2006), yachts (20 p. 2008) and Spanish gastronomy

(spons. Spain, 11 Apr. 2009). Political supplements covered 'the definitive guide to the Tony Blair era' (12 May 2007),[1130] the US elections (18 Oct. 2008), Obama's first 100 days (18 Apr. 2009) and Boris Johnson's first year as Mayor of London (25 Apr. 2009). In addition, the ambiguously named *Scoff* (edited by Jonathan Ray) covered food each quarter from summer 2009 to summer 2011. While there was evidently a desire to attract readers with material tangential to typical *Spectator* subjects, it was the hope of attracting more – and more lucrative – display advertising that prompted many of these dispensable accompaniments. *The Spectator*, of course, was by no means alone in responding to difficult financial circumstances (compounded by the ailing *Business*) with a scramble for additional corporate revenue.

In March 2009, d'Ancona acknowledged the hard-won value of *The Spectator* as an institution, adding that 'I have to

be very careful that I don't vandalise that brand.'[1131] Many will have nodded in approval. Whether it was a source of comfort or alarm that a piece appeared that month from the Conservative leader, David Cameron, on his party's readiness to replace the ailing Labour government is perhaps moot.[1132] However, readers were soon to be knocked for six. In June 2009, the magazine carried two supplements, authored by d'Ancona and his *Coffee House* colleague Peter Hoskin, on '*The Spectator*'s 50 essential films'.[1133] Though manifestly written by two men with deep passion for and knowledge of the medium, it jarred a little with the rest of the magazine. The next month two issues chronicled the 'Top 50 Political Scandals' – a series that profited from the labour of eager interns, but enjoyed the lavish support of a poster and YouTube campaign.[1134] The tabloid-style cover breathlessly advertised 'Those "moments of madness" in full', alongside the hitherto

Issues of 4 July (with tabloid insert) and 15 Aug. 2009

unexpected presence of a naked model seated on a chair. Appropriately enough, the supplement gave *The Spectator* its own red-top logo and layout. The rest of the issue contained interviews with Uri Geller and a star of the US drama *The Wire*. All rollicking stuff, it must be said, but hardly in character. Finally, in August, a month after *The Spectator* launched the first of its in-house poetry nights for subscribers, three issues hosted '*The Spectator*'s Guide to the 40 poems you should know', reprinting them in full – for those who did not know.

Yet such inventive *addenda* were not adding readers: the first half of 2009 saw a 5 per cent drop in sales, the sharpest fall in two decades. The magazine could, it seemed, profit from an editorial steer in a fresh direction. In August that year, d'Ancona was prevented from editorial activity by a bout of swine flu; by the end of the month, his departure from *The Spectator* had been announced. The issue

of 5 September 2009 thus recorded no editor, for the first time since this practice began in December 1996. But, before the press could even begin their speculation, the news came that Fraser Nelson, the thirty-six-year-old political editor, had been installed as his successor. When the news broke, d'Ancona was admirably professional. He expressed his genuine desire to pursue projects elsewhere:

After more than three-and-a-half delightful and rewarding years as editor, exciting opportunities are arising and I have decided to move on… It has been a privilege and an honour to lead and work with the best team of journalists in the business… Like the role of Bond or Doctor Who, *The Spectator* editorship is a precious trust to be held for a limited period of time and I had always envisaged moving on once my goals were achieved.[1135]

Nelson spoke warmly of d'Ancona' tenure, 'His legacy is a magazine whic has more verve, clout and readers than eve before – and with as much presence onlin as on the news-stands.'[1136] It is certainl true that, despite the encroachment o sponsored content into the magazine d'Ancona's *Spectator* ran some importan and influential stories. A small selectio would include the crisis of universit finance (Boris Johnson, 27 May 2006 a reminder of the world's unprecedente wealth and health (Allister Heath, 2 De 2006), the crisis of social mobility (Ann McElvoy, 5 May 2007), the iniquity global carbon-trading policies (Ros Clark, 11 Aug. 2007), the potential Cameron's education revolution (Frase Nelson, 1 Mar. 2008), the importance preserving the freedom of the intelligen services (Matthew d'Ancona, 15 Au 2009), and the scandalous treatme of wounded British soldiers (Jonatha Foreman, 22 Aug. 2009).

216

The great achievement of d'Ancona's tenure was its digital output. Aided by various round-table 'Digital Dinners', the website had taken on the advice of experts and readers to forge a trail-blazing way in a brave new world. When in early 2008 James Forsyth was appointed third in command ('deputy editor online'), Peter Hoskin arrived to take up the reins as online editor, helping push *Coffee House* over the next four years to the front line of intellectual debate. Even by 2009, unique visitors to the website had increased by 70 per cent, proving the template for *The Spectator*'s future dominance online. The stated rise in circulation through his tenure – from 61,000 to 75,000 – cannot, however, be taken quite at face value: the same period saw the increased issuing of free copies, and the introduction of double counting (i.e. of print and digital subscriptions) by ABC. The print circulation, which had reached the magazine's zenith (62,700) in the early stages of d'Ancona's tenure, i.e. the latter half of 2006, had fallen to 58,000 by mid-2009. D'Ancona's byline is yet to return to *The Spectator*. Instead, he has written for *The Guardian* and the *Evening Standard*, and helped launch two new challenger platforms: *Drugstore Culture* (2018–19) and *Tortoise Media* (2019–). A sense of his shifting politics is given by two monographs: *In It Together* (2014) critiques the Conservative-Liberal coalition, and *Post Truth* (2017) plots how to restore the global crisis in reporting and trusting facts.

With the appointment of the twenty-sixth editor of the magazine, in September 2009, we enter contemporary times. FRASER ANDREW NELSON (1973–) was at once a typical and unusual appointment. On the one hand, he had earned his stripes through many years of political journalism and principled debate, including three years' sterling work on *The Spectator*'s staff. On the other hand, unlike most of the magazine's editors, he had no overpowering interest in politics throughout his education – at Nairn Academy, his local comprehensive, at Dollar Academy, the private school he attended (courtesy of the MoD) while his father was posted by the RAF to Cyprus, and at the University of Glasgow (History and Politics, II.1). A successful spell in 1994 as editor of the *Glasgow University Guardian* (formerly edited by Neil in 1970) opened the door to the fourth estate. That October his first byline appeared in the *Glasgow Herald*. Nelson did not look back.

After a brief stint at the *Nottingham Evening Post*, he took a diploma in journalism at City University (1996). A few formative weeks at *The Independent on Sunday*, launched in 1990 by Stephen Glover, led Nelson to spend five years as a business reporter at *The Times*. It was during this period that he encountered a book by the self-same Glover, *Paper Dreams* (1993): the work opened Nelson's eyes to how broad the vista of possibilities was within the sprawling and evolving world of British journalism. Glover, he later recalled, 'made journalism sound so accessible that anybody could do it. I previously thought it was a world you could only get into if one of your family members were involved in it, and our profession is still quite nepotistic.'[1137] A general distrust of patrician patronage has, in fact, been a hallmark of his career.

Nelson's talents, nourished by Patience Wheatcroft at *The Times*, were already known to Andrew Neil, who had first met him in 1993, when returning to the sharp edge of Glaswegian student journalism for Radio 4's *Down Your Way*. In 2001, he was appointed as political editor of the *Scotsman*. A couple of years later, in November 2003, Nelson made his first landing on the pages of *The Spectator* to outline the crisis of NHS Scotland.[1138] After the magazine was acquired by the Barclays in 2004, however, his association with the *Scotsman* – then a fellow title in the Press Holdings group – held Nelson back from contributing to the sister journal regularly: before his appointment as associate editor in January 2006, he wrote only one other *Spectator* piece, on the Bush administration's respect for Thatcher.[1139] Although *The Business* went very much out of that in 2008, before its brief revival as *Spectator Business*, Nelson still wrote regularly for the *News of the World*, then enjoying a circulation comfortably above 3,000,000 readers.

And so, though he was born in Cornwall, Nelson became the fifth genuinely Scottish editor of *The Spectator*. Yet, despite his deep-seated interest in politics and economics, he saw himself as primarily a facts-and-figures man rather than a writer proper. In 2007, he claimed, 'I'm basically a numbers geek. Some guys are really gifted, I'm the type who sweats blood.'[1140] When reflecting on his initial appointment to *The Spectator* he expressed his surprise at 'even the idea that I was competent with words'.[1141] But he was clear from the outset that *The Spectator*'s kaleidoscopic outlook on the world should not be all statistics and politics: 'Actually, less than 10 per cent is about politics. And that is one of the things as an editor I would like to project

Issues of 2 Apr. and 2/9 June 2012, and 13 Apr. 2013

a little more. We're a journal of arts and manners.'[1142] Not long after, he reiterated that the magazine

> is about culture and books, arts, life. That is not obvious to our potential readers. A lot of people pass us in W.H. Smith and think 'These guys are wall-to-wall politics.' That doesn't help us. When we put Cameron on our front page we tend to take a sales hit rather than a sales jump.'[1143]

Little could anyone know that, despite the best editorial endeavours, the world was going to make an increase in political coverage almost inevitable.

In his first issue, Nelson reported in a programmatic Diary column that, alongside many a message of congratulations, he received the traditional request to keep things just as they are. David Cameron, too, sent the private plea that the 'Diary of a Notting Hill Nobody' survive any editorial cull; a Swedish

subscriber – the nationality, one notes, of Nelson's wife – simply said, 'Don't change a single thing. Least of all Taki.' He concurred:

> For decades it has been traditional for a new *Spectator* editor to be inundated with calls to show his commitment to civility by hiring a new High Life columnist. But this time, not a soul has asked for him to be sacked. All I hear is how the old rogue has never been in better form. This won't please him much, as he prides himself on calls for his resignation. But it's not that Taki is conforming to the world. The world, I think, is finally conforming to him.'[1144]

Taki has indeed continued to rib and rile readers ever since.

To settle any uncertainty about his political outlook, Nelson acknowledged to interviewers that he was a Conservative, even though he had (and indeed has) never been a member of the party that

'often drives him to despair'.[1145] Lik[e] many a predecessor at *The Spectator*, h[e] also revealed that as political editor of th[e] *Scotsman* he did not cast a vote in genera[l] elections, on the ground that journalist[s] should observe impartiality. He wa[s] particularly clear that he was not going t[o] replicate a different *Spectator* traditio[n] – achieved by five of the seven editor[s] who had attempted the feat – of using th[e] editorship as a route into Parliament: 'N[o] way will I ever enter politics! The mo[re] I see it the more I harden my resolve n[ot] to.'[1146] Although raised in the sort of fami[ly] where it was bad manners to discus[s] politics, Nelson became a *Spectat[or]* reader at a young age, attracted to t[he] magazine's liberal outlook. *The Spectat[or]*, he later recalled, 'had a magic of its ow[n.] My job is to protect and project that.'[1147] One of the most influential conversatio[ns] Nelson had as editor was with h[is] predecessor Alexander Chancellor, w[ho] told him to look for inspiration to t[he] Addison-Steele *Spectator*, which offer[ed] the quintessential blueprint of content, tone and good humour.

Readers were quick to get a sign of Nelson's sense of mission. For one of his earliest moves delighted the magazine's devoted subscribers, namely the restoration of the 'Portrait of the Week', which returned within a month in October 2009, with Christopher Howse properly back at the helm. It has continued ever since to provide the essential springboard into the magazine. But, despite the change of editors, the welter of supplements from previous years continued to appear. While some of these were engaging – such as a cartoons special (spons. Wiltons, 25 July 2010) and a 'Thatcher and *The Spectator*' special (spons. Intercontinental, 12 Apr. 2013), those on luxury and style (20 Mar. and 6 Nov. 2010, 2 Apr. 2011), summer drinks (spons. Tanqueray, 12 June 2010) and cruises (25 Sep. 2010, 17 Sep. 2011, 5 Sep. 2012) were of narrower interest. Mercifully, the brakes were applied early on, although it took some time for the advertising juggernaut to come to a halt. Substantial deals have since been struck with BAE Systems and Philips, who have sponsored several supplements that intersect with their commercial interests while posing bigger questions on humankind and its health.[1148] Nelson's policy soon evolved on this front: 'to bring the money to where the magazine is – not bring the magazine to where the money might be.'[1149] His overriding aim was to find sources of finance that would underpin but not undermine editorial quality. The proprietors, he reasoned, were not in pursuit of profit at all costs; a self-sufficient *Spectator* would be a worthy source of pride in itself. For his part, Neil repeatedly shared the welcome mantra: 'We are not a profit-maximising magazine.'

Nelson has steadily built up a dedicated team of foreign writers. Every issue reliably has one, sometimes two or three, pieces filed by freelancers based abroad: the primary correspondents include Gavin Mortimer and Jonathan Miller (France), Fredrik Erixon (Germany, Scandinavia), Nicholas Farrell (Italy), Christopher Caldwell and John R. MacArthur (USA), John R. Bradley (Middle East), and Daniel R. DePetris (global geopolitics); in recent years, Cindy Yu, the magazine's sparky broadcast editor, has been able to shed valuable light on her native China. These and a host of other writers chip in to provide rapid reaction to worldwide events via the *Coffee House* blog.

Over his ten years in post, Nelson has been able to introduce a broad church of fresh figures to the Diary. There have, of course, been politicians, albeit of a range that spans Jacob Rees-Mogg and Jess Phillips. But there have been plenty of academics (A.C. Grayling, Roger Scruton, Steven Pinker, Robin Lane Fox), public intellectuals (Christopher Hitchens, Richard Dawkins, Matt Ridley, Douglas Murray) and writers (Tom Holland, Anthony Horowitz, Irvine Welsh, Ian Rankin). While journalists and commentators have been ten-a-penny,[1150] Nelson has retained something of his predecessors' interest in celebrity: Ozzy Osbourne, Liz Hurley and Billy Bragg rub shoulders with Henry Blofeld and Pippa Middleton.

Nelson has described the magazine under his editorship as 'right of centre, but not strongly right of centre'.[1151] Although there was an initial suspicion that he would be a keen advocate of All Things Cameron, the healthy admixture of supportive and hostile articles on the Conservative government (elected to power in 2010) soon put paid to that. In fact, Nelson has been careful to protect the magazine from becoming a conduit for serving politicians – although *Spectator* readers had the novel opportunity of reading a piece by a serving prime minister for Christmas 2019.[1152]

Nelson is fond of quoting the colourful dictum of H.L. Mencken: 'journalist is to politician as dog is to lamp-post.' His *Spectator* has continued the tradition of allowing a broad range of political views to have their say, even if some find little favour with long-standing readers. It is telling that, in 2012, Jim Dowd, Labour MP for Lewisham West, confessed in the Commons that *The Spectator* was 'a magazine which, I am led to believe, is much read by Members on the other side of the House, although I have to say I have read it myself on occasion.'[1153] Although his initial target of 10 per cent politics proved untenable, Nelson has striven to keep the political element to no more than 15 per cent in a given issue, a proportion that is inevitably subject to seasonal flux. On occasion, the limit has flown out of the window: if the cover, the leader, the pol col, the double-page cover story, a columnist and the letters page all talk about politics, that accounts for more than a third of the magazine's front half. Nevertheless, the art of maintaining the right balance in the front of the magazine – between the political, the timely, and the timeless – remains one of the primary goals of *Spectator* editorial conferences.

After twenty-five years of almost no alterations, the magazine underwent, in September 2010, a significant redesign, led by Kurdish whizz-kid Kuchar Swara. Nelson told readers that this was done 'cautiously, taking the best ideas from past magazines, and refreshing the rest. Even the tidiest house needs a little spring-cleaning from time to time.'[1154] Careful to downplay the change, he told the press that this was 'a tidy-up … rather like restoring an old painting', adding that it would 'probably be the biggest change of the magazine under me.'[1155] The visual changes were more substantial than Nelson suggested to the press: the cover was spruced up, the masthead reworked into its pre-2008 form, and 'Est. 1828' proudly introduced in the top right. More space was given over to the cover artwork, increasingly a more important and arresting part of each week's issue. Inside the magazine, outmoded fonts were laid to rest, especially the sans-serif capitals that still exuded a distinctively Nineties feel; in their stead came the crisp and classical Goudy. One of the most bold and admirable decisions was to remove photographs – or indeed photo montages – not just from the cover but from the front half of the magazine, where they had always been rare. No other news magazine has tried such a counter-intuitive but strikingly effective policy – although this ban began to lapse in 2019.

The changes did not end there. The burgeoning contents were expanded to cover two pages, new caricatures were drawn by Jason Ford for the most frequent contributors, and the 'Barometer' column of often surprising and always telling statistics was introduced. This last feature was designed to be 'of the type that you'll read out to the person next to you on a Sunday afternoon';[1156] curated

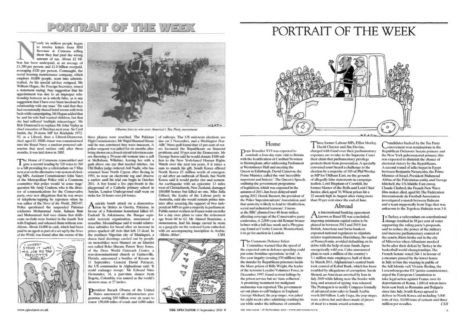

Portrait of the Week, 11 and 18 Sep. 2010

by Ross Clark, it has become one of the most reliably eye-opening features of the modern *Spectator*. The rear of the magazine was also sharpened up in appearance, with the addition of its own half-title page (when space allows), and a more prominent billing for the High and Low Life columns. Throughout all of the magazine, various accreted clutter that had built up over the last fifteen years was swept away, much to the approval of those who habitually read *The Spectator* from the back. Nelson – well aware of the outcry that followed the last major redesign in 1985[1157] – emphasised to readers the continuity of content:

And what of the character of *The Spectator*? We've changed it not one jot. We have no interest in striving to be modern, and no need to either. Our principles are the same in the 21st century as they were in the 19th. We adhere not to any political doctrine,

but to elegance of expression and originality of thought. We seek to offer a refuge from an often censorious and humourless world.[1158]

As far back as 2001, a former deput editor of *The Spectator* justly observed tha its covers 'need to shine more than the do'.[1159] Front pages under the Johnsons ar d'Ancona were – save for some outstandir examples – generally unattractive. Nelso however, differed markedly from rece editors in his degree of oversight in matte aesthetic. The modern magazine is inde uncommonly attractive. He recalls:

I wanted when I became editor to make covers a thing of beauty, above all. I sacked the art director (who had been a go-between with cover artists) and did it myself. I then found out there are artists who draw beautifully, are funny and on-point but only two who are all three: Peter Brookes and

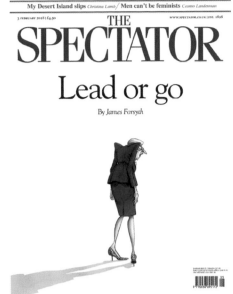

ssues of 4 Nov. 2017 and 3 Feb. 2018

Morten Morland. I genuinely think Morland is a new Gillray and my editorship might be remembered for his illustrations.[1160]

Morland, the Norwegian-born, London-ased artist, had long been a regular for *he Times* alongside the veteran Brookes *Spectator* cover artist since the Eighties). a fact, when writing his dissertation (for e Surrey Institute of Art and Design) on e history of British political cartoons, it as the curiosity shown by Brookes, his terviewee, that gave Morland the crucial eak in the national press. Having provided s first cover for d'Ancona (depicting rown's Cabinet as the living dead) in ne 2009, three years later he followed Brookes's footsteps by becoming chief ver cartoonist for *The Spectator* – a ange integral to Swara's redesign. Given ch a prominent billing, Morland is well are that, in the modern world

it's easy, very easy, far too easy, to offend. And people get offended on other people's behalf, which is even more annoying. They wilfully misunderstand what you're trying to say so they can be offended… You have people who are offended because you draw Theresa May in a certain way. That it's somehow sexist or misogynist. And again, you think, 'OK, should I not treat her in the same way I do male politicians? That would surely be sexist, if I treated female politicians differently?'[1161]

Happily, Morland has found no reason to hold back in satirising an increasingly odd world. And politicians are the gift that keeps on giving.

Since April 2011, Tanya Gold (one of a surprisingly large stable of *Spectator* writers who have written regularly for *The Guardian*) has been turning out deliciously biting reviews of restaurants, and pricking

the bubble of pretension with a mere fork-flourish. Her fortnightly 'Food' column alternates with another essential staple: Bruce Anderson had returned in 2011 – with bottle in hand – to discuss 'Drink' (in actuality Old World wines and whisky). The column shows how a supped-it-all-before palate can be blended with anecdote and wit to provide a fitting nightcap to the magazine.

But all *Spectator* readers will have rapidly sobered up on seeing, in November 2011, that a prize of £8,500 was in the offing: Matt Ridley, a frequent writer on the environment and science, offered a 'prize for environmental heresy' – the astounding cost of which was being met from his own pocket. The winner, Pippa Cuckson, saw her entry appear as the cover piece in September 2012: she coolly unearthed the woolly thinking behind the widespread supposition that hydro-electric power stations in the Highlands could be rolled out *pari passu* throughout the United Kingdom as a whole.[1162] She also exposed the environmental double standards rife in such 'green-friendly' operations. So pleased was Ridley that he ran the prize again, this time eliciting a winning piece, by Matthew Ware, on the excessive consumption of electricity that a 'greener' future presaged.[1163] Ever since an early special issue in Nelson's editorship,[1164] *The Spectator* has continued to tread a sceptical line about the green lobby's Panglossian belief in a single environmental panacea.

In order to profit from the support of high-end advertisers, but to protect the delicate ecosystem of the magazine proper from unwelcome intrusions, a set of quarterly supplements was devised in 2012

– on Life, Health and Money. The first issue of *Spectator Life* was launched in March 2012 under the editorship of Lucinda Baring, who had been involved with the magazine's previous lifestyle section, as well as *Spectator Business*.[1165] Headed 'Art, style, investment, jewels, travel', it carried as its cover piece an article by Toby Young and Rachel Johnson on 'The Right Stuff: the new breed of rebel MPs'. Appropriately enough, given its material aspiration, the new quarterly was launched in Asprey's on Bond Street. Baring was soon followed by Olivia Cole (Sep. 2012–Sep. 2015), who made the magazine a playful and wide-ranging companion. Her successor Toby Young (Sep. 2015–Jan. 2018) gave the supplement the feel of a separately issued magazine, which could run longer features and interviews than *The Spectator* proper could host. Young handed over to his deputy editor Danielle Wall, whose first issue included an important feature on the soi-disant 'Intellectual Dark Web' (Feb. 2018). Wall could call upon myriad connections across all sectors – including the two *Spectator* editors who had been her former employers. With the steady growth of online articles (life.spectator.co.uk) – ably edited by Will Gore and Joanna Rossiter – *Life* released its last print issue in December 2018.

In September 2014, the first *Spectator Health* supplement appeared, and the following month *Spectator Money*. Both series made the transition from self-standing supplement to magazine insert in 2016, becoming online-only in late 2018. A biannual physical supplement on schools (overseen by letters editor Camilla Swift) still appears in print, largely devoted to defending the independent schools who

sponsor it against their hostile reception elsewhere in the press.

Coffee House, which launched its own dedicated domain (blogs.spectator.co.uk) in July 2012, steadily grew in quality and influence to become a major player in British political and cultural comment. Over the last decade, its articles have been frequently cited in newspapers, on other websites, and on radio news. Its significant edge over the physical magazine, and indeed print media as a whole, is its ability to provide freely expressed criticism on a developing story without the daily business of running, printing and promoting a journal getting in the way. If a big story breaks in the morning, by the late afternoon three or more assessments will have appeared from *Spectator* writers online, establishing one or more positions to steer the national news that evening – to say nothing of the next day's papers.

To ensure such an efficient flow of news, *Coffee House* can call upon a large pool of trusted writers who file copy – for little, or perhaps no, payment. In addition, a small army of established *Spectator* bloggers stands ready in formation. Major contributors to the website in recent years have been Douglas Murray, Ross Clark, Isabel Hardman, Stephen Daisley, Ed West (son of Richard), Alex Massie (son of Allan), Brendan O'Neill (editor of the online bastion of free speech *Spiked!*), Nick Cohen and Robert Peston (whose breathless posts are syndicated from his ITV blog to avoid contractual conflicts). Lloyd Evans provides inevitably cynical parliamentary sketches with a dissection of character that only a theatrical critic can give. The financial reporting has been recently bolstered by the arrival of

the imperturbable Kate Andrews, who left the Institute of Economic Affairs to become *The Spectator*'s first 'economics correspondent' in January 2020. Without the restrictions of space that circumscribe a print journal, *Coffee House* has been able to run pieces of unwonted size: most remarkably, Dominic Cummings' straight-talking assessment of 'How the Brexit Referendum was Won' reached almost 20,000 words.[1166]

One of the great successes of *Coffee House* has been its role as a conduit for writers with a less established print profile to enter the fast-paced fray of online comment and establish themselves a leading voices in the nation's conversation. This has been the story for many political hacks, most notably James Forsyth (online editor, 2007–8), Isabel Hardman (*Coffee House* editor, 2012–14), Sebastian Payne (online editor, 2012–15) and Katy Balls. It was Hardman's innovation to introduce the 'Evening Blend' email round-up of the day's stories, along with a brief pol co on the day's major story. This has grow into the most read political email in the country, with over 75,000 readers signe up. Alongside the sleeve-rolling rom through the day's events, *Coffee House* does have a lighter, more playful outle In October 2012, *The Spectator* launche 'Steerpike', both as a new fortnight gossip column in the magazine and as a occasional blog online; given the need fo a speedy response to the curious quir of the diurnal news churn, Steerpik prudently became an online-only ventu in July 2013. This (multi-authored persona is the closest that *The Spectat* comes to the mischievous humour of ally on the Right, Paul Staines's *Gui*

Issue of 23 Mar. 2013

Hawkes (order-order.com).

Meanwhile, back in the magazine, Liddle was continuing to serve up increasingly popular – if increasingly controversial – columns, mostly about the hypocrisy of those in positions of power. On occasion, the line he trod was inevitably crossed, by loss of balance or judgment. In June 2012, *The Spectator* was fined £5,625 for comments Liddle made during the Stephen Lawrence murder trial of November 2011 that could have influenced its outcome.[1167] The article was referred to the Attorney General, and the jurors instructed not to consult that week's magazine. The deputy editor, Mary Wakefield, who visited the Old Bailey to witness the trial, was unexpectedly called upon to apologise to the court. *The Spectator* chose not to contest the fine from the Crown Prosecution Service. Of the offending piece, Neil said:

It's quite clear it shouldn't have been published, but if you are going to be a magazine like *The Spectator*, and take strong positions and be controversial, every now and then you may do something stupid.[1168]

Nelson concurred that it was 'a straight out-and-out mistake'.[1169]

Liddle has continued to press at the boundaries of what can (and, by turns, cannot) be said, and to push back against a top-down agenda of societal group-think. Unsurprisingly, his column has become both more popular and more divisive as the years have rolled on. In May 2018, *The Spectator* hosted the largest public event in its history: 2,300 people filled the London Palladium to see two journalists sit down and talk to each other. The only explanation for this curious gathering is that *The Spectator*'s editor was interviewing his most uncowed and unruly contributor. Liddle told the crowd that, of all the places he has written, he can get away with most at *The Spectator*, a statement that prompted spontaneous applause for the magazine's dogged defence of spleenful, doleful, lawful speech. Looking back on his first 500 issues, Nelson confessed that when he began as editor 'I thought I'd go down with Rod Liddle, that he and I would drive like Thelma and Louise over the cliff in the name of free speech. We've come close a few times, but stayed (just) on the right side.'[1170]

Yet any problem of free speech is minor compared to its suppression. In November 2012, following the Leveson enquiry, the British press was under the genuine threat of state regulation. *The Spectator* led the fight against that grim prospect, with Nelson declaring that it would play 'no part in any regulatory structure mandated by the state'.[1171] An accompanying leader said that

If such a group is constituted we will not attend its meetings, pay its fines nor heed its menaces. We would still obey the [other] laws of the land. But to join any scheme which subordinates press to Parliament would be a betrayal of what this paper has stood for since its inception in 1828.[1172]

In 2013, as a pointed gesture, the winner of the Spectator Parliamentarian of the Year award was a bumper crop: a cross-party cabal of fifteen MPs who had fought against restrictions of press freedoms. The fight rumbled on and, in early 2017, *Spectator* subscribers were encouraged to write letters of complaint; one enterprising reader even set up a website that provided a ready-made template for constructing such missives. But only after years of campaigning and sermonising was the prospect of such state regulation at last dropped, in the spring of 2018. Celebrating the achievement, Nelson told 'those readers who did join our petition, and reminded the government of its obligation to press freedom, thank you. It was you wot won it.'[1173] For his own part, Nelson was voted in 2013 'Editors' editor of the year' by the British Society of Magazine Editors.

In February that year, the magazine felt sufficiently confident about its online readership to introduce a paywall: after new visitors read three stories, they had to register to unlock a further five and delve any deeper into the site. Subscribers to the print edition already had access online, which provided content largely different from the magazine, but a digital-only subscription was available at a much-reduced cost. Paradoxical though it may seem, this decision has drawn more people to reading *The Spectator* online – and has guaranteed that advertisements are only tangential intrusions on the eye. It was telling that, in 2019, the *New Statesman* decided to make the same move.

In June 2013, *The Spectator* was able to gift to the nation something of immense (if still under-appreciated) importance. At great expense – and back-breaking labour – every page of every issue of *The Spectator* (from 1828 to 2008) was scanned and uploaded for consultation online (archive. spectator.co.uk); what is more, the text was combed through by OCR software, so that it was searchable and roughly indexed by topic. Although there were recurrent problems in reading the imperfect type of crabbed nineteenth-century print, and although some gaps in coverage emerged here and there,[1174] the insight into British history that this charitable act provided has been of incalculable importance. Some million pages – and towards a billion words – of *The Spectator*'s myriad opinions on the great, the good and the grotesque were opened up for instant consultation. No other major British publication has combined such a large-scale digitisation of their archive with a commitment to making it freely available. It is regrettable, therefore, that the archive was moved behind the subscriber paywall in 2019. The dust is yet to settle from this explosive emergence of material, but one man deserves especial thanks from those who seek to understand better the world in which they live: Andrew Neil, whose imagination and enthusiasm rolled out the project. This author, for one,

is ineffably grateful.

In September 2014, Sam Leith, previously literary editor of the *Telegraph*, and no stranger to *The Spectator*, replaced Mark Amory as the literary editor. Aided by the omniscient Clare Asquith, he has since brought admirable range to his coverage of books, having the crucially canny eye for inventively pairing them with a select team of people. The institution of a double-page 'lead book review' has helped maintain *The Spectator*'s reputation as one of the most read and revered critics among the periodical press – a quality it had eventually regained in the Seventies.

Alongside the literary firepower in the magazine's back half are the eye-poppingly honest cinema reviews of Deborah Ross (film critic since 2006), while the unpretentious reports of Martin Gayford (chief art critic since 2014) have cast a probing eye over the visual arts. Dance has gone freelance in the hands of Laura Freeman, whose curiosity and versatility prompt her to write on just about anything else. In 2015, Freddy Gray, deputy editor of the *Catholic Herald* and assistant editor of *The Spectator*, replaced Mary Wakefield as deputy editor, a post to which he has brought much mirth and mischief. In order to give him a good sense of the magazine's operational challenges, Nelson also appointed Gray managing editor. Wakefield meanwhile moved across to the new post of commissioning editor, maintaining her role as Rhadamanthine gatekeeper of the magazine's front half. For a two-year period (Oct. 2016–July 2018), Will Heaven joined the team as managing editor. It perhaps did not escape the notice of the Catholic proprietors that not just their editor but his deputy, commissioning

and managing editors shared that faith.

The Scottish Referendum of 2014 was potentially a watershed moment in the nation's history, but *The Spectator* had no real choice to make: the magazine has never been in two minds about preserving the unity of the United Kingdom. Despite the (historic and present) ubiquity of Scottish staff in the *Spectator* camp, the magazine gave its full backing to the 'No' campaign which crystallised in a heart-felt 'Scotland Please Stay' issue (13 Sep. 2014), following a public debate in Edinburgh where Alex Salmond, leader of the SNP, railed against George Galloway. These efforts had perhaps only a small and immeasurable effect on the victory for the Union.

By contrast, much the most important political decision of Nelson's tenure was made in 2016, when the magazine declared in support of Brexit. Although Nelson was late to reach that decision personally, and has described himself more than once as 'reluctant Brexiteer', the choice was very much in the *Spectator* tradition. Not only had the magazine fought hard for leaving the EU in the early 2000s, the early 1990s, at several flashpoints in the 1980s, and for the first half of the 1970s, but it has never ceased advocating the case for free trade. Although it has supported a complex mixture of constitutional changes within Britain, *The Spectator* has also doubted the fundamental principle that the country should always be able to govern itself, whatever pecuniary advantages that privilege may obstruct.

By 2016, Britain as a whole had fundamentally changed its attitude from the Seventies, with long-suffering scepticism infiltrating the blue-sky optimism of the first referendum. The

Issues of 18 June and 2 July 2016, and of 1 Feb. 2020

me round, several other titles in the press upported the Brexit cause, even if the kelihood of the people actually voting or it seemed low. *The Spectator* being *The pectator*, some of its staff were staunch emainers and were prepared to say so in o uncertain terms: Matthew Parris led e battle in the magazine, while Allan assie and Nick Cohen fought back the aysayers online. It should be noted that *he Spectator*'s conception of Brexit more liberal than that of much of the olitical right: it has argued for the removal a cap on student numbers, the right to main for all EU nationals, and – more ntroversially – an amnesty of illegal migrants currently in the UK.[1175]

To the surprise of almost everyone – d to the cataclysmic shock of (to use a *ector* term) The Establishment – the te for Out was victorious, at 52 per nt of 35.5 million voters (on a 72 per nt turn-out). *The Spectator* instantly ablished itself as the leading journal for discussing not just why Britain should make the exit it had decreed but how. As often in more recent years, the magazine has seen itself return to the role of a valued political counsellor – hectoring the short-sighted, encouraging the bold, and guiding the uncertain. Perhaps this was at its most evident in November 2018, when Theresa May's Withdrawal Agreement was submitted to a withering critique, summarising 'the top 40 horrors' of the deal.[1176] The usual carping of Steerpike, one may say. But when the piece went viral, shared some 40,000 times on Facebook (an all-time record), its influence was palpable. The article won over 300 new subscribers, and a record 1,000 new subscriptions were achieved that week. Astoundingly, the government felt such pressure as to respond directly, point by point, to this anonymous blog piece before the day was out: '10 Downing Street' was indeed a novel byline. Unconvinced, *The Spectator* issued a rebuttal of the rebuttal.[1177]

When the Withdrawal Agreement at last reached Parliament in January 2019, the government suffered the largest defeat in the history of that institution. As the prospective Brexit Day drifted farther into 2019, and Theresa May lost the confidence of her government, the field was open for a new leader to 'Get Brexit Done'. In the end, it was the combined team of Boris Johnson and Dominic Cummings – a former *Spectator* editor and a former *Spectator* online editor – who won a landslide Tory victory at the general election that December, allowing the government to pass the (slightly altered and abridged) Withdrawal Agreement with a formidable majority of 124 on 20 December 2019. Six weeks later, on 31 January 2020, the UK left the EU; *The Spectator*, having fought the campaign for precisely fifty years, found time for a well-earned drink.

Nelson has been an eclectic editor, happy to delegate much of the magazine's make-up to his core team: the commissioning editor (Mary Wakefield), the deputy and American editor (Freddy Gray) and the political editor (James Forsyth) in the front half of the magazine, and the literary (Sam Leith), arts (Igor Toronyi-Lalic, who in 2014 replaced Liz Anderson) and Life editors (Lucy Vickery) in the back. The columnists are, as ever, afforded the rope to do their own thing. As Nelson outlined to *The Guardian*, this free-form mix can prove a potent cocktail: 'we serve up cask-strength opinion, and by and large our readers like it. Even I as editor have one or two pieces each week I'd like to pull because I disagree with so much.'[1178] Despite the guaranteed disagreements among *Spectator* staff, the magazine preserves an uncanny *bonhomie*: Rintoul's wish for it to be a 'family' paper has been manifested by a heartening number of romantic unions.

In August 2016, the editorial team achieved a first in the magazine's history – or in the sixty-three years that the magazine had sported a separate cover: all of the stories making the front page were written by women. Nelson commented on the issue:

Our readers don't really care about gender, just good writing. It was our usual *Spectator* mix: life, with all the fun things left in… About two-thirds of the staff here are women but we have never had gender quotas. We just seek out the very best, and it just so happens that a lot of the very best happen to be women.

All true, but it was the sterling work of the production editor Peter Robins, supported by Emily Hill (acting as commissioning editor), that engineered this outcome. As chief sub-editor, Robins was renowned for his gentle corrections of minutiae that would elsewhere go unnoticed: Matthew Parris was once so impressed by a correction of his Latin that he sang Robins's praises in *The Times*.[1179] To his rueful question, 'In 50 years' time, will such paragons even exist?', Nelson gave a resounding 'Yes' on *Coffee House*: 'Having good sub-editors – nay, great sub-editors – is essential for any publication that takes good writing seriously. And not for nostalgic reasons, but for reasons of hard-headed capitalism: money follows quality.'[1180]

One other *Spectator* initiative that found plenty of favourable coverage in the press was, and is, the 'No CVs, please' policy for internships. Unlike many similar roles in the media, these positions are paid, and privilege the ability to edit and write over formal qualifications: the aim is to break the cliquey nepotism that can render the field of journalism so unattractive to outsiders. When an already well-connected character comes out on top, the conclusion is that meritocracy has won the day. One appointment achieved international coverage in September 2017: Katherine Forster, who at the age of forty-eight proved a strikingly successful *Spectator* intern and popular writer, online and in print. She commented:

I was concerned people would think that I was deluded or rubbish and didn't have a clue what I was doing. I know that if the application had been CV-based, they wouldn't have given me a second chance… It's been pointed out to me that I am one of the oldest people in the building, but I feel like I belong.

A year later, her place in the world – and workplace – was rather different:

When I got the placement, everything changed. My story seemed to capture interest: four BBC interviews, and a feature in the *Sunday Times* where I was interviewed by a young journalist called Leaf Arbuthnot. I'm now doing her job, while she has moved to the magazine… And no, I can't believe it either.[1181]

Nelson later told *The Guardian*:

We rejected CVs so that we can hire people from a deeper pool of talent, not out of a sense of do-gooding. No one, ever, is hired as an act of charity or social outreach. Journalism is about reflecting and reporting on the wider world, so it makes sense to avoid going for the same sort of person with the same sort of background. Of my senior colleagues now, one was a King's Scholar at Eton. Another left school at 16. It has never tended to matter.[1182]

A digest of the important stories th[at] have appeared in Nelson's *Spectator* ma[?] begin with his own account of how [?] spring the 'benefits trap' (19 Sep. 200[9?]) this topic, informed by his role as [?] advisory board member for the Cent[re] for Social Justice and the Social Mobili[ty] Foundation,[1183] was reprised five yea[rs] later with a cover piece on 'the road [to?] Benefits Street' (18 Jan. 2014). Other piec[es]

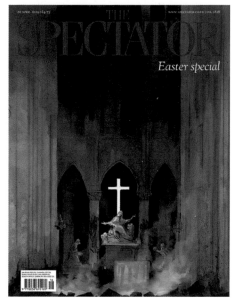

Issues of 22 Sep. 2018 and 20 Apr. 2019

hat won considerable traction include
ne 'fall of the meritocracy' (Andrew
Jeil, 29 Jan. 2011), obstructive political
orrectness in university education (Ross
lark, 2 Apr. 2011), phone hacking in the
ational press (Peter Oborne, 9 July 2011),
ne UK's need for quantitative easing
Nassim Taleb, 11 Feb. 2012), Christian
iffering in the Middle East (Douglas
avis and Ed West, 7 Apr. 2012), sexual
isconduct in Westminster (Julie Bindel
d Rod Liddle, 2 Mar. 2013), the 'Stepford
udents' (Brendan O'Neill, 22 Nov. 2014),
e migrant crisis in Italy (Nicholas Farrell,
June 2015), gender politics vs children
Melanie Phillips, 30 Jan. 2016), the rise
eugenics (Fraser Nelson, 21 Mar. 2016),
e broken system of aid for refugees (Paul
ollier, 25 Mar. 2017), 'The Jihadi next
or' (Tom Holland, Will Heaven, Rod
ddle, Mary Wakefield, 10 June 2017), the
yth of British decline (Robert Tombs, 8
ly 2017) and 'Putin's toxic power' (Owen
atthews, 17 Mar. 2018).

A remarkable coup came in April
2019, following the rapid dismissal of the
conservative philosopher Roger Scruton
from his role as a governmental adviser.
When George Eaton, a deputy editor of
the *New Statesman*, put into circulation
misleadingly edited quotations before his
interview with Scruton reached print, the
ensuing Twitterstorm caused predictable
outrage in predictable quarters. But
Douglas Murray, a tireless advocate for
intellectual fair play, somehow obtained
the original tape of their conversation: his
cover piece ('The Hit Job', 27 Apr. 2019)
revealed Scruton's remarks to be free of
the racism so rabidly alleged. Later that
year he was restored to his post, as co-chair
of the Building Better Building Beautiful
commission, a scintilla of justice before
his untimely death the following January.
His last published piece was a Diary of
his turbulent year in the Christmas issue
for 2019, which closed with prescient
poignancy: 'Coming close to death you

begin to know what life means, and what it
means is gratitude'.

Among influential non-cover pieces are
an article by James Bartholomew on the
rising societal blight of what he dubbed
'virtue signalling' (18 Apr. 2015),[1184] and
Miles Goslett's exposé of how the Kids
Company charity had been mismanaged
by Camila Batmanghelidjh (14 Feb. 2015).
Both these last two were commissioned by
Wakefield, the former popularising a term
that now has global currency, the latter
winning the industry accolade of 'Scoop
of the Year'. Perhaps the most significant
contributions online have come from James
Kirkup, who has since 2017 interspersed
his political blogs with outspoken and
principled pieces on the transgender
debate: these carefully researched blogs
have helped preserve open discussion
among communities far removed from
the magazine's typical readership. But
these and other pieces are only the more
serious part of *The Spectator*'s broader
campaign, reasserted in 2018, 'to foster
good-humoured debate. That's what we
strive to do today – because we feel our
country needs it.'[1185] Nelson, who shares the
task of leader-writing with Ross Clark, has
taken pains to keep the tone of the magazine
– from its opening page – provocative,
playful and (above all) readable.

Despite the large-scale changes at *The
Spectator* under Nelson's editorship,
circulation took some time to respond.
In fact, from 2009 to 2013, print sales
continued the gradual decline seen under
d'Ancona. But, for whatever reason, the
direction of travel changed and has not
stopped growing since. Including digital-
only subscriptions, from 2014 to 2019
circulation increased by a third. In 2020,

the magazine finds over 80,000 active purchasers: 50,000 print subscribers, 15,000 digital-only subscribers, and 15,000 forking out for a copy at the newsagent's. To its credit, *The Spectator* opted out of the double-counting used in the official ABC figures: the 'gross' number favoured by most publications includes free copies, bulk orders from the industry and – most misleadingly of all – 'allowable bundles', which count a print-and-digital subscriber twice. As a result, in 2019, *The Spectator*'s apparent fall by 20 per cent cloaked a real-terms rise of 9 per cent. When advertising revenue continues to be unsustainably low, *The Spectator* has the stability of almost 90 per cent of its income arising from magazine sales.

In the age of social media, Twitter has proved to be a potent tool for promoting the magazine's stories: the editor's account (@FraserNelson) has 235,000 followers, *The Spectator* (@spectator) 160,000, and Andrew Neil (@afneil) 1,000,000. But Twitter will always be a hotbed for unhinged ravers and ranters. One such harangued Nelson for a *Telegraph* piece he had written about an investigation into the behaviour of the England football manager Sam Allardyce,[1186] tweeting 'Why do we let half-educated tenement Scots run our English press?'[1187] The author, in fact, was the former flash-in-the-pan contributing editor to *The Spectator*, John Cleese. Matters did not improve when Cleese sought to defend his comments: 'Seriously, I'd rather have educated, cultured and intelligent people in charge. Sorry for the elitism. It's not casual racism, it's considered culturalism…

Issues of 23 Jan. and 23 July 2016

Another good question is: why are there no English journalists running Scottish newspapers? Xenophobia?' The mud struggled to stick. Cleese emerged as a buffoon, and Nelson did not need to say much – just as Rintoul did not when dismissed by envious colleagues as a 'cannie Scot of the worst description'.[1188] Aware of the parallel, Nelson retorted, 'funny thing is that *The Spectator* was created by someone who Cleese would disparage as a tenement Scot.'

An eye-opening insight into America has been provided since September 2017 by the novelist Lionel Shriver. Her fortnightly column replaced that of Hugo Rifkind, who served up witty cynicism (initially under 'Shared Opinion') for a decade. In fact, *The Spectator* – right back to the days of Townsend-Hutton in principle and of Strachey in practice – has been a keen supporter of America, save for some dramatic crises. In 2018, it seemed a clement time to bolster this

special relationship and launch a new initiative Stateside. *Spectator USA*, an online offshoot of the magazine with content tailored to an audience in the United States, was launched in March. The website (spectator.us), steered by *The Spectator*'s deputy editor Freddy Gray, fired up an array of bloggers – Paul Wood, Dominic Green, Helen Andrews, Kelly Jane Torrance, Daniel McCarthy and Jacob Heilbrunn. Its outlook was avowedly an extension of the twenty-first century *Spectator*:

The Spectator is pro-America and pro-Americans, though we aren't anyone's poodle. At a time when the 45th President often appears to have made the world go mad, we promise not to be crazily for or crazily against the Donald. We promise always to see that the world is far bigger than politics. *Spectator USA* will, like its mothership, look at all things. We will find life amusing, and we will never confuse the serious with the dull.[1189]

As a mark of its levity, the site runs a Steerpike-like gossip column, Cockburn, whose introduction was supported by the notably pro-American note that 'the ck is silent'. Still, the site has been serious enough to attract bloggers in the vanguard of progressive thinking, such as the pioneer of the 'wrongskin' movement, Godfrey Elfwick, a 'transblack genderqueer Muslim atheist'. But when his ally, the radical intersectionalist vegan slam poet Titania McGrath, was interviewed by *The Spectator*'s Tanya Gold (*Coffee House*, 2 Mar. 2019), she turned on the magazine for being 'a foul pro-Brexit rag. Every copy should be incinerated. Except the ones my name appears in.'

Cheered by the success of this venture, eighteen months later *The Spectator* made its boldest move for a generation. Despite the general struggle of *Spectator Australia* to grow, in October 2019 the magazine launched a print monthly: *The Spectator: US Edition*. Perfect-bound at eighty-two pages, and with a print-run of 30,000, it reflects the form and layout of its British counterpart, although all copy is specially commissioned. There is thus now an American *Spectator* in print, filling the space left by the *American Spectator* (no relation), which retreated online in 2014.[1190] The launch leader (written by Gray) declared that 'America is in *The Spectator*'s DNA, and imported copies of the *Speccie* have always appeared on the discerning American's reading list. It feels natural, therefore, to establish a presence here, and we dare to believe that we offer something that is lacking in

Spectator USA: Launch Edition (Oct. 2019)

journalism on both sides of the Atlantic.' As a closing coda, readers were reminded that '*The Spectator* reserves the right to say whatever it damn well pleases. What could be more American than that?' The tone of its outlook was established clearly enough by the cover story: Rod Liddle on Meghan Markle.[1191] And soon enough President Donald Trump was firing off a trademark Tweet in support of a *Spec. USA* piece (Donald McCarthy on the dangers of pursuing impeachment, 1 Oct. 2019).

At the close of 2017, print sales in the UK overtook the previous record of late 2006, at 62,940. By the end of 2019, they had climbed to new heights of 66,000. Total sales in 2020, at 82,000, are the highest they have ever been by any measure, making *The Spectator* the fastest growing current affairs magazine in Europe. Nelson regards the figure of dedicated, paid purchases as the true number by which his and other publications should be judged, so that editors 'concentrate

on making progress, not faking it'.[1192] To explain *The Spectator*'s marked achievement of recent years, he points to the magazine's successful orchestration of different media in harmony, rather than in competition: 'Digital is not a threat to print. In our experience, digital has led to the renaissance of print. Not just in the website, but social media and our range of podcasts'.[1193]

Thus far, *The Spectator* has mercifully avoided running either empty clickbait or invasive display advertising. Instead, by giving a wider audience than print can achieve a taste of typically vivid and varied *Spectator* fare, the website has proved to be a gateway drug for print subscriptions. Retention rates are monitored for those who become subscribers for six and twelve months after the end of a twelve-issue special offer. Astoundingly, that figure is around 80 per cent. 'If we give people a trial,' Nelson notes, 'the odds of their falling in love and staying with us for years are very high.'[1194] One reason for recent success is the virtuous cycle revealed by analytical tools: what is read with greater interest by subscribers influences the articles that are commissioned, which in turn compounds engagement. But the lively discussion of 'below-the-line' subscribers remains much the most direct method for telling *Spectator* authors what's what.

Coffee House is at the heart of this process, generating half of the digital subscriptions to *The Spectator*. In 2019 the *Spectator Life* hub (life.spectator. co.uk) started to incorporate articles from the *Money and Health* stables. But a major part of online success has come through the creation and expansion of

Spectator podcasts, which provide a fresh and unconstrained broadcasting medium of instant and global reach. During parliamentary sessions, the *Spectator* team releases a daily 'Coffee House Shots' podcast (usually of ten to fifteen minutes): these rapidly attract a wide and engaged following, not least because no other publication – magazine or newspaper – attempts to maintain a daily broadcast. A more important draw is the supremely well-connected gossip that Forsyth, Hardman and Balls can tap into – often literally on the buzzing phones at their sides. In fact, so closely involved is *The Spectator*'s political editor with the government of the day that the then prime minister, Theresa May, joked that there should be a 'James Forsyth app' to help cabinet ministers to leak details to their favoured recipient in real time.[1195] The magazine profits immensely from the depth and range of Forsyth's knowledge as well as his phone book. Nelson notes that 'James's degree of insider knowledge is something specific to him, and has not been achieved before by any political editor (myself included!).'[1196] Balls, appointed deputy political editor in January 2019, is increasingly hot on his heels in this regard, and has bolstered her online blogging and podcasting with pol cols for the magazine when Forsyth takes his well-earned holidays. Alongside these quotidian shots of proof-strength political discussion, Hardman rounds up the Sunday interview circuit each week with a sharp eye for what will count come Monday morning.

But rapid-response politics is only part of the digital picture. *The Spectator* has successfully launched a broad range of more detailed and devoted discussion

Issue of 7 July 2018 (cover by Morland)

outlets. In 2019, these were repackaged as *Spectator Radio*, which offers eight 'channels'. Alongside Coffee House Shots is the weekly *Spectator* podcast, 'The Edition', released on Thursdays in tandem with the new magazine: usually spreading three topical discussions over half an hour, it attracts an impressive and global audience. Weekly podcasts are conducted on books (with the literary editor Sam Leith), religious question ('Holy Smoke', with the associate edito Damian Thompson), American politic ('Americano', with Freddy Gray), an American culture ('The Green Room hosted by the life and arts editor of *Spe USA*, Dominic Green). More occasion are interviews with prominent fema figures ('Women with Balls', steered l deputy political editor Katy Balls) an

10,000 NOT OU

podcasts on food and drink ('Table Talk', with assistant editor Lara Prendergast and the cook Olivia Potts). While the main podcast attracts over 30,000 listeners each, the others garner another 30,000 between them. Total monthly listeners amount to an astounding 1.7 million. The multi-platform presence of *The Spectator* is bolstered by almost weekly events on the ground: in 2019, 18,000 subscribers gathered to hear, chat and argue with *Spectator* staff and guests, evidently reassured to rub shoulders in public with a like-minded crowd.

Despite the industry uncertainty and dog-eat-dog digital environment, *The Spectator*'s finances have likewise been knocked into shape: although certain initiatives (particularly software upgrades) required significant expenditure in some years (2012, for instance, saw a net loss of £500,000), the magazine is now more profitable than ever. In April 2018, record profits of £1.4m were announced – a remarkable achievement for an organ that has an editorial staff of twelve among some sixty employees. Evidently there is now sufficient security and stability on the balance sheet to allow funds to redound to the benefit of *The Spectator* and its readers. Perhaps it will be some time before the magazine (currently priced at 4.75) asks for the full five pounds? The final page of Simon Courtauld's narrative of *The Spectator* in the late-twentieth century closes with a pointed question: 'Is it unreasonable to hope that the profit motive at *The Spectator* will never be paramount?'[1197] More than twenty years on, that hope has not yet been dashed.[1198]

As the salutary news of *The Spectator*'s financial stability entered the public domain, Nelson overtook Chancellor as the title's longest-serving post-war editor. The following year, he celebrated ten years' service.[1199] Now, as the magazine reaches the historic milestone of its 10,000th issue,[1200] he has edited over 550 issues – a mere 1,000 behind Rintoul's total. *The Spectator* has long been the oldest weekly magazine in the world. This March, by surviving for 2,300 months, it also overtook the long-defunct *Gentleman's Magazine* (monthly between Jan. 1731 and Sep. 1922) to become the longest-lived magazine ever to appear.

The Spectator has never been more read, nor closer to political power. And yet politics has never been held in greater disdain, nor been a greater turn-off to many educated and sympathetic readers. Thrust into the limelight by its own success, *The Spectator* now spends much of its time on the other side of the lens – or the lash. At its best, however, the magazine finds space between its covers to foster and foment discussion and dissent, hosting the debates so rarely conducted in the public arena. While any prediction about the long-term future of the press is idle, it seems safe to say that, so long as the world is worth watching, and *The Spectator* is free to spectate, this magazine is set fair to retain a firm but forgiving readership into its third century and well beyond.

Coda

Such, then, is a sketch of *The Spectator*'s polychrome past. But, for all the change of almost two centuries, the tale is mostly one of continuity. Indeed, the modern *Spectator* still emerges as an amalgam similar to its very first number, 10,000 issues ago. Both begin with a concise summary of the week's news; whereas the first *Spectator* moved through national and global business to an account of parliamentary affairs, the 2020 *Spectator* gives its discussion of politics a specific column. The 1828 *Spectator* presents a series of editorial discussions of issues in the air: some give a steer on how to navigate the current political crises, others treat topics of a broader interest, though prompted by the news. In the modern *Spectator*, the most pressing of these subjects has been moved – since 1967 – to begin the issue, as the magazine's opening leader; the others have developed into the topical features that make up the front of the magazine. True, the modern *Spectator* now puts a name to the owners of these disparate views, but they still represent the same original mix of staff writers, occasional contributors and unsolicited spectators.

Charles Moore's 'Notes' represent the chattier 'Mr Spectator' elements of those original editorial asides; the 'Diary' that now appears each week is more akin to the dispatches from special correspondents, albeit with a more relaxed feel. The correspondence pages, as ever, see readers and rivals harangue the magazine for its assertions, or congratulate it for its veridical candour; letters that once were addressed to the editor on matters of morals and mores are now headed 'Dear Mary'. In a single column, 'Ancient and Modern' serves as an efficient tool for setting modern affairs in their classical context, something that percolated through (but never pervaded) the whole of Rintoul's *Spectator*. The 'Barometer' column reflects the interest in facts and figures that crops up from the very first issues of the 1828 *Spectator* (often headed 'Spectabilia', i.e. 'things worth taking a look at'). Business news has been given a personal spin, written up in a personal narrative (now by Martin Vander Weyer) rather than consigned to pell-mell news stories and the summary of the markets.

The main difference in the front half of the magazine is instead aesthetic: two columns of closely set and uninterrupted print have been replaced with three columns of text enlivened by red ink, colourful illustrations and arresting cartoons. In the back of the magazine, books and arts reviews, including theatre and opera, are fundamentally unchanged although they now cover the more new-fangled media of cinema, television and pop. Poetry intersperses the magazine's pages as it (almost) always has. The more laid-back tone of the modern *Spectator* is most obvious in the 'life' columns. High Life and Low Life remain entirely *sui generis*; Real Life and Wild Life overlap with the gripes of many an early correspondent at home and abroad. The unapologetically hedonic assessment of restaurants and of alcohol are the concessions of a happier age.

In fact, the only features of the original *Spectator* that have disappeared entirely are the reprints of articles from other journals ('The Press'), and the new gazette on the army, births, marriages and deaths. The modern *Spectator* has seen fit to replace these features with the novelties of a crossword, notes on bridge and chess and arm's-length surveys of sport.

The modern *Spectator* is connected with Rintoul's paper not just by lineage of descent and continuum of content, however. Its spirit returns to his very first paragraph.[1201] *The Spectator* of 202 still seeks 'to convey intelligence' – and in a manner that goes beyond that first number of 1828. The magazine wills its reader to take up and take on the facts, to confront new opinions – and, crucially, to *think*. It seeks not just to convey but to curate intelligence, in the hope that it will flower and flourish beyond. And if better arguments rebound or redound to knock sense into *The Spectator*, all the better for it.

The history of the British press is not one of linear progress, of news being discussed with ever greater accuracy and clarity, or of stories being weighed by ever more informed and open-minded readers. If anything, the mind-boggling expansion of media outlets across all forms of technology in recent decades has brought something of a regression in the journalistic world. Readers are now beset by the very real challenges of 'fake news', social-media echo chambers and self-imposed safe spaces. Now, more than at any point in the history of *The Spectator*, there is a pressing need for well-informed journalism and diversely opinionated comment. It is only sharp writing confident of where it is going that can cut through the clag.

Yet a serious purpose need not forgo wit or style. It was Graham Greene who famously proclaimed in the 1980s that *The Spectator* is the most entertaining and best-written weekly in the English language'. Evidently there is a solid crop of readers who feel that claim is still manifested each week. Fine writing needs to be enjoyed in its own space and left to speak for itself. A historical survey such as this cannot – through cruelly severed snippets – preserve the spark of an original article, nor translate the delicate and deft humour of the original. As a reminder of just how funny *The Spectator* can be, it is enough to flick through the two anthologies compiled by Christopher Howse and Marcus Berkmann.[1202]

Despite the embarrassingly recurrent prophecies that serious journalism is dying its inevitable death, there is plenty of scope for good cheer on Old Queen Street. *The Spectator*'s circulation looks set to continue climbing from its present zenith, so long as there is a demand in the English-speaking world for good writing. There is, perhaps, a perfect number of *Spectator* readers, whereby the magazine retains its intrinsic character but all to whom that character appeals are able to access it. That number is doubtless appreciably higher than 85,000, and very probably reaches into six figures, but it is a matter for keen debate about how high or low it actually is. Nevertheless, a blinkered obsession with that particular number, or with the financial success of the magazine more broadly, can become an unhealthy distraction. As one literary editor of *The Spectator* rightly recalled, 'a weekly paper is owned and run for pleasure rather than profit'.[1203]

Indeed, *The Spectator* survives because of those who delight in reading it, and see the joy that goes into making it. Compared to many of their peers, the staff of *The Spectator* work long hours for little pay. Yet their greater reward comes through joining a remarkably loyal and genial family, proud of its history and confident of its future. To close this account from one who has learned, laughed, debated and disagreed with *The Spectator* for not twenty years, it will suffice to repeat what the paper said of itself and its readers 162 years ago, after the death of the man who first brought it into being:

Such had always been felt to be the excellence of the *Spectator* as a reliable record of events, that even those subscribers who were most irritated by the course it pursued could find no substitute and continued their subscriptions. They swore at their leek, but they ate their leek too. By far the greater part of the regular readers of the *Spectator* have always been of a class that is not affected by partisan spleen: its circulation being chiefly, as it must always aim to be, among the men of culture, who like to listen to all sides of controversies, provided the argument is conducted with fairness and moderation.[1204]

Fair or unfair in its praise, moderate or immoderate in its criticism, this history of *The Spectator* has been written with one particular hope: that all those who disagree about issues of the modern day, however strongly and stridently, think and talk and write and reason about them whenever they can, in public as well as in private. *rem tene*, as a proto-*Spectator* reader once taught us, *verba sequentur*.

Endnotes

1. Disregarding the double or (occasionally) triple Christmas issues, only once has *The Spectator* failed to appear, during a troubled week of 1970: see pp.139–40.
2. See Appendix III.
3. *The Nation and Athenaeum*, 3 Nov. 1928, 168.
4. Sir W. Beach Thomas, *The Story of The Spectator, 1828–1928* (London, 1928): future references are simply to 'Beach Thomas'. Although the book proved to be an excellent introduction to the nineteenth-century paper, it contains many errors and omissions. I have in all cases returned to the original sources in researching this book.
5. S. Courtauld, *To Convey Intelligence: The Spectator, 1928–98* (London, 1998): future references are simply to 'Courtauld'. As a central figure of the magazine under Alexander Chancellor's editorship (1975–84), Chancellor helpfully reports plenty of material that is not otherwise available in print.
6. Rintoul was born on 12 January to John and Mary, who had moved a few miles north from the family home in Burnside near Forteviot. The Rintouls had been farming in the area since at least the fourteenth century. 'Rintoul' (which rhymes with 'BIN tool') is a Kinross-shire name, perhaps of Huguenot origins; the name developed in Ireland to 'Rentoul', and in America to 'Rantoul'.
7. The battle of Tippermuir/Tibbermore, fought on 1 September 1644, saw James Graham, 1st Marquis of Montrose, defeat the forces of the Scottish Parliament.
8. That Rintoul's services were soon in demand is attested by his publishing, in early 1809, the pamphlet *Rules adopted by the Physicians and Surgeons in Dundee for the Regulation of their Fees*.
9. R.M.W. Cowan, *The Newspaper in Scotland: A Study of its First Expansion, 1815–60* (Edinburgh, 1946) 28.
10. *Spectator* (henceforth '*Spec.*'), 1 May 1858. (This and all other references to the journal are given without specific pagination, in the hope that any citations given in this book are contextualised before being reprinted elsewhere.)
11. D.K. McKim and D.F Wright, *Encyclopedia of the Reformed Faith* (Louisville, 1992) 61.
12. He was also happy to publish two short-lived periodicals under the editorship of Mudie: *The Independent* (March–Sep. 1816) and *The Caledonian* (June 1820–Oct. 1821).
13. These nicknames are recorded in Kinloch's letters to his wife of 10 Dec. 1819 and 23 Jan. 1815 respectively (cited in C. Tennant, *The Radical Laird: A Biography of George Kinloch, 1775–1833* [Kineton, 1970] 60, 160).
14. Rintoul characteristically did not accept the gift until 1828, once its considerable cost had been fully paid off by the Guildry. The box was sold for £2,500 at Christie's of London on 8 Dec. 2011 (lot 89).
15. A legacy of £6,000 had been bequeathed by James Webster, the interest of which was to be used, in perpetuity, for the education of poor children in Dundee and its environs. Anderson was alleged to have lost this sum through financial malpractice. The full report on the trial by jury was published by William Bennet, Writer to the Signet, in 1824.
16. This otherwise unknown fact, heard from Rintoul at the *Spectator* office in autumn 1857, was reported by a journalist in *The Statesman*, 1 May 1858.
17. If the evidence of the Edinburgh Police Commissioners Minute Book (Edinburgh City Archives, ED9/1/5: 1823–7, p.268) is to be believed, a 'Mr Murray' was editing the title by Jan. 1826. As a lesson in how merciless the metropolitan press could be, the title merged after a year with the *Northern Reporter*, which soon merged with the *Edinburgh Star*, which before the year was out had become an advertising free-sheet; that was scooped up by the *Edinburgh Observer* in 1827, until that ship at last ran aground in 1845.
18. In his own record of publications (Mill-Taylor Collection, London School of Economics), Mill records that his 'article on wages and profits, capital & prices' appeared in May 1825. A copy has never been traced.
19. *Examiner*, 7 May 1826, 301.
20. From the original prospectus issued by the proprietors in May 1826. The full text was triumphantly reprinted twenty months later to demonstrate the project's successful delivery of its promises (see, e.g., the advertisements closing the *Edinburgh Review* for Jan. 1828).
21. *Atlas*, 21 May 1828, 8.
22. From the prospectus (as n.20).
23. The initial proprietors were James Whiting (publisher of John and Leigh Hunt, and a secret partner in *The Examiner*), his partner the engraver Robert Branston, and Henry Edward Swift. Whiting in due course became sole proprietor. After his exit, Rintoul would describe *The Atlas* as 'a pure commercial speculation by betting people in the city' (letter to William Blackwood, 11 Nov. 1828, NLS MS 4023.4).
24. *Atlas*, 21 May 1826, 11.
25. *Inspector*, Jan. 1827. Another early notice recorded that it was 'a very amusing journal, and will, we doubt not, succeed' (*Literary Magnet*, June 1826, 4).
26. 28 May 1826, 12.
27. W.M., 'On Public Opinion', *London Weekly Review*, 19 Jan. 1828: 'If the Editor of the "Atlas" will do me the favour to look over my "Essay on the Principles of Human Action," will dip into any essay I ever wrote, and will take a sponge and clear the dust from the face of my "Old Woman," I hope he will, upon second thoughts, acquit me of an absolute dearth of resources and want of versatility in the direction of my studies.'
28. Amongst his victories was a case, heard at the Court of King's Bench, on 10 July 1827: John Wright, author of an account of his time at Cambridge (*Alma Mater: Or, Seven Years at the University of Cambridge*, London, 1827) sued the paper for its unfavourable review (of 11 Feb.), which revealed the author's student nickname of 'Wretch Wright', pilloried his appearance, and mocked his uncouth arrogance. The presiding judge, Lord Tenderden, helped secure acquittal for *The Atlas* by noting that 'the man who thinks fit to apply the appellation of bear and beast to others, is not entitled to any very great compensation in damages for publications upon himself.'
29. 7 July 1828 (NLS MS 4023.1).
30. *Ibid*. Despite Rintoul's exit, *The Atlas* continued until 1869; for the years 1862–5 it bore the title *The Englishman*.
31. The first appearance was in the *Morning Post*, 1 July 1828.
32. The advertisement appeared in the *Globe* and *London Evening Standard* on 3 July, *The Times* on 4 and 5 July, and *The Examiner* on 6 July, the day the paper was born.
33. 7 July 1828 (NLS MS 4023.1). The request was later repeated on 19 Feb. 1829 (NLS MS 4020.73) with the more specific suggestion that Christopher North (i.e. John Wilson) mention *The Spectator* in the next instalment of his celebrated 'Noctes Ambrosianae' dialogues. Within a couple of months, the request was honoured (see pp.19).
34. The first run extended from 1 May 1711 to 6 Dec. 1712. It was revived in a thrice-weekly form by Addison alone for eighty issues from 18 June to 20 Dec. 1714. From 1712, these essays were published collectively in seven volumes, with the 1714 set providing an eighth. (A spurious 'ninth volume' was authored by other hands.)
35. It has now appeared in some 300 separate editions; see Stephen Bernard's online bibliography in the *Electronic British Library Journal* 2019.1.
36. For instance, *The Universal Spectator* 1728–46, *The Female Spectator* 1744–6, *The New Spectator* 1784–6, *The Country Spectator* 1792–3, *New York Spectator* 1797–1876, *The Boston Spectator* 1814–15, *Connecticut Spectator* 1814–15, *Edwardsville Spectator* 1819–26, *The Christian Spectator* 1819. 38. Among non-English titles were *Le Spectateur Français* 1719–21, *Le Nouveau Spectateur Français* 1723–5, *De Hollandsche Spectator* 1731–5, and *Den Danske Spectator* 1744–5.
37. Writing to John Cam Hobhouse on 2 July 1811.
38. For a survey of the evidence, see my article on Coffee House, 'How the Spirit of *The Spectator* dates back to 1711', 1 Mar. 2018. Rintoul's own correspondence shows that 'Spec.' was his preferred shorthand for his paper.
39. Interest in this giraffe endured, and on 4 July 1829, the first anniversary of the paper, an engraving the animal was offered up to curious readers.
40. 'The gliding fish that takes his play.'
41. Although it is difficult to reconstruct the circulation figures for the first few years of *The Spectator*, a rough sense of copies sold can obtained from occasional comments made by Rintoul and contemporary observers. For the slow and steady growth in circulation, see Appendix I.
42. 16 Aug. 1828.
43. 11 Nov. 1828 (NLS MS 4023.4). The emphases, these and other letters, are Rintoul's own.
44. 16 Sep. 1829 (NLS MS 4026.75). A letter Blackwood of 2 Dec. 1828 (NLS MS 4023.6) had been plain enough on this point: 'You will see a glance that the cost of production, as compared with other newspapers, must be very great; and that it will require a very large circulation

remunerate us.' Such costs did not decrease much with time: when giving evidence to a Parliamentary committee in 1843, Rintoul observed that it was 'very expensively got up,' at perhaps four times the cost of other Sunday papers (*Report from the Select Committee of the House of Lords Appointed to Consider The Law of Defamation and Libel* [June 1843] 162 §685.

45. Almost from the outset the paper had advertised itself as a 'family newspaper': an advertisement in *Aris's Birmingham Gazette* for 25 Aug. 1828 explained that the paper was 'calculated to afford innocent amusement to the various tastes of the different members of a family for the entire week. Politics are only treated historically.' By the end of the year, the public were told that the paper will, 'when bound, form the handsomest volume for the library, as, on grounds of morality and taste, it aims at being thought worthy of preservation, and of receiving the especial patronage of respectable families' (*Globe* and others, 26 Dec. 1828). Such language closely echoes the original Mr Spectator, who recommended his 'speculations to all well-regulated families' (no.10). When Rintoul advertised that his Spectator was 'not a sectarian or a partisan, in any sense, but a citizen of the world', readers would recall Addison's Mr Spectator fancying himself 'a Citizen of the World' at the Royal Exchange (no. 69).

46. Clayton was based at Windsor Court from 17 Dec. 1831, and began printing there on 14 Apr. 1832. The printing premises moved on 30 Mar. 1844 to Crane Court, off the north side of Fleet St. In October 1857, Clayton crossed Fleet St and began printing at 17 Bouverie St.

47. The paper was linked with 4 Wellington St from 27 June 1829 to 10 Dec. 1831; 9 (later 1) Wellington St was its base from 17 Dec. 1831 to 7 Aug. 1920.

48. Beach Thomas, 66; H.H. Asquith, *Memories and Reflections, 1852–1927* (London, 1928) I.82; John Buchan, 'Spectator memories,' *Spec.* 3 Nov. 1928, 20.

49. See p.86.

50. 2 May 1829.

51. J. Grant, *The Newspaper Press; Its Origin, Progress, and Present Position* (London, 1871) III.71.

52. Apr. 1829, 543.

53. 28 May 1829.

54. Letter to William Blackwood of 15 Jan. 1829 (NLS MS 4026.73).

55. 17 Sep. 1831.

56. 19 Mar. 1831.

57. 1 Jan. 1831.

58. *Ibid.*

59. The series ran for six weeks (12 Mar.–16 Apr. 1831) by the end of which the Parliamentary Candidate Society was dismissed as a misconceived and mishandled venture.

60. 10 Apr. 1831.

61. 14 May 1831.

62. 19 Nov. 1831.

63. 5 Nov. 1831.

64. 'Asmodeus at large. VIII', *The New Monthly Magazine*, Dec. 1831, 499.

65. 15 Nov. 1832.

66. 'To the Constant Reader,' 31 Dec. 1831.

67. 7 May 1831, after his dissolution of Parliament.

68. [J. Grant], *The Great Metropolis* (London, 1837) I.123.

69. *Blackwood's Magazine*, Apr. 1829, 543.

70. 22 Sep. 1838. Rintoul himself attended the meeting in Palace-yard of the 'working men of London' on 17 Sep. 1838, but was cautious in voicing outright support in the paper, instead describing Chartism as 'a natural and necessary result of having taught millions to read' (1 June 1839). An outspoken journal such as *The Chartist* realised that Rintoul's outlook was nevertheless in support of the Establishment: 'The only way, we imagine, by which the *Spectator* thinks it possible to save the nation is to make [William] Molesworth Prime Minister, [John Temple] Leader, leader of the House of Commons, and Mr. Rintoul Chancellor of the Exchequer' (2 June 1839).

71. *The Scotsman*, reported in *The Manchester Times and Gazette*, 17 Oct. 1835.

72. The proposal came from the radical diplomat John Crawfurd, an occasional *Spectator* writer who had publicly complained about the stamp duty that the paper suffered more than others (*Taxes on Knowledge*, London, 1836, 33). *The Constitutional* appeared as the first penny daily on 15 Sep. 1836 but collapsed within a year (1 July 1837).

73. The business was conducted privately, and evidence only survives in a letter from Grote's wife Harriet to Francis Place of 16 Aug. 1837 (BL Add. MSS. 35150, ff.279–80).

74. Letter to Francis Place of 16 Aug. 1837 (as n. 73).

75. 17 Dec. 1836.

76. 24 Dec. 1836.

77. 21 Oct. 1837. Even at the coronation of Queen Victoria a year later, *The Spectator* felt it could make merry: 'a distinguished foreigner was told that to roll down the steps of the throne at the coronation was the feudal tenure by which he held his barony and immense estates. The information was gravely recorded in a note-book.' This was par for the course in a ceremony which combined 'that love of noise and tinsel which barbarians and children are understood to share in common' (30 June 1838).

78. 12 Aug. 1837.

79. 2 Sep. 1837.

80. 22 Sep. 1838.

81. 21 Mar. 1840.

82. 15 Mar. 1840.

83. 21 Mar. 1840.

84. 17 Sep. 1842.

85. 3 Jan. 1835. Later that year a correspondent 'Nestor' wrote a withering open letter to Peel (21 Mar. 1835). One sentence will set the tone: 'I pity you, Sir, from the bottom of my heart; and I wonder at, while I regret, the supreme folly that led you to barter the tranquillity of your hearth for the tarnished honours of a few perilous and stormy days of power, disgracefully purchased and still more disgracefully held.'

86. 2 Jan. 1841.

87. 3 July 1841.

88. 17 Sep. 1842.

89. 31 Jan. 1846.

90. 9 May 1846.

91. *Ibid.*

92. 13 June 1846.

93. 21 Mar. 1835.

94. 6 July 1850.

95. 16 Jan. and 13 Mar. 1830.

96. Inserted as an 'appendix' in the issue for 3 Apr. 1830, with the last eight pages of the normal paper tacked on behind. Wakefield was tactful enough not to recall the ridicule that Rintoul's *Atlas* had directed at him after his arrest (see esp. 28 May 1826).

97. Review of *Facts Relating to the Punishment of Death in the Metropolis* (London, 1831), 23 July 1831.

98. 20 Jan. 1838.

99. 16 Feb. 1839.

100. 17 Dec. 1839 (NLS MS 4049.135).

101. *Dublin Evening Mail*, 26 Apr. 1858.

102. E.J Wakefield (ed.), *The Founders of Canterbury* (Christchurch, 1868) 180.

103. 28 Nov. 1841.

104. Wakefield recorded in his final work, *A View of the Art of Colonization* (London, 1849, 59), that 'by far the heaviest of my debts of gratitude is due to the proprietor and editor of *The Spectator* newspaper.'

105. Letter to Henrietta Rintoul of 8 Oct. 1852, reported in *Spec.* 3 Nov. 1928.

106. 1 Apr. 1848.

107. 8 Apr., 15 Apr., 22 Apr., 29 Apr., 20 May 1848.

108. Cited by R.D. Fulton, 'The Spectator', in A. Sullivan (ed.), *British Literary Magazines: The Romantic Age, 1789–1836* (Westport, CT, 1983) 394.

109. *London Saturday Journal*, 14 Sep. 1839.

110. 23 Aug. 1856; 8 Jan. 1848.

111. 18 Dec. 1847; 6 Nov. 1847; 9 Aug. 1828.

112. Review of *Fair Carew*, 18 Nov. 1851. The letter was first cited by C.K. Shorter in her edition of Gaskell's *Life of Charlotte Brontë* (London, 1914) 554 n. The reference is to the original paragraph of the *Spectator* review of 6 Nov. 1847, which began: 'Essentially, *Jane Eyre, an Autobiography*, has some resemblance to those sculptures of the middle ages in which considerable ability both mechanical and mental was often displayed upon subjects that had no existence in nature, and as far as delicacy was concerned were not pleasing in themselves.'

113. E.g., *Manchester Guardian*, 5 Feb. 1831.

114. S. Lee, G. Smith, L. Stephen, *George Smith: A Memoir* (London, 1902) 86.

115. Sometimes the law had to step in: in 1846, the Society of British Artists won damages of £100 for an article (of 11 Apr. 1846) that falsely claimed the organisers had misrepresented the support they enjoyed from the great and the good – notwithstanding the uncharacteristically grovelling retraction made the following week (18 Apr. 1846).

116. *Punch* vol. 4 (1843) 225.

117. *Ibid.* 29. Likewise, vol. 5 (1843) 4: 'The criticisms in the *Spectator* are very like muskets, for they all end with a heavy "but."'

118. *Punch* vol. 4 (1843) 29.

119. The tale is reported amid a strikingly vicious attack on Rintoul and *The Spectator* in *American Whig Review*, Dec. 1851, 511.

120. *Monthly Repository*, 1836.

121. *American Whig Review*, Dec. 1851, 511.

122. 'Pre-Raphaelitism', 4 Oct. 1851. The principles of the PRB had first found expression in the Brotherhood's own organ, *The Germ*, which produced four issues from Jan. to Apr. 1850 but failed to sell more than 100 copies. The first review of *The Germ* in the press appeared in *The Spectator* for 12 Jan. 1850, before Rossetti's arrival; it was not positive.

123. 17 Aug. 1850. Douglas Jerrold had spoken in Punch of 'a palace of very crystal' the previous month (13 July 1850).

124. *Mitchell's Press Directory* (London, 1846) s.v.

125. 9 Nov. 1833; 14 Dec. 1833; 9 May 1835; 3 Sep. 1836. For a detailed summary of the correspondence, see Beach Thomas 166–73.

126. Cited in *The Pilot*, 2 Apr. 1845.

127. Cited in the *London Evening Standard*, 13 Jan. 1847.

128. The first 'Letters' section appeared in the issue for 6 Apr., and was expanded to 'Letters to the Editor' the subsequent week.

129. 17 July 1852.

130. 10 Feb. 1855. The translation was made by de Tocqueville's correspondent, Harriet Grote.

131. *Fraser's Magazine*, May 1858, 611.

132. G.A. Macmillan (ed.), *Letters of Alexander Macmillan* (Glasgow, 1908) 96.

133. *Inverness Courier*, 24 Apr. 1862.

134. Quoted from John Hunter's unpublished diary in Iain Hamilton's 'Notebook', *Spec.* 7 Sep. 1962.

135. *Publishers' Circular*, 1 May 1858, 174.

136. W. Norrie, *Dundee's Celebrities of the Nineteenth Century* (Dundee, 1873) 177.

137. 1 May 1858.

138. *Cambridge Independent Press*, 1 May 1858.

139. No formal record of *Spectator* writers survives before Nov. 1874, after which there exist notes of contributors to the present day; given that the paper did not publish signed articles until the 1920s, hundreds of early commentators to *The Spectator* are now lost beyond reach. The records for the late nineteenth century were only discovered in the 1950s: see R.H. Tener, 'The *Spectator* Records, 1874–1897', *Victorian Newsletter* 17 (1960) 33–8. Most regrettably, their present location is unknown.

140. 'Ireland and the British Chief Governor' and 'Irish Regiments (of the New Æra)', 13 May 1848 (both signed). Clearly, Carlyle had moved on from his earlier opinion of *The Spectator* as a 'Radical and half-infidel', 'stupid enough' and 'dull crabbed paper' (letters of 10 Apr. 1830, 19 Dec. 1830, 26 Aug.1841).

141. Mill: 4 Apr. 1846, 5 June 1847, 10 Mar. 1849, 16 Mar. 1850. Other contributions by Mill include a review of Robert Tollens's critique of Peel (28 Jan. 1843) and an account of the 'provisional government of France' (18 Mar. 1848).

142. A series of seven letters was published from 4 Sep. to 16 Oct. 1847. Although given the pseudonymous initials 'A.B.', Grote published the collection under his own name later that year.

143. Three long letters appeared above Roebuck's signature on 3, 10 and 17 Nov. 1838.

144. 'Mr Rintoul being Scotch, of course his staff were all Scotch too; for Scotland is one large clique' (*Constitutional Press*, quoted in *Westmorland Gazette*, 15 May 1858).

145. Remark from *The Press*, reported in *Lincolnshire Chronicle*, 3 Jan. 1868.

146. R. Chambers and R. Carruthers (eds), *Chamber's Cyclopaedia of English Literature* (London, 1873³) 1.654 fn.*.

147. It is possible, but entirely speculative, that Rintoul met her during his 1819 visit to London. More likely is that they were introduced by a mutual acquaintance. This aspect of Mrs Rintoul's early life seems entirely unmentioned in print, although a curious remark appeared in the *Illustrated London News* after her husband's death (1 May 1858): as a 'hint' to his biography, the author writes that 'His great labour was the reform of the Royal Mint: for this he worked with an assiduity of purpose (even late in life) that shows he had but one object. Personally he may have missed his object, but his children … have not missed it.' The plural 'children' may hint at the knowledge that Rintoul's stepson, as well as his own son Robert, was involved in the Mint (cf. p.36).

148. Letter to Mary Scott Hogarth, 15 May 1836 (M. House and G. Storey [eds], *The Letters of Charles Dickens, Volume One: 1820–1839* [Oxford, 1965] 691).

149. Most harsh among the reviews of Dickens's novels was George Brimley's (anonymous) hatchet job on *Bleak House* (24 Sep. 1853), which made light of his vulgar wit, disparaged his improbable caricatures and even mocked his popular success.

150. Cf. *American Whig Review*, Dec. 1851, 511. It is unclear whether the nickname coined by the staff was ever used in print.

151. Letter to Douglas Jerrold, 24 Oct. 1846 (K. Tillotson [ed.], *The Letters of Charles Dickens, Volume Four: 1844–1846* [Oxford, 1977] 643).

152. Eleanor Smyth, *Sir Rowland Hill: The Story of a Great Reform* (London, 1907) 117. The account presumably refers to an episode in Henrietta's twenties. One obituary notice (*London Monitor*, 25 Nov. 1904, 5) similarly records that 'on one occasion she took entire charge of the paper for three weeks to enable him to enjoy a rare holiday.'

153. W.M. Rossetti, *Some Reminiscences* (London, 1906) 261. The couple spent regular holidays together on the Isle of Wight, under the watchful eye of Henrietta senior. Seven photographs of Henrietta, presumably taken by William, survive in the Rossetti family album in the National Portrait Gallery: P1273 (27a, c–e, g–i). The correspondence between the two does not survive. It was rumoured by the Rossettis that Henrietta had stipulated that she would only wed Robert if the marriage were platonic. The toll on both parties was severe: Christina Rossetti, who remained a close friend of Henrietta, told William how 'she held me fast kissing me and crying, and I could feel how thin she is and how she trembled in my arm.' (See A. Thirlwell, *William and Lucy: The Other Rossettis* [New Haven, CT, 2003] 215.) When William's translation of Dante's *Inferno* appeared in 1865, Part 1, *The Hell*, is dedicated simply 'To H.R.'

154. Rintoul's burial, on 1 May 1858, went unreported in the press. The shared grave plot was rediscovered in 2017: West Site #8839 (appointment only). Since there were no Rintoul descendants, the ownership of the plot transferred to three spinster sisters of Goldsworthy Lowes Dickinson: May, Hester and Janet.

155. As n.153, 99.

156. Constance Wakefield (later D'Arblay Burney), cited in R. Garnett, *Edward Gibbon Wakefield: The Colonization of South Australia and New Zealand* (London, 1898) 324.

157. E.J. Wakefield (ed.), *The Founders of Canterbury* (Christchurch, 1868) x.

158. Letter to Charles Redwood, 15 July 184[?] (accessible at carlyleletters.dukeupress.edu).

159. T.H.S. Escott, *Masters of English Journalism* (London, 1911) 238.

160. J. Grant, *The Newspaper Press; Its Origin, Progress, and Present Position* (London, 1871) III.72.

161. Cf. *Fraser's Magazine*, May 1858, 613: 'Beneath a somewhat cold exterior there ran a warm current of real human sympathy and affection.'

162. *Sphinx*, 24 July 1869.

163. W. Norrie, *Dundee's Celebrities of the Nineteenth Century* (Dundee, 1873) 178.

164. *Fraser's Magazine*, May 1858, 612.

165. *Spec.* 1 May 1858.

166. *Daily News*, 24 Apr. 1858.

167. *The Atlas*, 24 Apr. 1858.

168. 'His was essentially an opposition paper, and there was not enough left to oppose.' 'Town Talk (from our London correspondent)', reported in *Us[?] Observer*, 1 May 1858.

169. 19 Apr. 1856.

170. In a letter to Edward Taylor, leaving the post of music critic in 1843 after fourteen years' service Rintoul confided that 'the time is drawing on whe[?] with me, too, those pursuits that have occupied m[?] so busily for so many years must be relinquished (Cited in *Norfolk News*, 4 Apr. 1863.)

171. 6 Feb. 1858.

172. Rintoul always viewed the ancient universitie[?] of England and Scotland with the suspicion of peeved outsider. Years before, on 4 Dec. 1830, [?] had rankled many a *Spectator* reader by writing 'The truth is, it is not the *fashion* to learn at t[?] Universities; and the lecturers and tutors cann[?] procure attendance from the greater part of t[?] students, ONE DAY IN FIVE FOR AN HOUR [?] DAY.' A flurry of irate letters followed, especia[?] from William Whewell, then a tutor – but destin[?] to be master – of Trinity College, Cambridge.

173. In the dozens of reports of his death there w[?] some uncertainty as to whether he was seventy-o[?] or seventy; however, his birthday is recorded in t[?] parish records for 12 Jan. 1787.

174. 1 May 1858.

175. *Fraser's Magazine*, May 1858, 612.

176. *Social Economist*, 1 Apr. 1868.

177. Beach Thomas, 55.

178. *Worcestershire Chronicle*, 31 Dec. 1851.

179. 'The Lounger at the Clubs', reported in *Ar[?] Birmingham Gazette*, 19 Apr. 1858.

180. The first report, presumably penned by an [?] acquaintance, attributed Rintoul's retirement to [?] health: *Dundee Advertiser*, 2 Apr. 1858.

181. Two weeks later, a letter appeared from [?] historian Edward Freeman wishing the n[?] management the best success. He recorded

'deep debt of gratitude to the memory of Mr. Rintoul for the many opportunities which he has allowed me of arguing all sorts of points in the pages of the *Spectator*, even though my views often happened to be altogether at variance with his own.' (15 May 1858).

182. 15 Jan. 1876. Richard Holt Hutton, the author of the original piece 'The intellectual qualifications for chess' (8 Jan. 1876), was known to Scott as a former UCL colleague, and had a long-standing Friday ritual of playing chess with Walter Bagehot at their mutual club, the Athenaeum.

183. For many points of context and detail here I am indebted to the article of R.D. Fulton, '*The Spectator* in alien hands', *Victorian Periodicals Review* 24 (1991) 186–96.

184. See S.A. Wallace and F.E. Gillespie (eds), *The Journal of Benjamin Moran, 1857–1865* (Chicago, 1949) I.476, 480.

185. S. Dallas (ed.), *Diary of George Mifflin Dallas* (Philadelphia, PA, 1892) 293.

186. Reported in W.J. Linton, *Memories* (London, 1895) 117.

187. G.H. Holyoake, *Sixty Years of an Agitator's Life* (London, 1892) I.229. The passage continues, 'It was Mr. Rintoul's religion to produce a perfect newspaper, and in that sense he was the most religious man of his profession.'

188. Moran recorded, on the basis of his conversation with Hunt, that Rintoul 'was much noticed by the press and the *Daily News* spoke of his having suggested the generality of the Articles on his paper, whereas Hunt was the suggester, and Rintoul the simple repeater of these suggestions.' See Wallace and Gillespie (as n.184) I.299.

189. *Northern Whig*, 29 Dec. 1858.

190. In a letter of 15 Jan. 1829 (NLS MS 4026.73) to Blackwood, Rintoul claimed that Hunt wrote for a lower class of reader, and if he were then known to be contributing to the post-Rintoulian *Atlas* its sales would fall by 50 per cent.

191. 'The Occasional' ran from 15 Jan. to 20 Aug. 1859.

192. Fulton (as n.183) 188.

193. 19 Feb. 1859.

194. 16 July 1859.

195. 9 July 1859.

196. 3 Sep. 1859.

197. 19 Mar. 1859.

198. 28 Oct. 1859.

199. 3 Dec. 1859 (also printed in the national dailies). It is curious that The Spectator was content to cite this part of the speech without further observation: did (some of) the staff perhaps feel the same?

200. These sums, listed throughout the diary (as n.184), are conveniently summarised by Fulton (as n.183) 192.

201. Moran records the transfer in his entry for 2 Apr. 1860 in Wallace and Gillespie (as n.184).

202. See Moran's entry for 31 Jan. 1861 in Wallace and Gillespie (as n.184), although the editors were unable to identify the mysterious 'Delille'.

203. *Stirling Journal*'s London correspondent, reported by the *Dundee Advertiser*, 10 Apr. 1860.

204. See entry for 4 Apr. 1858 in Wallace and Gillespie (as n.184).

205. Moran met Delille through McHenry on 3 Dec. 1859: 'He is an American whose story is a wonder, and he is now here to purchase the *Morning Chronicle* for Louis Napoleon.' See Wallace and Gillespie (as n.184) ad loc.

206. Moran and McHenry met with Persigny on numerous occasions, perhaps first in April 1857.

207. G.F. Train, *My Life in Many States and in Foreign Lands* (New York, 1902) 273.

208. *Westmorland Gazette*, 23 June 1860.

209. Hooper has hitherto been entirely omitted from lists of *Spectator* editors.

210. 'London Correspondence' (sent from the Athenaeum Club) in *Trewman's Exeter Flying Post*, 24 Oct. 1860.

211. Entry for 15 Oct. 1860 in Wallace and Gillespie (as n.184).

212. 31 Mar., 2 June, 24 Nov. and 8 Dec. 1860.

213. 17 May 1890.

214. 24 May 1890.

215. Wallace and Gillespie (as n.184) ad loc.

216. *Ibid.* ad locc. The sale was first publicly announced on 5 Jan. 1861 in the *Carlisle Journal*.

217. 19 Dec. 1874.

218. *Caledonian Mercury*, 7 Jan. 1861.

219. *Nation*, 27 Mar. 1880, 270.

220. Reported in *Spec.* 3 Nov. 1928.

221. Henrietta senior had removed herself to Darlaston Hall, Staffs, the seat of Swyfen Jervis MP (grandfather, as it happened, of Thornton Hunt's children with Agnes), where she died in 1860. Occasional holidays were taken in the intervening thirty months at Freshwater on the Isle of Wight, to which Henrietta junior would frequently return in later years.

222. Cited in *ODNB*.

223. Just like Rintoul, Townsend had sought in India to set official papers and carefully sourced facts before the reader: he founded and edited the series of *Annals of Indian Administration*, a thesaurus of governmental documents, which began in 1856 and ran to nineteen volumes over the next twenty years. In 1855–7 he also found the energy to become proprietor and editor of the biannual *Calcutta Review*. At the end of his long career, Townsend published a digest of his wisdom under the title *Asia and Europe* (London, 1901: see n.296). The book sold in considerable quantities, and is still consulted today for its complex – if at times crude – assessment of Empire and the clash of civilisations.

224. He briefly edited the *Samachar Darpan* ('Mirror of News').

225. See Wallace and Gillespie (as n.184) I.770–1.

226. *Northern Whig*, 4 Mar. 1862.

227. From issue 98, of 15 May 1830, Clayton replaced F.C. Westley. Although his service as printer was constant for the next thirty years, from 30 Nov. 1833 to 26 Dec. 1835 Gustavus Arabin, later Justice of the Peace for Middlesex, was the publisher based at Wellington St.

228. Cited from Hutton's prefatory memoir to *The Works of Walter Bagehot* (5 vols, Hartford, CO) I.xxvii.

229. Diary of Henry Crabb Robinson, 30 June 1852 (MS Dr Williams's Library, UCL).

230. Reported by A.J. Church, *Memories of Men and Books* (London, 1908) 204.

231. As a Fellow of University College London (a post he held throughout his life), Hutton had seen *The Spectator* fail in the hands of his fellow Fellow, and former co-examiner, Scott. Whether or not they ever discussed the matter in person, Hutton was perhaps quietly confident that he knew how to make a success of it. For an account of Hutton's unconvincing tenure at *The Economist*, see R.D. Edwards, *The Pursuit of Reason: The Economist, 1843–1993* (London, 1933) 178ff.

232. H. Quilter, *What's What: A Guide to To-day, to Life As it Is, and Things As They Are* (London, 1902) 1124.

233. W. Robertson Nicoll, *British Weekly*, 16 Sep. 1897.

234. Townsend also wrote a weekly column for *The Economist*, which allowed him to range around domestic affairs more freely.

235. 26 Jan. 1861.

236. 1 June 1861.

237. *Ibid.*

238. 19 Sep. 1863.

239. 11 Oct. 1862.

240. Letter of 20 Feb. 1863: see M. Filipiuk *et al.* (eds), *The Collected Works of John Stuart Mill, Vol. XXXII: Additional Letters of John Stuart Mill* (Toronto, 1991) §589b, at 197.

241. 26 Aug. 1865.

242. 6 Feb. 1862. These columns were collected and edited by H. Mitgang in *Spectator of America* (Chicago, IL, 1971).

243. J. St Loe Strachey, *The Adventure of Living: A Subjective Autobiography (1860–1922)* (New York, 1922) 'Postscript' to preface of American ed.

244. *The Sphinx*, 24 July 1869.

245. 29 Mar. 1864.

246. 25 Dec. 1869.

247. 29 Apr. 1865.

248. *Northern Whig*, 4 Mar. 1862.

249. These were collected and revised by Hughes in *Vacation Rambles* (London, 1895).

250. Letter to E.A. Freeman of 11 Mar. 1863, cited in G.A. Macmillan (ed.), *Letters of Alexander Macmillan* (privately printed, 1908) 133.

251. Letter to Charles Wood of 1 Feb. 1863: see F.W. Cornish (ed.), *Extracts from the Letters and Journals of William Cory* (Oxford, 1987) 86.

252. 12 Apr. 1861. Another letter in which Galloway conveyed his failure to Collins was written on 9 Aug. 1862, but it was last seen at auction in 1909.

253. 4 Jan. 1874.

254. H.F. Jones (ed.), *The Note-Books of Samuel Butler* (New York, 1917) 161.

255. S. Colvin (ed.), *The Letters of Robert Louis Stevenson* (New York, 1911) III.285. He added what 'an able paper it is, and a fair one.'

256. *A Few Words on Criticism, Being an Examination of the Article in the* Saturday Review *of April 20, 1861, Under Dr Whewell's* Platonic Dialogues for English Readers (London, 1861).

257. 29 June 1861.

258. 1 Jan. 1870.

259. Reported in the *Edinburgh Evening News*, 18 Sep. 1897.

260. O. Chadwick, *The Victorian Church* (London, 1972²) II.123.

261. T.H.S. Escott, *Masters of English Journalism* (London, 1911) 239.

262. *The Sphinx*, 24 July 1869.

263. J.M. Capes, *The Rambler*, May 1857, 324.

264. 15 Feb. 1862.

265. Review of *Poems*, 13 Aug. 1881.

266. Beach Thomas, 234, cites an anonymous staff member's recollection that [D.G.] Rossetti and Tennyson contributed poetry to *The Spectator*, but I have not found evidence to sustain this intriguing claim, although Tennyson's 'A Call to Arms' was first published (posthumously) in *Spec*. 3 Oct. 1914.

267. 18 May 1878.

268. 22 Nov. 1873.

269. 12 Jan. 1861.

270. 'A song in time of order', 26 Apr. 1862; 'Before parting', 17 May 1862; 'After death', 24 May 1862; 'Faustine', 31 May 1862; 'A song in time of revolution', 28 June 1862; 'The sundew', 26 July 1862; 'August', 6 Sep. 1862. These poems were later reprinted in *Poems and Ballads* (London, 1866).

271. 24 May 1862.

272. Both Cossu and the equally fabricated 'Ernest Clouet' had successfully been slipped into his reviews of Parts II through V of *Les Misérables* (21 June, 26 July and 16 Aug. 1862).

273. C.Y. Lang (ed.), *The Swinburne Letters, Vol. 1: 1854–1869* (New Haven, CT, 1959) 72. Swinburne nevertheless wrote to the paper in later life, once to protest that he was deliberately misquoted (16 Aug. 1879), another time to declare the metrical origin of Tennyson's *In Memoriam* (4 Feb. 1899).

274. 7 Mar. 1863 (the marriage itself took place at St George's Chapel, Windsor, on 10 Mar.).

275. Of England: the Barings, Berkeleys, Cavendishes, Cecils, Clintons, Bentincks, Fitzroys, Fitzwilliams, Grenvilles, Greys, Grosvenors, Herberts, Lennoxes, Leveson-Gowers, Lowthers, Manners, Montagues, Osbornes, Pages, Percys, Petty-Fitzmaurices, Russells, Seymours, Somersets, Spencers, Stanhopes, Stanleys, Talbots, Vanes, and Villiers. Of Scotland: the Bruces of Elgin, Dalrymples of Stair, Douglases, Elliots, Gordons of Huntly and of Haddo, Grahams of Montrose, Hays of Erroll and of Yester, Ker(r)s, Murrays of Athole, Ramsays of Dalhousie, Scotts of Buccleuch, and Stuarts of Bute. Of Ireland: the Beresfords, Boyles, Brownes, Burghs/Bourkes, Butlers of Ormonde, Caulfields, Chichesters, Fitz-Geralds of Kildare, Hills, Jocelyns, Moores, Nugents, Ponsonbys, Stewarts of Mount Stewart, and Wellesleys.

276. 11 July 1863.

277. The series on England was later published by Townsend and the primary author, John Langton Sanford, as *The Great Governing Families of England* (2 vols, London, 1865). As a historian, the latter had been Hutton's colleague at UCL and co-editor at the *Inquirer*.

278. 1 Sep. 1866 ('The West Country') to 19 Mar. 1870 ('The Four Northern Counties', issued as a ten-page supplement).

279. J. Langton Sanford, *Estimates of the English Kings* (London, 1872) [vii].

280. The series ran in thirty-three instalments, published sporadically from 18 June 1870 to 27 Apr. 1872. They were subsequently published by their author, John Langton Sanford (as prev. n.).

A series on 'Leading personages of English history', advertised on 12 Mar. 1870, never materialised.

281. Frederick Greenwood had suggested Hutton as editor, but the proprietor George Smith preferred to appoint Greenwood himself.

282. Hutton (under his own name) collected seventeen sketches for publication in his *Studies in Parliament* (London, 1866).

283. *Fortnightly Review* 22 (Apr. 1866) 512.

284. A sign of his broader political interest is given by his contribution to the influential *Essays on Reform* (London, 1867): 'The Political Character of the Working Classes' (27–44).

285. W. Watson, *Excursions in Criticism* (London, 1893) 113.

286. Quilter (as n.232) 1123.

287. Charles Pearson in W. Stebbing (ed.), *C.H. Pearson, Memorials by Himself, His Wife, and His Friends* (London, 1900) 107.

288. Stephen Gwynn in *Fortnightly Review* 730 (Oct. 1927) 553.

289. Strachey (as n.243) 224–5.

290. The recollections of four staff members: Strachey (as n. 243), Buchan (*Spec*. 3 Nov. 1928), Beach Thomas (72), and Atkins ('The Spectator', *Nineteenth Century and After* 94 [Oct. 1923] 544–52, at 548).

291. 'Dreamy' occurs more often under Townsend's co-editorship than in the other 156 years of *Spectator* history combined; 'screamy' is thrice as common. It is characteristic both of his directness of phrase and his rough-and-ready affection for his co-editor that Townsend said 'Hutton is as blind as a bat, but has the courage of forty bloodhounds' (reported in, e.g., *Manchester Guardian*, 27 Oct. 1911).

292. E.E. Kellett, 'The Press,' in G.M. Young (ed.), *Early Victorian England: 1830–1865* (Oxford, 1934) II.3–97, at 50.

293. 'The snowstorm', 5 Jan. 1867; 'The gas explosion', 10 July 1880; 'The Calcutta cyclone', 12 Nov. 1864.

294. 'The purpose of 'pain'', 8 Oct. 1887.

295. *The Bookman* 5.28 (Jan. 1894) 110.

296. Townsend himself reworked contributions he had made on the Asian continent in the *Contemporary Review*, *National Review* and *The Spectator*. The resulting volume, *Asia and Europe: Studies presenting the conclusions formed by the author in a long life devoted to the subject of the relations between Asia and Europe* (London, 1901), sold well, passing through three editions before his death.

297. *Pall Mall Gazette*, 11 Sep. 1897.

298. 11 Sep. 1897.

299. *Common Reader* (London, 1925) 269.

300. T.H.S. Escott, *The Bookman* 13.1 (Oct. 1897) 6.

301. C.L. Graves, *Spec*. 3 Nov. 1928.

302. A long-standing (female) colleague recalled that Hutton's sympathies were 'naturally all on the side of woman. He felt the woman's point of view on every subject on which a woman's point of view can be said to exist' (Julia Wedgwood, 'Richard Holt Hutton', *Contemporary Review* 72 [1897] 457–69, at 468).

303. 13 Aug. 1892.

304. Strachey (as n.243) 225.

305. 16 June 1866.

306. E.g., 23 June (Ellen Drewry), 30 June (Frances Power Cobbe) and 14 July ('One of the petitioners') 1866; 23 Feb. ('A countrywoman'), 23 Mar. and 6 Apr. ('L.E.B.', i.e. Lydia Becker) 1867. Opposition to the movement came anonymously from 'An Englishwoman' (23 June, 7 July 1866) and the female 'S.D.C.' (2 Feb., 2 Mar. and 30 Mar. 1867).

307. 'Justice to women' [!], 13 Apr. 1867.

308. J. Grant, *The Newspaper Press; Its Origin, Progress, and Present Position* (London, 1871) III.71.

309. 21 Dec. 1872.

310. 12 Dec. 1872.

311. 7 Dec. 1872.

312. 14 Dec. 1872. *Punch* gleefully reset the letter to verse, whose first stanza read: 'My "dear old friend Homer" is sometimes caught napping; / What wonder if I were to nap now and then? | But observe, in this case 'tis not I that want flapping:– / The Scribe who reported made slip with his pen' (28 Dec. 1872).

313. Diary, 16 Sep. 1872: see H.C.G. Matthew (ed.), *The Gladstone Diaries, Vol. 8: July 1871–Dec. 1874* (Oxford, 1982) 211.

314. 21 Sep. 1872.

315. 5 Aug. 1876.

316. 15 July 1876.

317. For a list of Asquith's varied contributions, see H.C.G. Matthew, 'H.H. Asquith's political journalism', *Bulletin of the Institute of Historical Research* 49 (1976) 146–51, at 150–1.

318. See Appendix III.

319. Letter to Cicely Horner, 25 Sep. 1897, cited by Matthew (as n.317) 149.

320. H.H. Asquith, *Memories and Reflections, 1852–1927* (London, 1928) I.68.

321. J. Earle, *English Prose: Its Elements, History and Usage* (New York, 1891) 350.

322. Asquith (as n.320) I.82.

323. H. Quilter (as n.232) 1123–4. The most notorious feature of Quilter's criticism was his loathing of James McNeill Whistler.

324. Recalled by Alfred Everson, *Spec*. 8 Dec. 1928.

325. The tale is told by Church (as n.230) 199–20. Doubtless many more contributors of distinction could be listed, were any records to survive from before 1874. For a list of subsequent literary editors see Appendix I.

326. Remarks in 'Mr Congreve on the Anonymous', 3 Aug. 1867.

327. Remarks in 'The Prophet', 15 Mar. 1884. For more context on the practice, see R.H. Tener, 'Breaking the Code of Anonymity: The Case of the *Spectator*, 1861–1897', *Yearbook of English Studies* 16 (1986) 63–73.

328. These criticisms were first conveyed to the paper by Archbishop Whateley from private correspondence, and placed amid the book reviews for 24 Mar. 1860. A fuller and correct survey was submitted directly by Sedgwick – still anonymously – to the books pages of 7 Apr. 1860.

329. 'Darwinism and Theology', 7, 14 and 21 Sep. 1872.

330. It is certainly striking that he was the only protestant member of St George's, the Roman

Catholic Club on Savile Row. In 1891, Hutton published his one work of biography: *Cardinal Newman*.

. 7 July 1866; repeated 23 June 1883. On the death of Abraham Lincoln, Townsend used the phrase 'Providence governs, as well as reigns' (29 Apr. 1865).

. 3 Nov. 1888.

. *Fortnightly Review* 68 (1 Aug. 1872) 125–35.

. 6 July 1872. See also 'The efficacy of prayer', 17 Aug. 1872.

. 24 July 1875.

. 4 Sep. 1880.

. Quoted by Jack Atkins, *Spec.* 3 Nov. 1928.

. *Perthshire Advertiser*, 26 Aug. 1875.

. 23 Apr. 1853.

. 2 May 1846. Even on his election as prime minister in 1868, *The Spectator* rubbished him as 'the most incompetent administrator who ever gained power' (30 May 1868).

. 22 May 1886, Gladstone Papers, BL Add. MS 44215/332. One year later, on 26 Feb. 1887, Hutton made the very rare move of allowing his name to appear in *The Spectator* as part of his defence against an unduly critical work on Gladstone.

. 2 July 1886, Gladstone Papers, BL Add. MS 44548/106.

. 21 May 1887: the diary of Gladstone records on 5 May that he wrote letters to both *The Spectator* and Hutton, the latter presumably clarifying what should be done with the former. The choice of 'Y.' may be a gesture towards the initials deployed in the Addison-Steele *Spectator*, of which Gladstone was a devoted reader. Another letter from 'Y.' in support of Gladstone appeared on 30 July 1892. While such anonymity does not tally with the typical behaviour of the Grand Old Man, these were peculiar times.

. Reported in *The Speaker*, 4 Mar. 1893.

. Reported in *The Speaker*, 18 Sep. 1897, 310.

. Advertisement of 1887.

. Aug. 1896–Dec. 1897. Strachey always remained proud that, during such work, he was the first to 'discover' Walter de la Mare.

. Both published on 24 July 1886. Prior to this point Strachey had done some reviewing and, as a teenager, successfully submitted two sonnets for publication (the first was apparently anonymous, the latter appeared above 'St Loe' on 4 Aug. 1877), which he had also sent to Walt Whitman.

. It is telling that Strachey named the first chapter of his autobiography (as n.243), a book that covers some sixty-two years of his life, 'How I came to the *Spectator*.'

. In a letter of 30 Oct. 1890, Hutton confided to a friend, 'I have not much, if any, hope of a permanent recovery, but it is a great comfort to me that my wife takes some sort of satisfaction in playing chess with me every day, though at present she does not communicate with me at all.' (Letter in the author's possession.)

. Reported in *Spec.* 3 Nov. 1928.

. 11 Sep. 1897. Hutton was buried in Twickenham cemetery next to his second wife's plot.

. Bizarrely, all three were submitted in the same year: A.K. Stevens, *Richard Holt Hutton: Theologian and Critic*, Univ. of Michigan,

1949; G.N. Thomas, *Richard Holt Hutton: A Biographical and Critical Study*, Univ. of Illinois, Urbana-Champaign, 1949; R.A. Colby, *The Spectator as a Literary Journal under the Editorship of Richard Holt Hutton*, Univ. of Chicago, IL, 1949.

354. Despite this proviso, one did appear anonymously: *Richard Holt Hutton of 'The Spectator'* (Edinburgh, 1899). The author, John Hogben, was not a close associate of Hutton and the memoir lacks cogency.

355. 11 Sep. 1897.

356. *Sheffield Independent*, 13 Sep. 1897.

357. *The Speaker*, 4 Mar. 1893, 242.

358. H.C. Merivale, *Bar, Stage and Platform* (London, 1902) 32; letter of John Morley to Meredith Townsend, 14 Sep. 1897; W. Watson, cited in J.M. Wilson, *I Was an English Poet: A Critical Biography of Sir William Watson* (London, 1981) 86.

359. 11 Sep. 1897.

360. W. Watson, *Excursions in Criticism* (London, 1893) 119.

361. Pearson (as n.287) 107.

362. A proclamation made in 1893.

363. M. Oliphant, *Annals of a Publishing House: William Blackwood and His Sons* (Edinburgh, 1897) I.513.

364. 3 Mar. 1894.

365. *Saturday Review*, 18 Sep. 1897, 306.

366. *The Academy*, 22 Apr. 1899, 451.

367. *The Queen*, 18 Sep. 1897.

368. Harriet Jay's novel *Through the Stage Door* (1883), reviewed on 15 Dec. 1883 and 2 Feb. 1884.

369. 16 Feb. 1895.

370. Anon., 'To *The Spectator*', *Oxford Magazine*, 20 Feb. 1895.

371. 7 Dec. 1895.

372. 28 Dec. 1895.

373. See further M. Demoor, *Their Fair Share: Women, Power and Criticism in the* Athenaeum (Ashgate, 2000) 10. I am grateful to Dr Demoor for giving me permission to reproduce her image from Strachey's records (see p.72).

374. Cousins and Co. were declared as printers on 13 Aug. 1892, still producing the paper at 18 Exeter St; Wyman and sons took over on 1 Apr. 1893, and transferred printing to 74–6 Great Queen St (near Kingsway) at the start of 1894. John Campbell remained the publisher until 3 Feb. 1894, when he was replaced by John James Baker, likewise based at 1 Wellington St.

375. 12 Apr. 1899.

376. 'Looker on', *Country Life*, 29 July 1899.

377. J. Strachey (ed.), *Lytton Strachey: Spectatorial Essays* (London, 1965) 7.

378. *Pall Mall Gazette*, 11 Sep. 1897.

379. See Strachey (as n.243) 294–8.

380. Strachey had been deeply suspicious of Rhodes since his payment in 1888 of £10,000 to Charles Stewart Parnell in order to advance the lobby for Irish representation at Westminster.

381. 10 Aug. 1901.

382. The correspondence was published on 12 Oct. 1901, despite intense pressure being applied on Strachey during a meeting with Rhodes.

383. *The Spectator* of the years 1912–14 is filled

with withering critiques of governmental incompetence, disingenuous reporting and dishonourable conduct.

384. Recalled by his daughter Amabel Williams-Ellis, *Spec.* 24 Aug. 1962.

385. *Spec.* 3 Nov. 1928.

386. Strachey sold the paper in 1907, having overseen its merger with *Land and Water* in 1905. In 1920 it was incorporated into *The Field*.

387. 3 Dec. 1904.

388. 25 years later, Harold Massingham edited *Dogs, Birds and Others. Natural History Letters from 'The Spectator'* (London, 1921), a collection that Strachey was pleased to introduce.

389. *Record of the Speeches and List of Guests at The Spectator Centenary Dinner* (privately printed, 1928) 10–11.

390. From 'Elegi Musarum', the parody of William Watson in *The Battle of the Bays* (London, 1896).

391. *Punch*, Jan. 1904.

392. Introduction to Massingham (as n.388) 10.

393. *Harper's Magazine* 145, June 1922, 8.

394. 2 June 1903 (Churchill College Cambridge, CHAR 2/11/05).

395. 30 May 1903 (Parliamentary Archives STR/4/10/1).

396. 26 Sep. 1903.

397. Cecilia Townsend, *Spec.* 3 Nov. 1928.

398. Letter of 24 Feb. 1905 (NLS, Rosebery Mss. 10170 ff.16-17).

399. 15 July 1905.

400. Strachey (as n.243) 448.

401. Letter of 12 Feb. 1906, in E.E. Morison (ed.), *The Letters of Theodore Roosevelt* (8 vols, Cambridge, MA) V.151.

402. *Ibid.*, V.785 (letter of 8 Sep. 1907).

403. 15 Sep. 1906.

404. *Ibid.*

405. 31 Mar. 1906.

406. 21 July 1906.

407. 15 Sep. 1906.

408. 3 Feb. 1912.

409. Reported 15 Sep. 1906.

410. 5 Jan. 1907.

411. Letter to Ernest Dykes, 27 June 1911 (Parliamentary Archives STR/11/4/26).

412. Cited in *Spec.* 20 June 1908.

413. Reported in *The Times*, 24 Oct. 1910.

414. A fuller transcription of the speech was sent to *The Spectator* by an audience member, and published in the letters pages for 29 Oct. 1910.

415. *Ibid.*

416. 26 Oct. 1910 (Parliamentary Archives STR/33/1/58).

417. *Ibid.* Strachey later observed in private correspondence, 'It is wonderful what a large number of working-class readers we have. You would think it impossible that the working man would waste his sixpence in this way, but you see, nearly all the free libraries take the *Spectator*, and it gets read there on a very wide scale.' Letter to Theresa, Lady Thornberry, 13 Dec. 1918 (Public Record Office of Northern Ireland, Belfast, Thornberry Papers, D2846/1/10/8).

418. 24 May 1935. Perhaps the Welsh Wizard had forgotten that he had been called in the previous decade a 'species of political Vampire' (11 Mar.

1922).

419. J. Strachey (ed.), *Lytton Strachey: Spectatorial Essays* (London, 1965) 7.

420. *Ibid.*, 9.

421. A.G. Gardiner, *Pillars of Society* (London, 1913) 145.

422. Eric Sutton in *Week-End Review*, 1 Nov. 1930, 629.

423. 'Thoughts on morals,' *English Review* 8 (June 1911) 434–43.

424. 8 July 1911.

425. 28 Oct. 1911.

426. Cecilia Townsend, *Spec.* 3 Nov. 1928.

427. C.L. Graves, Ibid.

428. See esp. articles for 17 Feb. and 11 May 1912, along with copious correspondence. A collection of these contributions was soon published: *White Slave Traffic* (London, 1912).

429. Review, *The Sociological Review* 2.2 (Apr. 1909) 202.

430. By the end of his term in office, he was dismissed as a 'national ass' (16 Sep. 1916). For a detailed and lucid survey of Strachey's political outlook, see A.J.L. Morris, *A Study of John St Loe Strachey's Editorship of* The Spectator *1901–1914* (PhD thesis, Cambridge, 1986). In the absence of *Spectator* records, Appendix B (pp. [230–49]) provides a valuable record of several hundreds of leaders written by Strachey in these years.

431. 2 Aug. 1913.

432. 19 July 1913.

433. See his letter of 23 May 1914.

434. Williams-Ellis's motivations were not entirely architectural. As his much younger friend Gavin Stamp later recalled (*Spec.* 1 Sep. 1984), 'the young Clough was there at the meeting, had spotted Amabel and, "because I had immediately resolved that I must somehow contrive to meet and see more of this girl at whatever cost, I stood up and accepted her father's challenge directly it was formally announced."'

435. 1 Aug. 1914.

436. 8 Aug. 1914.

437. These were published in five instalments from 24 July to 21 Aug. 1915, before being issued in pamphlet form.

438. 19 Sep. 1914.

439. Roy Martin, of the *Associated Press*.

440. 23 Jan. 1915.

441. 30 Jan. 1915.

442. Hankey, then aged thirty-one, had read Theology at Corpus Christi, Oxford, and entered missionary work, first at Bermondsey, then in Australia.

443. 11 Dec. 1915.

444. 21 Oct. 1916.

445. Hardy's 'In Time of Slaughter' appeared on 12 Aug. 1916, Sassoon's 'Conscripts' on 17 Feb. 1917, and 'The Hawthorn Tree' on 27 Oct. 1917.

446. 23 and 30 Dec. 1916.

447. Strachey (as n.243) 460–1.

448. Letter to Joseph Fells of 30 July 1912 (Parliamentary Archives STR/17/3/11).

449. Gardiner (as n.421) 144. Five years Strachey's junior, he edited the *Daily News* from 1902 to 1919.

450. The column first appeared on 13 Mar. 1920, and above his signature on 4 June 1921.

451. 28 Nov. 1931.

452. 28 Feb. 1920.

453. 21 Oct. 1922.

454. 2 Dec. 1922.

455. Promotional pamphlet, 1924.

456. 22 June 1901; other letters cover the influence of Shakespeare (2 July 1898) and the First and Second Army Corps (5 Oct. 1901). For Hardy, see his poem 'After the visit' (13 Aug. 1910): although it was not clear at the time, these verses announced his passion for the novelist Florence Dugdale, whom he married after the death of his first wife Emma. The last piece published before Conrad's death headed up the article 'Is Europe Dead?' (31 May 1924), cited with permission from a letter to Strachey.

457. 4 May 1901; 4 July, 18 July and 1 Aug. 1903. On 26 Oct. 1912, Conan Doyle wrote in to clarify his belief in the innocence of Oscar Slater, convicted of murder in 1908.

458. Although Eliot's poem was later renamed 'Le Spectateur', he wrote in later life that he 'had no particular grievance against Mr. Strachey… 'directeur' and 'spectateur' happen to rhyme, that is about all there is in it' (letter to Amar Bhattacharyya, 22 June 1964).

459. 8 July 1922: the review is well worth reading in full, as Buchan defends a middle ground on tradition and innovation in poetry.

460. See, for instance, Pound's review of Harold Monro's collected poems (23 June 1933) and Eliot's article 'What does the Church stand for?' (19 Oct. 1934).

461. 'Literary Letter', *The Sphere*, 11 Nov. 1922.

462. 5 Jan. 1924.

463. *Ibid.*

464. 9 Oct. 1926.

465. In April 1924, Strachey took the opportunity, while touring Italy with his wife, of meeting Mussolini at the Chigi Palace in Rome, where they had 'an instructive and illuminating conversation', albeit via an interpreter. Strachey pressed the suggestion that Britain should enter into a common Mediterranean policy with Italy and Spain. It is unclear how amused the occupants of Chatsworth were at Strachey's recollection that Mussolini's manner reminded him of the Duke of Devonshire.

466. 27 Apr., 4 May, 11 May, 18 May 1923.

467. Ivor Montague, cited by R. Sitton, *Lady in the Dark: Iris Barry and the Art of Film* (New York, 2014) 84.

468. Quoted by Sitton (prev. n.) 85.

469. *Ibid.*, 91.

470. Strachey (as n.243) 321.

471. *The Forum* 72 (1924) 144.

472. Duff Hart-Davis, *Peter Fleming: A Biography* (London, 1987) 73.

473. 3 Sep., p.4. Previous instances commemorated King George IV (issues of 26 June to 24 July 1830), William IV (24 June to 8 July 1837), Prince Augustus Frederick, Duke of Sussex (22 Apr. 1843), Adelaide, Queen Consort (8 and 15 Dec. 1849), Prince Adolphus, Duke of Cambridge (13 July 1850), Arthur Wellesley, Duke of Wellington (18 Sep. and 20 Nov. 1852), Albert, Prince Consort (21 Dec. 1861), Victoria (26 Jan. and 2 Feb. 1901), President William McKinley (21 Sep. 1901), Edward VII (14 and 21 May 1910) and George V (24 Jan. 1936).

474. Beach Thomas, 96.

475. Asquith (as n.320) I.69.

476. *Times*, 10 Dec. 1925.

477. *Times*, 3 Dec. 1925.

478. 19 Dec. 1925.

479. Edward Hodgkin, *Spec.* 6 Jan. 1996.

480. 27 Dec. 1924.

481. 7 Feb. 1925.

482. The prize, proposed by the bookseller Gabriel Wells, was announced on 25 July 1925. The winning essays, restricted to a 1,000-word limit and chosen from a field of 800, came from Euphemia Alexander (who had recently studied the topic for her MA at Edinburgh) and W. Howard Hazell (a big beast of the printing world).

483. 27 Dec. 1930. Whether by chance or not, the preceding article described *The Spectator*'s oldest reader, born in 1820 and still being read the paper at 110.

484. Historical serialisations of this kind continued until the early 1930s.

485. 1 Oct. 1926 (Churchill College Cambridge CHAR/2/147/160). In connection with the General Strike, Atkins wrote, 'I feel more and more that Unionists have got to concentrate on this industrial peace if we are not to let in the Socialists. This involves many things which we used not to trouble very much about in times past.' A photograph from 1900 of the war correspondent team for the second Boer War survives, in which Atkins stands directly behind Churchill.

486. Atkins strangely wrote in later life: 'I was never Editor of *The Spectator*, though I am amused occasionally by being informed that I was' (*Incidents and Reflections* [London, 1947] 212). And yet *The Times* announced Atkins' appointment as editor on 3 Dec. 1925 (repeated elsewhere in the press), and *The Spectator* itself announced his resignation from that post on 2 Oct. 1926 (also reported in *The Times* of the same date).

487. Reported in *Spec.* 19 Mar. 1954.

488. W.A. Briggs (ed.), *Great Poems of the English Language* (London, 1928): the title page bears the otherwise undiscussed comment 'Presented by *The Spectator*'.

489. Cited in *Record of the Speeches and List of Guests at The Spectator Centenary Dinner* (as n.386). Elsewhere in his speech Baldwin revealed that the only letter to the press printed in his name appeared in *The Spectator*; its subject, left unmentioned, was in fact literary, tracing a feature of Spenser's poetry back to Plato and Arrian (8 Feb. 1902). It is true that Baldwin was behind the letter famously printed in *The Times* on 24 June 1919, in which he pledged to hand over a fifth of his income to the Chancellor of the Exchequer, encouraging others to do the same; however, he was there disguised by the initials 'F.S.T.', which took some time to be resolved as the 'Financial Secretary to the Treasury' – thus pointing squarely in his direction.

490. *The Sphere*, 10 Nov. 1928. The two earliest citations appear among many at the close of the pamphlet (prev. n.).

491. *Guardian*, 30 Oct. 1928.

492. *Times*, Oct. 1928.

493. The new committee was announced in *The Times* for 14 June 1928; details of its principles were recalled by Victor Mishcon, a board member, in *The Times* for 5 Nov. 1963. Several terms were

taken over *verbatim* from the trust of *The Times*, established in 1924.

494. *Guardian*, 8 July 1928.

495. 8 Dec. 1928.

496. 5 Jan. 1929.

497. 16 Feb. 1929.

498. Though claiming to be the offspring of King Ludwig of Bavaria and the Spanish dancer Lola Montez, the reality of Laura Jackson (a.k.a. Mrs Horos, Ellora, Madame Helena, Viva Ananda, Diss Debar, Claudia D'Arvie, Sister Mary, Editha Gilbert, Blanche Solomons and 'The Swami') was rather less exotic: a Kentucky-born fraudster who swindled single women out of their money before trapping them in the sex trade. She spent seven years in Pentonville.

499. Peter Fleming, *Gower Street Poltergeist* (London, 1958) 29. Karl Miller later described these as 'papier-mâché cells set in a kind of fuselage that poked out at the back' (*Spec.* 9 July 1988).

500. 23 Nov. 1929.

501. 11 Jan. 1930.

502. *Ibid*.

503. 15 Nov. 1930, 13 Dec. 1930, 17 Jan. 1931.

504. 9 Oct., 23 Oct., 6 Nov. 1936. The series was published in book form the following year.

505. 2 May 1931.

506. 12 Sep. 1931.

507. 24 Oct. 1931.

508. 6 Mar. 1942. Gandhi had also been the subject of a short piece by the Indian novelist R.K. Narayan ('Gandhi's Appeal', 11 Sep. 1936).

509. The weekly series ran from 14 Feb. to 4 Apr. 1931.

510. J.H. Reid, *Award-Winning Films of the 1930s* (Morrisville, NC) 119.

511. It was characteristic of 'YB' to launch a competition for the best philosophy of life that could be written on a postcard. The winner from a thousand entries used only eight words: 'Love, trust, dare, and go on doing it' (E. Dalzell, 2 July 1927). For a survey of *The Spectator*'s response to modernism in 1925–32, see C. Dawkins, *Modernism in Mainstream Magazines* (DPhil, Oxford, 2015) 116–49.

512. Quoted in E. Wrench, *Francis Yeats-Brown: 1886–1944* (London, 1948) 132.

513. 12 Mar. 1927.

514. 'What is Wrong with England?', 10 Oct. 1925; letter, 17 Oct. 1925.

515. H.W. Harris, *Life So Far* (London, 1954) 241.

516. Citations from a newspaper advertisement run throughout 1933–6.

517. *Spec.* 6 Jan. 1996.

518. 30 Jan. 1932.

519. 24 Jan. 1925.

520. 24 Sep. 1932.

521. 8 Oct. 1932.

522. His book *Modernism and Romance* appeared in 1908.

523. 'Aunt Eudora and the Poets', 31 Jan. 1936. Subsequent contributions came on 14 Feb., 28 Feb. and 19 June 1936.

524. 19 June 1936.

525. *Hansard*, 17 Nov. 1936.

526. '"The Spectator" and its readers', 12 Jan. 1934.

527. 3 Mar. 1933.

528. 14 Apr. 1933.

529. 25 May 1934.

530. 19 Jan. 1934.

531. 24 July 1936.

532. *Spec.* 26 Dec. 1952.

533. 3 Dec. 1943.

534. 5 Sep. 1947.

535. Greene began reviewing novels in Jan. 1932; his first article, on the late Charles Seitz, appeared the following year ('Death in the Cotswolds', 24 Feb. 1933). One of his most interesting pieces was a report on the atmosphere in Paris in the wake of the Stavisky Affair and the riots of 6 Jan. 1934 ('Strike in Paris', 16 Feb. 1934).

536. Reviews of *The Black Room* (20 Sep. 1935), *Destry Rides Again* (16 Feb. 1940) and *Secret Agent* (15 May 1936).

537. His columns were later published as *The Pleasure Dome: The Collected Film Criticism 1935–40 of Graham Greene* (London, 1972).

538. 19 Nov. 1937.

539. A smaller change, of altering article titles to block capitals, had already been made in March 1934.

540. 12 Feb. 1937.

541. From 7 June 1940, the topic of the first leading article was also advertised in a prominent position with the appearance of a second headline in the top right of the first page: the first such was 'Sequel to Disaster', in the wake of Dunkirk. That year the printers changed from Speaight & Sons to the St Clements Press, on Portugal St off Kingsway.

542. These columns appeared on 16 Aug. and 1 Nov. 1935, 24 Apr. and 13 Nov. 1936, and 12 Mar. and 29 Oct. 1937.

543. 12 and 19 Feb. 1937.

544. 19 Aug. 1938.

545. 18 Nov. 1938.

546. Harris (as n.515) 252.

547. 24 Nov. 1939.

548. *Ibid*. 242.

549. 11 Oct. 1940.

550. 11 Dec. 1942; 21 Mar. 1941; 20 Nov. 1942.

551. Janus, 12 Jan. 1945 (appeal first announced on 10 Nov. 1944).

552. 24 Aug. 1945. The inscription reads: 'Towards the cost of the altar, the editor of *The Spectator* raised the sum of £2,000 as a memorial to those who fought in the Battle of Malta 1940–1943.' The Archbishop of Canterbury, Geoffrey Fisher, visited the cathedral in Dec. 1946 to dedicate the shrine.

553. *Daily Mail*, 27 Feb. 1947.

554. See, for instance, Janus's thoughts of 7 Oct. 1949.

555. *Spec.* 6 Jan. 1996.

556. As per the announcement of 7 Sep. 1951, which blamed the increase particularly on the sharp rise in paper prices.

557. 15 Sep. 1950.

558. 26 Dec. 1952.

559. *Ibid*.

560. The printers had moved to Clerkenwell Green at the start of 1952, to the Steward St premises of George Berridge and Co.

561. *The Living Gide* (6 Apr. 1951), a translation of Sartre's *Gide vivant* that had appeared in France just a few weeks earlier. It is unclear how Sartre's involvement was secured.

562. Harris (as n.515) 232.

563. *Ibid*. Although evidently a careful reader of *The Spectator*, Eden – unusually among twentieth-century prime ministers – never wrote for the paper (cf. Appendix III).

564. *Times*, 13 Jan. 1955.

565. 14 Jan. 1955.

566. 10 Apr. 1953.

567. Alan Brien, *Spec.* 23 Sep. 1978.

568. Courtauld, 22.

569. *Ibid*.

570. J.D. Scott, reminiscing in *Spec.* 16 Apr. 1977.

571. 2 Oct. 1953.

572. 11 Mar. 1955.

573. First published in *Spec.* 24 Mar. 1950.

574. 16 Apr. 1977.

575. 1 Oct. 1954.

576. 8 Oct. 1954.

577. 18 Oct. 1954: see Z. Leader (ed.), *The Letters of Kingsley Amis* (London, 2000) 405. A month earlier, Amis (under the pseudonym 'Anselm Chilworth') had in fact mocked the growing trend of poetry in the Lallans dialect, by positing a 'Cockney Renaissance', which ended with a spoof reworking by 'Helfrid Uggins' of Baudelaire's *L'Albatross* into cockney stanzas – or 'The Helbatrawss, aht er Charley Bordilairs parleyvoo' (27 Aug. 1954). A mock Cockney-to-English glossary followed – as did a competition six weeks later for readers to submit their own Cockney renderings of Burns, Yeats and Eliot (15 Oct. 1954).

578. For instance, 'Wires', 2 Oct. 1953; 'Skin' and 'Age', 2 July 1954; 'Times, places, loved ones', 7 Jan. 1955; 'Church going', 18 Nov. 1955, this last under the tenure of the next editor, after the manuscript went astray for sixteen months.

579. Mallalieu had written occasionally on sports and games since the 1940s; sporadic contributions to this new column came from Bernard Darwin, C.B. Fry, John Arlott, Denis Brogan and Elizabeth Coxhead.

580. 6 Aug. 1954.

581. 20 Nov. 1953.

582. Cited by Courtauld, 29.

583. Iain Macleod (after Pooh-Bah), reported by Courtauld, 242.

584. A digest of the week's news followed the opening leader: it gained the heading 'News Summary' on 1 Apr. 1955, before settling with 'Portrait of the Week' from 29 Apr. The latter title still endures.

585. 7 Jan. 1955.

586. *Guardian*, 4 Nov. 1954.

587. 'A Special Correspondent' on 'The Political and Literary Weeklies', *Birmingham Daily Post*, 2 Dec. 1954.

588. 23 Sep. 1955.

589. 23 Dec. 1955.

590. 30 Dec. 1955. Four other pieces by Pepper exist: 6 Nov. 1953 (in praise of smog), 18 Nov. 1955 (against gourmet dining), 23 Dec. 1955 (a fake book review), and 22 Mar. 1963 (on the dispute between *Private Eye* and Randolph Churchill).

591. In 1987, 1988, 1991, 1992, 1994 and 1997–2005 a *Spectator Cartoon Book* appeared under Heath's editorship. In 2017, an Australian anthology of 135 Heath cartoons was published under the title of *The Battle for Britain*.

592. Cited by Courtauld, 242.

593. Simon Hoggart, *Guardian*, 22 Oct. 2004.

594. *The Listener*, 26 Sep. 1957.
595. 15 July 1955.
596. W. James, 2 July 1955.
597. *The Case of Timothy Evans: An Appeal to Reason* (London, 1956).
598. For a detailed survey of *The Spectator*'s support of this cause, see 'Persistent buggers: how *The Spectator* fought to decriminalise homosexuality', *Coffee House*, 27 July 2017, abridged in the magazine for 29 July 2017.
599. 14 Jan. 1955.
600. 1 Nov. 1953.
601. 25 Mar. 1952.
602. 25 Nov. 1955.
603. Leading article, 6 Sep. 1957.
604. 3 June 1960.
605. 12 Dec. 1958. The letter continued, however, to criticise *The Spectator*'s recent remarks in support of forceful police action against prostitutes.
606. 24 June 1955. A sporadic set of Scottish and Irish numbers had been introduced under the editorship of Wrench, first on 9 June 1928.
607. 19 Apr. 2008.
608. Since Feb. 1951, the rear pages (particularly the finance section) had been three-columned.
609. Murdoch reviewed Simone Weil (2 Nov. 1956) and French philosophy (12 July 1957); Leigh Fermor two translations of Colette (26 July 1957).
610. Ayer reviewed works on Wittgenstein (8 Mar.) and Russell (31 May 1957), Ryle the criteria of reasoning (23 Aug. 1957).
611. 'Divine Intervention', 5 Oct. 1956.
612. 'Meeting', 19 July; 'Parting' (later called 'September'), 2 Aug.; 'Secretary', 30 Aug.; 'Two Wise Generals', 6 Sep. 1957.
613. 18 Oct. 1957.
614. 1 Mar. 1957.
615. *Spec.* 20 Mar. 1999.
616. 30 Oct. 1959.
617. *Downstart: The Autobiography of Brian Inglis* (London, 1990) chs 16–22.
618. 20 Nov. 1959.
619. 'Crag Jack's Apostasy' and 'The Good Life', 4 July; 'The Retired Colonel', 22 Aug.; 'Things Present', 3 Oct.; 'Pennines in April', 26 Dec. 1958; 'Wilfred Owen's Photographs', 2 Jan. 1959; 'May Day on Holderness', 22 Jan. 1960; 'Her Husband', 24 Mar. 1961. Plath's 'The Companionable Ills' and 'Main Street at Midnight' appeared on 30 Jan. and 13 Feb. 1959.
620. *Times* advertisement, 18 Jan. 1960.
621. *Ibid.*
622. 13 Nov. 1959, covering pp.655–67.
623. 26 June 1959.
624. 2 Oct. 1959.
625. *Ibid.*
626. The highlights were published as a book in 1961, illustrated by *The Spectator*'s own Quentin Blake.
627. 15 July to 19 Aug. 1960.
628. 23 Sep. 1960.
629. 1 July and 30 Dec. 1960; 6 Jan., 17 Feb. and 15 June 1961.
630. Levin reported about the trial on 4 Nov. 1960, characteristically choosing to open with the quotation 'Shit and arse'.
631. 28 Apr. 1961.
632. Cited by Courtauld, 73.

633. *Times*, 2 Nov. 1961.
634. Inglis (as n.617), 253.
635. *Times*, 2 Nov. 1961.
636. Brian Inglis, *Spec.* 25 Mar. 1989.
637. 9 and 16 Mar. 1962.
638. 1 June 1962.
639. 23 Nov. 1962.
640. 'Politics and Sex', 3 May 1963.
641. Reported in *The Times* and elsewhere on 2 Nov. 1963.
642. *Ibid.*
643. *Ibid.*
644. 29 Nov. 1963.
645. The advertisement appeared during ATV's Sunday programme *Adult Education*, which was broadcast in London, the Midlands, Lancashire and Yorkshire. It was made by the advertising company Aspect, which was run under the aegis of *The Spectator*.
646. John Thompson's memorial notice, *Spec.* 25 July 1970.
647. The editorial secretary Joan Baylis, cited by Courtauld, 100.
648. Cited by Courtauld, 103.
649. 5 June 1964.
650. Crossword no. 1094 appeared on 17 June 1960, and was not followed by no. 1095 until 6 Dec. 1963.
651. R.S. Churchill, *The Fight for the Tory Leadership* (London, 1964).
652. Boris Johnson, *175th Anniversary Issue* (2003) 3.
653. The exact figure is unknown, but it did not exceed 69,000. Much of the readership came from the piece being syndicated elsewhere.
654. 24 Jan. 1964.
655. 18 Jan. 1964.
656. 2, 9 and 16 Oct. 1964; the comment had been made by Conquest in the issue before Macleod's arrival (29 Nov. 1963).
657. 29 Jan. 1965.
658. *Guardian*, 25 Sep. 1964.
659. *Times*, 8 Mar. 1961.
660. Thompson's obituary notice, *Spec.* 25 July 1970.
661. *Spec.* 20 Mar. 1999.
662. *The View From No. 11: Memories of a Tory Radical* (London, 1992) 892.
663. 22 Dec. 1967.
664. 31 May and 7 June 1968: the piece was well worthy of reproduction by *The Spectator* fifty years later, on 5 May 2018.
665. *Times*, 4 Apr. 1967.
666. *Times*, 12 Apr. 1967.
667. Third leader, 14 Apr. 1967.
668. Recalled by Charles Moore in the *175th Anniversary Issue* (2003) 12.
669. 23 Aug. 1975.
670. *Will This Do? An Autobiography* (London, 1991) 191.
671. Fildes was, however, absent from *The Spectator* between 1969 and 1984.
672. 26 Apr. 1968.
673. Kenneth Allsop, in his review of George Thayer's *The Farther Shores of Politics*, reported seeing a placard at the Dirty Speech Movement, which simply read 'FUCK' (10 May 1968). 'Cunt' followed, thus uncensored, the following year (Anthony Burgess, 21 June 1969).
674. 15 Nov. 1968.

675. 25 Apr. 1970.
676. 20 Feb. 1971.
677. *Times*, 9 Mar. 1970.
678. 21 Mar. 1970.
679. 11 Mar. 1970.
680. 21 Mar. 1970.
681. 13 Mar. 1971.
682. 11 June 1988 (Ali) and 10 June 2006 (Straw).
683. The first such appeared on 7 June 1969, and continued until the issue of 19 Sep. 1970.
684. 15 Feb. 1970.
685. *Another Voice: An Alternative Anatomy o, Britain* (London, 1986) 11.
686. Sarah Johnson, *Standpoint*, Jan/Feb. 2014.
687. When, in an early case of no-platforming, the University of Dundee cancelled Enoch Powell': visit to a student society, it was characteristic of the magazine to argue the case for freedom of speec (Robert Conquest, 18 Nov. 1972).
688. 21 Nov. to 26 Dec. 1970.
689. The first appeared, appropriately enough, in the first issue of the new year, 2 Jan. 1971.
690. 23 Oct. 1971.
691. It last appeared in the issue for 18 Mar. 1972 ironically, it was replaced from the following wee by an advert for what would appear in the next issu of *The Spectator*.
692. 25 Mar. 1972.
693. Cited in Thomas Teodorczuk, *Ultimat Vindication: The Spectator and Europe, 1966–7* (Bruges Group 41, London) 27. This pamphl carefully chronicles *The Spectator*'s evolvin attitude to Europe over the crucial decade of 196 to 1975.
694. *Ibid.*
695. 20 Feb. 1971.
696. 29 May 1971.
697. 29 July 1972; 22 Sep. 1973; 27 July 1973.
698. 21 Aug. 1971.
699. Letters of 28 Aug., 4 Sep. and 11 Sep. 1971.
700. 20 Feb. 1971.
701. 15 May 1971.
702. The first winner, announced on 2 Dec. 1972, w the future futurist critic Jon Margolis, writing '1984'.
703. The first winners were announced on 16 Ju 1973.
704. Nevertheless, the cover leader ran from 20 Ja 1973 to 21 June 1975.
705. Duncan Fallowell, pers. comm.
706. Repeated in *Spec.* 23 Sep. 1978, as part o recantation.
707. 11 Oct. 1970.
708. Courtauld, 154.
709. Teodorczuk (as n.693) 35.
710. *Irish Times*, 28 Jan. 1978.
711. 8 July 1972; cont. 15 July 1972.
712. 16 Nov. 1974.
713. 19 Oct. 1974.
714. 28 Feb. 1974.
715. 12 Oct. 1974.
716. 5 Apr. 1975. The context was at least reflexi Mosley reviewed Robert Sidelsky's 1975 biograp of his own life.
717. 18 Jan. 1975.
718. 8 Mar. 1975.
719. *Ibid.*

720. 7 June 1975.
721. For Creighton was certainly 'Editor'; and Moran, the co-owner in 1859–61, was pulling strings behind the scenes as a co-editor.
722. 23 Aug. 1975.
723. Teodorczuk (as n.693) 43.
724. 9 Aug. 1975.
725. 23 Aug. 1975.
726. *Ibid.*
727. 26 Apr. 1957.
728. Iain Hamilton, quoted by Courtauld, 242.
729. Nigel Lawson, *Spec.* 20 Mar. 1999.
730. The index for Vol. 138 (Jan.–June 1927) was the first to be sold separately, at 1s.
731. *Spec.* 1 Apr. 1995.
732. J. Lumley (ed.), *Peacocks and Commas: The Best of the* Spectator *Competitions* (1983). The title came from Competition no. 915, set on 12 June 1976: to complete a poem beginning 'It looks like a series of Peacocks and Commas'.
733. Christopher Howse, pers. comm.
734. 10 July 1953.
735. Charles Moore, *Spec.* 24 Mar. 1984.
736. After Seaton's death, the index to *The Spectator* continued to be produced until June 1998 by Jenny Naipaul, Seaton's successor as *Spectator* librarian.
737. 24 Jan. 1976.
738. A letter of Feb. 1979, cited by Courtauld, 190–1.
739. 12 May 1979.
740. 23 Aug. 1975.
741. Courtauld, 167.
742. 10 Jan. 1976, following on from the positive reception of a piece on Pinochet the previous week.
743. His first 'Postscript' appeared on 17 Nov. 1979, after John Mortimer had produced a single column the week before. It ran until 5 Mar. 1983, before P.J. Kavanagh took over the column, channelling the pleasures of his enviable existence in Gloucestershire. These gentle insights enlivened the magazine for three years, after which Kavanagh retreated to the back-benches of book reviewing.
744. 7 and 14 June 1980.
745. 7 Feb. 1976. Among the judges were the Directors of the Victoria and Albert and of Birmingham's Barber Institute of Fine Arts, and the artist Edward Lucie-Smith. The prize money had been donated by the American art collector Edward Goodstein.
746. P. Marnham (ed.), *Night Thoughts: The Spectator Bedside Book* (London, 1983) 8–9.
747. In a review of Peter Townsend's autobiography ('The Princess and the Peabrain', 18 Feb 1978).
748. 16 and 30 Oct. 1976.
749. The first column, on the Parisian club scene, appeared under the heading of 'Night Life' on 15 Oct. 1977; the 'High Life' column began on 12 Nov.
750. takimag.com, 29 Dec. 2011.
751. Taki was jailed in HMS Pentonville from 14 Dec. 1984 to 28 Feb. 1985, serving eleven weeks of a four-month term. His column did not appear in issues from 5 Jan. to 2 Mar. 1985. The suggestion of swapping columns was first made in a reader's letter, of 30 June 1979.
752. *Times*, 27 Apr. 1997.
753. The first 'Low Life' appeared on 12 Aug. 1978.
754. 12 May 1990.
755. J. Bernard in *High Life, Low Life* (London, 1981) 136.
756. See p.184.
757. The magazine at its current premises, Old Queen Street in Westminster, continues this tradition by its refreshingly enthusiastic patronage of The Two Chairmen.
758. Leader (as n.577) 828.
759. *Times*, 13 Sep. 2000.
760. Leader, 22 Sep. 1978.
761. 23 Sep. 1978.
762. *Ibid.*
763. *Ibid.*
764. Presumably by an unfortunate accident, the advertisement was mistyped as '150 years old is…', which required coy correction in the following week's *Spectator.*
765. Harry Mount, *Sunday Telegraph*, 29 Jan. 2017.
766. 7 Nov. 1981.
767. 24 Mar. 1984.
768. 20 Mar. 1999.
769. 19 Nov. 1979.
770. The first such summary appeared, without comment, on 13 June 1981; by 3 Oct. it was moved as the opening piece on p.3. Waugh had recently written a day-by-day account of the year in 1980, which he later published as *Auberon Waugh's Yearbook 1980* (London, 1981).
771. *Times*, 20 Mar. 1981.
772. Interview, bqlive.co.uk, 25 Sep. 2012.
773. 28 Mar. 1981.
774. 16 Jan. 1982.
775. 13 June 1981.
776. 20 June 1981.
777. 9 Oct. 1982.
778. 8 May 1982.
779. 12 May 1982: see Leader (as n.577) 945–6. The episode is recorded by Mount, *Cold Cream* (London, 2008) 291–3.
780. *Mirror*, 8 May 1982.
781. Charles Moore, pers. comm.
782. This had previously hung on Cluff's own walls. But everyone is now a winner, as in 2012 the painting was gifted to the (Irish) public as part of a collection owned by Allied Irish Banks.
783. *Guardian*, 27 Oct. 2004.
784. Andrew Gimson, *Spec.* 13 June 1987. A decade later came the unknowing remark, 'It is hard to imagine that the *Spectator* ever hands out promotional T-shirts. It probably dispenses free bonnets, the better that bees might be maintained.' (Ian Bell, *Herald*, 20 Nov. 1993.)
785. 11 June 1983.
786. So Bevis Hillier, *Spec.* 19 May 2010.
787. Mark Amory, *Spec.* 20 Sep. 2014.
788. Dominic Lawson, *Times*, 15 Mar. 1995.
789. *Ibid.*
790. Simon Courtauld, *Spec.* 4 Feb. 2017.
791. Charles Moore, *Spec.* 4 Feb. 2017.
792. 'Mr Prior in Ulster', 15 May 1982.
793. *Times*, 7 Feb. 1984.
794. Charles Moore, *175th Anniversary Issue* (2003) 10.
795. 31 Mar. 1984: 'Portrait of the Week' was restored to p.3.
796. *Ibid.*
797. The last 'Notes' appeared on 20 Apr. 1985; the leading article subsequently evolved towards one sustained article.
798. *Spec.* 7 Apr. 1990.
799. *Pall Mall Gazette* 9 (1896) 647.
800. 31 July 1959; later used on 16 June 1961.
801. 18 May 1984.
802. 23 Dec. 1989.
803. As n.670, 264.
804. S. Lowry (ed.), *The Young Fogey Handbook* (London, 1985) 10–11.
805. 9 Feb. 1985 – and raised at various points in the magazine in the following months.
806. 22 Aug. 1987.
807. 'Ten days that changed the world', 2 Dec. 1989. The piece was reproduced in full by Courtauld, 220–4.
808. Garton Ash gave a lively retrospective on the period in *Spec.* 4 Nov. 2009.
809. 6 Oct. 1984.
810. 23 Feb. 1985. I have failed to trace the subsequent career of Miss Gorman.
811. 9 May 1987.
812. 16 Apr. 1988; Alice Pitman.
813. A. Cluff, *Unsung Heroes* (privately printed, 2018) 60.
814. *Guardian*, 23 Jan. 1985.
815. 7 Apr. 1990.
816. 27 Apr. 1985.
817. 1 July 1985.
818. 4 May 1985.
819. *Ibid.*
820. His comments reveal that this must have been the issue for 9 June 1984.
821. 23 Feb. 1985.
822. 4 May 1985.
823. 5 Oct. 1985, on Susan Kay's Elizabethan novel *Legacy.*
824. *Spec.* 20 Sep. 2014; Jenkins on croquet can be found on 13 Apr. 1991.
825. *Evening Standard*, 21 Apr. 1999.
826. *Ibid.*
827. 19 Oct. 1985.
828. 15 Oct. 1988; on 29 Oct., 'Wallace Arnold' (Craig Brown), an imagined *Spectator*-reader but across-the-board bore, revealed some of the contents of 'Sod the Public III'. Among its barbs was: 'MIRRORS: Used to be perfectly all right, showing a perfectly decent and engaging young man. Now only show grumpy buffoons. Yet another example of the slovenly, contemptuous attitude for the needs of those it serves.'
829. 6 July 1991.
830. Peter Jones, *Times*, 5 June 1986. It was not without good reason that four anthologies of Ellis's *Home Life* were published from the magazine.
831. 24 Jan. 1987.
832. 7 Mar. 1987.
833. *Sunday Times*, 20 Aug. 1989.
834. *175th Anniversary Issue* (2003) 12.
835. *Guardian*, 7 Apr. 1988.
836. Sub-leader, 9 Apr. 1988.
837. 30 Jan. 1988.
838. 15 Mar. 1986.
839. 9 Apr. 1988.
840. 2 June 1984.
841. 2 Aug. 1986.
842. 9 Aug. 1986.
843. 25 Apr. 1987.
844. 27 May 1989.

845. 8 July 1989.

846. *Ibid.*

847. 14 Oct. 1989. Mrs Reddich was right to recall *The Spectator*'s predilection for 'judgement'. In 1931, a correspondent fired off a complaint to the paper about its breach of orthographic good sense: 'I was much surprised to see … that the word "judgment", which appeared several times in the article, was spelt "judgement". In view of your punctilious regard for spelling and grammar and the correctness of most things generally, I am rather surprised to see this glaring error in a paper of your standing, and merely desire to draw your attention to the same' (7 Nov. 1931). Fourteen months later, another purist wrote: 'I read the *Spectator* regularly every week, but I really think that as a leader of thought you should learn to spell correctly! In nearly every recent issue the word judgment is mis-spelt by putting an 'e' in the middle. Please correct in future' (6 Jan. 1933). (Letters followed next week politely noting that 'mis-spelt' had been misspelled.) Harris, of course, was not minded to let the matter lie: years later, his Janus column lamented the myriad letters which asked him 'to affix a special damn to "judgement", so spelled… Not for a moment. Judge + ment makes judgement, as atone + ment makes atonement. The O.E.D. gives both forms, "judgement" first' (27 Feb. 1942). This was an ill-chosen hill on which to die.

848. 13 Jan. 1990.

849. 20 Jan. 1990.

850. 24 May 1989.

851. *Ibid.*

852. Cited in *Spec.* 28 Oct. 1995.

853. *Times*, 15 Mar. 1995.

854. 15 Sep. 1989; 10 Mar. 1990.

855. 11 Apr. 1992 (but already available to read on polling day, 9 Apr.).

856. 30 June 1990.

857. 14 July 1990.

858. 18 Aug. 1990.

859. 7 July 1990.

860. *Ibid.*

861. 10 Oct. 1998.

862. 9 June 1990, 3 Nov. 1990, 15 Dec. 1990, 6 Apr. 1991.

863. Diana would later become godmother to Domenica, their second daughter.

864. The issue of 12 Dec. 1992 (which bore a torn royal standard on its cover) went to press on Wed. 9 Dec.

865. 'Black Mischief', 1 Jan. 1994.

866. 29 Oct. 1994. The outcry caused by these two pieces was retrospectively analysed in Lawson's long article 'Taboo or Not Taboo, That is the Question' (19 Nov. 1994).

867. 26 Nov. 1994.

868. 10 Dec. 1994.

869. *Independent*, 22 Jan. 1995.

870. 5 Feb., 5 and 19 Mar. 1994.

871. 12 Oct. 1991.

872. 26 Feb. 1994; Mount's piece of 29 Jan. 1994 was headed 'No Pontification in this Realm of England'.

873. Robinson's article appeared on 5 Oct. 1991, Edward Whitley's cover piece on 14 Sep. 1991. An attack on Ronald Reagan by Christopher Hitchens (20 July 1985) was cited in Black's first

874. 28 Nov. 1992.

875. Cited in Dominic Lawson's Diary, 9 Sep. 1995.

876. *The Spectator Annual 1993*, ix.

877. 26 May 1990. Dimbleby devoted his diary to defending the BBC, and particularly *On the Record*, which Lawson had recently criticised in the *Sunday Correspondent*.

878. *The Spectator Annual 1994*, ix.

879. 5 Sep. 1992; 20 Feb. 1993; 17 Oct. 1992. The first and third of these were the only two instalments of a planned series on the 'seven deadly sins' that appeared.

880. 25 June 1994, his last political column.

881. 30 Apr. 1994.

882. 'The Indignity of Elder Statesmanship', 11 Sep. 1993.

883. 'The Judgment of Salomon', 24 Aug. 1991; 'People in Glass Penthouses…', 13 Oct. 1990.

884. 'Nonsense, Nonsense', 2 Nov. 1991.

885. In fact, Wrench's *Spectator* had, in 1928–9, run a series of 'Spectator conferences for personal problems', in which a team of psychologists and doctors responded (anonymously) to a range of problems submitted to the paper.

886. Reported by Mark Amory, *Spec.* 20 Sep. 2014.

887. *Spec.* 7 July 2018.

888. See pp.56–7.

889. 18 Apr. 1992.

890. 23 Feb. 1991.

891. 30 Nov. 1991.

892. 14 Mar. 1992.

893. 30 Oct. 1993.

894. 22 Dec. 1990.

895. This extended account (available online), complete with faux-academic footnotes and hitherto-unreported sources, is a masterpiece of British spoofery.

896. 17 June 1995.

897. 24 June 1995.

898. 20 Aug. 1994; 19 June 1993; 3 Aug. 1991. As early as 1991 (Letters, 27 Apr.), the journalist Simon Carr pointed to the hypocrisy of publishing Vicki Wood's criticism of the sexual obsession of the rest of the UK press (6 Apr. 1991), while including elsewhere in that issue thirty-five mentions of sex, including phrases such as 'kinky sexual obsession', 'a good spanking' and 'whore'.

899. 31 Dec. 1994.

900. *Independent*, 22 Jan. 1995.

901. *Journalist's Handbook* 43 (Sep. 1995).

902. 25 Mar. 1995.

903. 'Second class justice', 18 Aug. 1979; 'Whose interest should prevail?', 9 Aug. 1980.

904. 21 Sep. 1996; 8 Nov. 1997.

905. 9 Sep. 1995; 12 Aug. 1954.

906. 28 Oct. 1995.

907. Atkins was fifty-three when he took up the editorship in 1926.

908. 'Liberals with nowhere to go', 25 Sep. 1976.

909. *175th Anniversary Issue* (2003) 10.

910. *Guardian*, 9 Jan. 1996.

911. 4 Nov. 1995.

912. 18 Nov. 1995.

913. *Guardian*, 9 Jan. 1996.

914. Lawson, pers. comm.; the following sentence

does indeed read as though intended to be a striking opener: '"The circulation will go down, of course," I congratulated the new editor in tones more of hope than prediction, "and you are the person to bring this about."'

915. *Ibid.*

916. *Ibid.* Johnson will have known that this was the degree of his predecessor, as well as of Lawson major.

917. *Ibid.*

918. 11 Nov. 1995.

919. *Independent*, 31 Mar. 1997.

920. *Ibid.*

921. 29 Oct. 1988. She had, in fact, cropped up in passing the year before as a successful tipper on the horses in a Charles Moore Diary (3 Oct. 1987)

922. 6 June 1992.

923. *Guardian*, 9 Jan. 1996.

924. 10 Feb. 1996.

925. 24 Feb. 1996.

926. 9 Mar. 1996.

927. *Guardian*, 9 Jan. 1996.

928. *Evening Standard*, 6 Sep. 1996.

929. 14/21 Dec. 1996.

930. The 1996 Christmas edition (as prev. n.) introduced the name of the editor (absent since 1975), which was deemed a sufficient prop to allow the name of the publisher to appear.

931. Repeated in *Evening Standard*, 5 Sep. 1997.

932. 23 Aug. 1997.

933. Reprinted in *Spec.* 20 Sep. 1997.

934. *Evening Standard*, 5 Sep. 1997.

935. 13 Sep. 1997.

936. Courtauld, 246 (cf. the title of ch.11: 'A Frothy Future?').

937. *Independent*, 31 Mar. 1997.

938. *Ibid.*

939. *Spec.* 27 Dec. 2006.

940. 6 July 1996: 'I believe the editor is Giannandrea Poesio. Is there proof to the contrary? Has anyone ever seen them together? We should be told.'

941. 15 Mar. 1997, responding to Anderson's article of 1 Feb. 1997.

942. 27 June 1998; Clark had praised the 'martial spirit' of the English hooligans on Radio 4's *Today* programme (17 June 1998).

943. 31 July 1999. Objecting to Gill's criticism of Germans, Taki had said in the previous week's *High Life*, 'I will ram my great uncle's first world war helmet – the one with the sharp spike on top – right up his bum.'

944. *Independent*, 10 Apr. 2001.

945. 4 July 1998.

946. 13 Dec. 1997, in response to the Diary of 6 Dec.

947. 16 Aug. 1997.

948. Cited in the *Irish Independent*, 15 Aug. 1997.

949. 7 Jan. 1995.

950. 8 Aug. 1998.

951. Gavin Stamp, 'Another vision of Britain', 13 Jan. 1990.

952. 13 June 1998.

953. *Independent*, 29 July 1999. The words may be Stephen Glover's.

954. *Ibid.*

955. *Guardian*, 29 July 1999.

956. 31 July 1999.

957. A. Gimson, *Boris: The Adventures of Bo*

Johnson (London, 2006) 156. The book has been extended steadily as Johnson's career has advanced.

958. *Guardian*, 2 Aug. 1999.

959. Boris Johnson, *Guardian*, 15 Dec. 2006.

960. Charles Moore, *Spec.* 27 Dec. 2006.

961. Gimson (as n.957) 156.

962. 29 July 1995.

963. Gimson (as n.957) 131, who made this comment to Sandra Barwick, but the line was later cited in certain quarters with 'ape' replaced by 'orangutan' or, rather more liberally, 'mentally defective monkey'.

964. *Times*, 30 July 1999.

965. *Ibid.*

966. *Guardian*, 29 July 1999.

967. *Independent*, 22 Sep. 1999.

968. *Ibid.*

969. Cited in Gimson (as n.957) 134.

970. 'Lovely little nippers', 18 Oct. 1998.

971. Gimson (as n.957) 140; he later recalled 'two- to three-minute' conversations' (*Guardian*, 15 July 2019).

972. 5 May 2001 and 9 Mar. 2002.

973. See p.223 below. The column was paused for most of 2006, on the arrival of a new editor.

974. Hoggart on *The Spectator*'s 175th anniversary, *Guardian*, 22 Sep. 2003.

975. The column recounting this event was reprinted in *Life in the Fast Lane: The Johnson Guide to Cars* (London, 2007) 72–7.

976. See p.154. In June 1989, *The Spectator* had challenged the Coach and Horses pub (chief haunt of *Private Eye*) to a cricket match. Captained by deputy editor and devilish bowler Lawson, *The Spectator* won the match on the very last bowl, thanks to a sterling performance from Giles Auty.

977. 1 Nov. 2000.

978. Entry for Fri. 11 May 2001, in B. Johnson, *Friends, Voters, Countrymen: Jottings on the Stump* (London, 2001) 3.

979. S. Purnell, *Just Boris: A Tale of Blond Ambition* (London, 2011) 190.

980. Gimson (as n.957) 157.

981. Anon., *Times*, 30 July 1999.

982. Gimson (as n.957) 134.

983. 13 Apr. 2002.

984. *The Journal*, 12 June 2002.

985. 'Why I must protest', 10 June 2000.

986. 17 June 2000.

987. 23 Sep. 2000.

988. 19 May 2001.

989. Pers. comm.

990. A more colourful but less credible account is given by Purnell (as n.979) 194.

991. 15 Sep. 2004.

992. 7 Sep. 2002.

993. 16 Mar. 2002. As a remarkable sign of technological advances in the journalistic world, Galloway was able to refer to Anderson's resignation from *The Spectator* in the last paragraph of the very piece that prompted that decision.

994. 7 June 2003.

995. 26 July 2003.

996. 26 Aug. 2004.

997. *Mirror*, 3 Oct. 2002.

998. *Times*, 27 Sep. 2002.

999. Reviews, 6 Nov. 2004 and 21 Oct. 2000. Benn, never treated with warmth by the magazine, was interviewed for the *Sun* by Susan Crosland in 1965: although Benn demanded it not appear, when it was mentioned in his published diaries twenty-two years later, *The Spectator* ran it in full ('The Bitchiest Thing I've Read', 17 Oct. 1987).

1000. 22 Sep. 2003.

1001. *Telegraph*, 13 Feb. 2003.

1002. *Times*, 14 Feb. 2003.

1003. *Hansard*, 27 Feb. 2002 (at 9.38 pm on a Wednesday).

1004. *Evening Standard*, 19 Feb. 2003.

1005. 17 May 2003.

1006. Everyone had been so busy, it seems, that the 9,000th issue (of 3 Feb. 2001) flew by without a word.

1007. *175th Anniversary Issue* (2003) 3.

1008. *Telegraph*, 4 July 2003.

1009. 25 Sep. 2003.

1010. *Ibid.*

1011. *175th Anniversary Issue* (2003) 3.

1012. Reported by Mark Amory, *Spec.* 20 Sep. 2014.

1013. 5 June 2004.

1014. 29 Apr. 2000 (Wateridge), 5 Feb. 2000 (Bell), 19 Jan. 2002 (Wateridge), 2 Feb. 2002 (Wateridge), 27 Apr. 2004 (Garland), 20 Nov. 2004 (Bell), 1 Mar. 2003 (Wateridge).

1015. *Margaret Thatcher, The Authorized Biography* (London, Vol. 1 2013, Vol. 2 2015, Vol. 3 2019).

1016. *Telegraph*, 1 Nov. 2000.

1017. 24 Jan. 2004.

1018. 25 Feb. 1989.

1019. 16 Oct. 2004.

1020. 19 May 2018.

1021. *Times*, 16 Oct. 2004.

1022. 23 Oct. 2004.

1023. *Independent on Sunday*, 24 Oct. 2004.

1024. *Telegraph*, 24 June 2004.

1025. It would take some ingenuity to parse the politics here of one newspaper embarrassing a sister title. One detail that may be relevant is the frustration that Johnson had caused by frequently selling *Spectator* stories to newspapers outside the Telegraph Media Group stable.

1026. Curiously enough, Johnson had used this exact phrase three years earlier in the *Telegraph* about any prospective attempt to intellectualise Portillo's failed bid for the Tory leadership (19 July 2001).

1027. 19 Nov. 2004.

1028. *Independent*, 11 July 2005.

1029. *Evening Standard*, 17 Aug. 2004.

1030. *Spec.* 5 Oct. 2019.

1031. Not all have recalled the atmosphere so rosily. In 2019, the journalist Charlotte Edwardes prominently alleged that it was at a *Spectator* lunch that Johnson found the opportunity to squeeze her thigh (*Sunday Times*, 29 Sep. 2019), a charge he has strongly denied.

1032. In 2001–3, Johnson and *The Spectator* had consistently 280–90 mentions in the British press each year; in 2004, the figure reached almost 1,000.

1033. The text has never been printed but can be found via www.nosacredcows.co.uk.

1034. *Daily Express*, 27 July 2005.

1035. *Times*, 23 June 2005.

1036. *Evening Standard*, 15 July 2005.

1037. *Independent*, 11 July 2005.

1038. 16 Nov. 2004.

1039. *Times*, 17 Nov. 2004.

1040. *Ibid.*

1041. *Guardian*, 3 Apr. 2005.

1042. 18 Sep. 2004. Hurd also conjectured that the novel was written in three days.

1043. 31 Apr. 2005.

1044. 'We're all in this together', 23 July 2005.

1045. 11 July 2005.

1046. *Ibid.*

1047. *Guardian*, 11 Feb. 2005.

1048. *Independent*, 14 Feb. 2005.

1049. *Independent*, 11 July 2005.

1050. 22 Oct. and 19 Nov. 2005.

1051. 24 Nov. 2012.

1052. *Evening Standard*, 14 Dec. 2005.

1053. 14 Feb. 2005.

1054. Sep. 2004.

1055. The present writer, in fact, only became a regular reader of *The Spectator* when this splendid (if short-lived) competition was thrust in front of him by a Lancastrian schoolmaster.

1056. 3 Oct. 2005.

1057. This happy phrase was used five months earlier by Johnson, when warding off such a prospect (*Independent*, 11 July 2005).

1058. 17/24 Dec. 2005.

1059. *Guardian*, 9 Dec. 2005.

1060. *Evening Standard*, 14 Dec. 2005.

1061. 15 Dec. 2005, cited by Gimson (as n.957) 244.

1062. *Ibid.*

1063. *Independent on Sunday*, 11 Dec. 2005.

1064. Cited in Purnell (as n.979) 191–2.

1065. *Ibid.*

1066. *Ibid.*, 192–3.

1067. Gimson (as n.957) 139.

1068. *Ibid.*, 156.

1069. Matthew Parris, *Sunday Times*, 12 Aug. 2018.

1070. The competition emerged after a German comedian faced prosecution for mocking the Turkish President Recep Tayyip Erdoğan. Johnson's entry (published on *Coffee House*, 18 May 2016) ran as follows: 'There was a young fellow from Ankara | Who was a terrific wankerer | Till he sowed his wild oats | With the help of a goat | But he didn't even stop to thankera.'

1071. Diary, 21 Dec. 2019 '(begun at 4.45 am and filed at 10.29 am, one minute before the magazine went to press)'.

1072. 4 Mar. 2006, courtesy of Nicholas Garland. Heath had already made such a move in 6 Apr. 1991, later followed by Wateridge (27 Oct. 2001, 28 June 2003, 30 Oct. 2004) and Garland (21 Feb. 2004).

1073. *Guardian*, 25 Sep. 2006.

1074. The online archive (exacteditions.com.) preserves images of every page of the magazine since 2 July 2005.

1075. Posted 2 Feb. 2006.

1076. A few days later, *Gair Rhydd*, the student paper of Cardiff University, did so – before it was rapidly pulped and its editor suspended.

1077. Mary Wakefield, cited in *Evening Standard*, 6 Sep. 2011.

1078. See p.184.

1079. Reported (but from an untraced source) in *Independent Media Weekly*, 9 Oct. 2006.

1080. See p.125.

1081. *Evening Standard*, 8 Feb. 2006.

1082. *Guardian*, 1 Feb. 2006.

1083. *Evening Standard*, 13 Feb. 2006.

1084. *Ibid.*

1085. *Independent on Sunday*, 26 Mar. 2006.

1086. *Evening Standard*, 15 Feb. 2006.

1087. *Independent*, 18 May 2009.

1088. *Independent on Sunday*, 26 Mar. 2006.

1089. Four of the last five editors, too, were Old Etonians.

1090. 'The new Shakespeare', 16 Oct. 1999.

1091. Hanger's words, reported by *The Guardian*, 25 Sep. 2006.

1092. 1 May 2006.

1093. *Evening Standard*, 9 Mar. 2006.

1094. Cf. Kite's retrospective, 'Why I decided to kill Tamzin Lightwater', *Spec.* 16 June 2010.

1095. 17 July 2006.

1096. *Independent*, 1 May 2006.

1097. *Guardian*, 9 May 2006.

1098. *Guardian*, 25 Sep. 2006.

1099. 17 July 2006.

1100. 7 Nov. 2007.

1101. *Ibid.*

1102. Martin Vander Weyer, pers. comm.

1103. 11 Jan. 2003, criticised by Liddle on 11 Oct. 2003.

1104. 8 Mar. 1997.

1105. 14 June 1997.

1106. 7 Oct. 2000.

1107. 6 Sep. 2003.

1108. 24 Feb. 2001.

1109. 3 Mar. 2001.

1110. 10 Mar. 2001.

1111. 21 Oct. 2006.

1112. *Guardian*, 3 May 2007. Like his successor in the editorial chair, d'Ancona welcomed the romantic notion that the magazine's origins really lay in 1711.

1113. *Independent Media Weekly*, 15 Sep. 2008.

1114. *Independent*, 28 Aug. 2006.

1115. Among these are a large portrait of R.S. Rintoul, donated to the magazine for its 150th anniversary, and (of infinitely greater value) the records of contributors and payments, which were kept by Hutton, Strachey, Wrench and Harris from 1874 to 1953. Does a reader have any lead?

1116. 7 July 2007.

1117. Two subsequent issues, published by an external team under Tom Rubython, were of a rather different character.

1118. A very large number – perhaps some 50,000 – must have been printed. Even at the magazine's 190th anniversary summer party, in July 2018, guests could be given surplus copies.

1119. *Guardian*, 31 Jan. 2008.

1120. See pp.30–1.

1121. See pp.31–2.

1122. 4 Oct. 2008.

1123. 22 Oct. 2008.

1124. 15 Dec. 2008.

1125. *Daily Mail*, 10 Apr. 2009.

1126. *Independent on Sunday*, 29 Mar. 2009.

1127. *Independent*, 13 Apr. 2009. Perry Worsthorne's 'As I Was Saying' column was ended by Boris Johnson in Apr. 2000.

1128. 'The real reason I had to join *The Spectator*', 25 Mar. 2009. Neil, in particular, was said to have been appalled by the appointment.

1129. See p.178.

1130. The radio advertisement for this supplement, aired on Classic FM, was censured by Ofcom because it lacked the approval of the Radio Advertising Clearance Centre. The advert spoke of 'Blair: A Modern Tragedy. The definitive guide to the missed opportunity of the Tony Blair era. Manipulator, communicator, fabricator. Only in *The Spectator*. On sale Thursday.' Two complaints were lodged.

1131. *Independent*, 18 May 2009.

1132. 'It is not enough for Labour to lose this election', 18 Mar. 2009.

1133. 20 and 27 June 2009.

1134. 4 and 11 July 2009.

1135. *Guardian*, 28 Aug. 2009.

1136. *Ibid.*

1137. *Independent on Sunday*, 14 Mar. 2010.

1138. 'Scotland is sick', 15 Nov. 2003.

1139. 'Why Bush won't back Howard', 19 Feb. 2005.

1140. *Guardian*, 14 May 2007.

1141. *Independent on Sunday*, 14 Mar. 2010.

1142. *Ibid.*

1143. *Independent*, 19 Apr. 2010.

1144. 12 Sep. 2009.

1145. *Independent on Sunday*, 14 Mar. 2010.

1146. *Ibid.*

1147. *Ibid.*

1148. BAE supplements include 'Britain's Skill Shortage' (5 Feb. 2011), 'The Cyber Threat' (30 June 2012), 'Exporting for Growth' (12 July 2014), 'Emerging Technologies' (9 July 2016), 'Prosperity Britain' (9 Dec. 2017), and '100 years of air power' (14 July 2018). Philips: 'The Future of Healthcare: The Digital Revolution' (25 Nov. 2017) and 'Fit for the Future: Medicine's New Frontier' (27 Apr. 2019). Other recent supplements have included 'What Europe Thinks' (spons. Project 28, 1 July 2017), 'Europe: Which Way?' (spons. Project 28 and Századvég, 24 Mar. 2018), 'Who's Afraid of Bitcoin?' (spons. BitMEX, 10 Nov. 2018), and 'The Smart Energy Resolution' (spons. The Campaign for a Smarter Britain, 28 Sep. 2019).

1149. Pers. comm.

1150. E.g. Paul Dacre, Max Hastings, Robert Peston, Nick Timothy, Nick Robinson, Kirsty Wark, Paul Mason, Jeremy Vine, Mishal Husain, Melvyn Bragg, Zoe Williams, Nick Cohen, and Petronella Wyatt. Conrad Black has also returned to the fold several times.

1151. *Guardian*, 18 Feb. 2013.

1152. Diary, 21 Dec. 2019. John Major's Allied Dunbar *Spectator* Lecture was published during his tenure, but was not a commissioned article (21 Sep. 1996): see Appendix III.

1153. *Hansard*, 3 Dec. 2012.

1154. 18 Sep. 2010.

1155. *Independent on Sunday*, 23 May 2010.

1156. *Coffee House*, 16 Sep. 2010.

1157. See pp.164–5.

1158. *Spec.* 18 Sep. 2010.

1159. Anne McElvoy, *Independent*, 10 Apr. 2001.

1160. Pers. comm.

1161. *Gentleman's Journal*, 3 Nov. 2017, 77.

1162. 1 Sep. 2012.

1163. 28 Sep. 2013.

1164. 'Global Warming: The Truth', special of 5 Dec. 2009.

1165. See p.213.

1166. *Coffee House*, 9 Jan. 2017.

1167. 19 Nov. 2011.

1168. *Independent on Sunday*, 15 Jan. 2012.

1169. *Guardian*, 17 Feb. 2013.

1170. *Spec.* 6 Apr. 2019.

1171. *Coffee House*, 28 Nov. 2012.

1172. 1 Dec. 2012.

1173. *Coffee House*, 1 Mar. 2018.

1174. The online archive currently lacks volumes for the latter halves of 1857, 1862 and 1933, and the first half of 1999. Some thirty-two other disparate issues are missing.

1175. Leader, 14 Mar. 2019; Fraser Nelson, 21 Apr. 2018 and 31 Aug. 2019; Leader, 9 Nov. 2019.

1176. 'The top 40 horrors lurking in the small print of Theresa May's Brexit deal', *Coffee House*, 17 Nov. 2018 (published at 9 am).

1177. 'The Brexit deal: 40 rebuttals to Mr Steerpike's 40 horrors', 17 Nov. 2018 (published at 8 pm) countered by 'May's' Brexit deal: 40 rebuttals to Downing Street's 40 rebuttals', 19 Nov. 2018. It is premature to give a historical judgment of May's tenure at No. 10, but Bruce Anderson has set the tone by comparing her to a wine that 'you would pour down the sink, not even fit for cooking' (2 June 2018).

1178. *Guardian*, 17 Feb. 2013.

1179. *Times*, 26 Mar. 2014.

1180. 'The genius of *The Spectator*'s Peter Robins', *Coffee House*, 26 Mar. 2014.

1181. 12 May 2018.

1182. 24 Aug. 2018. Nelson later expanded on the principle of being open to writers of all ages: 'What about these people who have had the talent but for whatever reason, they started a family, they haven't been able to let their journalistic talent shine? You don't need qualifications to be a journalist. You just need a hunger, an aptitude, a love of language, a love of words. And I think there is a lot our profession can do to open the doors to talent from places that we don't expect.' (Interview, mediamasters.fm, 12 Sep. 2019).

1183. Nelson later explored these topics in two documentaries for Channel 4's *Dispatches* on 'How the rich get richer' (17 Nov. 2014) and 'Britain's wealth gap' (10 Oct. 2016).

1184. The same phrase was first used (positively) in 2010 by the Australian professor of religious studies Joseph Bulbulia, who was influenced by the work of Thomas Schelling and Robert Frank (pers. comm.). Nevertheless, as with Fairlie and 'The Establishment', Bartholomew is certainly responsible for giving the term its (pejorative) public prominence.

1185. Leader, 7 July 2018.

1186. 'The value of our threatened free press is the real Sam Allardyce exposé', *Telegraph*, 29 Sep. 2016.

1187. @JohnCleese, 3 Oct. 2016.

1188. See p.33.

1189. *Coffee House*, 9 Mar. 2018.

1190. The first *American Spectator* (1932–7) was founded as a monthly 'literary newspaper' by George Jean Nathan, and took much of its character and outlook from its London counterpart. The current magazine of the same name bears no formal relationship with Nathan's journal: it was first founded by R. ('Bob') Emmett Tyrrell Jr in 1967 as *The Alternative*, a monthly paper for students of Indiana University; it, too, directly copied some features of *The Spectator*, and duly renamed itself in 1974 *The Alternative: An American Spectator*, before becoming simply *The American Spectator* in 1977. The magazine grew considerably when it moved to Washington DC in 1985, and was a major force in the early Nineties, before plummeting to near-bankruptcy at the turn of the millennium. The title became an online-only affair in mid-2014, but still continues as a bastion of uncompromising Conservatism.

1191. 'The Meghan Nightmare', *Spectator USA*, Oct. 2019.

1192. Pers. comm. *The Spectator*'s sales, compared over 2013–18 with 36 European current affairs titles, revealed that only eight magazines grew, of which six were British: *Private Eye, Prospect, The Economist, The Oldie,* the *New Statesman,* and *The Spectator*, whose growth at 26 per cent placed it at the head of the field.

1193. *Coffee House*, 15 Feb. 2018.

1194. Cited by Lucinda Southern, 'In the pivot to paid, publishers fear the churn spiral', digiday.com, 16 May 2018.

1195. Westminster Correspondents' Dinner, 28 Feb. 2018.

1196. Pers. comm.

1197. Courtauld, 252.

1198. In October 2019 the Barclay brothers let it be known that they were contemplating the sale of the *Daily* and *Sunday Telegraph*; unsurprisingly, rumours circulated that *The Spectator* could be on the market too. At the time of writing, there is no sign that this is the case.

1199. Notebook, 6 Apr. 2019. Nelson's notice of this book attracted that of its present publisher, for which the author is grateful both to generous editor and attentive subscriber.

1200. The precise date for the 10,000th issue is not entirely without complexity. 10,000 weeks after 4 July 1828 is 22 February 2020. But, according to the modern numbering of issues, #10,000 appeared on 25 Apr. 2020. The numbers started to fall out of sync with the first double edition, for Christmas 1976, which was given a single number. The same single-numeration of a Christmas issue occurred anomalously in 1978, 1995, 1996, 1997, 2006 and 2007; in 1996 and 2007 the Christmas issue was a three-weeker, meaning the loss of two issue numbers over those three weeks. (In Jan. 1982, Jan. 1985 and Jan. 1989, the mistaken single-numbering of the preceding Christmas editions was corrected by leap-frogging an issue number: there are thus no issues #8009, 8167 and 8376.) The result is that the current *Spectator*'s number is nine weeks lower than the number of weeks in which it has appeared.

1201. Quoted on p.14.

1202. C. Howse (ed.), *The Wit of The Spectator* (London, 1989); M. Berkmann (ed.), *The Spectator Book of Wit, Humour and Mischief* (London, 2016).

1203. G. Wheatcroft, *Times*, 21 Sep. 1978. The piece was entitled 'The Survivor'.

1204. [William Weir], *Spec.* 1 May 1858.

Picture Credits

Images of the magazine's cover, contents, advertisements and website are reproduced by kind permission of *The Spectator*. Title-page roundel adapted from *Spec.* 24 Aug. 1962; p.9 reproduced courtesy of DC Thomson Media, Dundee; p.10 portrait reproduced from *Spec.* 23 Sep. 1978 (original miniature untraced); signature reproduced from NLS 4028.160r; p.11 photographed from British Library; p.12 left image adapted from Ackermann & Co. print; right image taken by author; p.19 reproduced by permission of Historic England (EHC01/141/1931/031; no 19th-century image of the West side of Wellington St South appears to survive); p.21 reproduced from *Spec.* 7 July 2018 (original held by British Museum); p.22 reproduced from Google Books; p.36 reproduced from NPG P1273(28c); p.37 reproduced from Getty Images Open Content; p.41 reproduced from cradleylinks.com (original held in Shuker Collection, Shropshire Archives, 3798/5); p.43 photographed from Samuel Laurence's portrait of Hunt reproduced in G. Haight, *George Eliot: A Biography* (Oxford, 1968) (original in Ashmolean Museum, Oxford); p.45 photographed from *Illustrated London News*, 31 May 1890; p.48 reproduced from Strachey (as n.243); p.59 photographed from *Punch*; p.61 photographed from *Punch*; p.68 both images photographed from prints by Frederick Hollyer, c.1890 (copies held in Victoria and Albert Museum); p.72 reproduced by permission of Prof. Marysa Demoor from her photocopy of the original notebook (current location unknown); p.77 reproduced from Strachey (as n.243); p.78 photographed from *The Sphere*, 21 July 1906; p.84 reproduced from NPG 4795; p.85 upper image sourced online from unknown photographer (a copy is held in the London Metropolitan Archives: SC/PHL/01/490/71/4430); lower image taken by the author; p.86 cover of *Spec.* promotional pamphlet (1924: as n.455); p.96 collage compiled by author from *The Sphere*, 19 Dec. 1925, NPG x85095 (1937), and Courtauld (as n.5), who gave generous permission for reproduction; p.99 taken by the author; p.111 photographed from the *Daily Mail*; painting by Arthur Butler, frontispiece of *99 Gower Street* (London, 1943); p.126 collage compiled by author from Courtauld (as n.5); p.128 photographed from *Private Eye* 12 (1 June 1962); p.147 cover by Michael Heath for Courtauld (as n.5); p.148 collage compiled by author from Courtauld (as n.5); p.176 cover cartoon by Peter Brookes, photographed by author; p.182 collage compiled by author from *Spec. Coffee House* 11 May 2007, and sundry Twitter images; p.201 Lloyd Evans (image supplied by Alida Campbell); p.213 reproduced from Wikimedia Commons, uploaded by Philafrenzy; p.247 *Spectator* cartoons by Grizelda (28 Feb. 2015), Bernie (Stephen Hutchinson, 3 Nov. 2018), K.J. Lamb (5 Apr. 2014), and (Peter) Dredge (6 May 2017), reproduced with artists' kind permission. Sincere thanks, too, to Rhys Williams for some technical wizardry.

'What a great list! Have you considered a career in journalism?'

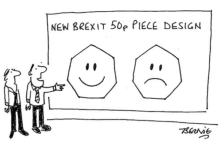

'At the moment we're torn between these two...'

'What's wrong? You've hardly touched your phone.'

'Come on! Come on!'

Appendices

I: **Editors of** *The Spectator*

Editor	Term	Proprietor
Robert Rintoul	July 1828 – Feb. 1858	Robert Rintoul
John Addyes Scott	Feb. 1858 – Dec. 1858	John Addyes Scott
Thornton Hunt	Jan. 1859 – Mar. 1860	James McHenry and Benjamin Moran
George Hooper	Mar. 1860 – Jan. 1861	
Meredith Townsend	Jan. 1861 – Dec. 1897	Meredith Townsend and Richard Hutton
with Richard Hutton	July 1861 – Sep. 1897	
St Loe Strachey	Sep. 1897 – Dec. 1924	St Loe Strachey
Jack Atkins	Jan. 1925 – Oct. 1926	Evelyn Wrench and (from 1930) Angus Watson
Evelyn Wrench	Oct. 1926 – Sep. 1932	
Wilson Harris	Sep. 1932 – Mar. 1953	
Walter Taplin	Apr. 1953 – Nov. 1954	
Ian Gilmour	Dec. 1954 – Mar. 1959	Ian Gilmour
Brian Inglis	Apr. 1959 – Feb. 1962	
Iain Hamilton	Feb. 1962 – Oct. 1963	
Acting editor Tony Hartley	Oct. 1963 – Nov. 1963	
Iain Macleod	Nov. 1963 – Dec. 1965	
Nigel Lawson	Jan. 1966 – June 1970	Ian Gilmour (to Apr. 1967); then Harry Creighton
Acting editor John Thompson	June 1970 – Sep. 1970	
George Gale	Sep. 1970 – Sep. 1973	
Harry Creighton	Sep. 1973 – July 1975	
Acting editor Patrick Cosgrave	Sep. 1973 – July 1975	
Alexander Chancellor	Aug. 1975 – Mar. 1984	Henry Keswick (to Apr. 1981); then Algy Cluff
Charles Moore	Mar. 1984 – Apr. 1990	Algy Cluff (to Jan. 1985); then John Fairfax Ltd (to May 1988); then Conrad Black
Dominic Lawson	Apr. 1990 – Oct. 1995	
Frank Johnson	Nov. 1995 – July 1999	
Boris Johnson	Aug. 1999 – Dec. 2005	Conrad Black (to July 2004); then David and Frederick Barclay
Acting editor Stuart Reid	Jan. 2006 – Mar. 2006	
Matthew d'Ancona	Mar. 2006 – Aug. 2009	
Fraser Nelson	Sep. 2009 –	

Deputy Editors

Although there were figures deputed as assistant editors from the title's foundation, the post of deputy editor was not formalised until after 1945.

Walter Taplin, 1946–53; Iain Hamilton, 1953–6; Brian Inglis, 1956–9; Bernard Levin, 1959–62; Tony Hartley, 1962–3; John Thompson, 1963–70; Michael Wynn-Jones, 1970–1; Patrick Cosgrave, 1971–5; George Hutchinson, 1975–80; Simon Courtauld, 1980–4; Andrew Gimson, 1984–7; Dominic Lawson, 1987–90; *hiatus*; Simon Heffer, 1991–4; Anne Applebaum, 1994–5; Anne McElvoy, 1995–7; Petronella Wyatt, 1997–9; Stuart Reid, 1999–2008; Mary Wakefield, 2008–14; Freddy Gray, 2014–.

Literary Editors

For the period 1861 to 1922, books wer[e] handled successively by Richard Hutton (unt[il] the 1880s), Alfred Church (until the 1900s) an[d] St Loe Strachey.

Amabel Williams-Ellis, 1922–3; Marti[n] Armstrong, 1923–4; Alan Porter, 1924–[?]; Francis Yeats-Brown, 1927–31; Cel[ia] Simpson, 1931–2; Peter Fleming, 1932 (fi[ve] months); Frank Pakenham, 1932 (four months); Derek Verschoyle, 1932–40; Graham Greene, 1940–1; Walter Turner, 1941–7; James Pope-Hennessy, 1947–9; Derek Hudson, 1949–53; Anthony Hartley, 1953 (two months); J.D. Scott, 1953–6; Iain Hamilton, 1956–7; Robert Kee, 1957–8; Karl Miller, 1958–61; Ronald Bryden, 1961–2; Robert Conquest, 1962–3; David Pryce-Jones, 1963–4; David Rees, 1964–7; Hilary Spurling, 1967–70; Trevor Grove, 1970 (four months); Maurice Cowling, 1970–1; Christopher Hudson, 1971–3; Peter Ackroyd, 1973–7; Geoffrey Wheatcroft, 1977–81; Patrick Marnham, 1981 (eight months); A.N. Wilson, 1981–3; John Gross, 1983 (a few days); Patrick Marnham, 1983–4 (six months); Ferdinand Mount, 1984–5; Mark Amory, 1985–2014; Sam Leith, 2014–.

Political Editors

Although there were various dedicated commentators on political affairs between 1920 and 1950, a formal political correspondent was not established until 1954.

Henry Fairlie ('Trimmer'), 1954–6; Charles Curran, 1956 (four months); Bernard Levin ('Taper'), 1956–9; *hiatus*; Julian Critchley, 1960–2; *hiatus*; David Watt, 1963–4; Alan Watkins, 1964–7; Auberon Waugh, 1967–70; Peter Paterson, 1970 (six months); Hugh Macpherson, 1970–2; Patrick Cosgrave, 1972–6; John Grigg, 1976–7; Ferdinand Mount, 1977–82; Colin Welch, 1982–3; Charles Moore, 1983–6; Ferdinand Mount, 1986–7; Noel Malcolm, 1987–91; Simon Heffer, 1991–4; Paul Johnson, 1994–5; Bruce Anderson, 1995–2001; Peter Oborne, 2001–6; Fraser Nelson, 2006–9; James Forsyth, 2009–.

: Anthologies of *Spectator* articles

St L. Strachey (ed.), *Dog Stories from the 'Spectator'* (1895)

St L. Strachey (ed.), *Cat and Bird Stories from the 'Spectator'* (1896)

J. Massingham (ed.), *Dogs, Birds & Others: Natural History Letters from the Spectator* (1921)

Fleming & D. Verschoyle (eds), *Spectator's Gallery: Essays, Sketches, Short Stories, &*

Poem from The Spectator 1932 (1933)

H.W. Harris (ed.), *The Spectator Booklets* (I: Parliament or Dictatorship?; II: The Next Ten Years; III: After Death?; IV: Christianity and Conduct; V: Hitler's First Year; VI: Aspects of England) (1934)

H.W. Harris (ed.), *Christianity and Communism* (1937)

E. Wrench (ed.), *The Voice of Under Thirty* (1937)

W. Harris (ed.), *Spectator Harvest* (1952)

I. Gilmour & I. Hamilton (eds), *Spectrum: A Spectator Miscellany* (1956)

B. Inglis (ed.), *John Bull's Schooldays* (1961)

B. Inglis (ed.), *Points of View: A Selection from the Spectator* (1962)

G. Hutchinson (ed.), *Spectator's Choice* (1967)

K. Amis (ed.), *Harold's Years: Impressions from the 'New Statesman' and 'The Spectator'* (1980)

J. Lumley (ed.), *Peacocks and Commas: The Best of the Spectator Competitions* (1983)

P. Marnham (ed.), *Night Thoughts: The Spectator Bedside Book* (1983)

C. Moore & C. Hawtree (eds), *1936 as Recorded by the Spectator* (1986)

C. Howse (ed.), *The Wit of The Spectator* (1989)

P. Marsden-Smedley & J. Klinke (eds), *Views from Abroad: The Spectator Book of Travel Writing* (1989)

F. Glass & P. Marsden-Smedley (eds), *Articles of War: The Spectator Book of World War II* (1989)

P. Marsden-Smedey (ed.), *Britain in the Eighties: The Spectator's View of the Thatcher Decade* (1989)

F. Glass & C. Moore (eds), *The Spectator Annual 1990* (1990)

F. Glass & D. Lawson (eds), *The Spectator Annual 1991* (1991)

D. Lawson (ed.), *The Spectator Annual 1992* (1992)

D. Lawson (ed.), *The Spectator Annual 1993* (1993)

M. Killen (ed.), *Dear Mary: The Spectator Book of Solutions* (1993).

D. Lawson (ed.), *The Spectator Annual 1994* (1994)

D. Lawson (ed.), *The Spectator Annual 1995* (1995)

M. Bell (ed.), *The Quotable Spectator* (2004)

M. Berkmann (ed.), *The Spectator Book of Wit, Humour and Mischief* (2016)

Appendix III: Prime-ministerial contributions to *The Spectator*
(* denotes serving PM)

William Gladstone: *Letter clarifying the time he spends reading Homer (14 Dec. 1872: see pp.61–2).

Robert Gascoyne Cecil, 3rd Marquess of Salisbury: Letter correcting a mistaken report (29 July 1893).

Archibald Primrose, 5th Earl of Rosebery: Letter correcting a mistaken report of his speech (30 May 1874); signatory of petitions to establish a Tennyson Museum (20 Nov. 1915) and an Eton War memorial (24 Feb. 1917).

Arthur Balfour, 1st Earl of Balfour: Signatory of a petition to establish an Eton War memorial (24 Feb. 1917).

Sir Henry Campbell-Bannerman: Letter rejecting allegations about Cecil Rhodes's donations to the Liberal Party (10 Aug. 1901: see pp.73–4).

Herbert Asquith, 1st Earl of Oxford and Asquith (leader writer, 1876–85): some sixty unsigned 'Topics of the Day' appeared over nine years (see p.63, and H.C.G. Matthew, 'H.H. Asquith's political journalism', *BIHR* 49 (1976) 146–51, at 150–1).

David Lloyd George, 1st Earl Lloyd-George of Dwyfor: 'The case for public works' (24 May 1935).

Andrew Bonar-Law: Letter on naval and military contracts (23 Nov. 1901).

Stanley Baldwin, 1st Earl Baldwin of Bewdley: Letter tracing back an aspect of Spenser's poetry to Arrian and Plato (8 Feb. 1902: see n.489).

James Ramsay MacDonald: 'The purpose of an opposition' (17 Nov. 1923); 'Continuity in foreign policy' (6 Dec. 1924); letter correcting the misreporting of a speech (19 July 1913).

Arthur Neville Chamberlain: Letter on state maintenance of canals (27 Sep. 1913).

Sir Winston Churchill: Letter defending Government's right to shape military strategy in South Africa (9 Nov. 1901).

Clement Attlee, 1st Earl Attlee: 'Not wholly in vain' (review of book on Gallipoli, 27 Apr. 1956); 'Orthodox at last' (review of book on socialism, 3 Aug. 1956); 'The two sides of colonialism' (review, of books on Rhodes and Lugard, 28 Sep. 1956); 'Jan Masaryk' (review of biography of Masaryk, 11 Jan. 1957); 'The dissidence of dissent' (review of A.J.P. Taylor on foreign policy, 28 June 1957); 'Big three' (review of Herbert Feis on Churchill, Roosevelt and Stalin, 3 Jan. 1958); 'Never smell a college spoon' (part of *John Bull's Schooldays* series, 21 Nov. 1958); 'In and out of Chambers' (part of *John Bull's First Job* series, 13 Dec. 1963).

Maurice Harold Macmillan, 1st Earl of Stockton: 'The objectives of foreign policy' (20 May 1955).

Alexander Douglas-Home, Baron Home of the Hirsel: 'Time for a Rhodesian settlement' (26 Feb. 1977).

Sir Edward Heath: 'Where do we go from here' (a 'Financial Survey', 25 July 1965); 'A policy for the environment' (10 Apr. 1970); letter clarifying his view on HMY Britannia (15 Mar. 1997: see p.185).

James Callaghan, Baron Callaghan of Cardiff: Letter in tribute to Nicholas Davenport (9 June 1979).

Margaret Thatcher, Baroness Thatcher of Kesteven: Two-part interview on her education policy (8 and 15 July 1972: see p.145).

Sir John Major: *'Taxation: it is a moral issue' (Spectator and Allied Dunbar Lecture 1996, 21 Sep. 1996); 'Why we must veto this alien constitution' (on the EU Constitutional Treaty, 24 May 2003); 'My lifelong love affair with the Oval' (22 July 2017).

Anthony Blair: 'Second class justice' (on immigration law, 18 Aug. 1979); 'Whose interest should prevail?' (on the Steel Papers case, 9 Aug. 1980); 'The Conservative Party seems neither to understand nor to act upon the concept of duty' (Spectator and Allied Dunbar Lecture 1995, 25 Mar. 1995).

Gordon Brown: 'Outward bound: the British nation state has a future in Europe' (Spectator and Allied Dunbar Lecture 1997, 8 Nov. 1997).

David Cameron: 'It is not enough for Labour to lose this election' (18 Mar. 2009); Cameron was interviewed on 25 Apr. and 12 Dec. 2015

during his tenure as prime minister, and on 21 Sep. 2019 afterwards.

Theresa May: 'We're all in this together' (on the need for reform in Tory leadership elections, 23 July 2005).

Alexander Boris Johnson (political editor 1994–5, editor 1999–2005): 'Of pornography and protection' (31 Aug. 1991); a dozen articles followed over the next three years before he became political correspondent. In that post he wrote weekly from 15 July 1994 until 11 Nov. 1995, publishing 67 pieces. Over the next four years six articles appeared until he became editor in Aug. 1999. As editor, he published another 67 pieces, until stepping down at the end of 2005. Ten articles appeared under the editorship of d'Ancona (2006–9): fifteen – and one limerick (see n.1070) – have appeared under that of Nelson (2009–). He was interviewed during the Tory leadership race on 6 July 2015, and during his tenure as prime minister (2019–) on 30 Nov. 2015. *Most recently, as PM, he filed the Diary on 21 Dec. 2019 (see n.1071).

IV: Print circulation of *The Spectator*: 1828-2020

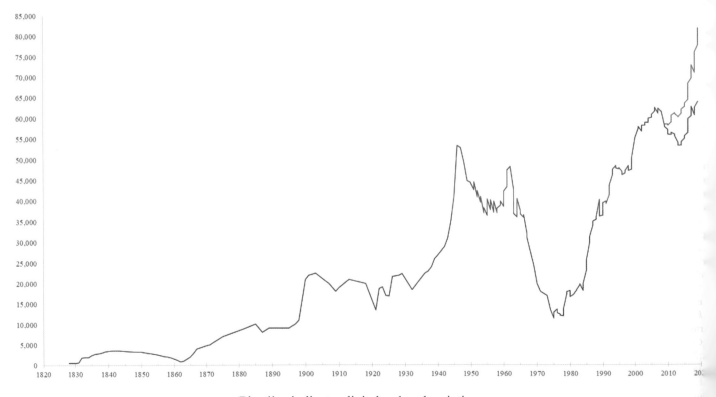

Blue line indicates digital-only subscriptions

Index

Acknowledgments

First and foremost, I wish to record the geniality and good humour of the *Spectator* team. Many have generously accommodated over recent years all manner of queries that have interrupted the incessant business of editing an incessant weekly. Among staff past and present, particular thanks are due to Simon Courtauld, Charles Moore, Dominic Lawson, Matthew d'Ancona, Algy Cluff, Christopher Howse, Martin Vander Weyer, Morten Morland, Mary Wakefield, Danielle Wall, Lynne Wall, Shez Shafiq and Fiona Williams. The editor, Fraser Nelson, has inspired me with his genuine passion about the magazine's history, an enthusiasm that must be rare in the trade. I am also grateful to his deputy, Freddy Gray, for giving me the excuse to pursue a book-length history.

Next I must record my gratitude to those genuinely expert, who answered enquiries with enviable clarity and rapidity: Kirsty McHugh of the National Library of Scotland, Lucinda Lax of the Scottish National Portrait Gallery, Susan Keracher and Anna Robertson of The McManus Gallery Dundee, Eva Bryant and Ian Leith of Historic England, Peter Guillery of University College London, Prof. Marysa Demoor of the University of Ghent, Dr Mary Shannon of the University of Roehampton, Richard Fulton of the University of Hawaii, and Justin Bickersteth of Highgate Cemetery. Important help also came from David Powell of DC Thomson, Dr Malcolm Woodfield of SAP Labs, and Dr William Oliver of Bath. Dr Tony Morris – once of Pembroke, Cambridge – volunteered extraordinary generosity in lending me his own copy of the best doctoral thesis written on *The Spectator*'s most invested editor. The meticulous indexes compiled by the first and last *Spectator* archivist, Charles Seaton, often helped me find the way forward when a trail went cold.

Writing a book should never be easy. But this one would have been impossibly difficult without the fine staff of Cambridge University Library, G. David's bookshop, Christ's College, The Champion of the Thames, Blyth Service Station, Ravenbridge stores, Addenbrooke's Hospital – and of Southey, Bow and Irving Street. Broader encouragement has come from elsewhere: to all *Spectator* readers, to *Telegraph* letter writers, to below-the-line commentators on the sites that suffer them, and to those that draw a firm line at Twitter, I tip the hat that I cannot pull off. To my trusty laptop I begrudgingly offer the handshake that betrays at once my personal guilt and incipient RSI.

To all those who make Queens' College the most perfect of communities – far transcending the wildest fancies of Erasmus – I will always be immeasurably grateful. From the College's historians – Richard Rex, Andrew Thompson, Gareth Atkins and Craig Muldrew – I have learned too much to remember. Life in Cambridge and beyond has introduced me to many men whose company has been precious and formative: David McKie, David Thomas, David Vermont†, David Damant, Colin Sydenham, Bill Fitzgerald†, James Diggle, J. Andrew Smith, Benny Harvey†, O. St J. Machell, and Hubert Picarda. But it was through sheer serendipity that I came to know the best of men Alex Middleton and Peter McDonald, and the best of teachers Richard Hitchings and Myles Tracey. To the quondam Kottabistae I raise a public glass, as I do to the Flaccidae; and to those not mentioned here for reasons they will understand I give a private toast. More generally, I am grateful in the extreme to all those students, friends, colleagues and strangers endowed with the curiosity to ask and to answer questions, to have their ear bent and their head scratched, and to demand better explanations than are currently on offer; I relish all those wiser folk who know the frontiers where pedantry becomes pettiness or particulars become trivialities, yet who take real pride and pleasure in ranging far and wide within.

For all my blind enthusiasm, it was the staff at Unicorn who successfully reified this book. The publisher Ian Strathcarron shared my passion for its subject and so gamely took on a tome that is unlikely to be piled high at entrances and exits of the duty-free WHSmith. To the designer Jonathan Christie I record my wonder at his ability to create an attractive page in the *Spectator* tradition while suffering my unbounded tinkering with such good grace. And to all the rest of Team Unicorn I return sincerest thanks. My copy editor has been paradigmatically perfect: Elisabeth Ingles is as good as the trade gets, reading my text with the eye, ear, taste and verve seldom found in 2020. By removing my own inconsistencies, but agreeing to preserve those of authors cited, she helped me greatly. Any errors in fact, and many infelicities in style, are shortcomings that rest firmly against my door. I am acutely aware that there exist better people to have written a better book. But, as a classicist ranging into a frightfully modern era, I have at least enjoyed piecing together a new narrative as far as my powers allowed.

Yet this book is built on firmer foundations than its research. To my darling, patient wife Rhiannon I owe everything that is tangibly good in my life; to our sons Arthur and Alfred everything that gives me hope. Without these three all text would fall from the page and empty leaves rustle in the wind.

Queens' College, Cambridge, 1 ii